MW00800971

FROM ASHBY TO ANDERSONVILLE

The Civil War Diary and Reminiscences of

GEORGE A. HITCHCOCK

Private, Company A, 21st Massachusetts Regiment
August 1862—January 1865

Edited by
Ronald G. Watson

Manufactured in the United States of America

From Ashby to Andersonville: The Civil War Diary and Reminiscences of George A. Hitchcock, Private, Company A, 21st Massachusetts Regiment, August 1862-January 1865

edited by Ronald G. Watson

Copyright © 1997 Ronald G. Watson
Copyright © 1997 of maps Mark A. Moore

Includes bibliographic references and index

Printing Number
10 9 8 7 6 5 4 3 2 1
(First Hardcover Edition)

ISBN 1-882810-18-X

Savas Publishing Company
1475 S. Bascom Avenue, Suite 204,
Campbell, California 95008 (800) 848-6585

This book is printed on 50-lb. Glatfelter acid-free paper. It meets or exceeds the guidelines for permanence and durability of the Committee on Production Guidelines for Book Longevity of the Council on Library Resources

Unless otherwise noted, all photos and illustrations, including the jacket image of Private George Alfred Hitchcock, are courtesy of the Fitchburg Historical Society.

For the Fitchburg Historical Society,

George Alfred Hitchcock's beloved association

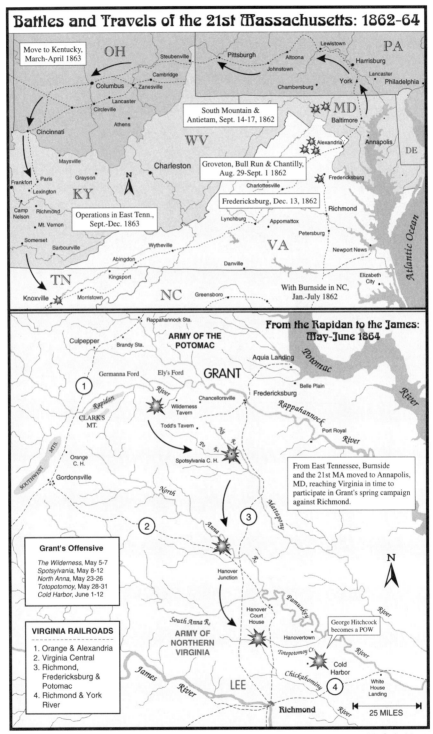

Battles and Travels of the 21st Massachusetts: 1862-64

Move to Kentucky, March-April 1863

OH

Lewistown

PA

Steubenville
Pittsburgh
Altoona
Harrisburg
Johnstown

Cambridge
Lancaster

Columbus
Zanesville
Chambersburg
York
Philadelphia

Lancaster
Circleville

South Mountain & Antietam, Sept. 14-17, 1862

MD

Athens
Baltimore

Cincinnati

WV

Alexandria
Annapolis

DE

Maysville

Charleston

Groveton, Bull Run & Chantilly, Aug. 29-Sept. 1 1862

Fredericksburg

Frankfort
Paris
Grayson

N

Charlottesville

Lexington
KY

Fredericksburg, Dec. 13, 1862

Richmond

Camp Nelson
Richmond

Operations in East Tenn., Sept.-Dec. 1863

Lynchburg
Appomattox

Mt. Vernon

Somerset

Petersburg

Barbourville
Wytheville

VA

Newport News

Abingdon
Danville

TN

Kingsport

Elizabeth City

With Burnside in NC, Jan.-July 1862

Knoxville
Morristown
NC
Greensboro

Atlantic Ocean

From the Rapidan to the James: May-June 1864

Rappahannock Sta.

Culpepper
Brandy Sta.

ARMY OF THE POTOMAC

Aquia Landing

Potomac

Germanna Ford
Ely's Ford

GRANT

Belle Plain

River

1

Rapidan
River
Chancellorsville
Fredericksburg

CLARK'S MT.

Wilderness Tavern

Rappahannock

Todd's Tavern

Port Royal

Orange C. H.

Spotsylvania C. H.

River

From East Tennessee, Burnside and the 21st MA moved to Annapolis, MD, reaching Virginia in time to participate in Grant's spring campaign against Richmond.

Gordonsville

North

Mattapony

SOUTHWEST MTS

2

3

Anna

Grant's Offensive

The Wilderness, May 5-7
Spotsylvania, May 8-12
North Anna, May 23-26
Totopotomoy, May 28-31
Cold Harbor, June 1-12

Hanover Junction

N

Pamunkey River

Hanover Court House

George Hitchcock becomes a POW

VIRGINIA RAILROADS

South Anna R.

ARMY OF NORTHERN VIRGINIA

Hanovertown

1. Orange & Alexandria
2. Virginia Central
3. Richmond, Fredericksburg & Potomac
4. Richmond & York River

Totopotomoy Cr.

River

James
River

Chickahominy

LEE

Cold Harbor

4

White House Landing

Richmond

River

25 MILES

Mark A. Moore

Table of Contents

continued. . .

Table of Contents (continued)

List of Maps and Illustrations

Twenty-year-old Private George Alfred Hitchcock,
21st Massachusetts Infantry

Foreword

A happy combination of circumstances beginning in August 1993 has led to the publication of *From Ashby to Andersonville: The Civil War Diary and Reminiscences of George A. Hitchcock, Private, Company A, 21st Massachusetts Regiment, August 1862-January 1865,* by Savas Publishing Company. This book will be welcomed by a broad constituency of Civil War enthusiasts, be they scholars, armchair buffs, or confirmed battlefield stompers.

The genesis of *From Ashby to Andersonville* dates to an August 1993 visit to the Fitchburg Historical Society by Ronald Grover Watson, a Fitchburg native long interested in genealogical research. As chance willed it, Ms. Ruth Ann Penka, recently appointed the Society's Executive Director, apprised of Watson's interest in the Civil War, retrieved from a walk-in vault "The Army Diary of George A. Hitchcock." She inquired of Watson, "have you read the journal?" He had not, and, after perusing the document for more than an hour requested permission to copy the manuscript for possible publication. Ms. Penka responded, she must bring Watson's request before the Society's Board of Directors.

In mid-September, Ron Watson received a letter from Executive Director Penka informing him that her Board of Directors "heartily approved" his proposal to edit the journal for publication. The diary had been donated to the Fitchburg Historical Society more than 60 years before by Miss Anne Louise Hitchcock, the only daughter of old soldier George A. Hitchcock. Anne Hitchcock had been dead since December 12, 1936.

Ron Watson, besides a deep interest in the Civil War, possessed excellent credentials for evaluating and carefully editing the Hitchcock journal. Born in

Fitchburg, he graduated from the local high school in 1946 and matriculated at Hartford's Trinity College, graduating with a B.A. in history in 1950. He taught school for one year at Ashby High School in Ashby, Massachusetts.

After pulling two years duty in the U.S. Army's counter-intelligence corps during the Korean Conflict, Watson returned to school in 1953, graduating the next year from Springfield College with a M.Ed. in secondary school education. Beginning in September 1954, Watson spent the next 30 years as an educator, initially as a teacher, and then as an administrator in high schools, first in New Hampshire and then for the next 28 years in New Jersey. Upon retiring in August 1984 as principal of West Windsor-Plainsboro High School in Princeton Junction, Watson and his wife Carolyn relocated to Pittsboro, North Carolina, at Fearrington Village, seven miles south of Chapel Hill.

Watson's retirement years have been fruitful. A master gardener, he has completed three graduate courses in history at the University of North Carolina, immersed himself in voluntary community service, and has been an active member of the North Carolina Civil War Round Table. A past president of that organization, he has written a number of articles for the group's newsletter.

Watson, in editing *From Ashby to Andersonville*, learned that he and George A. Hitchcock shared a number of experiences. He found that Hitchcock had been a member and deacon of Fitchburg's Calvinist Congregational Church and in 1901 authored the church's history. This was the church in which Watson taught Sunday school. Hitchcock lived at 46 Arlington Street in Fitchburg, two houses from Watson's paternal grandfather's home. His father was ten years old when the old soldier died. Watson had lived briefly at 45 Arlington Street; George Preston Hitchcock, George's son, had taught chemistry and was principal of Fitchburg High School from 1893-1905, a school from which Watson's paternal grandmother had graduated in 1894.

Employing the skills learned in college and honed in more than three decades in public education, first as teacher and then administrator, with a love and appreciation of history, Watson carefully transcribed and edited the Hitchcock journal. In doing so, he avoided the pitfall of too many editors—a heavy hand. Explanatory notes were informative but concise, not calculated to overwhelm the reader.

On Saturday, January 20, 1996, I met Ronald Grover Watson. I had traveled to the Raleigh-Durham area to speak to the Civil War Round Table of North Carolina. At the dinner preceding the presentation, I was introduced to Watson. Also present was Mark L. Bradley, the author of *Last Stand in the Carolinas: The Battle of Bentonville* (Savas Publishing, 1996). Knowing of my special interest in the Civil War, Andersonville, and the tragic prisoner-of-war story, Watson told me about his project and his desire to have the Hitchcock writings published. He had submitted the manuscript to the editor of the North Carolina University Press, he said, and the response had been less than enthusiastic. What I heard in our brief chat, reinforced by Watson's sincerity, satisfied me that the Hitchcock journals were not just another Civil War diary, and I told him I welcomed the opportunity of reading and evaluating his manuscript.

Within a week after my return to Northern Virginia, I received the edited and transcribed diary. Several weeks were spent with old soldier Hitchcock, and it struck a responsive chord. Few if any Civil War diarists with whom I was familiar had a better eye or talent for describing the countryside or the people. For example, in the days immediately following the battle of Antietam, Private Hitchcock wrote on September 26:

> Orders received again today for us to move out at eleven and we move down Antietam Creek where it empties into the Potomac. Here we are joined by the remainder of the brigade and proceed into camp, two miles from our former one, very near General Burnside's headquarters. The entire 2nd Division is encamped in a large level field and as we expect to remain here several days, proceed to erect tents and comfortable shelters of boughs. One great inconvenience is that all the water for the entire division has to be brought from a large spring, half a mile away. Since the spring is ample for the thousands of troops in the vicinity, it is constantly surrounded by great crowds of men, mules and horses.

Then, on October 3:

> The 21st was ordered out at seven in the morning and to slick up nice to meet the President. The various brigades, divisions, infantry, cavalry and artillery were drawn up in long lines and at half past ten the bands struck up "Hail to the Chief," as a great cavalcade came down the lines.
>
> I quickly distinguished "Honest Old Abe" with General McClellan by his side at the head of a long line of notables. He rode a spirited horse but handled him in a masterly fashion. He wore a democratic black suit and stove pipe hat. As he passed up and down the lines I had a fine opportunity to see his features which were homely but lighted up with a kindliness which would make the plainest person attractive. From us he rode away in the direction of the Potomac where the rest of the army is encamped.

Hitchcock's description of the great battles, such as Fredericksburg, in which he was a participant, are focused and evocative. In an afterword to what he wrote at the time, the old soldier added in 1890 his pungent comments regarding the leadership of the generals who commanded the Army of the Potomac. Late December 1862 found the 21st Massachusetts on picket duty near Chatham, the home of Horace Lacy, a Fredericksburg landmark then, and now an historic property administered by the National Park Service. On December 30, Hitchcock wrote:

> I came off my first beat so I was quartered with the officers for the remainder of the time in the parlors of the Lacy House.
>
> This mansion, owned by Horace Lacy—a Virginian aristocrat and a rebel officer—stands on a commanding eminence overlooking Fredericksburg and a wide extent of country. Three large parlors on the main floor are connected by folding doors which when thrown open make a grand hall. The whole place with its numerous outbuildings, barns, and slave quarters give an air of grandeur and elegance. Being a central point, it is used as the headquarters for the general picket; the result has been that the furniture had received rough usage at the hands of the soldiery. Among these was a grand piano with an organ combination which, during the night, was torn to pieces and "confiscated" by unmusical hands for relics.

The Ninth Corps, on February 4, 1863, was detached from the Army of the Potomac, and, after duty in Southside Virginia, was reassigned to the Department of the Ohio. What happened during these months, particularly when the 21st Massachusetts and the other units assigned to the corps' Second Division were on occupation duty in Central Kentucky, is not well known. Hitchcock's journal provides excellent insights into how the Yankees interacted with the civilians in a "loyal" state where slavery was legal.

On the trip west, there was a riot during a stopover in Columbus, Ohio. While en route, a number of soldiers had secured a barrel of whiskey at Newark. Our diarist on March 30 described what ensued:

> As a preventative for further mischief, the provost guard of Columbus was instructed to prohibit any of our men from leaving the vicinity of the depot. In their attempt to get more liquor, this restraint only served to madden the raging devils; they attacked the guard with stones and brickbats knocking down and severely wounded two or three. The whole provost guard was then ordered out and ordered to load and fire a round of blank cartridges into the crowd. Instead of frightening back the mob, it only served to madden them the more.

The commander then ordered ball cartridges to be loaded. I lost no time in getting away from the crowd and when this volley was fired into the crowd, several men were wounded and one killed. A grand rush was made for the cars to secure arms with which to retaliate. In our car men struggled with each other, the orderly ones striving to restrain and calm the excited ones. In midst of all the confusion, Colonel Clark sprang on the engine and ordered the train forward with all speed. Many were left behind who were properly cared for as we afterward learned.

In mid-September, the Ninth Corps began the long march that took Hitchcock and his comrades deep into East Tennessee. The marches, camps, battles and personalities that characterized Maj. Gen. Ambrose E. Burnside's successful campaigns in the region are described in an intelligent and insightful manner that enlightens and entertains.

On January 7, 1864, the regiment, having reenlisted, set out in a "blinding snow storm" back to Kentucky by way of Cumberland Gap. Some three months later, the peripatetic Ninth Corps was back in Virginia. After a stint in a Kentucky hospital and a furlough, Hitchcock rejoined his regiment on May 29 near Totopotomoy Creek. The regiment since May 5, when it crossed the Rapidan, had been an active participant in Lt. Gen. Ulysses S. Grant's bitter Overland Campaign. Hitchcock, as a casual, found the 24-day trip south from Boston to the Richmond approaches vexing, irksome, and fraught with red tape. On May 12, having reached Arlington, Virginia, he noted:

I was detailed for fatigue duty with a lot of others and went out to work on the road near Fort Runyon. The day was hot and there were numerous complaints by the chronic growlers, who doubtless supposed they ought to be transported immediately on beds of roses to their regiments, instead of handling the pick and shovel and building roads for Uncle Sam. With blistered hands I worked until near noon when a heavy shower drove us back to camp. The place is called Camp Convalescent and is a large village of barracks. At night I drew a new canteen, haversack and shirts.

Hitchcock was back with his unit less than a week before he was captured by the Confederates on June 2 after a bitter fight at Bethesda Church. The Rebels, always looking for an opportunity, took advantage of sloppy coordination between the Union Fifth and Ninth corps, dooming our diarist to spend the next six months as a prisoner-of-war.

Prisoner-of-war stories, with the theme of man's inhumanity to man, command public attention far beyond the Civil War community. More than 40 years ago, MacKinley Kantor's *Andersonville* hit the best sellers' list and earned a Pulitzer Prize for the author, and in March 1996 Ted Turner's *Andersonville* attracted a national audience of television viewers. I am no exception, finding Hitchcock's diary entries describing his experiences at Libby Prison, Camp Sumter (Andersonville), Camp Lawton (Millen) and Florence soul-searing.

In the years since President Richard M. Nixon signed into law on October 16, 1970, legislation establishing Andersonville National Historic Site, I have been professionally involved with the site of the nation's most infamous military prison. To facilitate plans for development and interpretation of the site by the National Park Service, I visited the area on several occasions in the early 1970s. In doing so, I became familiar with the history of the prison, its administration, and the prisoners. Out of my research came the *Historic Resource Study and Historical Base Map: Andersonville National Historic Site*. Then, in the mid-1990s, I was honored to be chosen to be one of the "talking heads" for the hour-long segment of A&E's "The Civil War Journal" with its focus on Civil War prisons. Prior to the showing of Ted Turner's "Andersonville," I returned to national television on a program intended to provide an understanding that all Civil War prisons, whether Union or Confederate, were hell holes.

It was with this background that I evaluated Hitchcock's trials and tribulations, and came to understand its importance as a primary source. Hitchcock's diary, unlike most prisoner's accounts, is a day-to-day record instead of a reminiscence. As a World War II combat veteran, on returning to reunions, I have learned too often the hazards of reliance on old marines' memories.

After reading and annotating the draft manuscript, I returned it to Watson on March 19, 1996. In encouraging its publication, I wrote:

> The diary. . .is one of the best and most informative. . . that I have been asked to read and comment upon." Particularly enlightening is Hitchcock's description of his service with the IX Corps during the period January 1863 to February 1864 and of the occupation and campaigns in Kentucky and East Tennessee, focusing on a theater of war that has not received the attention it warrants.
>
> Unlike the reminiscences of most Andersonville prisoners, Hitchcock's diary presents a balanced account of the more than four months he spent there. Not as well known are what the prisoners experienced at Camp Lawton and at Florence, how the exchanges were effected, and how the soldiers were processed upon reaching Camp Parole, Maryland. Now, thanks to Hitchcock's journal and your notes these can become common knowledge.

Ron Watson, upon return of the manuscript and my comments, discussed with me by telephone on several occasions possible publishers. I told him of the pros and cons of University presses vis-a-vis specialty presses. Among the specialty publishing houses, the best insofar as I am concerned were Morningside Bookshop and Savas Publishing Company. For additional information on Savas Publishing, I suggested that Watson contact Mark Bradley, whose *Battle of Bentonville* had been published by Savas Publishing. Bradley was the catalyst that brought Ted Savas and Ron Watson together, resulting in *From Ashby to Andersonville*, a Civil War enthusiast's dream.

Edwin C. Bearss
Historian Emeritus, National Park Service

"Ashby was never a utopia, simply a plain, common sense,
healthy outgrowth of democratic ideas."

Editor's Preface

Ashby, Massachusetts, a small town forty-two miles west of Boston in the
northwestern extremity of Middlesex County and bordering on New Hampshire,
was incorporated on September 4, 1767. The picturesque land offers a variety of
hills and vales with rich pastures and farmland marked by meandering streams.
In the 1860s, a majority of the people were engaged in agricultural
pursuits—wheat, potatoes, corn, oats, barley, apples and dairy products.[1] The
1,091 residents listed in the 1860 census were comprised of 532 males, 559
females and no free men of color.[2] Ashby area residents were noted for their
industry, frugality and hospitality. December 22, 1869 *Ashby Evening Gazette*
editorialized that "the town early took measures to administer justice, or at least
to correct violations of good order, especially on the Sabbath." This small town
of farmers and merchants ultimately furnished 109 soldiers to the cause of the
Union, including Pvt. George Hitchcock. Eighteen of his fellow townsmen
never returned.

George Alfred Hitchcock was born in Ashby on January 15, 1844, the third
child of Eliza Sparhawk and George Loring Hitchcock. Three of the Hitchcock's
seven children died in their early youth. George inherited from his parents a
strong "Yankee" conscience with an abiding sense of duty and responsibility.
His uncompromising moral standards were rooted in Victorian values and
enhanced by what he described as "strong parental love." His wheelwright
father, he noted in his diary, was his "congenial companion," an abolitionist and

member of the free soil party who believed in "free soil, free speech, free labor and free men."

In *Memoirs of Ashby in 1850*,[3] George Hitchcock wrote after the war that his home was located on the main road running north and south between southern New Hampshire and Fitchburg, Massachusetts. Adjoining his home was his father's carriage and wheelwright shop with its medley of old wheels and parts of wagons. Throughout the village, each home had its connecting shop: boots and shoes, harnesses, blacksmith, coffins, rope, carpet and dressmaker. During the decade between 1840 and 1850, Ashby boasted of two unusual industries: Whitney's organ shop (one of the first in the country), and Willard's clock shop, which provided time pieces that remain today a cherished heirloom. There were four stores in Ashby including an apothecary. The southern part of town was called "Mill Village" with its dozen mills of various industries: tub, pail and saw mills.

Farming was a cherished way of life in Ashby. According to Hitchcock, the farmer was the "captain of industry." Outside the village the entire township was dotted with large farms with well-kept barns stocked with all kinds of domestic animals. The large families provided the necessary labor and Hitchcock noted that "no unreliable hired help was then known." Before the railroads were built, Ashby was relatively important on the great Boston and Burlington (Vermont) stagecoach road with its two enterprising hotels. An old tavern, "Children of the Woods," furnished rest and refreshment for passengers and animals before the journey through the hills of Rindge, New Hampshire.

As his journal attests, the young Hitchcock was well educated. He attended the Ashby public school and continued his academics at Appleton Academy in New Ipswich, New Hampshire and Templeton (Massachusetts) High School, all with the intention of attending college. He recalls with some fondness the small ungraded-school near the Ashby Commons crowded with 60 to 70 pupils. "The town was indebted for the high standard of excellence of such teachers as Mrs. Sara Wyman and Miss Susanne Augusta Wallis (afterward Mrs. Amasa Norcross)." Academic results were reflected in the high character of citizenship and domestic virtues of the scholars who were pupils of those teachers. "No more perfect discipline had ever since been attained and at the same time the development of individuality—an attainment well nigh impossible by the present graded methods. And with both of these teachers, the dominant trait which controlled was the law of love."

Ashby never harbored or claimed an aristocratic taint, a fact Hitchcock believed differentiated it from other towns in old New England. Many communities of eastern New Hampshire and northeastern Massachusetts, whose settlements had been fostered by royalists, boasted of their highbred families. Neighboring towns pointed with pride to some dominant masterful family who bequeathed its spirit to later generations and gave it a character which Oliver Wendell Holmes depicted as the "true New England aristocracy." Hitchcock took pains to stress that this was not so with Ashby, and no aristocracy or plutocracy could ever buy anything but "an excrescence or offense in any true American community." Hitchcock felt that "the blossom and fruitage of Ashby in the 1850's was the sterling common sense which called no man master." The people looked to their ministers of God as their moral leaders and their physicians were their leaders in educational thought—all men of superior intelligence and judgment. Yet Ashby was "never a utopia, simply a plain, common sense, healthy outgrowth of democratic ideas." Towns like Ashby "helped to make this nation the foremost in the world."

On August 7, 1862, the 18-year-old Hitchcock left Ashby to volunteer in the 21st Infantry Regiment of Massachusetts Volunteers, the same regiment that his older brother, Henry Sparhawk Hitchcock, had joined almost a year earlier. From August 7, 1862 until January 1, 1865, Hitchcock composed in a series of pocket diaries a compelling personal narrative, a meticulous detailed record of his daily activities. By 1890 he had transcribed the diaries into a single document, to which he added additional reminiscences and commentary. His journal, which was not published for personal reasons, was presented to the Fitchburg Historical Society by his daughter, Miss Annie Louise Hitchcock, on April 7, 1932, four years before her death. And there the diary remained, hidden away in a walk-in vault.

The first portion of this vividly written and well-organized journal includes accounts of: the Army of the Potomac's battles from South Mountain and Antietam through the disastrous action at Fredericksburg. Transferred west with his corps, Hitchcock details his journey by rail through York, Pittsburgh, Columbus and Cincinnati to Paris, Kentucky, and his interesting service in that region, including the skirmishes and engagements in Ambrose Burnside's Knoxville campaign and the arduous return march to Camp Nelson during a severe winter with Confederate prisoners. Unfortunately for Hitchcock, his corps was transferred back to Virginia in time to take part in Ulysses S. Grant's Overland Campaign. His diary entries offer a captivating description of his capture at Cold Harbor and subsequent imprisonment at Andersonville and other Southern stockades.

Private Hitchcock's original journal expresses a remarkably fresh point of view with a minimum of hostility. Such objectivity is seldom found in Civil War diaries. His personal reminiscences and commentary written after the war, when he was struggling to secure a pension and reevaluating his capture and imprisonment, are somewhat more partisan in tone. His daily record provides today's readers with a descriptive account of a Union soldier's activities and a fascinating chronicle of a soldier-traveler who spent free moments exploring cities, attending church services and observing the local environment.

Acknowledgments

I wish to express my sincere appreciation to Ruth Penka, executive director of the Fitchburg Historical Society, for providing me with access to George A. Hitchcock's Civil War journal. Ruth and all her dedicated volunteers have always been extremely pleasant and helpful. Ruth's professional expertise and the Fitchburg Historical Society's excellent resource library provide Fitchburg, Massachusetts, with an ideal historical society for the Civil War historian. The collection of Massachusetts regimental histories is very comprehensive.

I was privileged to have access to two outstanding reference libraries which provided the major portion of the research material in this book: Davis Library at the University of North Carolina at Chapel Hill and the Perkins Library at Duke University. Many staff members extended valuable aid and great kindness.

The library and archives at the Andersonville National Historic Site in Georgia were very informative. I appreciated the help from Alan Marsh, Fred Sanchez, Mark Ragan and Bill Burnett. The Archives/Library Division of the Ohio Historical Society at Columbus was an outstanding resource. Steve Gutgesell, who I met during a tornado drill, offered many good suggestions. The archives and library at the U.S. Army Military History Institute, Carlisle Barracks, at Carlisle, Pennsylvania, were very valuable resources. Archivist Richard Sommers was helpful identifying and researching material related to the conflict on June 2, 1864 near Bethesda Church. The Georgia Room at the University of Georgia in Athens was also a very valuable resource.

Martina Hines, Data Specialist, Kentucky State Nature Preserve Commission at Frankfort, Kentucky, was very knowledgeable about the Camp Nelson area and identified the Daniel Boone Cave in Jessamine County. Martha

Sink, research librarian at the Central North Carolina Regional Library at Burlington, was helpful through the use of the "Library Stumpers" on the Internet.

Additional resources which provided important information included: Fitchburg, Massachusetts, Public Library, especially the materials in the Henry A. Willis Room; Mercer University Main Library at Macon, Georgia, especially the excellent microfilm collection; Lexington–Fayette County Historic Commission in Lexington, Kentucky; and the invaluable General Reference Branch of the National Archives in Washington, D.C.

Many people were exceedingly generous with their time and expertise: Jane Matthews at the Thomas Public Library at Fort Valley, Georgia; Ruth Spiers at the Jenkins County Memorial Library at Millen, Georgia; Walter A. Gray, Jr., Director of the Beaufort National Cemetery, at Beaufort, South Carolina; Janie Morris at the Special Collections Library, Duke University; Jeanine Bruce at the Lake Blackshear Regional Library at Americus, Georgia; Thomas Blake at the Florence National Cemetery, Florence, South Carolina; the research staff of the Florence County Library, Florence, South Carolina; Nick Zeigler, a resident of Florence, South Carolina; Donald Norton, historian in Ashby, Massachusetts; Marja Leena LePoer at the Ashby Public Library; Archivist Margot Karp at the Reference Library at Pratt Institute, Brooklyn, New York; and Joseph F. von Deck, teacher from Ashburnham, Massachusetts. I am grateful for the valuable technical assistance provided by David Watson and Doug McMahon.

I offer a special thanks to former National Park Service Chief Historian Edwin C. Bearss for reading the entire manuscript and for offering many valuable suggestions. His evaluation and comments were very encouraging and supportive. In addition, Ed took time from his busy schedule to pen an excellent and informative Foreword, a valuable addition to this book.

Mark A. Moore, of Wilson, North Carolina, provided the excellent maps to accompany Hitchcock's work. There is no one better working today. Appreciation is also due to Lee Merideth for his indexing, and David Lang for all of his computer assistance.

And finally, I wish to thank Mark Bradley, author of *Last Stand in the Carolinas: The Battle of Bentonville* (Campbell, 1996), for highly recommending Theodore P. Savas and Savas Publishing Company.

Ron Watson

Introduction (1890)

A quarter of a century has rolled away since the events recorded took place. Of the great leaders whose faces I have looked upon, Lincoln, McClellan, Burnside, Grant, Sheridan and Hancock have gone to their last roll call. Of the comrades with whom I marched into battle, bivouacked by the camp-fire or suffered in prison-pens, nearly all are gone, either scattered or dead.

The heritage of disease, bequeathed from Southern swamps and battlefields, reminds me daily that the record for me is not to last forever. As the events in which I then bore a humble part recede, they increase in interest and I am inclined to transcribe them from the old worn-out blotted pages, adding occasionally incidents which memory has kept written for me. Yet the record will be mainly identical with that which was made from day to day while in participation of the events.

When the shock of war came, it found the lines of opinion sharply drawn at the Mason-Dixon line: the North for the Union of States and the freedom of the slave; the South for the independence of the State and the perpetuation of slavery. Yet on both sides were multitudes who divided on these questions. Thousands of northern soldiers disclaimed any desire to interfere with slavery but were loyal in their devotion to the Union.

We now understand that thousands in the South were anxious to remain in the Union but devotion to the cause of slavery drew them into the rebellion. From our standpoint today we can see that it was not as some claim, that might made it right to overthrow the doctrine of state rights. Aside from the moral wrong of slavery which no one questions now, the beneficent power of a firm national union is proved to be the destiny of our country in the worlds history and a Divine hand is guiding the helm of state to carry out this own purpose.

What ever may be the undercurrent of politics today we realize that the part taken by the Union soldier twenty-five years ago was in the grand line of human progress and we have only to compare the wonderful growth in wealth and prosperity of our country to the condition which we imagine might have been if the South had been victorious. It is with peculiar satisfaction then, that we see in this year of grace 1890, one of our number at the head of the nation, and the "soldier element" recognized as a potent factor in its government, not from any martial spirit or desire for military government but that the loyal hearts that stood the test when it was sorely needed, have the right to demand (not plead) that the government shall be administered in the spirit of righteousness which exalteth a nation and the results of the war, especially in restoring manhood to the freedman shall be completed.

Among the earliest recollections of my life was the picture indelibly stamped upon my mental vision of various heated discussions between my father and certain very estimable neighbors of ours who always found my father's workshop a very convenient lounging place and my father a very congenial companion. The topics of conversation ranged from the ordinary topics of daily life to religion and politics and invariably instructive. The point of divergence began when our Whig neighbors, with the assurance which characterized that powerful and highly respectable party, upbraided my Freesoil father for his "factious and heretical theories."

As an abolitionist, he was sincere and consistent—as various poor fugitive slaves could testify, who in seeking the land of promise, always found a welcome at my father's door, a sort of underground railway station. From these early lessons my interest in the burning questions of those historic days began, so that when the news of the defeat of Freemont and Dayton in 1856 came to us in our quiet country home, it was almost as a personal affliction to me, then a boy of only a dozen years.

As the following years rolled by freighted with so many history-making events, it is not strange that the year 1861 found me with more zeal than discretion when as a lad of seventeen I was determined to go to war. I first essayed to enlist in the 12th Massachusetts, when a certain Captain Ripley came into our village [Ashby] seeking recruits for Fletcher Webster's regiment. To march to the front under command of the son of the great Daniel Webster seemed a special inducement, but the fiat of wise parent kept me back, as it did two months later when the 21st Massachusetts was formed. This was a peculiar disappointment to me for in it a company was recruited by George P. Hawkes of Templeton in whose family I had lived; my brother Henry was a sergeant in the company and many of its members were my companions and acquaintances.

When the disastrous campaign of the Peninsula forced President Lincoln to call for 500,000 more men, father, whose patriotism had nothing selfish in its composition, yielded his second son to his country's service.

Nearly twenty-eight years have passed away and the sacrifice he then made, is now better appreciated then when on a calm summer's afternoon in July 1862, the die was cast and I enlisted from Ashby's quota under B.W. Seaman as recruiting officer. My companion in arms was Lemuel Whitney, an old acquaintance, somewhat older than myself, whose subsequent career proved him to be as fine material as ever was furnished for citizen soldiery—calm and cool in the excitement of battle, patient and cheerful in trying hardships, prompt to obey his superior officers—I take pleasure in giving him this tribute, for the stimulus which these qualities in him, gave me in my boyish impetuosity and inexperience.

Backed by strong parental love which would not yield me until I had first yielded my allegiance to the source of all authority, I went out from a happy home life into the fearful and thrilling experience of the war of so momentous results in the worlds history. As a unit in the myriad which made up the Union army I was lost from sight, but I may be forgiven the pride of believing that I had a part in sealing the doom of human slavery in our country.

Although most of Ashby's quota of the call went into the new 83d Regiment, I decided to go as a recruit into the 21st. Governor John Andrew secured an exceptional privilege from the War Department, which was granted to no other state. In order to fill up the veteran regiments, inducements were offered to those who joined such regiments that their term of service would end with the regiment and their status would be the same as though they had gone into service when the regiment left Massachusetts. Subsequent events however denied me the opportunity of returning to Massachusetts with the regiment and the last acts of the drama were being played when I stepped off the stage.

George Alfred Hitchcock

Sergeant Henry Sparhawk Hitchcock,
Company A, 21st Massachusetts Infantry

One
Apprenticeship to Uncle Sam

When George Hitchcock left Ashby, he looked forward to a reunion with his brother and membership in a proud regiment. His older brother, Henry Sparhawk Hitchcock, a resident of Templeton, Massachusetts, enlisted as a sergeant in Company A, 21st Massachusetts Infantry on July 19, 1861. The regiment was organized and trained during July and August at the Agricultural Fair Grounds in Worcester, Massachusetts. Henry received leave to marry Mary Miller Chamberlin on August 21. Prior to heading south, the soldiers were issued old smoothbore muskets, altered from flintlocks, to replace the makeshift, crooked-barrel guns they had used for drilling.

On August 23, 1861, after being mustered into the United States service for three years, the regiment was presented with a silk regimental flag from the ladies of Worcester. The Bay Staters left for Norwich, Connecticut, by train, traveled to Jersey City by boat, and again boarded a train to Havre-de-Grace by way of Philadelphia. They were finally issued ball cartridges for the first time, since the regiment expected a hostile reception in Baltimore. On August 25, the 21st Massachusetts arrived at Baltimore before noon, filed quietly from the train with fixed bayonets and loaded guns, and marched through the crowded streets to Patterson Park—with neither a welcome nor insult heaped in the unit's direction. Three days later the regiment arrived at Annapolis, Maryland, for temporary garrison duty. More reliable Enfield muskets from Massachusetts reached them just before their first Christmas of the war.

On January 6, 1862, the 21st Massachusetts boarded the steamer Northerner bound for Hatteras Inlet as part of Ambrose Burnside's expedition to North Carolina. *Brigadier General Ambrose Everett Burnside led a joint army-navy force to gain control of the Pamlico and Albermarle sounds. The 12,000-man land force (the Coast Division of the Army of the Potomac) was organized in three brigades, with the 21st Massachusetts part of Brig. Gen. Jesse L. Reno's Second Brigade. Three battles would turn the raw recruits into veterans. The strong Union force was victorious at the Battle of Roanoke Island on February 8, 1862, where the regiment received it baptism of fire. Of the 700 soldiers from the 21st engaged on Roanoke, 13 were killed or died of wounds and 44 others were wounded. The 21st also saw action in the March 14, 1862 Battle of New Bern, where 675 soldiers engaged the enemy and suffered 23 killed or died of wounds and 35 others wounded. The Battle of South Mills, on April 19, 1862, closed out the campaign for the Massachusetts soldiers. The regiment managed to engage 500 of its soldiers, of which four were killed or died of wounds, 11 others were wounded, and one was taken prisoner.*

After the close of Burnside's campaign, the 21st Massachusetts left North Carolina and went into camp at Newport News. A month of drilling and target shooting followed, during which the regiment became part of the newly organized IX Army Corps. The corps left Newport News on August 2, and arrived at Fredericksburg, Virginia, two days later.

*   *   *

August 7, 1862

It was a fine, warm morning that dawned on the little town of Ashby nestled among the hills of Middlesex [County]; the farmers were busy in the hay-fields on each side of the road as father carried me to Townsend where I boarded the train for Boston.

Provided with the "official documents" by Mr. Seaman and countersigned by the selectmen of Ashby, Lemuel Whitney[1] and I proceed to the State House, find the office of Adjutant General William Schouler to whom we report in person. After disposing of a roomful of persons, he greeted us cordially and after a few pleasant words of praise and encouragement, gave us passes to Camp Cameron, which was situated in North Cambridge six miles from the State House; thither we proceed in the horsecar.

Reaching there just before sun-down, we have but little time to look about us and find the headquarters. Lieutenant Jordan, who is commander of the camp, is absent and we are unable to have our quarters assigned to us. We therefore return to Cambridge and secure lodgings at the Market Hotel.

August 8

We are aroused early in the morning by the sounds of a heavy thunder shower. After breakfast we return to Camp Cameron and make several ineffectual attempts to secure recognition. We remain until afternoon and somewhat losing patience we leave camp, go into Boston, catch a train on the Boston and Maine Railroad and proceed to Lynnfield where we find the Ashby boys who left home a week earlier and are now joined to Company E, 33d Mass of which Colonel Maggi is commander. He was Lieutenant Colonel of the 21st and commanded that regiment in Roanoke and Newbern—a brave Italian officer who fought with Garibaldi for Italy's freedom.

Two regiments, the 33d and 35th, compose "Camp Staunton," a beautiful camping ground with a fine grove of trees in the rear and a large, clear sheet of water near by. We find our boys all in fine spirits who urge us to go in with them, but we remain firm in our purpose to join the 21st. We witness the Dress Parade for the first time with great interest, after which the boys share with us their soldiers fare and we try a soldiers bed in a large "Sibley" or bell tent with the boys. Tired out, we sleep soundly as only healthy boys can.

August 9

The next morning opens with showers; heavy sea-fogs are wafted in upon us for we are near the salt water. Returning to Boston in the forenoon we dine at Campbells and go out to Camp Cameron again. This time we are successful in gaining a hearing; at half past four we (Lem and I) are ushered into a tent where a U.S. surgeon orders us to strip naked; he puts us through various evolutions, thumps us freely and declares us "perfectly sound."

Quarters are assigned to us in barracks number six. The camp is composed of ten long sheds with two rows of bunks on each side the entire length. Our first army ration is a chunk of bread which we relish and then weary and lame we lie down on the hemlock boards of our bunk; using our coats for pillows we find refreshing rest without blankets or covering.

August 10

We awake on our first Sabbath in camp to find a beautiful day and being so near the great city, swarms of Sabbath-breakers overrun the camp all day bent on sightseeing. No religious exercises were held but during the morning the entire camp of recruits was ordered out and formed in a hollow square where the articles of war were read to us. These give instruction in the duties and laws governing each member of the army. The knowledge of them gives me new feeling of the important responsibility of even a private.

A great deal of drunkenness and many arrests during the day have made the sacred hours seem profaned to me since I have never before been away from the quiet and holy influences of a genuine New England Sabbath.

August 11

As the night was chilly and we had no covering, I slept only four hours. No duties were assigned us and as we are now regularly enrolled, we cannot leave camp and the hours hang heavily. Nearly three-hundred recruits were sent away to Washington, but the numbers are so great that their absence is not felt. New men are coming in rapidly.

August 12

The morning is cloudy, threatening rain but soon breaks away and the sun shines out warm. Lem and I procure passes, go into Boston and try to get sworn into service there so as to be able to secure blankets and rations. In this we were unsuccessful and next stroll into the Tremont Temple which is being used as a recruiting office for the Boston quota. Here we are urged and sorely tempted to enlist but do not yield.

Returning to Camp Cameron once more, we are somewhat out of temper having been here nearly a week and nothing apparently accomplished. We are quite sure that our Uncle Sam is treating us very shabbily and testing our patriotism unnecessarily.

August 13

Today finds us more successful. Lem has his mustering-in papers made out and he secures the necessary supplies; mine are also made out but I, being a minor, must procure my father's written consent. This is to be accomplished by his countersigning my enlistment papers; I take them down to Porter's Station and forward them to Ashby by express. Another large squad of recruits left camp tonight for Washington.

August 14

Lem shares his blanket with me. I go down to the Cambridge Post Office seeking my papers, but I do not find them. I stroll through Cambridge to Charlestown to the top of Bunker Hill monument, to the Navy Yard and into Boston; get a good dinner and return to Porter's where I was happily surprised to meet father and brother Arthur who give me my needed papers. Then I go on to Campello to visit Rev. C.W. Wood[2] while I trudge back to camp where I am at last duly installed.

August 15

The morning was rainy but as soldiers are not supposed to know any changes of weather we are ordered out into line and marched to headquarters to receive our bounty money; after some delay we are ordered back without it. Father returned from Campello this afternoon and called on me. After some faithful words of advice and a sad farewell, he returned home. Recruits for the seat of war left tonight for the 2nd, 18th, and 22nd regiments.

August 16

The sergeant and corporal in charge of our barracks went away today, leaving us in charge of inexperienced men. I wrote letters and in the afternoon went with a squad of men out to Spy Pond, West Cambridge, to bathe. Received tonight, twenty-five dollars, the first installment of our bounty money.

August 17

The Articles of War were again read to us in the morning. In the afternoon a large number of us accepted an invitation from the Baptist Church, North Cambridge, to attend service. I know not how soon I may have another opportunity to see the inside of a church so the occasion is an impressive one.

August 18 and 19

Had my first experience in guard duty on the camp guard. We form a living fence—each man having a "beat" of some three or four rods [one rod equals five and one-half yards] on which he tramps back and forth. Guard mounting begins at nine in the morning. First relief stands from nine to eleven; second from eleven to one; third from one to three and continuing through twenty-four hours. The occupation was not hard but very tedious and during the night the desire to drop to sleep was well nigh irresistible, but a healthful fear of the dread penalty kept me awake.

August 20

The monotony of camp life is broken by various peddlers who scent the soldiers bounty money and various articles, some useful, some useless, are exchanged for "shinplasters." I purchased a stencil with which I mark my various articles of wearing apparel:

GA. HITCHCOCK

Co. A, 21st Reg't MV.

August 21

I receive a box of goodies from home in which is a letter from Henry written from Culpeper, Virginia, where the 21st has been engaged with the enemy. The selectmen of Ashby—Joseph Foster, Levi Burr, D. Ware and Boyden of Boston came out to camp to see us in the afternoon.

August 22

We receive news of the evacuation of the peninsula by McClellan. Eighty men for the 17th Mass left for the seat of war tonight.

August 26

I was drilled in battalion drill for the first time today. Edwin Whitney and Henry Burr from Ashby visited us bringing a home-box—especially acceptable in the change we get from the camp rations. I found prayer meeting in progress in number nine barracks conducted by Rev. Goodhue of North Cambridge; great interest was manifested.

August 30

No furloughs were allowed today and the momentous day has arrived. I received my government clothing and equipments which I donned and I am now a "truly soldier boy." Packed up my citizens clothes which I gave in charge of the corporal of the barracks to be sent home, after which I packed my knapsack in the most approved style which may not always be so thoroughly done.

After noon orders were issued for the recruits of the 2nd, 11th, 21st, 24th and 27th to leave for the seat of war. We harness up and realize at once that a heavy knapsack will be no boys plaything to carry about. March out of camp and load into horsecars—a long line being provided to transport us into Boston.

Several hundred of us march across the city through Washington Street. The Germania Band serenaded us as we passed and rendered very sweet and stirring music. The day was fine as were our spirits and thousands crowded the streets to bid us "God speed."

Embarked on the Old Colony Railroad for Fall River and at sunset roll out of the city. Enjoy the ride, stopping only once at Bridgewater until we reach Fall River at 9:30 P.M. Went on board the fine steamer, Empire State, and after finding a comfortable place in the grand saloon, where I deposit my accouterments, I explore the vessel which is a wonderful new world to me.

The novelty of sailing out on the broad ocean in a floating palace, with genuine Yankee curiosity—examining every part, from the huge engine to the luxurious cabins and from the hurricane decks watching the receding shores, all inspire me with an intense interest. At last I lie down on the soft carpet in the warm main cabin and sleep soon draws the curtain until early day light finds us sailing up the Long Island Sound and nearing New York harbor.

August 31

Multitudes of vessels of all descriptions are on all sides and as we near "Hell Gate" [section of East River, New York, a channel 200 feet wide at narrowest part], we pass under the shadow of the Great Eastern,[3] the largest vessel in the world which lies at anchor, its huge black hulk towers high above our decks and we get a fine idea of its immensity.

Arrive at the pier at foot of Cortlandt Street at 10 o'clock and march up Broadway to the "Soldiers Rest" on Franklin Street which is apparently a large old-time mansion converted to the use of government for lodging place for soldiers who are passing through the city and delayed awaiting transportation. This evidently is our lot, for we remain through the day and night. It is the Sabbath but we are not allowed to leave our quarters.

After drawing rations we while away the hours trying to reconcile ourselves to the noise of so many rollicking and profane fellows, card-playing, singing, munching rations and the like; while the din of rattling wheels on the pavement rack our country-bred ears and brains, we bid farewell to the New England Sabbath.

September 1

We awake to find a stormy day and march to the Jersey Ferry, cross to Jersey City, and wait three hours in the depot for transportation. Start at noon for Philadelphia; cross the Delaware River on a ferryboat and reach the city at half past nine in the evening. The rain was pouring and the streets comparatively deserted as we marched to the Soldiers Refreshment Saloon; at the "Cooper's Shop" we find an excellent supper, clean white tablecloths and lots of pretty girls to look after our welfare.

After this we take up our march to the Philadelphia, Willmington and Baltimore Railroad Station; here we find two new regiments ahead of us awaiting transportation. After some delay we are provided with quarters in the hall of a hose company nearby and at midnight stretch out our tired limbs until morning.

September 2

Leaving Philadelphia at half past eight, we pass out of the immense station of the PW&B. I caught sight of Mr. H. F. Kenney with whom I spoke. Mr. Kenney was a Fitchburg boy who went out to Philadelphia several years ago and has now the responsible position of Master of Transportation for the PW&B Railroad; he provides for the moving of the immense bodies of troops which pass through to the front.

The day was beautiful and I enjoy the ride through fertile fields and beautiful country. At noon the train arrives at the banks of the broad Susquehanna–opposite Wilmington, Delaware. Here at Havre de Grace our train is divided into three sections and run side by side onto great ferryboats, and transferred to Wilmington. Immediately on reaching the mainland I see negro slaves in large numbers and realize that we have left free land behind, and a feeling that we are in some sense in the enemy's country.

Arrive in Baltimore at 2:30, unload at the same place where the mob attacked the 6th Mass last year; and march across the city to the Soldiers Relief Building, where there are eight hundred others awaiting transportation. Our quarters are comfortless and crowded; evidently the policing of the building is not sufficient for the great numbers who have to be accommodated.

September 3

We are all glad to leave Baltimore on a very long train at near noon; a part of our load is a Zouave regiment in their showy uniforms. As we draw out of the city we meet a long train filled with wounded men from the battlefields of Bull Run and Chantilly.[4] The sight of them is sickening to many of us and we realize that the curtain is beginning to rise upon the dread realities of war.

From Baltimore to Washington we move very slowly and the warlike aspect increases as we approach the capitol forts and fortifications are on either side of the railroad and soldiers guarding the entire line. Reach Washington at noon and disembark near the Capitol building which we discern looming grandly above the trees–surmounted by the great white dome not yet finished.

Our long band of patriots march down Pennsylvania Avenue attracting but little notice and our consequence naturally diminishes in the same ration. However, I am too much interested in the scenes around us to care; soon we are in sight of the Potomac and gaze on the hills beyond. They appear delightful enough to the eye to remind us of Beulah land [name applied to the land of Israel or Jerusalem] but fancy gives way to the stern fact as we see several gunboats loaded with troops sailing up the river.

Learn for the first time that the rebel army is attempting to get north of our army and is already crossing into Maryland. We are taken across the river to Alexandria, Virginia, in a steamer where supper is furnished us after which we march out two miles to Chestnut Hill, a continuation of Arlington Heights and a short distance from Fort Elsworth.

At last our commander orders a halt and to camp for the night, adding the caution, "Lookout that you do not bump your heads against the rafters when you get up in the morning." Here we are at last on the sacred soil of Virginia and as darkness settles down upon the earth, the impression upon me is most thrilling.

From our elevated point of observation we see the countless fires of McClellan's great army dotting the valley thickly from Alexandria far out for miles on the Fairfax road which runs along the base of Chestnut Hill, while myriads of drums and bugles fill the night air with their martial sounds as they play the tattoo. McClellan is evidently concentrating his great army around Washington for its defense.

September 4

From our camping place as morning light breaks, we look out northward upon Washington as it lies spread out before us with its great marble Capitol as a central figure seven miles away: Alexandria almost at our feet two miles away and the Potomac with its broad stream sweeping around in a grand curve for ten miles down to Port Washington. Westward and back of us a circle of hills which must once have been picturesque but now almost entirely denuded of trees and dug up with fortifications.

News came in to us that the 21st Mass was badly cut up in the late battle, and that Colonel Clark and all his staff were lost—either captured or wounded;[5] Lieutenant Colonel Rice of Ashburnham was killed; members of the 21st serving in the convalescent camp near us report that the regiment was not far away—some two miles out toward Fairfax.

September 5

I started out to find the regiment but had not gone a mile when I learned that it went to Chain Bridge, six miles up the river. A rough looking, wiry grisly man strolled into camp who was said to be "California Joe" of Berdan's Sharpshooters.[6]

September 6

The sun shone down very hot, so Lem and I rigged a shelter with our rubber blanket.

*   *   *

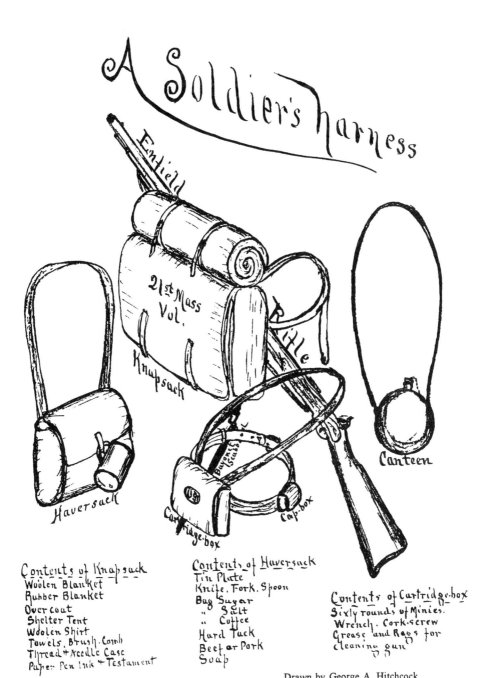

Contents of Knapsack
Woolen Blanket
Rubber Blanket
Overcoat
Shelter Tent
Woolen Shirt
Towels, Brush, Comb
Thread & Needle Case
Paper, Pen, Ink & Testament

Contents of Haversack
Tin Plate
Knife, Fork, Spoon
Bag Sugar
" Salt
" Coffee
Hard Tack
Beef or Pork
Soap

Contents of Cartridge-box
Sixty rounds of Minies.
Wrench, Cork-screw
Grease and Rags for
cleaning gun

Drawn by George A. Hitchcock

Capt. George P. Hawkes

Hawkes was taken prisoner at the Battle of Chantilly on September 1, 1862, and although was soon released on parole, he was not exchanged for several months. He was promoted to major on September 2, 1862, and to lieutenant colonel on December 18, 1862. He resigned due to a disability on July 3, 1864.

"I quickly distinguished "Honest Old Abe" with General McClellan by his side at the head of a long line of notables. He rode a spirited horse but handled him in a masterly fashion. He wore the democratic black suit and stove pipe hat. As he passed up and down the lines I had a fine opportunity to see his features which were homely but lighted up with a kindliness which would make the plainest person attractive. . . ."

Two
The Maryland Campaign

On September 1, 1862, after the Union army retreated to Centreville, the Second Bull Run Campaign came to a violent end during a tremendous thunderstorm. Two Federal divisions fought a bloody but successful rear guard action at the Battle of Chantilly at Ox Hill, Virginia, against Thomas "Stonewall" Jackson's troops, which were attempting to crush the retreating Union right flank. Two of the more promising commanders of the Union army were killed in the engagement: Maj. Gen. Philip Kearny, who commanded the First Division of the III Corps, and Maj. Gen. Isaac Ingalls Stevens, the commander of the First Division of the IX Corps. The 21st Massachusetts was hotly engaged at Chantilly, where Hitchcock's regiment suffered the heaviest casualties it would experience during the war.

President Abraham Lincoln removed Maj. Gen. John Pope as commander of the Union army the following day and replaced him with Maj. Gen. George Brinton McClellan. The soldiers were jubilant about the change of commander and the troops, notwithstanding their loss of morale from the debacle on the plains of Manassas, were prepared to challenge the Confederate forces within a matter of days.

Shortly after Lincoln reinstalled McClellan at the head of the Army of the Potomac, Gen. Robert E. Lee embarked on a bold raid north of the Potomac River. His 55,000-man army moved north to Leesburg, Virginia, on September 4 *and crossed the Potomac River at White's Ford. The vanguard of the Army of Northern Virginia arrived in Frederick on September 6. When Lee's plan to resupply his army and recruit soldiers failed, he evacuated the city on September 10 and marched toward the South Mountain gaps. The Federals, however, refused to abandon Harpers Ferry as Lee had anticipated. Lee divided his army, sending Jackson's troops to capture the 2,500 Union soldiers at Martinsburg and some 11,000 others at Harpers Ferry. McClellan's advance arrived in Frederick on September 12, where the next day XII Corps soldiers discovered Special Orders 191, which detailed the position and strength of the various segments of Lee's army. McClellan moved against Lee with more alacrity than usual, and on September 14, 1862, attacked three well-defended gaps in the South Mountain range: Crampton's, Fox's and Turner's.*

The 21st Massachusetts went into action at Fox's Gap, where the fighting lasted until 10:00 p.m. Major General Jesse Reno, commander of the IX Corps, was killed during the fighting, and his loss devastated the men of the 21st. According to Augustus Woodbury, there was not a man in the regiment who did not love him. "He had a magnetic kind of enthusiasm," he wrote, "and, when leading on his men, he seemed to inspire his followers and make them irresistible in action—a dauntless soldier, whose like we rarely see."

Late on the afternoon of September 15, McClellan halted the Army of the Potomac on the east bank of Antietam Creek near the village of Sharpsburg. The Federal right wing (the I and IX Corps) was commanded by Maj. Gen. Burnside; the center (the II and XII Corps) by Maj. Gen. Edwin V Sumner, and the left (the VI Corps and Darius Couch's division of the IV Corps) by Maj. Gen. William B. Franklin.

By the following evening General Lee had most of the Army of Northern Virginia deployed on the heights crowning the west bank of Antietam Creek. Lee's army, unofficially composed of two corps commanded by Maj. Gen. James Longstreet and Maj. Gen. Thomas J. Jackson, was concentrated in front of Sharpsburg. Jackson's troops arrived on the field on September 16, one day after the surrender of Harpers Ferry. At sunrise the following morning the divisions of Lafayette McLaws and Richard Anderson arrived from Harpers Ferry. About 40,000 Confederate troops confronted some 87,000 Federals.

The Battle of Antietam was fought on September 17, 1862. The fighting lasted from sunrise until after dark and resulted in the bloodiest single day battle of the Civil War. Union losses were 12,882 (2,157 killed, 9,716 wounded and 1,009 missing), while Confederate losses were only slightly less at 11,530 (1,754 killed, 8,649 wounded and 1,127 missing).

The 21st Massachusetts was engaged in the afternoon phase of the battle at the lower bridge—popularly dubbed Burnside's Bridge—over Antietam

Creek. Five hundred Georgia riflemen from the 2nd and 20th Georgia regiments stalled the Union advance over the narrow span during the morning hours. When Burnside's troops finally crossed the creek in the early afternoon, the Georgians withdrew toward Sharpsburg. As Burnside's Federals were driving across the fields and hills toward Sharpsburg, Maj. Gen. Ambrose P. Hill's Confederates division arrived from Harpers Ferry and drove the Union troops back to the heights near the bridge. Hill's tactical victory was the last significant fighting at Antietam. Lee, whose army had come within hair's breadth of being demolished, brazenly held his position the following day and began withrawing south of the Potomac River later that evening.

Although the battle's results were not readily apparent (and are still hotly debated today), several diplomatic, military, political and social implications eventually flowed from the fighting. Robert E. Lee had failed in his bid to duplicate his successful string of battles north of the Potomac River. President Lincoln's political support, which hinged largely on military successes, solidified with the blunting of Lee's offensive and his subsequent retreat. Lincoln had stated in 1861 that "we must settle this question now, whether in a free government the minority have the right to break up the government whenever they choose." He utilized the "victory" at Antietam as a means of enlarging the purpose of the war beyond simply saving the Union. On September 22, 1862, Lincoln issued the preliminary Emancipation Proclamation, which would take effect January 1, 1863. The document purported to free slaves held in those parts of the nation still in rebellion. The brilliant political document all but ended the threat of European intervention in the war and the movement overseas for diplomatic recognition of the Confederacy waned.

George Hitchcock finally managed to link up with the 21st Massachusetts on September 9, 1862, in Maryland, a rather untimely association that cast him into one of the war's bloodiest contests. On September 14, 225 soldiers in the regiment were lightly engaged at South Mountain, with four suffering wounds. Three days later 150 of the regiment's soldiers marched with Ambrose Burnside across the creek and against the Sharpsburg heights. Almost thirty percent of these were killed or wounded (10 killed and 35 wounded).

*   *   *

September 7, 1862

As I sat under our shelter reading this Sabbath morning, orders came for us to pack up and march. At noon we left Chestnut Hill and proceeded to Long Bridge[1] where we wait fore 14 hours and then cross what is said to be the longest bridge in the world, up Pennsylvania Ave to the "Soldiers' Rest" between the railroad station and the Capitol building where we lodge for the night. On our way through the streets we saw General Casey,[2] a large gray haired man of about sixty, who is commander of the post.

September 8

On arising from our rough quarters, I had my first introduction to the "soldiers companion," which sticketh closer than a brother, loveth darkness rather than light because his deeds are evil. He also loveth a warm comer and every cleanly soldier would gladly consign him to a very warm region (LICE). I found Herbert Leland,[3] drummer for Company A of the 21st, with several who had been taken prisoners at Chantilly and were now paroled enroute for Annapolis.

At one in the afternoon our squad marches out of Washington northward on the road to Annapolis Junction. March all the afternoon, halt in the evening by the side of the road until eleven when news is received that our 21st is only three miles ahead; we press forward until we find the distance increased to five and at last we discern in midnight darkness the "tented city;" an inquiry soon leads us to General Burnside's headquarter's tents and a few minutes later to the 21st.

September 9

At one o'clock at night, I find myself groping among the sleeping thousands seeking my brother [Henry S. Hitchcock]. There was a weirdness in the surroundings which impressed me; in the midst of so much life, how silent, and my own voice almost startled me as I inquired from tent to tent of the heavy-breathing sleepers to find the Sergeant's tent. Reaching it, I called Henry's name and he answered me immediately. My anxious inquiries were soon checked by him since we would have only three hours to sleep; I therefore drop down on the ground by his side and am soon asleep.

At half past four I am aroused for coffee. The daylight reveals to me the effects of the terrible hardships upon my old friends in their worn pinched features and battered uniforms. My own new uniform at once reveals me as a "fresh fish" by its comparison. I am also sadly impressed by the depleted ranks of the company whose fortunes I have so closely watched during the past year.

After taking a genuine campaign breakfast, I harness up (knapsack, haversack, canteen, gun and equipments) and take my place in the ranks. Lem and I are in the first file of fours on the right of Company A—being two of the tallest [5'11"]. We are now full-fledged soldiers of the Army of the Potomac, but after a short spurt of brisk marching I feel like an unfledged chicken.

Tripping gaily along through verdant meads [meadows] and by bubbling brooks and all that sort of things may sound well in romance, but wriggle as I may, I do not find the soft spot on my shoulder or back where the harness does not chafe and the fifty pounds of load soon becomes a ton. How a fellow can ever "dash furiously" against the enemy in this panoply seems very grim humor.

We are also cheered and comforted by our veteran comrades with the assurance that this is nothing compared to the "Camden march" (the Camden chestnut was constantly hurled at us throughout the service whenever we passed through any severe marching).[4] We accept in silence all advice, consolation or jibes but keep up a busy thinking.

Burnside's whole corps are on the road marching in a north-westerly direction. The occasional halts are very welcome to me. Soon afternoon we file out into a field and go into camp in a hollow ground after an eight mile march, near Brookeville. I feel well used up.

September 10

We did not move today, lying about in the scorching sun. We see a constant stream of troops moving past, some on the divert road to Frederick City [Frederick, Maryland], others going due west . I feel much refreshed after the day's rest.

September 11

The reveille arouses us at half past four and at half past six we move out on the road to Frederick City. March all day, halting after every two miles. Meet some of our cavalry pickets bringing in a rebel prisoner who tells us that the enemy is about six miles away. After a fourteen mile march we go into camp in a fine level field. I try my luck at cooking meat for the first time; it is done in primitive style by impaling on a stick and held over the fire. I am too dainty yet to relish the style.

September 12

Rained nearly all night and I was lying in a hollow place; result, wet as a drowned rat. We march fifteen miles and when we're miles from Frederick, find that the enemy is but a short distance ahead. Hear cannonading as we approach the city. The road is filled with troops hurrying forward to the scene of action. Arriving within two miles and in sight of the city, we camp for the night.

September 13

Our division [Second Division of the IX Corps commanded by General Samuel Davis Sturgis] is under orders to move at a moments notice and to be prepared for fighting. I therefore go to work and acquaint myself with my new friend, my Enfield rifle; take it to pieces, clean it up and then harness up and lie on arms until four in the afternoon when we are ordered forward.

The cannonading, which has kept up very briskly during the day, slackens. As the sun goes down behind the lofty Blue Ridge, we march briskly through Frederick City with drums beating and colors flying, then out across a long level tract and as darkness settle down upon the scene, we begin to climb the Blue Ridge. Up, up, four long weary miles when it seems as if I could not take another step. At last we reach the Gap which has been held all day by the enemy.

We see signs of the struggle on each side of the road. Although trapped in darkness, we gain a faint idea of the grand view before us. Signal lights flashing from distant heights and outlines of lofty ranges far away beyond the Potomac. We do not stop but hasten down the mountain side and go into camp near Middletown after a ten mile march. We have marched over seventy miles within a week—a good test for a raw recruit.

September 14

We lie on arms all the morning, listening to the battle of the artillery up the side of South Mountain. The serious faces of my comrades warns me that I may soon have to receive my "baptism of fire." At half past one in the afternoon, the fated order comes to us: "Forward Second Brigade"—this is composed of the 21st Mass, 51st New York and 51st Penn. Our division marches rapidly through the streets of Middletown and we see the village given up to the uses of the army.

Churches are filling up with wounded as they are rapidly brought in on stretchers and in ambulances. From their steeple-tops the signal corps is busy with its waving signals. The streets are packed with troops hurrying forward and into battle. Passing out toward the sharp and constant rattle of musketry, we meet a steady stream of wounded pouring down the mountain sides. Up half a mile ahead we see the dense smoke where is the center of conflict, long black lines are sweeping across the open space or moving out of the woods.

As we begin to ascend the hill groaning and screaming men covered with blood, blackened with smoke lie on each side of the road. Officers and orderlies mounted and galloping frantically about. The sights and sounds fairly sicken me but John Wallace,[5] the corporal who has us under his direct command, cautions us to keep our eyes straight ahead. At last we file out into a field and form in line of battle [Fox's Gap - Wise's field: part of the struggle was for the wooded crest on the left of the field; Confederate soldiers were posted behind a stonewall near the Wise's house; on the left of Wise's house is the ridge road].

With no delay we rush forward at double-quick-step to save a battery. Our part of the line swings around into the grove of trees on the left of the field, when suddenly a sheet of flame a few rods in front from out of the trees beyond greets us, a united volley of musketry and artillery. Instantly the order comes, "Lie down," and as instantly obeyed. An eternity of time it seems as we receive the withering fire but possibly twenty minutes elapses when it is seen that an attempt is being make to flank us.

We are ordered across the road to the left which is called Fox's Gap. The sunken road is literally packed with dead and dying rebels who had held so stubbornly the pass against our troops who have resistlessly swept up over the hill. Here the horrors of war were revealed as we see our heavy ammunition wagons go tearing up, right over the dead and dying, mangling many in their terrible course. The shrieks of the poor fellows were heartrending.

Our brigade is moved forward into an open field on the summit of the mountain [South Mountain] between two wooded pieces and again formed in line of battle when we receive a waking fire from the enemy who is strongly posted behind a stone wall a half dozen rods in front. Falling flat for a few moments until the volley is over, then rising up, charge across the field reaching the stonewall, we find the 51st New York who were halting for orders. Our position is so far advanced and exposed that some little time elapses before any of the field officers appear. Captain Richardson,[6] the senior officer present, at last orders us back to the woods in our rear and not finding any superior officers, we retreat still further to a corn field where Colonel Clark finds us. General Sturgis immediately orders us up to the stone wall.

We learn that General Reno[7] has just been killed and this accounts for the temporary disorder of the brigade. His death is a terrible loss for he was considered one of the finest, bravest and most popular officers of the army.

Soon after breaching the stone wall, darkness settled down over all and the Battle of South Mountain has passed into history. We remain in position all through the chilly night expecting a renewed attempt by the rebels to force the pass. As the hours slowly pass by, I review the events of the past week and personally am not ashamed of my participation in them. Have succeeded in keeping pace with veterans in the long severe march which intercepted General

Lee's Army in its attempt to carry the war North. Have not flinched in this my first battle and now my comrades tell me the next one will come easier.

What were my feelings when first under fire? I was fearfully that the rebels would hit somebody and I wished they would not hit me. How did I feel? My brain was constantly telegraphing to my legs to take me down the hill. Yes, strange as it may seem, I did not want to be shot and I thought I might be if I remained. I was not brave and I did not want to be a coward so I watch the others and did just as they did, carrying on a conflict on my own private account in my heart and with the help of God I won a victory.

September 15

As daylight slowly lifts the curtain we begin to realize the heavy loss to the enemy. The first sight to meet our gaze was a dead rebel hanging over the wall. Just over the other side the ground was thickly strewed with dead who had been our silent companions through the night. We find the enemy has retreated but were startled just before sunrise by hearing the report of the guns of our pickets just in front of us in the woods.

We were double-quicked into the woods and take two or three rebels who by mistake came into our lines supposing the summit was in possession of the rebels. We lay on arms through the morning; many of our boys venture out beyond the lines and secure trophies of the conflict from the rebel dead. The faces of many have changed color to a dusky hue, which gives them a frightful appearance. It is said to be caused by drinking a concoction of whiskey and gunpowder.

At noon General Burnside and a large escort rode by us down the Boonesboro Road amid the hearty cheers of his men. He was followed by division after division. Fitz-John Porter's Corps [Fifth Corps] composed largely of U.S. regulars also passed us. At last we start and South Mountain is left behind. March until dark through a beautiful, fertile country, the boys in good spirits singing the rebel song, "Maryland, My Maryland," and go into camp near Boonesboro.

Reports to the effect that the rebel army is cornered between us and the Potomac, that General [John Ellis] Wool is engaging them from Harpers' Ferry, that they are much demoralized and that Stonewall Jackson is killed.[8]

September 16

The morning is foggy, but our artillery is hard at work, the various batteries moving from one position to another. The whir of shells and scream of solid shots are constant and painful to listen to. Often the rebel batteries range becomes uncomfortably close for us as their "railroad iron" comes screaming and burying in our midst. The scarcity of heavy ammunition is said to cripple the enemy and the standing joke of our boys as the unusual sound made by the supposed blacksmith's tools greets us coming from their batteries is: "Look out for the blacksmith, they'll be sending him over next, to get his tools."

General Burnside rode up and addressed a few encouraging words to his men, saying that our artillery had forced back the enemy a mile. During the afternoon as we are lying in a field by the side of the road, the sounds of cheering is heard away back in our rear; it is taken up and comes nearer when soon General McClellan, followed by a long staff of officers in brilliant uniforms and escort of cavalry, rides rapidly past us. I had expected to see a dark-complexioned man but instead, find him fair-haired and light complexioned.

At four in the afternoon our brigade moves forward about a mile and rests on arms, supporting a battery for the night. Rations are furnished us as our wagons have succeeded in reaching the army.

September 17

Get a good nights rest and early in the morning we are moved forward to support Captain [Samuel N.] Benjamin's battery. The roar of artillery is incessant and seems to come from far and near, evidently the two great armies are getting to work in earnest. We received a large mail from home; Colonel Clark learns that extensive preparations were being make for his funeral in Amherst as he had been reported killed at Chantilly.

At one o'clock the terrible order is received by us, "Forward and charge down the hill to the banks of the creek." Up over the brow of the hill in face of a terrific artillery fire sweeping past Benjamin's battery which reserved its fire until we had descended below its range. The long sheet of flame poured its leaden hail upon us, but we rush forward at double quick until we reach a cornfield where we halt to close up ranks. Benjamin's battery sends its shells screaming uncomfortable close over our heads and we can see the havoc they make among the trees beyond Antietam Creek.

Filing out of the cornfield we charge down to within twenty rods of the creek and the rebel line just beyond. Here we halt in clear view of the whole rebel line, load and fire as rapidly as possible. In this way we draw the rebel fire from the 51st New York which is charging across the bridge. The struggle on the side-hill may have lasted nearly half an hour before the charge was made on the bridge. Here our loss was heaviest—scores of our men were swept down, some pitched headlong down the hill, some dropped with a "thud" and lay motionless, others lay writhing in death agony, others ran bleeding back up the hill.

Among the number was Dan Dailey,[9] an old Ashby boy somewhat older than myself [22 years old], a big jolly Irishman who, in time gone by, when we were together in the old district school house, taught me to chew my first and last quid of tobacco. The memory of it still lingers and I seem to see him in an uncontrollable fit of laughter as I had surreptitiously taken and swallowed the sickening juice, the agonized look on my face partly from a deathly sickness and partly from fear of exposure to the teacher. But my time was too fully occupied to take notice of falling friends. My only duty was to take sure aim into the rebel ranks and forget the carnage; yet I was conscious of the magnitude of the battle from the sounds of the roar and rattle far and near, and the sight along toward our right on the elevated lands.

When the 51st New York is fairly on the bridge, we push forward to the stonewall and pour a volley into the rebels; we see their sharpshooters drop from the trees and soon the whole rebel line is flying up the hill and out of sight. Then we tear down the rail fence and follow the 51st Penn. As soon as we are across the bridge we halt to reform, being in inextricable confusion. Out of range of the musketry for the moment, the comrades of the three regiments fraternize and congratulate each other on securing the bridge which had been hotly contested all day.

The remainder of the 2nd Division soon follows us and General Burnside dashes across with two or three orderlies, hastily scans the situation, orders the division into position and sweeps in a long line of battle up over the brow of the hill where we find the rebels who again fall back to the edge of a large cornfield where they rally behind a rail fence. A withering fire from us again sends them flying and we take position on the opposite side of the fence. Here we lie down and give them more of Uncle Sam's kills.

Lem and I are now full of enthusiasm and so busy loading and firing that we forge all else. We are not as expeditious in emptying our cartridge boxes as our more experienced comrades and amid the din and crash of exploding shells, the flying of splintered fence rails, we do not see the regiment retire down the hill; after a few minutes we realize that we are alone with the killed and wounded so we crawl back and find the boys under the brow of the hill, slightly protected from the musketry fire.

It seems that the new 35th Mass regiment has been joined to our brigade and had just been placed on the left of the old brigade. The 21st had been pushed too far front so that the enemy's lines overlapped ours and giving the 35th a raking flank fire doubled them back hence the necessity of reforming our line further back. The sun had now set and the battle lulls. We rest on arms during the night by the banks of the creek. During the earlier part of the night the gloom is lighted by the burning of Sharpsburg, half a mile away inside the rebel lines. The ghastly light added to the groans and screams of the wounded render the night truly hideous.

September 18

While catching a few naps, the surgeons and their assistants can be heard all about as attending to their sad duties. The losses must have been very heavy on both sides. One voice whose groans had been heart rending all night long, gradually grew weaker until daylight when we saw that death had hushed it.

Soon after daylight our regiment is ordered out on the skirmish line and I have my first experience in that line. We are deployed in front of our most advancing line of yesterday - further to the left. The day is dark and cloudy; no attack is made from either side; although exposed to the bullets of the enemy's line of skirmishes, there seems to be a recognized or tacit agreement not to fire, so we sit all watching each other like two bulldogs. It is very evident that the enemy have suffered fearfully, and rumors at night say they are retreating across the Potomac. From my position I see rebel officers ride out and take observations but too far away for a bullet to reach. Fresh troops relieve us at night and we return across the creek encamping in an apple orchard. It was here we first learn of Dailey's death—being shot in the leg and bleeding to death.

September 19

Wrote letters home in the morning. The 21st mustered seventy-five men, two captains, and one field officer—Colonel Clark. [Casualties suffered by the 21st in the battle of Antietam: killed—one officer and nine enlisted men; wounded—three officers and thirty-two enlisted men; a heavy loss since there were less than 150 officers and men involved; Companies B and F went back to Frederick to guard the prisoners taken at South Mountain].

The enemy is supposed to have retreated into Virginia so before noon our regiment is sent forward as advance guard of the division. Deploying about a rod apart, we advance as a line of skirmishers some four miles when we come in sight of the Potomac and our advance is checked by shells from rebel batteries on the opposite bank. Finding shelter behind a hill, we ascertain the fact that the enemy is strongly posted. At night we are relieved and retire beyond the rang of the enemy's artillery, supporting Captain Benjamin's battery.

September 20

We did not move today and General Burnside promises us two weeks rest, which is welcome news. Fighting has been reported a few miles up the river where it is said that two or three regiments were captured while trying to escape into Virginia. Stragglers have been coming in all day and our regiment now numbers nearly two hundred men.

September 21

The day has been spent in washing clothes and body, writing home letters and strolling about short distances from the regiment. The routine of camp duties has been established and dress parade held for the first time since I joined the regiment. Religious services were held by Chaplain Ball,[10] reading the scripture, prayer and touching remarks eulogizing Lieutenant Colonel Rice, who was a Christian and beloved by all the regiment. Colonel Clark read a message from General Burnside tendering his thanks to the 21st for their bravery in the late battle.

September 22

Have been cleaning up and trying my hand at cooking. Several regiments passed by us in the direction of Harpers Ferry where rumor says we are soon to go. The new 36th Mass regiment has just arrived and been has been placed in our division. There is a company of Templeton[11] boys in it which we have been visiting.

September 23

Our bugle sounded before light, rousing us to pack up and prepare to march. After waiting in the scorching sun until noon we again spread our blankets and in the afternoon the order was countermanded. We were visited by a delegation sent out by the town of Fitchburg to look after the wounded belonging to that town. They were Dr. Hitchcock, Alvah Crocker, Porter Kimball, Norman Stone and Benj Prentiss.[12]

September 24

A smart shower in the forenoon but I kept dry under our rubber shelter. Wrote and received letters from home. The fireside patriots of the North are getting excited over the nine months enlistments. I have just read President Lincoln's emancipation proclamation freeing the slaves after the 1st of next January. Good!

September 25

The morning is cold with heavy dew. We are drummed up before light and prepare to march. At noon orders are received to move at one o'clock when we move away from camp some twenty rods and rest in line until half past four; again the order was countermanded and we return to camp for the night. The New York Herald containing accounts of the late battle have been received in camp with great interest.

September 26

Orders received again today for us to move and at eleven we move down across Antietam Creek where it empties into the Potomac. Here we are joined by the remainder of the brigade and proceed into camp, two miles from our former one, very near General Burnside's headquarters. The entire 2nd Division is encamped in a large level field and as we expect to remain here several days, proceed to erect tents and comfortable shelters of boughs. One great inconvenience is that all the water for the entire division has to be brought from a large spring, half a mile away. Since the spring is ample for the thousands of troops in the vicinity, it is constantly surrounded by great crowds of men, mules and horses.

September 27

Camp duties have been established: roll call twice a day, camp guard detailed, guard mounting at nine in the morning, and dress parade at six at night. Orders, lamenting the death of General Reno, were read at dress parade. The monotony of camp-life is hard to bear—by its great contrast from the exciting times of the past month.

September 28

Roll was called at five in the morning, breakfast at six, inspection of arms and equipments at eight, after which there are no duties until dress parade at five in the afternoon. Wrote letters home; Henry Cobly[13] of the 36th Mass called on us. Have just heard of the deaths of Captains Frazer[14] and Kelton[15] who were wounded at Chantilly. The band of the 9th New Hampshire discoursed some very fine music at sunset.

September 29

Today the 21st was detailed to go down to the Potomac and posted at the confluence of Antietam Creek as reserve picket. We lounged about in the shade near the picturesque ruins of an old mill and a stone bridge over the creek. We could discern the black mouths of cannon beyond the Potomac but "all was quiet on the Potomac" as on former days. Returned to camp at night.

September 30

Company drill in the morning; recruits drilled separately; part of the regiment was out on picket. Burnside came into our camp to look after his boys. He is very popular with all. In the afternoon the regiment received orders to pack up, but as soon as we were ready, they were countermanded. The hot sun affects us unfavorably; Lem Whitney is sick with diarrhea and excused from duty.

October 1

Heavy thunder shower at night but we keep pretty dry under our rubber blanket shelter. Received a most welcome mail of letters and papers from the North.

October 2

Company drill at eight, battalion drill at half past three. Wrote home, read in the Boston papers a thrilling account of the battle of South Mountain. Rumors that we are to have a visit from President Lincoln.

October 3

The 21st was ordered out at seven in the morning and to slick up nice to meet the President. The various brigades, divisions, infantry, cavalry and artillery were drawn up in long lines and at half past ten, the bands struck up "Hail to the Chief," as a great cavalcade came down the lines.

I quickly distinguished "Honest Old Abe" with General McClellan by his side at the head of a long line of notables. He rode a spirited horse but handled him in a masterly fashion. He wore the democratic black suit and stove pipe hat. As he passed up and down the lines I had a fine opportunity to see his features which were homely but lighted up with a kindliness which would make the plainest person attractive. From us he rode away in the direction of the Potomac where the rest of the army is encamped.

October 4

I was detailed for guard duty today for the first time since I joined the regiment. Saw the great army balloon. Company A drilled in skirmishing. Heavy cannonading in the direction of Harpers Ferry and shortly afterward dense black smoke arose from the same direction, but we do not learn of its meaning. By the middle of the afternoon dark wind clouds arose with spiteful gusts accompanied with light rain swept over the camp threatening destruction to our frail shelters but cooling the atmosphere by night.

October 5

Mail arrived but I miss my expected letter so sit down and write in return. Supplies of clothing and shelter tents arrive. Lem and I each draw a piece which we put up and find it a very acceptable home using one rubber blanket at one end and the other laid on the ground. Chaplain Ball gave us an excellent talk at dress parade, with reading scriptures and prayers, after which the regiment joined in singing Old Hundred [Psalm 100]. Company A has several fine singers in its ranks and leads the regiment in that branch of worship so that it has acquired the nickname of the "Psalm-singing Company A." Much enjoyment is had from the exercise of that talent by both singers and listeners.

October 6

The night was so cold I could not sleep and I therefore sat over the cook's fire most of the night. Battalion drill was omitted as we are under marching orders with one day rations in our haversack. Lem and I closed up our tent at night thereby securing a comfortable nights rest.

October 7

The 2nd Division was roused at three in the morning, got breakfast and packed up before day light, and left camp at eight marching in the direction of Harpers Ferry. The road was very narrow and rough, winding up the side of the mountains making very slow progress. At half past one in the afternoon, we reach the summit of Maryland Heights, from which an extensive and magnificent prospect is spread out before us. A long range of the Blue Ridge stretching from far up into Pennsylvania down across Maryland into Virginia; nearer to us in the southeast is another range running parallel with us, inclosing Pleasant Valley (truly named), picturesque in its beautiful country scenes, farm houses dotting the landscape with fertile cultivated fields.

As the eye follows this valley down toward the Potomac, it meets the rugged cliffs of Bolivar Heights, rising perpendicular back of Harpers Ferry, beyond which lies the Shenandoah Valley. From these same heights and wilds where we are looking, John Brown and his daring band were hounded. Today "his soul is marching on" in us, the great Union Army, and slavery is doomed.

After a long rest during which we feast the eye on the sublime and lovely prospect, we descend into Pleasant Valley and go into camp in a fine large field sloping to the south some three miles from Harpers Ferry. The camp is laid out with regularity, the four regiments arranged as sides of a hollow square with a large parade ground in the center.

October 8

Camp guard was instituted and the usual duties for perfecting us in military life established. The sun shines down upon us very hot. I can hear the sounds of railway trains and the whistle of locomotive down on the Baltimore and Ohio Railroad, the first time for more than a month and a pleasant reminder of peaceful times. Mail was received in which I was remembered.

October 9

I was detailed as guard and posted at the Quartermaster's and Commissary's tents. My duties were not arduous, simply to keep off intruders and thieves, but the sun was scorching. Brother Henry was officer of guard; Lem Whitney was posted at General Sturgis' Headquarters, protecting an orchard of ripe apples (wish I could protect it).

October 10

The day has been cloudy and mild. Came off guard at eight and had no duties until battalion drill at three in the afternoon. A new full regiment, the 11th New Hampshire, Colonel Harriman[16] commanding, was joined to our 2nd Brigade. The men were a large brawny looking set, enlisted from the central and northern part of New Hampshire. We think they will make fine material for soldiers, sandwiched in with our veterans. Several of the 21st boys were arrested by the provost guard for stealing apples.

October 11

A fierce northeaster broke upon us during the night. A small tornado awoke me just in time to save our tent from destruction but many others were blown down. But little rain fell during the day yet the air was so chilly that we bundled ourselves in our overcoats and closed up our tents. Major Foster[17] joined the regiment from Massachusetts where he has been since the battle of Roanoke Island where he was severely wounded in the leg. He is still very lame. Received mail in the evening.

October 12

Chilly, cloudy day; was detailed for guard and got a soaking as it rained hard all night. Sunday morning inspection by General Ferrero.[18] Companies C and F were excused from all duties for the day and night on account of their neatness and clean equipments. Heard heavy cannonading all day down the river. Wrote home asking for a box of supplies. Religious services were omitted as Chaplain Ball has gone to Washington.

October 13

The cold northeaster continues with but little rain, and as I can't keep warm, I am "blue." We learn that J.E.B. Stuart's cavalry made a dash into Pennsylvania and returning, made a circuit of our army. In his attempt to recross into Virginia, he met with resistance. This explains the cannonading heard yesterday at Point of Rocks. [19]

A corn field discovered not far away received a general harvesting by our Yankee soldiers who do not want to forget their farm education. Result, hasty pudding for dinner. If inquisitive minds seek to know where the corn was ground, leave the Yankee alone to find out the way. Our tin cartridge-box cases were punched full of holes with our bayonets forming a grater and meal produced after the fashion of grated nutmeg.

October 14

The weather cleared up somewhat although still chilly and cloudy. Feasting on hasty pudding and molasses for breakfast, stewed beans for dinner and pudding and sugar for supper: highly relished as a change from the everlasting, indomitable, indestructible hardtack. Major Foster commanded the regiment at battalion drill. He is a dashing officer skillful in handling his high spirited horse, in spite of his "game leg." Our candle ration fell short so Lem and I spend the evening in darkness shut up in our tent.

October 15

Am feeling nearly sick today. Was on guard at the Quartermaster's tents. Letter from home—father has gathered twelve barrels of apples (wish I was there). He writes that the Ashby quota of nine months men has been raised and gone into camp at Groton in the 53rd Mass. Henry received letter from Captain Hawkes[20] who is at Camp Parole in Annapolis, not yet exchanged. He was captured at Chantilly.

October 16

Clouds and sunbeams have fought for mastery all day. Cannonading above Harpers Ferry opened at seven in the morning and continued all day. The 1st Brigade received marching orders and ours are expected tomorrow. Brigade guard mounting and no one allowed outside the lines without a pass. Announcement at dress parade that we are to have full supplies of clothing.

October 17

Heavy thunder showers during the night. McClellan began moving his army across the Potomac into Virginia at Charlestown where it met with resistance but succeeded after hard skirmishing. J. Clapp[21] received his discharge papers tonight. General Burnside visited the 21st just before dress parade. He has a way of showing a fatherly interest in the boys which makes him much beloved.

October 18

A beautiful but cold day. General Ferrero commanded the brigade dress parade. It was a fine sight - regimental drill was omitted so that we prepare for Sunday morning inspection. A bundle of letters and papers for me in the mail.

October 19

Rained at intervals through the night; day inspection at eight. Dress parade omitted on account of rain.

October 20

Detailed for guard duty; my post was in the valley below the camp but the cold penetrating wind made me very uncomfortable; therefore made a fire on my beat. Brigade drill in the afternoon. A straw stack was discovered in the vicinity and transferred to camp and no questions asked.

October 21

Suffered from cold during the night on guard and the morning revealed a heavy white frost. Company drill at ten, regimental drill at two, and dress parade at four fill up the day's duties. I begin to feel quite proficient in soldier's duties. The wintry blast has caught us unprepared—changing so suddenly from summer s heat.

October 22

Fred Sanderson[22] was captain of the guard today; Henry commanded Company A at drills and dress parade. Several members of our regiment have enlisted into the regular army cavalry.

October 23

At dress parade a circular was read notifying us that, "owing to the impending movement" no more clothing will be given out. This looks as if we were to leave here soon. Henry stopped with me overnight.

October 24

Another heavy frost this morning. Was on guard at Col Wild's[23] headquarters of the 35th Mass. Regt. Regimental inspection of arms and equipments in the afternoon. Have been reading in Massachusetts papers of the excitement occasioned by the draft in various places. The home patriots are very willing to enjoy the fruits of others' struggles but are unwilling to bear their share of the sacrifice. The regular army enlistments are causing great havoc in the veteran regiments; many have already left our regiment.

October 25

Preparations for early marching are being made; all surplus baggage and supplies have been sent to Washington. In the afternoon orders were issued for marching at daylight with two days cooked rations, but just before bed time the orders were countermanded. Albert Davis[24] of the 6th N.H. called to see me; his brigade is under marching orders.

October 26

Storm began at nine in the morning and at ten orders came to march; these were countermanded owing to the very heavy rain. No camp duties, so we staid close under our shelters all day.

*   *   *

Major General Ambrose Burnside,
George A. Hitchcock's favorite commander

Three

The Fredericksburg Campaign

On November 5, 1862, President Lincoln relieved George McClellan from command of the Army of the Potomac; Maj. Gen. Ambrose Burnside assumed command two days later. McClellan had adopted what Lincoln viewed as an extremely cautious policy. His steadfast refusal to undertake offensive action against his opponent resulted in his removal. The fact that he was recognized as a prominent opponent of the Lincoln administration and its policies did not assist his cause.

Burnside reorganized the army into what he styled three "grand divisions," with each wing composed of two corps of three divisions plus artillery and cavalry brigade. Major General William Franklin commanded the Left Grand Division (47,000 men including the I and VI Corps with 100 pieces of artillery); Maj. Gen. Joseph Hooker commanded the Center Grand Division (40,000 men including the III and V Corps with 100 pieces of artillery) and Maj. Gen. Edwin Sumner commanded the Right Grand Division (30,000 men including the II and IX Corps with 60 pieces of artillery). The 27,000 men of the XI and XII Corps, with the mission of covering Washington, constituted the army's reserve. Burnside moved his mammoth 120,000-man army to Falmouth, across the Rappahannock River from Fredericksburg, one of the country's most historic cities. His plan was to cross the river quickly and drive his army to Richmond. The Federal navy, solidly in control of Virginia's tidal rivers, would secure his supply line. Union generals were obsessed with the emphasis of "on to Richmond," while Lincoln repeatedly stressed that their objective was the defeat of the Confederate army.

General Sumner's Right Grand Division reached Falmouth by November 17, and by the 22nd the entire army had arrived before Lee could shift substantial numbers of Confederate troops to block a river crossing. The 21st Massachusetts was assigned to Sumner's Grand Division as part of Brig. Gen. Edward Ferrero's brigade, Brig. Gen. Samuel D. Sturgis' division, Brig. Gen. Orlando B. Willcox's IX Corps. The Massachusetts men moved slowly through a drizzling rain and entered Falmouth at noon on November 19. They eventually went into camp near the river opposite Fredericksburg. Sumner was anxious to cross the river at one of the fords and occupy Fredericksburg and the adjoining heights. Hooker suggested that his troops could cross at a ford above Fredericksburg. Since the pontoons needed to bridge the river had not yet arrived, Burnside rejected the recommendations because the army, he believed, was not sufficiently supplied for such an undertaking. He also feared that heavy rains might cause the river to flood and isolate any troops that had crossed. Although the bridges across the Rappahannock River had been burned, their stone foundations were in good condition. Federal engineers could have built temporary structures across these piers within hours if Fredericksburg was secured. Two days later, James Longstreet's troops arrived in the town and the river rose rapidly because of heavy rains. Lafayette McLaws' Division arrived on November 25 and William Barksdale's Mississippi Brigade, 1,600 strong, occupied Fredericksburg. Realizing the serious threat that confronted him, General Lee requested support from Jackson's divisions that were operating in the lower Shenandoah Valley. Jackson's men arrived on December 1 after marching 150 miles.

On November 22, while waiting for the pontoon trains to arrive, Burnside wrote to Brig. Gen. George W Cullen, Chief of Staff in Washington:

> *It is very clear that my object was to make the move to Fredericksburg very rapidly, and to throw a heavy force across the river before the enemy could concentrate a force to oppose the crossing and supposed the pontoon train would arrive at this place nearly simultaneously with the head of the column. Had that been the case, the whole of General Sumner's column—33,000 strong—would have crossed into Fredericksburg at once over a pontoon bridge in front of the city. Had the pontoon bridge arrived even on the 19th or 20th, the army could have crossed with trifling opposition. But now the opposite side of the river is occupied by a large rebel force under General Longstreet. The pontoon train has not yet arrived, and the river is too high for troops to cross at any of the fords. The President said that the movement, in order to be successful, must be made quickly, and I thought the same.*

By the time the pontoons arrived, however, Longstreet's Corps was entrenched on the slope of the heights above the city holding a position of great natural strength. Burnside was cognizant of the serious dissension that was spreading among his subordinates. A majority of the corps and division commanders who had been designated to assault Marye's Heights disapproved of attacking the Confederate army through Fredericksburg. Lee had established a permanent position around Fredericksburg and could remain there all winter if he chose; the pressure on Burnside from the Lincoln administration and the northern public, however, was intense: offensive action was expected.

In the predawn darkness of a cold and foggy morning on December 11, Union engineers began laying three pontoon bridges in front of Fredericksburg while two additional pontoon bridges were constructed two miles below the city. The work opposite Fredericksburg faced an immediate problem when Barksdale's Mississippi and Florida sharpshooters, firmly rooted in buildings and rifle-pits, began picking off the engineers. A heavy artillery bombardment failed to deter Barksdale's men. After considerable delay, the 7th Michigan, 19th and 20th Massachusetts and 89th New York regiments crossed the river in boats and successfully dislodged the Confederates in house-to-house fighting. The two bridges at Franklin's crossing below Fredericksburg had been completed by eleven that morning with little opposition from the Confederates, but Burnside prevented Franklin from crossing until all the bridges were completed. That evening a third bridge was constructed at Franklin's crossing. On December 12, after the Union army had entered Fredericksburg, soldiers looted the town, destroying much of what they found in the houses abandoned by the city's 5,000 inhabitants.

While Burnside remained at his headquarters, Lee visited his corps and division commanders, inspecting his 275 guns and correcting faulty battery positions. Longstreet's corps of 40,000 men was entrenched with a frontage of almost five miles, while Jackson's corps of 39,000 men was positioned in depth along a more narrow two mile wide front southeast of the city.

On December 13 Franklin's troops attacked Jackson's Corps at Prospect Hill. Major General George G. Meade, commander of the Third Division, led the assault and achieved temporary success before being driven back to his original position. Franklin, who utilized less than a quarter of his men during the attack, failed to send additional troops after Meade and Brig. Gen. John Gibbon's troops had penetrated the Confederate line. Franklin later refused to renew the attack even after receiving orders from Burnside to do so.

The second thrust was focused against the heart of Lee's defenses on Marye's Heights, directly beyond Fredericksburg. Union soldiers attacking the heights were savaged by fire from enfilading artillery on Lee's Hill and by the four ranks of Confederate infantrymen standing in a sunken road in their front. Longstreets infantry, massed behind a four foot high 500-yard long stone wall, *was also well supported by artillery emplaced along the hill he defended. From late morning until dusk, fourteen brigade-size attacks were thrown against Longstreet's position, assaults as courageous and hopeless as any made during the war. Wave after wave of Union soldiers charged toward Marye's Heights, crossing open ground broken only by small ravines and a canal. Approximately 6,000 Confederate soldiers and twenty guns withstood the attack of seven divisions. More than 7,500 Union casualties lay like a thick blue blanket on the cold December ground. When the day ended, Lee had won his most one-sided victory of the war. All told, the Army of the Potomac lost 12,653 men, while the Army of Northern Virginia suffered 5,377 casualties. The 21st Massachusetts suffered heavy battle losses. The regiment went into the action with 200 soldiers and ended the day with 134, a loss of one-third of its battle strength. Of these 66 men: 13 were killed, 52 were wounded and one was captured.*

A distraught Burnside was dissuaded by his commanders from leading a final charge with his old IX Corps on December 14. Lee fully expected Burnside to renew the attack by attempting a turning movement, but instead, during the rainy and windy evening of December 15 following a truce to allow for the burial of the dead and recovery of the wounded, the Union forces withdrew across the river. The harshest criticism leveled at Burnside dealt with his continuous attacks on the stone wall and his failure to coordinate Franklin's attack on Lee's right flank (Jackson's Corps). Burnside had labored under extreme physical and mental exhaustion, and although he had remained at his headquarters and thus was unable to witness the battle, he failed to communicate with his commanders and to sufficiently delegate duties. Burnside had turned down command of the Army of the Potomac on two previous occasions because he did not consider himself qualified for the position.

*   *   *

October 27, 1862

After an uncomfortable night during which many tents were demolished by the gale, we received our expected orders at ten in the morning. At eleven we broke camp and marched out of Pleasant Valley facing southward, leaving the monotony of camp life behind and bound for new scenes and untried experiences.

After a two mile tramp we arrive at the banks of the Potomac at Sandy Hook, a small station on the B.& O. Railroad. Here we pass by some of the grand scenery of America. Under lofty rocky precipice, hundreds of feet in height, we look up in a perpendicular line and see far above us trees and shrubs growing out of the rocks. Between this lofty wall and the waters of the Potomac, there are but a few feet, entirely utilized by the turnpike, the railroad and the canal. Before turning our faces southward we catch a distant view of Harpers Ferry: the heights back of the town, now celebrated as the scene of John Brown's raid; also the ruined bridge. We see where the Shenandoah meets the Potomac and beyond it, the far famed Valley of Shenandoah, running away into the distant blue.

Plodding through the sticky mud, we cross the railroad pass through Knoxville and straggle along the tow path of the canal some three miles to Berlin [Brunswick]. Here we cross the Potomac on a pontoon bridge near the solid abutments of the burnt bridge at Berlin, march up through a piece of woods and pass a new regiment of stalwarts of Down-Easters [Maine soldiers]. They complain bitterly of their hardships, one of which is that they have had no soft bread for three days and another, that no straw has been furnished them for even a longer time on which to rest their weary limbs! They receive the sincerest sympathy from our wicked veterans. At sunset we go into camp near Lovettsville [Virginia].

October 28

We suffer much during the night from the cold; and daylight reveals a heavy white frost. As we look out from our sightly camp, a grand and beautiful landscape is spread out before us. The lofty Blue Ridge running away to the southwest is lost in the hazy blue while a wide sweep of the notable fertile and charming country of the Old Dominion rivets our delighted gaze. We are camped on the great broad pike leading to Leesburg and Winchester; therefore, it may be said that we have entered the gates of the Southern paradise. Lieutenant Sanderson made the descriptive lists for Lem and myself so that we can draw government pay with the rest of the regiment.

October 29

At noon, orders come to march and at two we are on the road to Leesburg; passing through Lovettsville we find it almost entirely occupied by general officers and their staffs. With no hint of the plans or intentions of a campaign, the soldier in the ranks is very busy in surmising. If we can flank the rebel army, we may soon be fighting our way into Richmond.

The country through which we pass is under a high state of cultivation and is very beautiful. After a march of eight miles we encamp for the night. Before breaking ranks Major Foster warns us to be on the alert as the enemy is right in front of us. Henry has been appointed acting Adjutant for the 21st in place of Lieutenant Howe[1] who has been promoted to Quartermaster.

October 30

Drummed up at three in the morning and at sunrise we are marching toward Leesburg through the same lovely country as yesterday. At noon we halt near Wheatland, seven miles from Leesburg. Long lines of troop pass by our camp during the afternoon showing us that the entire Army of the Potomac is on a forward movement. A lot of home boxes arrived at the regiment but none for me. Henry formed the regiment at dress parade.

October 31

The rough ground and frosty weather keep sleep from my eyelids most of the night. I was detailed as supernumerary-guard; result, only two hours guard duty during the night—spent most of the night by a large fire in a grove near Ferrero's headquarters. Brigade was mustered in for pay, which is expected next week.

November 1

Brigade drill at ten in the morning. At dress parade, orders were read for us to march at daylight, after which Company A was detailed for picket duty. We were posted at a crossroads three-quarters of a mile from camp. Secured a good nights rest standing guard only two hours. Although we realize we are in the presence of the enemy, I was far from feeling lonely. A continual chuckle of coons in a neighboring cornfield, dogs baying far and near at the numerous farm houses, hooting owls and singing whippoorwills all combine to furnish an interesting serenade.

November 2

At sunrise returned to camp and at ten o'clock our division was on the march. Cannonading began quite early and continued through the day a few miles in our front showing that our advance is being disputed. After a short march we struck off the Leesburg road leaving it on our right and march in an easterly direction; very soon we meet three ambulances loaded with wounded which sobers down the mirthful spirits in our ranks.

The sounds of artillery grows near and we are warned of the possibilities in store for us. Although our route was very circuitous, the firing persistently keeps in our front when we should prefer to have it somewhere else. At night we halt and camp two miles from the scene of the days action after a twelve mile march.

November 3

Slept soundly although a chilly wind arose during the night. A rebel prisoner belonging to Stuart's cavalry was captured in a house near our camp. He says Lee's army is moving down the valley on our right. Took up the march at half past two in the afternoon; move ahead five miles, encamping on the same ground of the enemy of last night in the village of Bloomfield. Several commissions for our regiment were received today, among which was one making Henry a 2nd Lieutenant.

November 4

Marched at half past nine. Hooker's corps[2] arrived during the night and is with us on the road, so whenever we come to any long stretch of road we see the road filled with the dark moving mass for miles in both directions, while the lines are keeping pace with us on the other roads. I saw General Couch[3] with his staff, passing him on the route. We go into camp near Ashby's Gap outside the village of Upperville. Receive supplies of bread, meat, coffee and sugar. The heavy booming of cannon reverberates up through the mountains occasionally through the day. A large persimmon tree is discovered near camp, laden with ripe fruit. The easiest way to secure the luscious treasure is the "soldiers way"—cut the tree down; I get a good share, but like the manner of Scripture, it loses it sweetness by hoarding.

November 5

Another cold and frosty night. The enemy is apparently keeping ahead of us some six miles all the time evidently intent on securing a good position before accepting battle. Broke camp at half past seven; marched through the rebel village of Upperville; as the inhabitants show unmistakable signs of hostility; our bands salute them with "Yankee Doodle" and "Down with the Traitors." March is a southerly direction; cross the Manassas Gap Railroad at Delaplane and halt after a brisk march of seven miles. We have passed several fine mansions, evidently homes of the wealthy planters of this fair and fertile valley. Rest during the afternoon and receive a mail in the evening.

November 6

A dark chilly windy day; left camp at ten and after filing into the road we are ordered to halt and allow the 2nd and 12th Corps to go ahead. Hour after hour passes by as does the endless procession while our corps is lying on knapsacks by the roadside. Little "psalm-singing"—Company A led by Jimmy Carruth[4] beguile the time in singing patriotic, sentimental and negro melodies. The spirit of music catches and spreads until far down the line as far as can be heard, swells out the grand chorus. Never before has the haughty Virginia farmer listened to such a mighty choir and doubt if he world have dared to be disloyal if had known the fervor of patriotism which found expression in these melodies. Certainly he would not, if he could have had the prescience to see the miles of burning fences which we left as we took up the line of march at half past one—but our hands and feet must be kept warm. March briskly until six and after a most wearisome tramp of twelve miles encamp near Salem. Tried to sleep but failed so I spent the latter part of the night hugging the campfire.

November 7

At nine in the morning a snow storm began - continuing until four in the afternoon when we take up the march. After a dismal, disheartening tramp of three miles through the snow, darkness settle upon us just as we reach the ford of the Rappahannock. It proves to be too deep for us, and very fortunately too, as it proves later that the enemy was awaiting to entrap us. After standing an hour or more in the snow and darkness, it is ascertained that we are under the guidance of a very drunken General Sturgis.[5] We then about face and march back two miles; then on another road and finally, worn out, discouraged, mad and cross, we turn aside into some woods and drop down into the mud. I get three hours rest between two fires.

November 8

At nine o'clock in the morning, we move out on the Warrenton turnpike; march three miles and stack arms near the edge of woods and get coffee. After an hour's halt, resume the march; cross the Rappahanock on a bridge built by the pioneer corps; make a hurried march of six miles; pass through the villages of Glen Mills and Jeffersonton; camp just outside the deserted village of Jeffersonton—contains only three families and a slave-pen.

November 9

Snowed during the night. I was on guard. The sun melted the snow before noon. We are now advanced beyond the main army and are not more than a mile or two from the rebel army in the direction of Culpeper. As this is the Sabbath, chaplains of the 21st and 11th N.H. held religious services in the village church. Suppose it would be called an exchange of pulpits. Prayers, giving thanks for Burnside's victories, were made at dress parade.

November 10

The day was bright and mild. General Ferrero with a company of cavalry made a reconnaissance during the morning finding the enemy's pickets two miles from our camp. They were fired upon and one frightened cavalryman came dashing into camp arousing us. The long-roll was beat and the brigade formed in line of battle to resist the attack. After a few shots from our battery we were dismissed to quarters. Brisk cannonading was heard in the gap up in the mountains and away toward Culpeper where the rebel army is concentrated—evidently waiting and watching for us.

November 11

Another pleasant day and another reconnaissance in which our cavalry was driven in, after which our battery went out and forced back the rebel pickets re-establishing our line of pickets. Our rations are getting short and our supply train of seventy-five wagons is reported captured.

November 12

Awoke at one o'clock in the night and found the regiment very silently preparing to depart. At four we silently stole away marching swiftly in a northeasterly direction toward Warrenton. Five miles of this ghostly marching in the darkness brought us to the famous Sulphur Springs at daylight. This was a favorite summer resort for the southern aristocrats before the rebellion. Nearly all the large buildings and hotels are now in ruins, a result of the war.

We encamp by the side of the broad pike leading to Warrenton—seven miles distant. Rations have given out and we shall not get any until tomorrow when the supply teams return from Warrenton. We learn that our small force at Jeffersonton was not withdrawn any too soon for the enemy had been quietly surrounding us intending to capture us this morning. The 1st Brigade came in at night and encamped on the opposite side of the road from us.

November 13

An Indian summer day. Rations of hardtack and salt pork were given out this morning; a dinner of pork and beans made the boys happy. The rebels came out in sight of us on the hills about a half a mile distant and sent a few cannon shots at us, doubtless to inform us that they had occupied our ground of yesterday. Two shots from our battery, planted squarely in their midst, sent them back out of sight. Received a call from Albert Davis.

November 14

Fair and Mild. Our division is being supplied with provisions. A very novel sight was seen by us this afternoon. Clouds of black passed over us southward which we discern to be countless myriads of crows going to winter quarters. The hum of their innumerable "caws" and the strange appearance of the sky is very remarkable.

November 15

High wind. Roused at five and resume our march eastward. After we had gone about a mile the enemy discovered our movement and open fire on our wagon train. The various batteries of our corps are hurried into position and a brisk artillery duel is inaugurated. The infantry is drawn up in line of baffle to support and protect the guns. After four hours action their guns are silenced during which our regiment received the fire of two or three guns; several are killed or wounded but mostly are artillery men. The inaction of the infantry was aggravating as we have to lie and see the effects of bursting shells all about us. At eleven o'clock our march is resumed and after marching five miles encamp near Fayetteville.

November 16

Started at nine in the morning moving toward Warrenton Junction. Pass by immense camps of different corps through a woody, level tract. A brisk tramp of seven miles brings us to the Orange and Alexandria Railroad two miles from Warrenton Junction where we encamp. Our forces hold the railroad as far as the Rappahannock fifteen miles below.

November 17

Stormed during the night and today is cloudy. At last the fact is developed that McClellan has been superseded by General Burnside[6] and the plan of campaign is to attempt to reach Richmond by way of Fredericksburg, thereby flanking the rebel army. Resumed the march at half past twelve proceeding in a southeasterly direction in three columns: one in the road and one on each side tramping through the fields. Ten miles of marching and we encamp on a rough piece of ground on a hillside in sight of thousands of troops.

November 18

Rain during the night; roused at four; on the road at daybreak. Our route lay through a most dreary country. Burnside passed by us with his escort; halted at one after a thirteen mile march and go into camp seven miles from Fredericksburg. I was on guard from eight till ten in the evening at the Quartermasters tent.

November 19

Move at seven; our division takes the road while others are on each side, but the road is blocked by the immense trains and troops; our progress is therefore very slow through the deep sticky Virginia mud. At half past twelve we arrive at Falmouth, a mile above Fredericksburg on the north bank of the Rappahannock while Fredericksburg is on the south side of the river. Pass General Couch's Corps in which is the 15th Mass where many old Fitchburg acquaintances are found and salutations made. The 2nd Division goes into camp opposite Fredericksburg on Falmouth Heights at two in the afternoon; the day is dreary and dark, which sets the boys to thinking of the comforts of absent northern firesides.

The 21st Mass was detailed to support a battery which was planted of overlook the city, only a stone's throw from the river. On the curiosity to take in the situation many of us, before pitching tents, go out by the banks of the river where we find the rebel pickets on the opposite banks and their cavalry riding about the streets but apparently not in large numbers.

Considerable bantering conversation was carried on with the rebel pickets and a tacit agreement between both sides to withhold firing. It is rumored that the pontoons for crossing the river, which were expected to be here so that our army could get by this strategic position of the enemy, have failed to arrive and that the failure is due to Washington authorities. If this be true, our forced march to this point will be of no avail.

November 20

Rained hard all day. A long train of cars could be seen by us moving away from the flour mill and our battery fired several shells into it. These heights of

Falmouth extend all along the river front opposite the city of Fredericksburg furnishing commanding positions for our batteries which have been moving into position all day.

November 21

Storm continued throughout the night and day with great severity. Our frail shelter tent would not shed the rain; I am therefore soaking wet and have a cold settled on my lungs with cough. Was excused from duty by the surgeon and took medicine. The regiment has been taken out by squads and discharged pieces; returning to camp, we take them to pieces, clean them up and put them in fighting trim.

The camp of the 21st is evidently a temporary one in a sheltered nook, a few rods below the brow of the hill where is planted the battery which we are supporting. As the darkness of night settles upon the scene we are thrilled by the sight beyond the city back of the circle of hills surrounding it. The bright reflection upon the clouds for a long distance plainly indicate that the great rebel host is at last planted squarely between us and Richmond and all flanking business is out of the question.

November 22

Today the weather has cleared somewhat although clouds still shut out the sun. A bountiful mail arrived. Among commissions published in the Massachusetts papers: Captain Hawkes is promoted to major and Foster to lieutenant colonel. Our battery fired a few shells into a departing train in Fredericksburg but without apparent effect. In our present camp we are isolated from the main body of the army and are therefore in ignorance of its plans or movements.

November 23

A clear cold day which brings on the chills and I feel like a sick chicken. Sunday morning inspection at ten o'clock. Lieutenant Fred Saunderson has been promoted to captain. For a change we get a ration of "salt horse"—quite a luxury after a month with fresh meat. The boys are nearly all writing letters home.

November 24

Cold, frosty morning; the battery which we have been supporting, left us, another taking its place. I was again excused from duty and am under doctor's care—dosing for my cough. A small building, the home of some rebel who is doubtless in the army over beyond the hills, fell prey to our northern vandalism. It stood almost in the limits of our camp and as wood is very scarce, everything not fastened down has been transferred to camp: furniture, books, papers, furnishing much amusement for the boys. I received a long delayed letter from home written a month ago notifying me of a box having been sent which I have not received.

November 25

Frosty morning; answered my home letters and received another mail tonight. The commissions for the new officers arrived, dated September 25th—Henry's with the rest. The 2nd Brigade moved into camp about two miles back leaving the 21st alone. Several members from hospitals joined the regiment.

November 26

Rained hard during the night and cleared off cold today. Regimental inspection in the morning at ten o'clock. Our division wagon-master informs us that twelve days rations have been issued, which indicates a prolonged stop; I am therefore encouraged to send home for a few needed articles like mittens; we are face to face with winter and will find a new experience on these bleak Virginia hills. Lieutenants Clark[7] and Hill[8] joined the regiment from the hospital.

November 27

Thanksgiving day in Massachusetts and several other states. Chaplain Ball at dress parade read Governor Andrew's[9] proclamation accompanying it with excellent remarks and prayer. The adjutant read an order from General Wilcox,[10] praising the troops for their patient endurance during the march through Virginia, expressing the hope and conviction that the coming campaign would end the war. Captain Davis[11] joined the regiment—returned from Massachusetts.

November 28

Was on guard at night but felt so miserable that was again excused from duty in the morning. Colonel Clark came down from Aquia Creek this morning on the first train that has run over the road since our army retreated last summer. The enemy run everything south and burned the bridge over the Rappahanock so that our government has sent down locomotives and cars for the use of the army. Captains Goss[12] and Parker[13] returned with Colonel Clark just from Camp Parole, Annapolis; Clark is looking finely. Brother Henry having secured a new officer's uniform has given me his nice warm dress coat which is highly appreciated; my thin army blouse was not sufficient warmth for me in my debilitated condition. Orders came at night for us to join the brigade tomorrow.

November 29

Roused before light; ate a breakfast of hasty-pudding; struck tents at daylight and at sunrise being relieved by the 2nd Michigan; march back and join the brigade; we pass by large camps, all laid out with great regularity. Find the 2nd Brigade encamped on a broad upland plain entirely denuded of trees, and in the form of a hollow square (51st Pennsylvania, 51st New York, 11th New Hampshire, 35th Massachusetts, and 21st Massachusetts).

The bleak, wintry winds sweep over our exposed camp and all our wood and water has to be brought nearly half a mile. The water is from a large spring under a great old tree and furnishes an abundance of the purest water for thousands on thousands of men, horses and mules. The usual camp duties are established.

Brigade religious services were held at eleven, conducted by the chaplains of the different regiments. Rations of beans, rice, molasses, salt pork, vinegar, hardtack, sugar and coffee were issued to the companies. Dress parade under command of Colonel Clark. The new Lieutenants were assigned to different companies: Henry goes into Company I, Pittsfield boys; George C. Parker and Lawrence[14] to Company A.

December 1

Cloudy and variable; company drill at ten; brigade guard mounting at nine; battalion drill in the afternoon was omitted as the paymaster was in camp. I signed the pay roll for forty dollars and sixteen cents and drew pay in the evening; consequently the boys turn in to bed in great glee; although—what to do with the money is a quandary as we have no sutler in camp.

December 2

Fair and cold. Get up early and start out to find a much desired sutler—craving for a change of diet is common to all. Found one at a neighboring camp of the 18th New York before whose tent stood a line of several hundred men in single file awaiting their turn to exchange greenbacks for buffer crackers, cheese and pigs-feet—the extent of his merchandise. Colonel Clark commanded at battalion drill; we were drilled in the fighting manual in anticipation of what seems to be the inevitable. Chaplain Ball goes to Massachusetts and carry money for the boys; I send home thirty dollars. Read the President's message in the Baltimore Clipper.

December 3

Clouds with cold wind. I help build a fireplace for Captain Sanderson of mud and pine sticks. A disgraceful row occurred on the parade ground. Several lawless fresh members of the 21st Mass caught sight of an applecart which had previously been charted by some 11th N.H. men, and attempted to capture it— in the melee a shower of brickbats flew; the officer of the day [Major Mitchell] drew his revolver on the crowd which threatened to kill him if he fired. Three companies of the 11th N.H. were then called out and the mob dispersed. Loss—one applecart.

December 4

Fine day. Permits for leaving camp are daily issued to one commissioned officer, two non-commission staff and three privates. I received one today and made a tour through the camps of the Army of the Potomac. Sutlers are in great demand but very scarce; I have no doubt it is quite as well that it is so for they would easily get away all the terribly hard-earned wages of the boys and our commissary is abundantly supplied. The 5th Army Corps had a grand review a mile southeast of our camp.

December 5

Snow and rain. I was detailed for guard and was supernumerary; being on the third relief, my post was at guard headquarters where there was a nice warm fire—very highly appreciated on such a disagreeable day. A supernumerary's duties are to be ready to respond to any call - similar to a policeman's in a civil life.

December 6

During the night the weather cleared and grew very cold. I was on guard when the moon came out from behind the clouds. I then witnessed its total eclipse which lasted four hours. Suffered severely from the cold but a teamster's tent near the guard line had a fire in it; my neighboring sentinel and I therefore took turns in doubling the beat while the other tended the fire; that is what is called "volunteer militia." All the camp duties were omitted for the day on account of the severe cold weather.

December 7

Another very cold, zero day. Much suffering on account of lack of warm clothing and poor shelter. A large portion of the regiment was excused from duty by the surgeon for lack of good shoes. Company A reported only ten men fit for duty.

December 8

The cold snap continues. Everything freezing hard. General Ferrero ordered all duties omitted for today and tomorrow that the men may fit up winter-quarters. Three teams for each regiment were detailed to draw logs and boughs. Corporal John Wallace tents with Lem and myself, we therefore build a miniature log house—three feet high using our three shelters for a roof. Having received a pass, I went down to Falmouth, a dingy looking village, seemingly entirely occupied by our army officers for headquarters.

December 9

Weather moderated and quite mild. I was again detailed for guard duty. We build a fireplace and chimney of pine sticks and mud. The Virginia clay makes a fine substitute for mortar; great care has to be used to keep the inside constantly covered with the mud which is liable to crumble off. Mail arrives regularly each evening. Our brigade has orders to keep constantly on hand three days cooked rations preparatory to marching at any hour, and a detail of one hundred men from the 21st has been organized for fatigue duty, presumably to lay the pontoon bridges. The camp is alive with talk about the expected attack.

December 10

Mild thawing day. Charles Wyman visited camp in the morning, having left Ashby three weeks ago [owned Charles Wyman Hotel near the Common in Ashby]. He is employed in the Quartermasters Department. Brigade inspection was held at one o'clock and everything ordered to be put in fighting trim; packed and prepared to march at daylight.

December 11

At four o'clock we are drummed up and pull our new winter-quarters to pieces. In the darkness of the chill wintry morning, lighted only by the numerous company-cook fires, we take up the duties with anxious hearts. Suddenly at half past four the still night is broken by a terrific thunder from more than a hundred cannon. All the Union batteries along the heights open simultaneously upon the doomed city of Fredericksburg—the roar reverberating far up and down through the gorge of the heights where the Rappahannock runs.

This startling and deafening opening was the signal for throwing our pontoons across the river directly opposite the city for there the banks were so steep that the workers could be protected from the rebel artillery which was posted a mile back from the river on Marye's Heights. Although this was all begun before daylight, we discern the sound of musketry firing which develop the fact that the attempt was contested and soon the fires from the burning city light up the country.

The roar of artillery continues incessantly until noon, bringing destruction on this aristocratic seat of the Old Dominion. At daylight we see great volumes of smoke rising over Falmouth Heights which hid the city from our view. At half past eight we join the great columns of troops which are moving toward the city and massing behind the shelter of the hills. We lay on arms all day long witnessing the moving back and forth of the immense Army of the Potomac settling down into all the defiles and sheltered approaches near the river. We gain no idea of the extent of battle which all this noise indicates, but lying there all through the long hours of the day doing nothing, our thoughts are shaped into words and anticipations of a deadly struggle in which many of these moving thousands will be stilled forever beyond that fated and fatal city.

At one time during the day some of the 21st boys recognized a mounted staff officer, the well known features of Colonel Augustus Morse,[15] the original commander of our regiment—a pompous, spread-eagle style of man, who was so big a coward that he allowed his regiment to leave Annapolis without him, rather than face the dangers and hardships which he knew would be their inevitable lot. As he had always been a harmless, good natured fellow, he was greeted by various members in a pleasant but half contemptuous manner.

The mild sunny day passed by without any successful attempt to effect a crossing so that at near nightfall some of those regiments, who were near their old quarters, were allowed to return to them; the 21st therefore turned in to its old quarters and I got a good nights rest.

December 12

Before I had awakened, the pontoons were laid and a large force of our army were occupying the city, having driven out all the sharpshooters which had filled all the buildings along the river front. At daylight the 9th Corps was sent across the river. As we move rapidly out and down to the pontoon bridge, there was an ominous silence from both sides. Looking out beyond the city to the hills that skirt the horizon a mile and a half away, there was not a sight or sound that would indicate the presence of our brave and deadly foe, only the smoking ruins of many buildings and torn and ragged roofs.

As we cross the "Rubicon" the same feeling of awe which has been our experience twice before possesses us. The rapid firing of skirmishes on the opposite side of the city shows that the enemy's lines are not far away. We file to the right and halt in the area recently vacated by Barksdale's Mississippians [sharpshooters]. We settle down in the mud and are under shelter of the river bank. Looking backward we witness the long columns of our soldiers come out of the defiles and cross, massing all about us. Occasionally the enemy open their artillery upon our advancing lines which is responded to by our batteries, but no serious attempt is made to rake the city. Their intention is evidently to spare the city, relying on the strength of their fortifications, being fully satisfied that they must be taken by an assault if at all.

The streets are filled with troops which have been plundering stores, banks and dwelling houses. Much of it seems to be wanton destruction, but according to all rules of war, that which may contribute to their comfort can be rightfully taken from the enemy; and that, the city of Fredericksburg certainly is.

As we are not allowed to leave the ranks, I have no opportunity to inspect the city but see an immense quantities of all kinds of eatables, drinkables, wearables and furniture which is brought down to the banks of the river. While lying here, various startling scenes are witnessed. A few steps from us, lying propped against a shed is a "grayback" whose head has been taken clean off by a shell exposing his chin and the mutilated portions of throat and spine—a horrible sight truly. He was on the rebel side of the shed and had evidently been taken in the act of firing as he was close by the corner looking down toward the pontoon bridge.

During the afternoon a Union regiment came out over the hill directly by one of our batteries instead of more prudently marching around through the defile whence most of us came. Being in plain sight and in good range of the enemy's guns, a shell was sent over the city and across the river, bursting squarely in the midst of its ranks. No formality or red tape was used, but the liveliest skedaddle—every man for himself rushing to the foot of the hill, some even taking to the water. We could see two or three prostrate forms left to care for themselves either wounded or killed.

Still later, a mounted band rode down to the river bank and supposing themselves out of sight and range of rebel guns, struck up the impudent tune "Bully for you," much to the amusement of their immense audience on the opposite bank. Suddenly a solid shot came screaming over and struck in the edge of the water throwing spray in their very faces. No musical director could ask for more prompt obedience to the command: "Stop!" In less time than it takes to tell it, not a horseman was to be seen: some had galloped up the hill, some down, all had "got." All this, amid a perfect storm of yells and cheers from our side. It was an encore that was never responded to.

December 13

The comfortless night was passed lying on our arms in the mud with equipments strapped to us; as the dull gray light of winter morning broke, I arose and asking no question took a quiet stroll through the principal business streets, witnessing the strange and awful spectacle of a desolated, plundered and ruined city. Streets and sidewalks packed with sleeping soldiers, burning ruins of great solid blocks of buildings everywhere. Streets and yards strewed with furniture and articles of every description. I pick up a few books, a piece of a magnificent broken mirror three fourths of an inch in thickness, and an account-book from the steps of the ruined Bank of Virginia; explored a large bookstore on Carolina Street where every man was his own clerk. These mementos I afterward delivered to "Julie," our company cook who went back to the Falmouth side laden with stuff from different members of the company which was eventually sent home.

About nine o'clock we were ordered up and through the city; halt in a small back street on the side nearest the rebels and deposit knapsacks, shelters and extra baggage in a vacant house; meanwhile the din of baffle increases. Shells from the rebels works crash through the streets and into buildings all about us. We stand or sit along the sidewalk awaiting the dread orders. This is the time that tries men's courage. Few words are spoken by any one. A few reckless ones improve the minutes by eating their rations but most are looking into each others faces in silence, wondering, no doubt, if they have come to the end of their earthly career.

Soon our troops come pouring in long lines out of the city and form in lines of battle a few rods beyond us. We hear the orders for charging and know that the storm has at last broken in all its fury. The main point of attack was Marye's Heights nearly half a mile away. These heights were crowned by a noble Virginia mansion set in the midst of a magnificent grove of trees. From this position strongly entrenched the enemy was able to completely sweep the city in all directions. One continuous crash and raffle of musketry, the roar of all the rebel artillery concentrating its deadly fire at this point, and after a few moments the shrinking line of wounded and frightened men rushing past us to the rear.

At no time in all the horrors of the day was there such a sickening sense of war's realities while we awaited the orders sure to come. For my own part, I cannot understand how a soldier gifted with reason and given time for reflection can prepare himself for battle as our men did at this time without having the thought cross uppermost. Am I prepared for eternity. Fast and earnestly went up the silent prayers to God for courage, strength and deliverance, as I heard General Ferrero shout: "Forward 2nd Brigade."

Relieved of most of the luggage which we had carried into our other engagements, we filed rapidly out into the open fields where the others had preceded us and find not a tree, fence or building to obstruct the view between us and that line of belching fire before us. Quickly forming in line of baffle, we stand face to face with the long line of rebel earthworks crested with a sheet of flame from the well protected troops behind them. All over the field is strewn the dead and wounded, but we do not stop an instant to consider the spectacle. With the grand Union cheer the veteran 2nd Brigade move swiftly up without a break only as we close up the fast thinning ranks. It was a glorious sight that I could well be proud of, to see our men facing such an ordeal so cool and fearless.

One shell or shot swept down a dozen of the 21st boys and I saw one man's head fly off from his body, the force of the concussion of this same shot threw me and my comrade Lewis[16] down, but quickly springing up kept our place in line. We are ordered to halt at a slight rise of ground within a few rods of a stonewall, the first line of rebel infantry. Here we are partially protected when lying flat, but we immediately begin firing at the line of heads which can partially be seen through the dense smoke.

Joseph Collins[17] of Company A, the color sergeant of the regiment was shot and another man grasping the colors was also shot down. Sergeant Plunkett[18] then seizes the colors when a bullet strides him in the arm; with the other he forces the staff into the ground and again pulls it aloft; very soon a shell takes off the other arm and sends him reeling down the slope, his bleeding form dyeing the stars and stripes which he had so gallantly held.

The rapid firing has soon exhausted our ammunition and it apparently has no effect in silencing the deadly musketry fire from behind the stonewall. We are ordered to lie flat and see the leaden hail spatter about us. We see brigade succeed brigade in moving out of the city, form in line of battle and pass through the same fury ordeal which we had passed through. A few lines of evidently new troops would break and "skedaddle-daddle," but most of them did bravely, moving up to where we lay, halt just in front of us and keep up fire unabated.

Through all the long afternoon we laid, watching the butchery of thousands of brave boys. We looked for orders to storm the works, but concluded that it was deemed too reckless an undertaking. Just before sunset the famous Irish Brigade came up over the plain in a perfect, unbroken line, although receiving the concentrated fire from batteries which had hitherto been engaged in other directions. With a reckless bravery they dashed past us almost up to the stonewall but were soon forced back to the same light shelter which we had.

During the afternoon our batteries on Falmouth Heights could not be used without endangering us, but one battery was sent out on to the fatal field. Before they had time to unlimber, two or three horses had been shot down when they prudently retired. All day long the great Army balloon could be seen high up over Falmouth Heights and repeated attempts by the long rang guns of the enemy to bring it down but without success.

Thus, through all that fearful day, we laid in this exposed situation and before darkness fell upon us, the twenty-five members of Company A were found reduced to ten; all the rest were killed or wounded. The entire brigade seems to have suffered in the same proportion. Under the friendly cover of darkness we steal off the field, receiving a parting volley and the battle lulls. Stumbling over dead bodies all the way along the exposed field, we reach the city and find it a vast charnel house; pass down to our position of last night by the river and drop down, thoroughly exhausted; sleep putting away all remembrance of the terrible defeat we have suffered.

December 14

Sunday opens, a bright mild day passed without any general engagement, but the roar of artillery and rattle of musketry was incessant. The stupendous events of yesterday, the absence of the many familiar faces from our ranks, and the severe strain both mental and physical have a paralyzing effect upon us and the day passes by almost as a dream.

John Wallace, Lem and I find a feather mattress in a backyard which we appropriate early in the evening and find it a fine substitute to the mud which we have laid in for two nights. At half past seven we had turned in and sleep almost instantly came to me and a few moments later, the sharp, clear familiar voice of General Ferrero brought me to my senses, with the order: "Fall in Second

Brigade!" Up we spring and rapidly march through dark streets out over the fatal field, very silently we creep up to the outer limit of our yesterday's position relieving the skirmishes of today.

We are so near the enemy's line behind the stonewall that we can hear their voices and raffle of their equipments. We remain in position all through the night: cold, sore, weary and comfortless. The sleep which we had welcomed earlier was driven from our eyelids, and at midnight we were startled by a volley from the stonewall. A pig had wandered from our lines towards the enemy who had mistaken it for a stealthy attack by us. No damage was done by it.

December 15

About half past one, we were ordered to throw up a slight earthwork using our bayonets to loosen the dirt and cups or plates to remove it. Although no protection from the enemy's fire, it serves as a screen. As daylight approaches whispered instructions as to our actions for the day are sent from mouth to mouth along the line. This, then, is the situation: The Union line lying flat, one solid line for a mile in length behind a ridge of dirt about a foot in height; the rebel line a few rods from us behind a high stonewall, a perfect defense, while a quarter of a mile up the hill the impregnable Marye's Heights frowns down upon us, which if they should choose to, could sweep us out of existence.

As the sun rises, the raising of a head, an arm or drawing up the knee is the mark for a rebel shot and is quickly improved. In the position which we are lying, with heads up against the little earthwork, we can look back over the battlefield and take in its horrors. Although the wounded had all been removed, it was thickly strewn with all manner of soldiers toggery, fragments of human bodies, horses and artillery. I counted the dead which came in the range of my vision without moving my head: more than seventy-five all within the space of two or three acres. How many hearts in far off Northern homes must soon bleed as the news goes to them of these loved and fallen heroes.

The sad sight was that of a wounded horse fastened to an artillery wagon, which had been shot somewhere in its hindquarters. From time to time it would raise itself up on its forward feet, look toward us in a most imploring way, appealing for help with a groan like a human being—most heart-rending; then falling back in exhaustion, slowly dying by pain, starvation and thirst. A few careless heads were picked off during Friday, which, forgetful or in spite of the knowledge that they would draw fire, were in torture lying so many hours in one position.

Just before sunset the enemy succeed in planting a heavy gun on our right so as to sweep our line. One shot went squarely through our line, killing and wounding several but before they could get as good a range again, the friendly darkness came to our relief and what a relief! We could hardly wait for it so that we might change from our one terrible position. It was, in its way, a more terrible ordeal than the baffle itself.

As night drew on we look anxiously for the relief. Hour after hour passes on and none comes, At last Colonel Clark goes back into the city to hunt up General Ferrero and near midnight orders come for us to leave the field—one by one. Each man crawling off silently to the left of the line rendezvousing in the railroad cut. We learn that we are the last skirmish line on the field and our army has retreated across the river.

After waiting an hour in the railroad cut until the entire brigade has been drawn off in this slow manner, we march through the city passing through streets crowded with our ambulance trains filled with wounded—all headed toward the river. We reach the pontoon bridge, find it thickly covered with sawdust so as to deaden the sound of retreat. It was hardly necessary however as it was found that the enemy was in full knowledge of it, and many of the rebels followed, almost joining our ranks as we passed through the city. Moving back into our old camp, we pass through the great bivouac of wounded where rapid preparations were in progress for erecting tents for their shelter.

December 16

Reach our old quarters at three in the morning; everybody worn-out, discouraged and sadly out of temper. Drop down without attempting to spread our shelters and after sleeping a couple of hours, awake to find the rain pouring upon us. Pitch tents and as there were no duties, wrote home and remain very quiet throughout the day. The army was moving all day back to its former quarters. Lem with twenty others were detailed to go over to the battlefield under a flag of truce to bury our dead.

Comments in 1890:

General Burnside assumed the responsibility for the defeat in these chivalric words in his report to the President: "For the failure of the attack, I am responsible, as the extreme gallantry, courage and endurance, shown by our troops was never exceeded and would have carried the points had it been possible. To the families and friends of the dead I can only offer my heartfelt sympathies, but for the wounded I can offer my earnest prayers for their comfort and final recovery.

Looking backward twenty seven years, we have found that the responsibility must be shared by the treacherous subordinates who failed to give him the willing help which they ought in the flank movement on the left. It must also be shared by the authorities in Washington which failed to have the pontoons ready on his arrival but forced him to make the advance at an inopportune time.

It is futile to suggest what might have been the result if the cooperation had been hearty. Yet, granting all this the country still claims that his judgment was in error in attempting to throw his brave troops against an impossible barrier, forgetting that General Grant found equally impossible barriers two years later at Spottsylvania and Petersburg with as equally terrible slaughter. All the previous and later triumphs of General Burnside failed to place him in the first rank by an indiscriminate public. A callow youth may be forgiven the effusive homage paid to his commander for those qualities which deservedly render him popular; namely, a dashing, magnificent presence combined with a cheerful, gracious temperament; a watchful interest in the welfare of his men and a pride and confidence in their prowess (as evinced in his determination to send the veterans of the 9th Corps to accomplished what the whole army had failed to perform); but he is not to be judged by such a tribunal. Neither is he to be judged by the critics who passed judgment adversely on every one of the leaders of the Army of the Potomac excepting General Grant.

Perhaps not one of them suffered this unrighteous judgment more than General Pope, who accepted the unwelcome position with soldierly obedience with full knowledge that he was to be the victim of the damnable spirit of revenge on the part of the satellites of General McClellan. From this standpoint of history we claim for General McClellan the credit of organizing the grandest army of modern times out of an unwieldy mob of self-asserting Yankees. This mission ended with the Peninsula campaign, but the nation's gratitude should be cheerfully rendered for what he did.

General Pope's soldierly qualities and ability should in no sense be dimmed for the failure which a discriminate people rests upon the heads of General Fitz-John Porter and others whose names are not worthy. And this also in face of the defense pleaded by them, because their loyalty (in spirit) was withheld from their rightful commander.

General Hooker's failure may be said to have the least excuse, for with whatever talents he may have possessed must ever be associated the criminal folly of drunkenness at a critical hour. As a "chain is only as strong as its weakest link," so he was weakest of all. No finer generalship was displayed with grander results than that of General Meade in the culmination of the war, in the Gettysburg campaign and its credit is solely due to him, but in its stead, he received the cruel letter from General Halleck which he justly resented.

But how the country has almost forgotten him in eulogizing General Grant. We would take no laurels from General Grant which belong to him; but many have been bestowed which belong to others. General McClellan as an organizer; General Pope by his example of obedience; General Burnside by his bravery and sturdy patriotism in the midst of the darkest hours of the rebellion and a disloyal army; General Meade by skillful tactics overwhelming the invincible General Lee; all had a share in turning over to General Grant an army perfected by discipline, and an administration willing at last to bestow autocratic power upon him.

The Supreme Arbiter of events gave each his appropriate work, but myriad causes united to end the war and General Grant was only one instrument in its accomplishment. The error of judgment then rests with the critics of General Burnside, and we therefore claim for him as high attainments as any commander of the Army of the Potomac.

*   *   *

As I lie down to sleep in my fine comfortable quarters, I cannot help thinking of the thousands of poor fellows up the river, lying shelterless in this horrid Virginia mud and I feel almost ashamed of this "parlor soldiering."

Four

Winter at Falmouth

Morale of the Army of the Potomac plummeted after the Fredericksburg disaster. As the days passed the events of December 13 became known throughout the army, many Union soldiers became discontented and demoralized. Large numbers fell out for sick call and daily desertions increased to 100 or more. Several unscrupulous and self-serving high level commanders disseminated negative information about General Burnside both within and outside the army that further damaged Burnside's already tarnished reputation.

By contrast, General Lee's prestige regained some of its luster that was lost in the Maryland Campaign. With the intent of developing his opponent's intentions, Lee sent Maj. Gen. J.E.B. Stuart and 1,800 cavalry on a raid deep behind Union lines. Stuart returned on New Year's Day without news of Union plans. Lee continued to strengthen his defenses fronting Fredericksburg with his left anchored on Taylor's Hill and his right on Hamilton's Crossing. The Confederate army spent a bleak Christmas in shelters on the heights and in the woods near Fredericksburg. Union pickets, accepting an invitation by the Confederates, crossed the river at the rocky ford above Falmouth and celebrated Christmas at huge campfires with Southern pickets. When fifty Confederate soldiers returned the visit a few days later, they were seized while smoking and joking around the fires with Union pickets. They were returned to their side of the river shortly thereafter and stringent orders against fraternization were issued and enforced by Union commanders.

Despite the drubbing he had suffered, Burnside still believed the Confederate position could be flanked. With weather favorable he made preparations for a cavalry raid bypassing the Confederate lines with the mission of interrupting communications and creating alarm in Richmond. On December 30, the day the raid was scheduled to begin, Burnside received a dispatch from Lincoln that stated: "I have good reason for saying you must not make a general movement of the army without letting me know." Two dissident officers, who had been granted leaves for personal business, traveled to Washington to convince officials that Burnside was incompetent and that all planned actions must be stopped. The two malcontents, Brig. Gen. John Newton, commanding the Third Division in the VI Corps, and Brig. Gen. John Cochrane, commanding the First Brigade in Newton's division, met with Lincoln on the issue. Later, Burnside met with the President and offered his resignation. On January 8, Lincoln wrote to Burnside: "I do not yet see how I could profit by changing the command of the Army of the Potomac, and if I did, I should not wish to do it by accepting the resignation of your commission." Fortified by Lincoln's support, Burnside prepared a new plan to cross his army over the fords above Fredericksburg and turn Lee's left flank.

On a cold and sunny January 20 following an unusually dry month, Franklin's and Hooker's troops headed for Banks' Ford, five miles above Fredericksburg, while Sumner's troops delayed a day before their planned crossing in front of Fredericksburg. Unfortunately for Burnside, a fierce three-day winter-storm struck. Rain fell in torrents and the roads were reduced to ribbons of mud, the long columns of blue troops, wagons and artillery pieces almost unable to move. On the morning of January 22, Burnside ordered the soldiers back to their camps. For the next twenty-four hours, muddy and tired soldiers slowly plodded back to their quarters. Coming on the heels of the Battle of Fredericksburg, the "Mud March," sealed Burnside's brief command tenure. Hooker openly denounced the commanding general. When Burnside heard the negative rhetoric, he traveled to Washington and submitted General Orders No. 8 for Lincoln's consideration. The order dismissed from the service Gens. Joseph Hooker, W. T. H. Brooks, John Newton and John Cochrane, and relieved Gens. William Franklin, W. F. "Baldy" Smith, Samuel Sturgis, Edward Ferrero and Lt. Col. J. H. Taylor. Instead of a wholesale dismissal, on January 25 Lincoln relieved General Burnside from command of the Army of the Potomac and named General Hooker to assume command. General Franklin was also relieved and, at his own request, Lincoln relieved General Sumner.

A popular choice with the rank and file, Joe Hooker, reorganized the cavalry into a separate corps using the Confederate model, curtailed corrupted quartermasters, improved rations, cleaned up the winter quarters and granted more leaves. Although there was an immediate improvement in morale, the efficiency of the command had been seriously impaired by the internal dissensions and by a lack of cooperation from subordinate officers. These discordant elements persisted in the Army of the Potomac until Maj. Gen. George Gordon Meade assumed command on June 28, 1863.

Morale on the opposite bank of the Rappahannock River was high by comparison. There was a consciousness in the ranks of the Army of Northern Virginia, however, that the persistent and determined Union army had an unlimited supply of men and materials to replace its egregious loses.

*   *   *

December 17, 1862

The army is at last back in its old quarters on the north side of the Rappahannock and the enemy have reoccupied the city of Fredericksburg; the pickets of the opposing armies face each other on its opposite banks. J. L. Hildreth of New Ipswich, New Hampshire, called on us and said Albert Davis was shot dead on the battlefield. Several exchanged prisoners from Annapolis returned today.

December 18

Very cold, blustering day; ground froze hard. Major Hawkes arrived from Massachusetts bringing shirts, stockings and welcomed letters for me. It is the first time I have seen him since I joined the regiment. I dined with Henry on soup and gingersnaps from Templeton.

December 19

Major Hawkes brought to my tent a pair of nice warm mittens that had been knitted by Aunt Lee of Templeton—a most acceptable gift for me in my guard and picket duties. Colonel Maggi of the 33rd Mass, our former Lieutenant Colonel, called at the regiment headquarters and held an impromptu reception—many of the boys calling on him. He was very popular in the regiment. At night I was detailed with two others from the 21st to report to the Division Hospital, a mile from camp.

December 20

It was cold but clear; were quartered in a large hospital tent and today we fixed up around the tents of the wounded, putting them in comfortable shape for winter. Returned to the regiment at night.

December 21

Very cold; Sunday morning inspection at 10:30. At dress parade orders were read from General Ferrero thanking the regiment for its bravery in the late battle. The 21st and 35th Mass and part of the 11th N.H. were detailed to go out on picket at the river tomorrow morning at eight. Spent the evening at Captain Sanderson's tent with Major Hawkes, Henry and others, having a fine sing.

December 22

Weather moderated today. I was excused from duty on account of poor shoes. Spent most of the day in my tent reading and writing. The army balloon was up at three this afternoon.

December 23

A load of express boxes arrived via Harper's Ferry—one for Henry and me from home. A grand review of the Ninth Corps by General Sumner[1] near our camp today. Our regiment came in from picket in season to join in the review. Colonel Maggi brought over the 33rd Mass Regimental Band to serenade us this evening.

December 24

Pleasant and thawing. The regiment was again detailed for picket duty and I was again excused by the surgeon. John Mayo[2] and Elias Churchill[3] of the 33rd Mass called to see me. Saw the army balloon up in the afternoon. This is the night before Christmas and the reckless Irish Company B, securing a lot of whiskey from Falmouth, prepared to celebrate the event by getting fighting drunk. Their street is next to ours and during the evening numerous knockdowns occurred; several tents were demolished—my own among the number. The row was quieted by the efforts of its officers—Captain Walcott[4] and others.

December 25

A mild day. The regiment came in from picket and at 12:30 went as escort for a load of wounded to the depot enroute for Washington. Henry and I send home a box of books. Rations of whiskey with which to celebrate Christmas were served to the regiment; it is unnecessary to say that I refused mine.

December 26

Letters from home tell me the cold is very severe in Massachusetts with hardly any snow. Brigade drill by General Ferrero. Commissions for Whitney[5] and Sampson[6] were announced at dress parade. Colonel Foster resigned. I drew clothing—pants and shoes.

December 27

I was on guard at the brigade commissary headquarters.

December 28

Very mild; E. Churchill of the 33rd came over to see me again. Rev Mr Paim of Holden, Massachusetts, addressed the regiment at dress parade. He was the first chaplain of the regiment but resigned on account of poor health.

December 29

Drilled two hours by squads in skirmishing and an hour and a half in battalion drill. Received a bundle of papers from Mr. Seamans.

December 30

We were roused before light and at eight went down by the river (two miles) on picket. I was on the first relief—my post being near the edge of the river and my nearest companion a rebel picket—only a stone's throw across the river. We did not speak as conversation is strictly forbidden. Major Hawkes detailed me to act as his assistant after I came off my first beat so I was quartered with the officers for the remainder of the time in the parlors of the Lacy House.[7]

This mansion, owned by Horace Lacy—a Virginian aristocrat and a rebel officer, stands on a commanding eminence overlooking Fredericksburg and a wide extent of country. Three large parlors on the main floor are connected by folding doors which when thrown open make a grand hall. The whole place with its numerous outbuildings, barns, and slave quarters give an air of grandeur and elegance. Being a central point, it is used as the headquarters for the general picket; the result has been that the furniture had received rough usage at the hands of the Union soldiery. Among these was a grand piano with an organ combination which, during the night, was torn to pieces and "confiscated" by unmusical hands for relics.

December 31

The weather cleared up during the night—very cold. As the regiment returned to camp at eleven, the mischievous members created a sensation with the organ pipes of the Lacy house, each one blowing for all he was worth, creating most discordant sounds. Henry found a valise full of goodies from home containing apples, cake, jelly, brown bread, pies and butter—a most acceptable New Year's present.

Major Hawkes commanded at dress parade. The 11th N.H. band serenaded the field and staff officers of the different regiments of the 2nd Brigade in the night. The hospitality with which it was received became very marked after each succeeding treat, so that, when the last headquarters had been "done," each member was playing on his own hook regardless of time or harmony.

January 1, 1863

The day was made a holiday and all drills were omitted. Henry and I feasted on the contents of our home box in his officer's tent.

January 2

Company drill in the morning; brigade drill in the afternoon. A part of the 9th Corps was reviewed on the parade grounds. Henry received a box via Newbern from Templeton having been on the way six months. Its contents excepting shirts were valueless.

January 3

Lieutenant Colonel Foster came to the regiment last night and today Lieutenant Parker.

January 4

Fair and mild; John Mayo visited me.

January 5

Warmer. Grand review of Hooker's Corps on our drill ground by General Burnside.

January 6

General Burnside reviewed the 9th Corps near General Sumner's headquarters—Phillips House.[8]

January 7

The 21st and 35th Mass went on picket at the river; my post (third relief from eight to ten) gave me opportunity to see large numbers of rebel soldiers on the other shore. Most of the night was spent on the filthy cold brick floor of one of the slave quarters belonging to the Lacy Mansion.

January 8

My miserable quarters gave me a sore throat.

January 9

Skirmish drill in the morning; in the afternoon division drill commanded by General Nagle;[9] it included a great deal of heavy standing still.

January 10

Rain poured all day; passed the hours in our leaky tent reading, singing, cooking and eating.

January 11

Cold and clear; Sunday morning inspection.

January 12

In obedience to orders, tents have been cleaned and aired, ditches dug around each tent and streets cleaned; this is necessary as a sanitary measure: vermin flourish in the warm tents so that personal cleanliness is important. Heard that Charles Wyman has been sent to Washington; sick with fever. Received letter from Rev. C.W. Wood of Campello.

January 13

Threatening weather with rain. Captain John Proctor and Otis Ruggles of Fitchburg visited the regiment. Proctor carried an open umbrella which seemed so very effeminate and odd that he was made the victim of the "sassy" ones by hooting and ridicule. I was on guard at the brigade commissary tents.

January 14

Regiment on picket at the river. Sidney Heywood[10] rejoined the regiment.

January 15

Cloudy, high wind, warm. Saw a pontoon train moving toward Falmouth and it is rumored that another attempt is to be made to cross the river above Falmouth.

January 16

Raw, chilly wind. Lem and I visited Falmouth and after great hunting found the 33d Mass where we saw old acquaintances. Our division has received marching orders and rations accordingly, so we are thinking of more fighting—well, that's what we are here for.

January 17

Cleared away cold. Skirmish drill in the morning. Three days rations are to be kept constantly on hand.

January 18

Very cold. Learned that all the Union Signal Corps' books and codes were captured at Murfreesboro, Tennessee. Lieutenant Asahel Wheeler[11] has been promoted to Captain of Company G.

January 19

Company and battalion drills. Lem is on guard at General Ferrero's headquarters.

January 20

At ten o'clock in the morning, batteries began moving through our camp toward Falmouth and continue until noon after which Hooker's and Franklin's Corps followed in a continual stream all afternoon. We are ordered to march early tomorrow morning. Began to rain at night.

January 21

A deluging rain continued all night and day. As no general movement of the army seemed possible in the flooded condition of the country, the 21st was ordered to relieve the picket at the Lacy House. Major Hawkes, commander of the picket, detailed me to wait upon him (a slight attack of nepotism). Instead of standing on guard in the drenching storm, I was quartered with the officers in the parlors of the Lacy House. Much interest was manifested by officers coming to inspect the commotion of the rebels over the river. Horsemen could be seen riding hurriedly through the streets of the city northward preparing to meet our advance. As I lie down to sleep in my fine comfortable quarters, I cannot help thinking of the thousands of poor fellows up the river, lying shelterless in this horrid Virginia mud and I feel almost ashamed of this "parlor soldiering."

January 22

The storm continued with heavy fog. Mud, mud everywhere; streams very high and the Rappahannock overflowing its banks. The elements seem to be in league against General Burnside. I saw a "Richmond Examiner." The rebel pickets stuck up an effigy on their line with this placard: "Burnside stuck in the mud."

January 23

Cleared away in the night and today the army again returned to its old quarters. Burnside's plan was to suddenly flank the rebel army on our right some two miles above here before they could fortify, but the storm completely overthrew this plan.

Late in the evening, muttered words and mysterious movements among the unruly members of the regiment in which Tim Donahue[12] always figures, broke out in a riot near the brigade sutler's tent. Large numbers from other regiments joined them. They made a grand charge on the sutler's tent but were checked for a few moments by the occupants who showed resistance, but soon returning they surrounded them, took down the tent and carried off all the merchandise. Two of the roughs were shot during the melee.

January 24

Major Hawkes has been promoted to Lieutenant Colonel and Captain Richardson to Major.

January 25

Sunday morning inspection. Have been reading the Life of Adjutant Stearns[13] of the 21st who was killed at Roanoke. He was the son of President Stearns of Amherst College.

January 26

My time was fully occupied: washing clothes, company drill, battalion drill and dress parade; the brigade welcomed General Ferrero back from his furlough with cheers and music.

January 27

I was detailed with forty others to build a corduroy bridge over a swollen stream near Quartermaster Thompson's[14] tent. Orders were read at dress parade notifying us of the change of command of the Army from General Burnside to General Hooker and the 9th Corps from General Sumner to General Couch. So our old commander leaves us much to our regret.

January 28

Severe storm began last night and snowed all day. The regiment went out on picket by the river. I was on guard during the day—two hours at a post half way between Falmouth and Fredericksburg on a knoll exposed to the piercing winds which swept up the river. The air was filled with driving sleet and snow; there was nothing near with which to make a fire, so binding my overcoat cape tightly over my head, my rubber blanket over the whole, I trotted swiftly back and forth on my beat until completely exhausted, when I would sink down in the snow and rest a few moments, then up and go it again.

The only human being in sight was the rebel picket on the opposite bank of the river within talking distance, who sat during the whole time crouching over his faint, struggling fire. "Misery makes all nature kin" and although no words passes between us, I could not help a friendly feeling for this companion in suffering, although a deadly enemy.

I cannot remember that I ever suffered so much from the cold, and it seemed as if I was near perishing when I espied a solitary man come plunging through the snow to relieve me. Owing to the severity of the storm the ordinary rules were dispensed with in taking the entire guard around and dropping off a man at each post, but each one was sent out singly to his respective post.

I return to the rendezvous of the picket which is a cave in the side of a steep bank adjoining the grounds of the Lacy House. We were relieved and returned to camp at night. Mrs Ide of Fitchburg wrote me, saying she had sent me a box of delicacies (which was never received).

January 29

Wallace, Whitney and I crawled under our blankets and snuggled closely together to keep out the cold; early in the evening we dropped into a dreamless sleep and did not wake until broad daylight when we found the sun shining brightly and the snow piled in a small drift over our blankets that added warmth to our nest. Drills and dress parade were omitted on account of the snow. Henry came to see me.

January 30

A court martial was held in the hospital tent, trying the men engaged in the riot at the sutler's tent. Wallace and I have been fixing up our quarters.

January 31

Received papers from home. Orders were read at dress parade announcing the assumption of command of the Army of the Potomac by General Hooker.

February 1

Sunday morning inspection by Colonel Hawkes. Furloughs for officers and privates of our brigade are being granted.

February 2

I was detailed for the river picket with detachments from the different regiments of our brigade. My post was on a terrace below the Lacy House which overlooked the river and Fredericksburg. My orders were to give notice to the officers at the House if anything unusual occurred in our front: flag of truce, boats or suspicious movement in the streets of Fredericksburg. These duties were unnecessary during the day; therefore, I stood only during the night.

February 3

The weather grew very cold during the night, the air very clear and nipping, and the moon came out from the clouds full and bright giving me from my elevated position a beautiful picture. In one direction the stately Lacy mansion with its noble shade trees, shrubbery and pretty arbors. In the opposite direction the afflicted city with all its spires and towers standing out in dark relief against the sky. Beyond and above, the dark forests fringe the horizon seem doubly gloomy as I think of the many thousands who are hidden behind their shelter ready to meet us in deadly conflict. Then in the foreground down at my feet flows the swollen Rappahannock with its sullen roar as if chiding the warring multitudes which it separates. Standing thus, hour after hour in this silent night, it is hardly strange that the soldier on picket finds time for moralizing.

February 4

The morning was the coldest of the year but before night it had moderated and threatened snow. A brigade bakehouse is being erected in the rear of our regiment.

February 5

A cold stormy day, snow and rain. Duties omitted. Heard that Sigel's German Corps[15] was moving. Brooks[16] of the 2nd Mass, a Templeton boy, called on us.

February 6

The 9th Corps has received marching orders; there is great wonderment among us as to its meaning.

February 7

Henry has been appointed aid-de-camp to General Hartranft,[17] commanding our brigade; General Ferrero takes the division. Orders were received to march at a hour's notice with our knapsacks packed.

February 8

Sunday morning inspection at ten o'clock.

February 9

At four in the morning our drums and bugles sounded out the orders: "Prepare to march." We understand we are about to leave the Army of the Potomac—destination unknown. After a hasty breakfast our brigade leaves its old camp at daylight wondering if we shall ever return to these familiar sights.

* * *

"I was on guard near the beach. From my post in the night I kept knowledge of the time by the cry of the "navies" on their watches on the *Minnesota* as they sung out: `alls well.' When off beat I found comfortable quarters nestled among the numerous bales of hay which are piled on the wharf."

Five

Removal to Newport News

On February 6, 1863, George Getty's division of the IX Corps left winter quarters on the Rappahannock River, near Falmouth, proceeded by train to Aquia Creek, was transported to Fort Monroe, and then proceeded to Newport News, Virginia. Edward Ferrero's division left on February 9 and Orlando Willcox's division followed the next day. On February 10, 1863, the IX Corps, commanded by Maj. Gen. William F. "Baldy" Smith, was separated from the Army of the Potomac, and remained inactive for the next six weeks.

On January 30, 1863, 1,800 Confederate troops in Brig. Gen. Roger A. Pryor's Brigade, defending the lines of the Blackwater River, engaged Brig. Gen. Michael Corcoran's 4,800 Union troops at Deserted House (Kelly's Store), Virginia, nine miles west of Suffolk. The Confederate troops were forced to retire because of a shortage of both men and ammunition. Both sides claimed victory. There were 39 Confederate casualties (8 killed and 31 wounded), while the Union forces suffered 143 casualties (23 killed, 108 wounded and 12 missing).

In March, Brig. Gen. Getty's division was sent to Suffolk, about twenty miles southwest of Norfolk, where Confederate troops threatened Union works. Getty's division never rejoined the IX Corps, being reassigned on March 2, 1863, to the Department of Virginia. On March 19, Maj. Gen. John Grubb Parke assumed command of the corps.

*　*　*

February 9, 1863

Embarked on freight cars for Aquia Creek. As the day was bright and the air mild, we enjoyed the ride very much which was a novelty to veterans who had paced up and down through Virginia here to fore. Along our route most of the way laid the camps of the various divisions of the Army of the Potomac.

Arrived near Aquia Creek early in the afternoon; left the cars and march about a mile through a very lively scene. This being the base of supplies for the two hundred thousand soldier of the Army of the Potomac, it has the appearance of a busy city hundreds of moving army wagons, immense storehouses and large camps of quartermasters tents.

We reach one of the wharves and after some delay embarked on the large steamer "Louisiana" with the 51st Penn and 35th Mass. At four o'clock in the afternoon the vessel swings out into the middle of the broad Potomac and casts anchor. There is much confusion while so large a number of men are appropriating their quarters; Company A finds quarters in the fore part of the lower deck.

February 10

Early in the night two schooners loaded with the remainder of the brigade are taken in tow by our steamer; anchors are weighed and we move slowly and grandly down the river. There was too much noise and excitement for us to sleep very much. Early in the forenoon we enter the Chesapeake Bay when the steamers "Georgia" and "North America" pass us laden with the 1st Brigade. The day is fine and the men drink in the enjoyment of the holiday excursion, lying about on the sunny side of the decks reading, writing, singing and playing cards. The officers appropriate the staterooms of the steamer for their use so Henry finds grand quarters with brigade staff officers.

February 11

The weather changed during the night and the morning dawns cloudy with a chill northeaster blowing in from the Atlantic. Arrive off Fortress Monroe by midnight and cast anchor where we lay till daylight when we sailed up Hampton Roads passed the ripraps and landed at Newport News upon a long pier near the scene of the terrible combat between the Monitor and Merrimac [battle between ironclad ships on March 9, 1862].

The half submerged hulk of the *Cumberland* [30 gun frigate] lay a short distance out and nearer still, the masts of the buried *Congress* [50 gun frigate].

Pitched camp a quarter of a mile from the coast on very level land. I was detailed to unload baggage from the schooner.

It is unnecessary to say that the War Department did not give us information in regard to its plans or the reasons for the removal of so large a body of disciplined troops from the front of Lee's Army on the eve of Hooker's advance. In the absence of definite information, the rank and file are not fully united in their views. One theory was that Burnside was to return to North Carolina with his 9th Corps and resume offensive operations. Another was that a strong force at this point would so threaten Richmond from the same lines of McClellan's old campaign that Hooker would have less opposition.

February 12

The morning opens with fog and a strong sea breeze. The camps have been laid out with great precision the tall straight pines in the rear of the camps split up so nicely that we make fine stockades for our tents. Soft bread was issued and camp duties established.

February 13

The fine broad plateau between the camps and the beach furnish an excellent place for drill and parade, overlooking Hampton Roads and James River and across to the mouth of the Elizabeth River and Norfolk a dozen miles away. I was detailed to unload express boxes from a schooner at the wharf.

February 14

I was kept busy getting out fuel and stockade stuff from the pine forest and unloading schooners.

February 15

The Monitor and several gunboats have been cruising about the mouth of the James River, a mile or two away picketing the river.

February 16

Captain Hill[1] of Company D commanded us at squad drill. I was detailed to shovel around headquarters and was therefore excused from battalion drill. Was also detailed to unload hospital tents from a steamer. General Ferrero has resumed command of the brigade and Henry had returned to the regiment.

February 17

Colonel Clark returned from a ten day furlough in Massachusetts. An incessant deluging rain began in the night and our level camps were flooded. I had to fill in with mud to keep myself and trappings out of water.

February 18

Storm continued unremitting all day and night. All duties were suspended and all blankets, clothing and knapsacks were soaked with water. I sit all day under my shelter unable to find any occupation in such a storm.

February 19

Weather cleared. The brigade has received the A tent. I have gone in with Freeman Cole[2] and we have been fitting up our quarters in weather proof shape. Lem Whitney has received a box from home in which were valuables for me in shape of dried apple, cakes, and sausage.

February 20

Went out on picket. The line extends along the edge of a tall pine forest. Our part of the line is about a mile back of camp. As there is no enemy in any force for many miles, the duties were light and dull.

February 21

Cleaned up equipments for tomorrow's inspection. We pitched our A tent and settled in.

February 22

Snowed all night which turned to rain at daylight which continued till afternoon. Our tent barely escaped overthrow from high winds. We were kept busy bailing water out of our flooded tents.

February 23

I exchanged tents and tentmates with Osgood[3] and have gone in with Wilbur Potter[4] in a shanty made of slabs and several pieces of shelter. The 51st N.Y. had a presentation of a stand of colors at dress parade.

February 24

On guard at the parade ground. Brigade drill under General Hartranft. Stood on my beat from one till five in the night and as I had no fire, suffered from cold.

February 25

About nine in the morning, batteries and regiment began to march into position of the parade ground and at ten our brigade marched to its place in line. Soon the whole 9th Corps was stretched out in a long line over a mile in length. Then the guns of the Frigate Minnesota at anchor in our front belched out salutes to General Dix,[5] who is commander of the Fortress Monroe department. He landed with his staff and accompanied by General Smith,[6] Commander of the Corps, rode up and down the lines amid the cheers of the troops and music of many bands. Then the whole corps passed in review before him. I had an excellent opportunity to see the old soldier, a gray haired man of sixty. Crowds of army and navy officers and many ladies came up from Fortress Monroe to witness the review.

February 26

I built a chimney and fireplace of split sticks and mud for our tent bringing comfort again.

February 27

Received a letter from home containing pictures of all the loved ones.

February 28

Regiment was mustered in for its pay. Inspection by Colonels Clark and Hawkes. I was detailed for guard at General Ferrero's headquarters.

March 1

Regimental inspection by a regular army officer.

March 2

Regimental squad drill in the morning and brigade drill in the afternoon.

March 3

On guard in front of camp; stood four consecutive hours during the night. General Ferrero drilled the brigade. Lieutenant John F. Lewis[7] resigned on account of fever and ague [a malarial fever marked by successive cold, hot and sweating fits] and received an honorable discharge.

March 4

Company drill in afternoon; Captains Sanderson and Aldrich[8] received furloughs and went home. Jack Reynolds[9] returned to Company A from the hospital; received letter from home.

March 5

Detailed with a hundred others to unload a schooner of baled hay. Brigade drill in the afternoon.

March 6

Very cold last night. Drilled by squads in the facings. Witnessed a sad and impressive sight. A young man of the 35th Mass was buried with military honors. The regiment marched past our camp to the burial place with arms reversed, at slow step, muffled drums and bands playing the dirge, "Pleyel's Hymn" [Ignaz J. Pleyel melody written in 1791].

March 7

Drilled without arms. Colonel Hawkes and Henry went down to Fortress Monroe on the mail boat which makes two trips daily. Received a package of papers at night.

March 8

Cleaned up gun and equipments; inspection at one o'clock. Warm and mild. Furloughs have been granted to several in the regiment who have gone home.

March 9

Company and battalion drill in facings under Captain Walcott who is acting adjutant.

March 10

It was rumored that Burnside was in camp today and that possibly we are in for active duty soon.

March 11

On guard at Colonel Harriman's 11th N.H. tent.

March 12

Company drill in the afternoon.

March 13

The 3d Division left Newport News for Suffolk where Corcoran[10] is said to have retreated. Company drills all day.

March 14

Brigade guard mounting was changed to regimental as the 51st N.Y. and 51st Penn have gone into barracks half a mile below here, which the 3d Division vacated. Duties and drills were omitted in honor of the anniversary of the Battle of Newbern.[11]

March 15

I went out on picket; my post was the farthest one on the line on the beach below the promontory. An interesting scene was spread out before me. Seven miles away, over the water, the trim and massive gray walls of Fortress Monroe rose out of the blue ocean. The low sandy beach connected it with the main land further to my left where lay the village of Hampton prominent in which arose the shining dome of the seminary; back of this and running almost up to the beach in the intervening distance was a low level of unbroken pine forest. Off to the right of the Fort in the middle of the "Roads" arose the black ragged rocks composing the ripraps solitary and low. Away to the south partially exposed to view was the city of Norfolk. A large fleet of vessels laid at anchor around Fortress Monroe. The weather was mild so that my picket duties were very easy and lazy.

March 16

Received a Congregationalist [church bulletin] from home.

March 17

Lieutenant Lawrence drilled us. Received a pair of pants from the quartermaster. The 21st broke camp and moved a mile further down where there is better water and better conveniences generally.

March 18

I fixed up my quarters, strolled down to the wharves, sutlers' shops and walked about the beach. The officers of the 2nd Brigade accepted invitations to a grand ball on board the steamer lying at the wharf opposite camp. It was an elegant affair.

March 19

I was on guard at some old barracks to prevent them being torn down by the men who try to get the boards to use for tent flooring. The 1st Division has embarked for Baltimore enroute for the Dept of Ohio. We are anticipating therefore that we may follow them soon. One of our batteries left this morning for Hampton. Began to snow at night.

March 20

Snowed all day and is very cold. As we have no fireplace here we had no fire so Potter and I laid abed all day the only way which we could keep comfortable. The 27th New Jersey which is awaiting transportation, occupied the old barracks.

March 21

Storm continued. Several returned from furloughs. More troops went away.

March 22

Clear and warm. Snow went off rapidly. Colonel Hawkes started for a ten day furlough in Massachusetts. Inspection at ten o'clock. Several frigates and ironclads are anchored off the beach in our front, the Minnesota and Keokuk among the number.

March 23

Our regiment is performing provost duty at the wharves and storehouses. The 36th Mass embarked for Baltimore. Fixed up our tent.

March 24

I was on guard near the beach. From my post in the night I kept knowledge of the time by the cry of the "navies" on their watches on the *Minnesota* as they sung out: "alls well." When off beat I found comfortable quarters nestled among the numerous bales of hay which are piled on the wharf.

March 25

The 1st Brigade left for Baltimore and orders were read at dress parade for us to leave tomorrow. Five days rations are being cooked for our journey.

March 26

At eight o'clock we are packed and down to the wharf. At noon went on board the steam transport *Kennebec*. I was then detailed to assist in loading officers' baggage which was completed at three in the afternoon when we moved out into the stream amid the cheers of those left behind and Newport News with its quiet scenes recedes from sight. We sail down the "Roads" through a fleet of vessels carrying the ensigns of various foreign nations; just touch at Fortress Monroe for mails and then put out to sea.

*   *   *

"Whiskey has been smuggled on board and the reckless portion of the regiment is crazy with drink. From one end of the vessel to the other all is boisterous confusion. Many were fighting and life was fairly in danger. Those officers who were sober worked long and late to keep their men from doing harm to others but there were many bruised faces."

Six

Transfer to the Department of the Ohio

On August 19, 1862, the Union Department and Army of the Ohio was reorganized by the War Department. The new department included the states of Ohio, Michigan, Indiana, Illinois, Wisconsin and that part of Kentucky east of the Tennessee River, including Cumberland Gap. On August 23, Maj. Gen. Horatio G. Wright assumed command of the department with headquarters at Cincinnati. This reorganization was made in response to a resurgence in Confederate fortunes that began in mid-June. Southern armies had boldly seized the initiative along a 1,000-mile front, extending from Virginia's tidewater to the Indian Territory.

President Lincoln intuitively understood the importance of keeping Kentucky in the Union and was aware of the long-heard pleas of East Tennessee Unionists to free them from the "heavy hand" of Confederate despotism. These circumstances provided President Lincoln with the means to rescue General Burnside from oblivion and give him a meaningful mission. After his dismissal as commander of the Army of the Potomac, Burnside was directed on March 16, 1863, to resume command of his beloved IX Corps and relieve General Wright as commander of the Department of the Ohio. He was also to take the IX Corps to Ohio with him. Burnside arrived at Cincinnati on March 23 and assumed command on March 25.

Confederate raids coincided with Burnside's arrival. On March 22, the 8th Kentucky Cavalry (a detachment of Brig. Gen. John Hunt Morgan's cavalry), commanded by Col. R.. S. Cluke, raided Mount Sterling, Kentucky, taking 300 prisoners and seizing horses and supplies. Cluke reported that his "command is elegantly mounted and clothed—in better condition than they ever have been." On the following day Brig. Gen. John Pegram led a 1,500-man cavalry expedition to obtain beef cattle for the Confederate army. He attacked Danville, 40 miles southwest of Lexington and forced five Union regiments to retreat.

These raids caused alarm and anxiety among the inhabitants of Kentucky and Ohio. Burnside recognized the need for a larger military force in the area. Such a force would serve to restore the peace in Kentucky, impress the "Peace Democrats," "Copperheads" and other antiwar activists in Ohio, Indiana and Illinois with the presence of military authority, and accomplish the deliverance of East Tennessee.

On March 26, soldiers of the IX Corps, including the 21st Massachusetts, boarded the steamer Kennebec at Newport News, arrived at Baltimore on March 27 and headed west the next day on the Northern Central Railroad. The troops had an unfortunate clash with local militia at Columbus, Ohio, on March 30, which was never officially reported by the military. The IX Corps was welcomed by Burnside at Cincinnati on the final day of March before being transported to Paris, Kentucky, some 70 miles south. The soldiers were surprised that the inhabitants showed no open hostility and seemed to be glad to see them.

*   *   *

Comments in 1890:

It was definitely announced at last that the 9th Corps was to be transferred to the Department of the Ohio. General Burnside having been assigned to its command, he desired that his old soldiers should go with him. The 9th Corps was formed out of the original "Burnside expedition" and its peculiar mission rendered it, if not somewhat clannish, at least exclusive in its interests and purposes from the Army of the Potomac; certainly it acquired none of its jealousies and rivalries.

General Burnside widely discerned that such a body of men loyal to each other and to their commander would be a very effective force in the independent line of action laid out for and by him. Subsequent results proved his wisdom of choice and gave success to the plans of the East Tennessee campaign. Although withdrawn from participation in the glorious Gettysburg campaign, a portion of the Corps took part in the equally glorious Vicksburg campaign, but the grand strategic value of its work was the East Tennessee campaign.

Although Sherman's march to the sea received the wider admiration, one object attempted and accomplished was the same with each army, namely: severing the Confederacy and thereby forcing each part of fight without the assistance of the other. By the whole sale transfer of so large a body of veteran fighters into the heart of the Confederacy, our government was also able to open up a large section of the South notable for its Union sentiment.

The summer of 1863 found bodies of "Yankee" soldiers scattered through Kentucky engaged in the missionary work of converting its citizens to the knowledge that the Union had the power and would eventually conquer the rebellion. It was this experience that made Kentucky the first state to swing solidly back into the Union.

When the reunited 9th Corps reached the valley of the Holston [river in East Tennessee], it was planted squarely in the pathway between Lee and Johnston. At the nearest northern base of communication and supplies was two hundred miles away, separated from it by natures great barriers of lofty mountain ranges and broad rivers.

March 26, 1863

The air is mild and the sea calm and before dark we are out of sight of land the first time in my experience. I remain on deck long after the night has closed down upon us, enjoying the new and strange scene. "Out on the ocean all boundless we ride" is the refrain caught up and sung by the boys on deck.

March 27

When I go below, the scene changes. Whiskey has been smuggled on board and the reckless portion of the regiment is crazy with drink. From one end of the vessel to the other all is boisterous confusion. Many were fighting and life was fairly in danger. Those officers who were sober worked long and late to keep their men from doing harm to others but there were many bruised faces.

Company A found quarters in the gangway and in the coal bin opposite the engine room where there was constant movement. With the present condition of the men we were constantly being trampled upon, but no resistance or protest was ventured. At last I crawl up into the coal bin, spread a blanket on the coal, draw my overcoat over me and retire to my "downy couch." In this strange bed I shut my eyes at midnight from all worldly trials and vanities and wake at daylight after a truly refreshing sleep.

We are allowed by the good natured firemen to boil our coffee by setting our tin cups in the mouth of the great furnaces where but a moment was needed of its intense heat to boil. Going on deck we find ourselves sailing up the broad Chesapeake Bay with the low sandy reefs of Eastern Maryland on our right. We continually meet and pass vessels of all descriptions among which a massive screw propeller went rushing past us with astonishing rapidity. Before noon we passed by Annapolis, though several miles away from it; about two in the afternoon we drew near the granite walls of Fort Carroll which guards the entrance to the Patapsco River; passing this, we approach the enlivening scenes of the great city of Baltimore. After many months absence from scenes of civilization the sight is truly refreshing.

We plow up to the wharves right under the guns and parapets of Federal Hill and Fort McHenry which frown down upon us in a threatening manner and we are reminded of Key's lines, "By the rockets red glare and bombs bursting in air; Gave proof through the night that our flag was still there." Before the boat had fairly touched the pier, scores of enterprising ragamuffins swarm about us in boats bringing pies, cakes and fruit to sell, who find ready purchasers.

Owing to the intoxicated state of many in the regiment, we are not allowed to land; the authorities wisely deeming it safer for us on the vessel than awaiting transportation about the city. At nine o'clock at night we land, and march across the city through many of the principal streets two miles to the depots of the Northern Central Railroad. Here we are again detained ,several hours while the trains are being made up. The soldiers catch the undisturbed minutes of waiting: some to secure a nap and many others to secure a "sip" in the neighboring saloons. I found a comfortable nook in the bulkhead of a block of dwelling houses, where I dropped to sleep and was roused by the sound of tramping footsteps. I discovered the last of the brigade moving away. I barely escape being left behind, but at last succeed in finding the car where Company A is loaded.

March 28

At two in the morning the long train moves out of Baltimore. We were huddled into freight cars so closely that all could not lie down at the same time so we take turns in sitting up; in this manner I secure a little sleep before daylight which finds us entering free Pennsylvania and the accursed slavery left behind. The train was delayed sometime in the morning at Glen Rock and later at York. Early in the afternoon we came in sight of the Susquehanna River which we followed as far as Bridgeport, stopping here a few minutes we get a fine view of Harrisburg across the river with the towering dome of its State House.

After leaving here we approach and enter the mountains. Nearly every mile presents an active scene of the mining region. Little wooden railways run from some hole far away in the mountains to the main line. In some places they are only a few rods in length, running up a steep inclined plane into some over hanging cliff; on these are numberless trucks laden with coal that will be transported to every part of the Union. The day has been cold and stormy and the old and rickety car leaks badly so that our interest in the country through which we pass is divided in attempts to keep dry and warm.

At dusk we enter the enterprising town of Mifflin up in the mountains where we stop sometime and then proceed to climb the Allegheny Mountains; darkness however shuts out this interesting country.

March 29

Our weary bones ache from the constant jolting of the cars and on account of our cramped positions. As each man's misery is of more importance to himself than to anyone else, we present a seriocomic appearance such a medley of snarls, whines, growls and scolds. Amid such discordant music of unruly tongues, I am lulled to sleep.

After a night of broken rest, daylight finds us approaching Pittsburgh. At nine o'clock we disembark and march into the city. After several halts we meet the 51st N.Y. and 51st Penn and all march to the city hall where we were feasted by the bounteous hospitality of patriotic ladies and gentlemen. Toasts were responded to by General Ferrero, Colonel Clark and Dr. McCook of Pittsburgh. After a rousing "three times three and a tiger," we march back to the depot to await transportation.

In a surprisingly short time all three of the regiments had dissolved to a mere corporals guard; evidently the guards were in league with our men. After awhile they began to come scattering back and each one seemed to have taken to himself a raging devil. A more disgraceful sight could hardly be imagined as our regiment marched or staggered to the depot of the Columbus Railroad. Fully nine tenths of the regiment were under the influence of liquor—officers and men, and the remaining sober ones were all busy helping their drunken comrades into the cars.

March 30

Our train load of drunken freight went speeding out of the mountains of Pennsylvania into the broad prairies of Ohio. Riding all night, daylight found us near the town of Coshocton. The storm had at last broken and the sun shone out mild and spring like. Many of us exchanged our crowded quarters for the tops of the cars where the clear air and swiftly moving panorama made a most acceptable change.

Much of my time was occupied during the forenoon in keeping a drunken Company C man from rolling off the top of the car where he persisted in riding. The train halted a few moments at Newark where some of our men discovered a barrel of whiskey in a store cellar near the depot. Without asking leave of the proprietor they began rolling it toward the train but the train had already begun to move off. Some of the men ran and caught on the train, and succeeded in cutting off three or four of the rear cars while the rest of the train moved on before the ruse was discovered and a connection again made. The liquor was concealed in the rear car.

Reaching Columbus in the afternoon the generous and patriotic citizens met us and treated us with abundance of sandwiches and boiled eggs. I suppose a popular historian would pass lightly over those acts which reflected unfavorably upon his own regiment. No one could be more proud of the record of his comrades than I and this is why their only great disgrace seemed more shameful and I am prompted to notice it so fully here. It might be an easy matter to single out a certain set of contemptible fools in the regiment as there is in any community and rest the shame on them, but where so large a number join with them and attempt to dignify these shameful orgies as a jolly prank of a set of happy go lucky fellows and many commissioned officers join them.

The disgrace falls on every member of the regiment. Charity for a liquor drinker has never been one of my virtues so that when my individual record was stained by association with the lawless drunkards which made up the 21st Mass Regiment, I must be permitted to say that, no matter how bravely they may have done their duty in the past, I gladly welcomed the time when the regiment was purged of their companionship.

As a preventative for further mischief, the provost guard of Columbus was instructed to prohibit any of our men from leaving the vicinity of the depot. In their attempt to get more liquor, this restraint only served to madden the raging devils; they attacked the guard with stones and brickbats knocking down and severely wounded two or three. The whole provost guard was then ordered out and ordered to load and fire a round of blank cartridges into the crowd. Instead of frightening back the mob, it only served to madden them the more.

The commander then ordered ball cartridges to be loaded. I lost no time in getting away from the crowd and when this volley was fired into the crowd, several were wounded and one killed.[1] A grand rush was made for the cars to secure arms with which to retaliate. In our car men struggled with each other the orderly ones striving to restrain and calm the excited ones. In midst of all the confusion, Colonel Clark sprang on the engine and ordered the train forward with all speed. Many were left behind who were properly cared for as we afterward learned.[2]

We stop a few minutes at dusk at London and then another night shuts us in. A majority of the men were sleeping off their potions while the inventive minds of the unfortunate ones who can't find places to rest, construct a sailor's hammock out of their shelter tents, swinging them across the top beams of the cars. By ten o'clock our car is filled with them and we are vexed that the idea had not been put in practice before. Very soon however the insecure fastenings give away and down plunges its occupant upon the sleepers underneath. "Curses both loud and deep" are the response and before the hammock is again secured, down goes another man head first. "What's fun for one is death to another" but this sort of thing keeps up through the night.

March 31

We are not sorry to hear the train stop at three in the morning; looking out we find ourselves in sight of the Ohio River in the confines of Cincinnati. At daylight we unload and march from the Miami Railroad depot to Fifth Street Market where breakfast was waiting after which we proceed to the river, halting a few minutes in front of the Burnet House where General Burnside speaks to us words of hearty welcome and praise, which was responded to with enthusiasm. Cross the Ohio on ferry boats, march through Covington [Kentucky] to the depot of the Kentucky Central Railroad. At night we continued into Kentucky and bring our hammocks into use. During the night we arrive at Paris and our long journey by rail is ended.

*   *   *

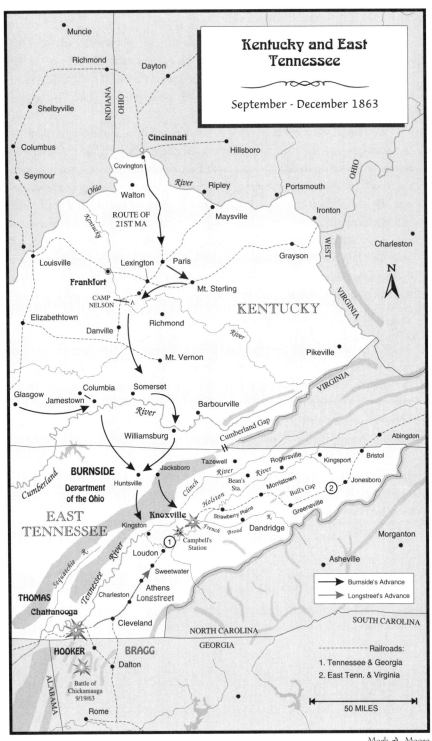

Kentucky and East Tennessee

September - December 1863

Muncie

Richmond

Dayton

Shelbyville

INDIANA OHIO

Columbus

Seymour

Cincinnati

Hillsboro

Covington

Ohio River

Walton

Ripley

Portsmouth

OHIO

ROUTE OF
21ST MA

Maysville

Ironton

Kentucky River

Louisville

Lexington   Paris

Grayson

WEST

Charleston

FrankFort

CAMP
NELSON

Mt. Sterling

VIRGINIA

N

Elizabethtown

Richmond

KENTUCKY

Danville

River

Mt. Vernon

Pikeville

Glasgow   Columbia   Somerset

Jamestown

River

Barbourville

VIRGINIA

Williamsburg

Cumberland Gap

Abingdon

BURNSIDE

Jacksboro

Tazewell

Rogersville

Kingsport

Bristol

Department
of the Ohio

Cumberland

Huntsville

Clinch River

Bean's
Sta.

Holston

Morristown

Bull's Gap

Jonesboro

Greeneville

EAST
TENNESSEE

Knoxville

Kingston

Strawberry Plains

R.

French   Broad   Dandridge

Morganton

Sequatchie R.

Tennessee River

Loudon

Campbell's
Station

Asheville

Sweetwater

THOMAS

Charleston   Athens
Longstreet

Chattanooga

Cleveland

NORTH CAROLINA

SOUTH CAROLINA

HOOKER   BRAGG

GEORGIA

Dalton

Battle of
Chickamauga
9/19/63

ALABAMA

Rome

➡ Burnside's Advance

➡ Longstreet's Advance

- - - - Railroads:
1. Tennessee & Georgia
2. East Tenn. & Virginia

50 MILES

Mark A. Moore

". . .the consciousness of the unseen danger of lurking guerrillas furnish just enough excitement for stimulus."

Seven

Spring and Summer in Eastern Kentucky

General Burnside assigned the troops of the IX Corps to various locations in Kentucky, including Lexington, Paris, Mount Sterling, Liberty, Glasgow and Frankfort. The Daily Ohio State Journal, *published in Columbus on March 31, 1863, reported that the IX Army Corps had been "quietly transported by regiments, without attracting particular attention, by different lines, to their destination." The newspaper also reported that "with these troops in Kentucky all apprehensions of an invasion of that State may be set at rest." The 14th Kentucky Cavalry, about 300 men, together with the 21st Massachusetts, about 400 men, were stationed together at Mount Sterling.*

Slavery was a delicate problem in Kentucky, especially with the release of the Emancipation Proclamation. Slaves residing in the areas of Kentucky occupied by Union troops were not included in their declaration, and the Union army was forbidden to interfere with any civil process in the state. Although all freed slaves were entitled to their freedom, Union soldiers were not allowed to aid or to abet the escape of those still held in bondage.

While the IX Corps troops offered at least the assurance of security to the harassed citizens of Kentucky, the New Englanders were not cordially welcomed. There was a strong prejudice against "Massachusetts Yankees," including the 21st Massachusetts, that resulted in barely-concealed displeasure and even open insults. These "abolitionists" were simply not wanted in the Kentucky communities. Such prejudices waned after a regiment was garrisoned within a town. The Union soldiers changed the popular attitudes by their discipline, intelligence, general good conduct and the gentlemanly demeanor of their officers.

Augustus Woodbury, writing in 1867, identified the 21st Massachusetts Regiment as one noteworthy example:

> *It was sent down to Mount Sterling, on the 5th of April, to hold the place and, with other troops, to secure the neighborhood against the occurrence of rebel raids, to which that section was peculiarly open. The regiment was very coldly received. It remained at this post for three months, and during that brief period, coldness was changed to cordiality, contempt to unwonted esteem, aversion to hospitality and kindness. When the regiment was to be ordered away, the inhabitants of the town actually petitioned the commanding general to allow the troops to remain for their protection. Two loyal cavalry regiments raised in the vicinity had been stationed near the town, and were still to hold the position. But the citizens were even more ready to trust themselves to the care of the Yankees than to the keeping of their own neighbors.*

George Hitchcock personified the "Massachusetts-Yankee" soldier who impressed the people living in Mount Sterling.

*   *   *

April 1, 1863

In the morning we march with flying colors through the very neat and pretty town of Paris, and encamp on the fairgrounds a mile from town. After our tents had fairly been pitched, Company A was detached from the regiment and sent into the town as headquarters guard for Colonel Clark, who occupied a large solidly built old mansion, the former residence of an ex governor. Paris is a place of considerable importance: several churches, three hotels and many stores scattered about town. I took the opportunity to attend a prayer meeting in a neighboring chapel in the evening.

April 2

I was on guard at the stables in the rear of headquarters in the night. Received orders at night to march in the morning with three days rations. Attended a Methodist prayer meeting in the evening. Suffered with a toothache.

April 3

Roused at five. Fine day. Packed up and when the regiment came along, fell in with them, marched out of town eastward passing the residence of Congressman Garret Davis.[1] The 21st march as rear guard for a wagon train on a fine broad pike. Teams and horses were pressed into service which were loaded with our knapsacks and company luggage. After a weary march of twenty one miles through a beautiful country passing through the small village of Middletown, we go into camp at dark in a pleasant grove, worn out and most of us footsore.

April 4

Slept but little during the night on account of the cold. The brigade marched through Mount Sterling and pitched camp two miles beyond. We learn that a rebel guerrilla band had a running fight with the Union cavalry along this road last week. It appears that the country is infested with guerrilla bands composed chiefly of rebel inhabitants of eastern Kentucky and as

April 5

A very mild spring like Sunday. "Better the day better the deed." Washed up clothes and body; cleaned up about our tent preparatory for inspection which took place at 10:30. Two from the 10th Kentucky Cavalry came in from the mountains and report a rebel force in the vicinity.

April 6

General Ferrero arrived from Lexington where he has been acting commander of the division. He now assumes command of the brigade. Various orders restricting the liberty of the soldiers were promulgated at dress parade. This is necessary for the discipline must be of vital importance now that the corps has been broken up into detached forces and great caution is taken to guard against the guerrilla bands which will attempt to surprise us.

April 7

I was on guard at the residence of a Union army officer who was murdered by the rebels when they passed through here. We realize that the method of warfare is quite different from what we have been accustomed. Kentucky was called the "dark and bloody" ground and she still retains the animosities of a passionate people. Assassinations are frequent occurrences and we shall do well to be watchful.

April 8

Colonel Hawkes rejoined the regiment from Massachusetts; he brought a bundle for me from home. Major Richardson drilled the regiment in the manual today. Orders were issued instituting regular camp duties.

April 9

A spring like day with birds singing. Squad drill in the manual. Rations getting scarce and the hardtack almost gone.

April 10

I was on picket on the Jefferson Road a mile out from camp with a half dozen others in charge of a corporal. Half rations were dealt out and we are anxiously looking for the supply train.

April 11

Warm and smoky. The expected supply train did not arrive until night. We, therefore, starved through the day. We anticipate that this may be one of the discomforts of our isolated position. Many of the boys have been out among the farm houses foraging for food. A citizen who came in today reports that five Union men were kidnaped by guerrillas eighteen miles from here.

April 12

Sunday inspection of guns and knapsacks at nine o'clock. A squad of men from the regiment attended church in town carrying arms in the old Puritan style to be prepared for guerrilla surprises. Our camp has swarmed all day with negro slaves mostly women and children bringing in pies and cakes for sale. Sunday is their great holiday and the Union soldiers are their great attraction. All seem to be in the happiest frame of mind.

April 13

The contrast between this and our Virginia service seems very great. The charming country, the mild spring weather and our distance from any rebel force make it all seem like holiday soldiering while the consciousness of the unseen danger of lurking guerrillas furnish just enough excitement for stimulus. Two guerrilla spies were found concealed in a barn near by and arrested by a squad of the 35th Mass. Their place concealment was disclosed by a negro slave belonging on the premises. General Ferrero was present at dress parade accompanied by a lady; music was provided by the 11th N.H. Band.

April 14

After sleeping soundly a few hours we were roused up at midnight, ordered to pack up in light marching order and started off at one in the morning with the 51st N.Y. for Sharpsburg, 13 miles in a northeasterly direction. Marched swiftly along through the darkness wondering what the object of the secret expedition may be. Halt only at rare intervals and then but for a very short stop when sleep would overcome nearly all; this made lively work for the officers to rouse the men and not overlook any sleepers in the pitch black night.

While marching toward morning, Sergeant May[2] of Company D was found to be sound asleep although keeping up with the regiment. His walk was unsteady and he only awoke when we halted for a rest and was told to stop and sit down.

As light began to dawn in the east we approached the town and the object of our visit became apparent. Silently and quickly one half of the troops were drawn off to the right and the left through the fields with each detachment making a half detour of the village, thereby forming an unbroken skirmish circle around it. As soon as the circle was complete the remaining portion of the force marched into the town. The people were taken completely by surprise.

Sharpsburg had been a convenient rendezvous for guerrilla bands, being near the mountains and wilderness of eastern Kentucky where such parties could easily escape capture. It was a regular rebel nest and the few Unionists were easily overawed. As we marched into the town the people looked out upon us wonder struck. Far from rail or telegraph communication few had any idea that any Union army could have any designs upon this quiet retreat. It was as if a ghostly band had risen out of the earth to them. We soon disabused them of any such notions, for we were soon invited to breakfast by our officers and there was nothing ghostly about our appetites.

The cordon of soldiers around the town securely kept anyone from leaving and the earlier part of the day was occupied by detailed squads of men searching the various houses. At some places the snappish and fiery rebel women attempted to resist the work. It was their first experience of what a hostile invading army meant and their disgust and amazement was great as they saw our men "go through" their homes from cellar, parlor, chamber and attic with perfect freedom and doubtless in some instances our lawless members appropriated more than they should; yet this is one of the necessary lessons of war, and if war in itself is right, these methods can easily be justified. Without a doubt we left the people at night with a wholesome fear of the power of the government which they had believed was already destroyed.

Information was given that a guerrilla was concealed in one house near the edge of town. Lieutenant Lawrence with a squad of Company A was sent to search the house but found that the bird had flown. During the forenoon about a dozen guerrillas were unearthed and put under guard. The remainder of the day was spent arraigning and examining prominent citizens suspected of complicity with the guerrilla bands.

Meanwhile the soldiers lounged about the streets and stores gaining a good idea of the intelligence of this typical backwoods, Jeff Davis worshipping place. We also visited the town house college academy meeting house where we remained during a hard shower until half past five when we gather up our trophies including a delegation of rebels; we escort them out of town and back to Mount Sterling where they were lodged in the county jail. We arrive at our camp at ten—weary and foot sore. "Here endeth our first lesson" to "Kaintuck rebs."

April 15

Went on guard; Lieutenant Hitchcock was officer of the guard. The paymaster has arrived. Learned by a home letter of the deaths of Lyman Holt[3] and Martin Gilson[4] in Louisiana.

April 16

General Ferrero's farewell address was read at dress parade; the command of the brigade now goes to General Hartranft, former Colonel of the 51st Penn. Ferrero was a dashing officer of rather small stature whose appearance reminded me of pictures I had seen of Bonaparte. We were always proud of him as a show commander for his fine military appearance but his habits of dissipation and immorality were such that he could not command the respect which an officer of his rank ought to have. The regiment received orders at night to march at once to Winchester, fifteen miles distant.

April 17

Very warm. Instead of marching to Winchester, the morning finds the 21st left alone while all the rest of the brigade has gone and we learn that the 9th Corps has been scattered all through Kentucky, posted at important places.

Mount Sterling is the place which has fallen to our lot; we break camp, march into town and take up quarters in the Court House, a large two story brick building, surmounted by a steeple and standing on an eminence in the center and overlooking the town. Being the county seat and having a large number of stores, it is a very busy center for a wide extent of territory. The nearest point to a railroad is Paris, twenty one miles away; the only mode of conveyance is horseback riding. Consequently every day finds a long row of horses tied to the railing which surrounds the courthouse grounds. The jail stands in the rear of the courthouse. Four companies occupy the lower floor and six the upper floor while the line officers have tents pitched on the lawn outside.

The regiment was paid off after which I was detailed with six others to go out and picket the Paris pike, a mile from town. The regiment is required to throw out pickets on all the roads leading from town of which there are the Paris pike, Paris dirt road, Winchester pike, Lulebegruel dirt road, Ticktown pike, Maysville pike, Sharpsburg pike, Owingsville pike and Hinkston pike. The pikes are made of macadamized stone smooth and hard as a floor which the rains cannot affect; the dirt roads are inferior, passable enough in dry weather but miserable in wet weather.

The day is beautiful and our picket post is in a shed adjoining the tollhouse. Our duties are light during the day: simply to demand a pass signed by the commander of the post of everyone going out of town. In the night two men are placed: one a few rods beyond the tollhouse and the other a quarter of a mile further away at a gate opening to a private road through which guerrilla bands have succeeded in passing into town when it was picketed by the home guard cavalry. We have to demand the countersign from everybody we see or hear, and in case of refusal, powder and ball are to be given.

This is a beautiful country but in the silent night watch I forget all this as I stand with wide-open eyes strained to pierce the darkness for the creeping crafty and treacherous bushwhacker is a kind of enemy which I have not had to deal with, and they have within a few days laid out more than one man in cold blood on this very picket post. However, I was undisturbed during the night.

April 18

We were relieved at half past ten. Cincinnati papers inform us that General Cox[5] takes the Department of the Ohio and General Burnside is wanted in the field. There was considerable drunkenness in quarters tonight.

April 19

I was on picket on the Ticktown pike near our old camp ground under Lieutenant McKabe.[6] A rebel bushwhacker, who had murdered a Union citizen a few miles out, was brought in by our picket during the day. When we were off duty, we went out to the neighboring farm houses and buy milk, eggs and poultry and get the negro women to bake biscuits for us; prices are very cheap. The weather is fine and we are unanimously agreed that this is truly "parlor soldiering."

April 20

The brigade band left us today. County court is in session under our quarters. Lieutenants Parker and Valentine[7] returned.

April 21

The provost guard is very strict arresting every man found outside the court yard without a pass. Many are confined in jail (now used as a guard house) for drunkenness. Henry has been assigned to Company K.

April 22

I was on picket at the Winchester pike under Sergeant Gethings.[8] We were notified that a spy had sneaked into town by our post and to lookout for him when he returned. We scattered out into the fields and watched for him but he eluded us, escaping back of the hills. A squad of cavalry was sent out to catch him and succeeded.

April 23

In the morning the spy was carried past us in irons, accompanied by the Sharpsburg crowd of a dozen rebs which we brought from there when we made our raid upon it. They were sent to Cincinnati.

April 24

Today has been a pruning day for the 21st Mass. Colonel Clark returned from Cincinnati with his resignation accepted and read his farewell address at dress parade. We lose a most efficient, highly cultured and fine appearing officer. It was claimed that he was disappointed in not receiving the appointment of brigade commander in place of General Hartranft, which was the cause of his resigning. Colonel Hawkes takes command of the post and Captain Clark the regiment.

All but two of the captains have resigned, also several lieutenants. It is rumored that they received hints that they were not wanted longer on account of their complicity with the rioters in Columbus, Ohio. They were certainly not in harmony with the present commander on the temperance question. This action on their part was wise, if not patriotic. Company A took possession of the jury room on the southeast corner of the court house for its quarters. It is a high, light, airy room, and shut off from the rest of the regiment. Received papers from home.

April 25

On picket under Sergeant Koster[9] on the Winchester pike. A squad of 21st boys were sent out on the Sharpsburg road to search for concealed rebels but returned unsuccessful.

April 26

Sunday: attended the Episcopal Church in the afternoon Rev. Mr. Tompkins, rector. Captains Sanderson, Hill, Wheeler, Walcott and Aldrich received honorable discharges [Captain William T. Harlow was also discharged].[10] Captain Sanderson came in and bade us good by; he starts for Massachusetts via Lexington tomorrow morning at four. We shall miss him as he was a happy, jovial fellow rather reckless, but popular with the boys.

April 27

A deserter from the 14th Kentucky, who was caught burning the house of a Union man and stealing a negro, was brought in and confined in the jail. The 14th Kentucky Regiment was raised in this section and is made up of a wild, reckless, unsoldierly set. Their camp is a mile out of town and they seem to enjoy bushwhacking their hated neighbors rather than undertaking more disciplined service for the Union. The adjutant was put under arrest for drunkenness.

April 28

On picket on the Lulebegruel road: this a lonely back road and only three privates (Lem Whitney, Jack Reynolds and Hitchcock) and a corporal (Alvin Humiston[11]) are posted here today. Visited a neighboring farm house where we purchase eggs (price five cents per dozen), butter (ten cents per pound) and other produce at equally low prices. During the night we were startled by a shot fired nearby. On investigation we found it was by a negro who was killing sheep; we return to our post much relieved.

April 29

Citizens from Sharpsburg this forenoon brought news that a force of rebels entered that place and drove out Union men. After a good deal of excitement on the street, Major Williams[12] of the 10th Kentucky Cavalry gathered up a force of four hundred citizens on horseback and set out to change the tune; Williams' own cavalry was out in the mountains scouting.

April 30

I was roused up in the night and with nine others under Lieutenant Howe went out scouting in a suspicious locality a few miles from town but returned to town at day light unrewarded with any trophies. Two Union families came in from the mountains, driven away by the rebs. They were in a state of great destitution. This peculiar style of warfare, while rather novel to us, is sufficiently exasperating. At night the regiment received orders to march tomorrow to Columbia, 150 miles southwest.

May 1

The citizens of Mount Sterling hastened a very urgent petition to General Burnside that the 21st be held at this place. Its importance as a center with the whole region infested by guerrillas demanded it. So the orders were countermanded temporarily. I was a picket on the Ticktown pike with Sergeant May. Many of the boys are on a high spree tonight over milk punch, eggnog and the "undiluted;" large numbers have been shut up in the guardhouse.

May 2

There was news of fighting seven miles from here between some of our cavalry and a force of fifty guerrillas. Reinforcements were sent out to them. They returned in the morning.

May 3

On picket on the Ticktown pike under Sergeant Curtis.[13] The regiment again received marching orders for tomorrow morning so we returned from picket at dusk.

May 4

Our marching orders were again countermanded. The 10th Kentucky Cavalry passed through town headed for Owingsville with two mountain howitzers. A rebel spy and a female letter carrier were arrested in the town this afternoon. Heard that General Hooker had advanced across the Rappahannock and the Army of the Potomac was at Culpeper.

May 5

Two howitzers of the 10th Kentucky passed through town today. Criminal court opened session at the Presbyterian Church.

May 6

On guard in the rear of the court house. News from General Hooker that he has captured Fredericksburg with 5,000 prisoners.

May 7

News says that General Sedgwick has fallen back from Fredericksburg and the enemy again holds it.

May 8

News that General Hooker has recrossed the Rappahannock; that the slaughter has been terrible on both sides [Battle of Chancellorsville on May 14, 1863]. I went to town on a pass.

May 9

On picket on the Maysville pike under Sergeant Miller.[14] General Hooker has again returned to his old Falmouth quarters. General Stoneman made a circuit of the rebel army and joined General Dix's force two miles from Richmond.

May 10

Sunday. Attended Episcopal church in the afternoon and Methodist in the evening. Some of our good singers of the 21st assisted the parson's pretty daughters in the musical branch of the service.

May 11

Received a pass and visited the MacPhelah Cemetery half a mile north of the town. It is situated on a high hill overlooking the town, from which we have a fine view of a wide sweep of charming country: fine farms and farmhouses dotting the landscape. This is on the confines of the famous blue grass region and is remarkably fertile. John Wallace, who has been on duty with the provost guard, has been promoted to sergeant and has returned to the company. Although the reported capture of Richmond by General Dix is not credited, the citizens have been celebrating the supposed victory by firing skyrockets.

May 12

On picket on the Paris pike under Corporal Dyer.15 Colonel Hawkes visited our picket post during the afternoon.

May 13

News of the deaths of Stonewall Jackson and Van Dorn[16] in the late fighting in Virginia.

May 14

Colonel Hawkes went to Lexington on official business; Major Williams of the 10th Kentucky commands the post in his absence.

May 15

On picket on the Paris pike under Sergeant Sperry.[17] Lieutenant Hayward[18] has been dishonorably discharged from the army for drunkenness and left for Massachusetts today.

May 16

Lieutenant Fuller,[19] our quartermaster, left for home on a fifteen day furlough. Colonel Hawkes returned from Lexington.

May 17

Sunday. Inspection at eight. Attended Episcopal service in forenoon, dinner at noon, church again in afternoon, dress parade at five where the Rev. Tompkins addressed the regiment, and church again in the evening.

May 18

On picket on the Owingsville pike under Sergeant Cummings.[20] The weather is fine and warm. We lie about under the shade of the great walnut trees when off duty, reading, chatting, cooking and eating. Several rebel soldiers and two officers were brought in past our post while I was on duty.

May 19

Called on Henry who is commander of the provost with headquarters downtown. He has a detail of fifty men from our regiment who have to guard the county jail and various public buildings: principally to keep order throughout town; especially to keep the soldiers from disturbing the peace. The quiet arcadian existence is strangely non conducive to good order and morals among our men. News of the imprisonment of Vallandigham[21] at Fort Warren.

May 20

Several hospital bummers returned to the regiment from Lexington. Hear that the rest of our brigade is stationed at Lancaster seventy miles south of here. I went out of town on a pass to bathe.

May 21

On picket on Ticktown pike under Lieutenant Goodrich.[22] A citizen came in and reported a force of rebels forty miles from here.

May 22

Very warm and sultry. Spent most of the time reading.

May 23

Attended a musicale at the Episcopal church; Miss Tompkins presided at the organ. Among the male singers were officers Hawkes, Davis, Hitchcock, Goss and Valentine and private Carruth.

May 24

On picket at Sharpsburg tollgate under Sergeant Wilder.[23] Spent most of the day writing letters.

May 25

Received a pass and went bathing near the house of the "swamp angel," a notorious character.

May 26

Very warm and dusty. I have been calling at Henry's rooms down town. He is considered quite a prominent character; he is a very efficient and faithful officer occupying a position similar to that of police chief in a northern city.

May 27

On picket on the Owingsville pike under Sergeant Wallace. Our drum corps has developed considerable musical talent and this evening held a minstrel show and concert in the courthouse hall.

May 28

Colonel Hawkes has gone to Cincinnati. I went out on a pass tonight. The New England Minstrels repeated their concert to accommodate the pickets on duty yesterday. It consisted of comic and sentimental songs; dances, jigs and witty dialogues were accompanied by an excellent orchestra of violins, guitars, flutes and bones.

May 29

Dress parade was omitted on account of rain. These occasions have become the great attraction of social life of Mount Sterling. All the elite turn out to honor us with their presence; multitudes of negroes and backwoodsmen make up a great crowd which inspires the 21st to do their best, and it seems as if they had become perfect in the manual.

May 30

On picket at the Sharpsburg tollgate under Sergeant Curtis. Colonel Hawkes returned from Cincinnati. Rumors that General Burnside has been relieved.

May 31

Sunday. Attended the Methodist church; heard an itinerant preacher who was very smart. Heavy thunderstorm in the evening.

June 1

Regimental inspection of knapsacks and equipments this afternoon. Twelve rebel soldiers came in and gave themselves up to the 10th Kentucky Cavalry. Quartermaster Fuller returned from Massachusetts. Received papers from home.

June 2

On picket at the Sharpsburg tollgate under Sergeant Muzzey.[24] Several men have gone home on furloughs.

June 3

Grand match game of baseball[25] was played just outside of town on the Ticktown pike.

June 4

Very warm. Lem and I received passes and took a long and interesting tramp out on the Lulebegruel road. Stopped at several farmhouses and held conversation with the natives: typical Kentuckians great brawny men and healthy looking women. Went in swimming before we returned. Orders were received this evening from General Hartranft for the 21st to report at Paris tomorrow. It is supposed that we are to go to Vicksburg with the 9th Corps. Heard a sermon by the Reverend Tompkins this evening; he has become a great friend of the regiment; he is a staunch Union man, and being a person of great influence, it is believed that he will succeed in keeping us here.

June 5

Our marching orders were countermanded during the night. I was on guard at the courthouse. Considerable excitement and indignation was caused today by the public execution of a negro slave. He had been convicted on Kentucky testimony of trying to kill his master, being aggravated by cruelty. The master was well and present at the trial. When all arrangements had been made for the execution, Henry as provost commander was called on to furnish guard. This he refused to do.

As there was an ominous muttering among the Yankee soldiers, the authorities after a long delay succeeded in getting a squad of the 14th Kentucky Cavalry to escort the poor man out of town where he was hung. A small drum cord was used which broke when the drop fell; although strangled, he lived and was conscious while another rope was procured from town after half an hour waiting in agony. He was then launched off into eternity in the presence of a crowd of people, many of the 21st witnessing the horrid scene. I chose to keep out of sight of it.

As our government's policy is to refrain from interfering in all loyal state governments, Colonel Hawkes wisely remained neutral in the affair, but a little effective outlawry by our boys might have been winked at if the opportunity could have been found.

The paymaster arrived with our payrolls.

June 6

Twelve rebel prisoners were brought in. I attended a choir rehearsal this evening at the Episcopal church.

June 7

Sunday. Attended church at which the sacrament was administered. In the afternoon I went with three others out to the negro church on a back street at the edge of town. After wild chanting and singing, the unlearned minister exhorted his flock to "git religion." Then the circus began: First an old negro women would jump up, shout, and singing in a wild discordant way march up the aisle, shake hands with the minister; then another would take up the march and at last the whole audience would be shouting, dancing and working itself into a fine frenzy. This would be called "getting religion." The ludicrous actions were too much for my visibilities and I vowed to keep away from them in the future on the Sabbath.

The army telegraph has arrived, bringing us into quick communication with the rest of the world.

June 8

On picket on the Hinkston road under Corporal Goodness.[26] This is a quiet romantic road leading away through the hills to the north; the only individuals passing through were a few negroes. Eight prisoners were sent to Cincinnati today.

June 9

The regiment was paid; I received two months pay $26.[27]

June 10

We learn that the 9th Corps and part of the 23d has been sent to Vicksburg and that our regiment with a few others are to remain in Kentucky to perform garrison duty. The Union people fear that the guerrilla bands of East Tennessee and in the mountains of this state will now be emboldened to push forward into the heart of the state and make trouble.

June 11

On picket on the Hinkston road under Corporal Barney McNulty.[28] The 10th Kentucky passed through here from Owingsville to Lexington. Freeman Cole returned to the company from provost duty.

June 12

A grand match game of baseball: Adjutant Parker is leader for one side and Lieutenant Kelt[29] for the other. They play for a supper which is won by Parker's side; they have a grand carousal at the Sterling House in the evening. I sat for an ambrotype [a glass negative with a thin density made to give the impression of a positive when placed against a dark background].

June 13

On picket at the Owingsville pike under John Wallace. At noon I went into town on an errand and as I was returning to the picket post the startling news was brought in that the scouting party composed of a portion of the 14th Kentucky Cavalry had been attacked by a superior force of a guerrilla band a few miles out on this Owingsville pike.

When I reached the post I found a scene of wild excitement. Large numbers of stragglers and cowards of the 14th Kentucky came galloping in, bringing conflicting and improbable reports of terrible slaughter and that their command had been completely wiped out. They told us that we might expect them at any moment. Our picket force of eight men was formed across the road with fixed bayonets and for a short time found lively work in keeping back the poltroons from rushing past us into town.

Our post was in a sightly place commanding a view of more than a mile of the pike beyond and the clouds of dust from the retreating cavalry kept us in suspense for awhile, thinking it might be the approaching enemy. Soon the 21st came hurrying out at double quick step, and as they pushed forward, the weak kneed cavalry boys began to pluck up courage and about faced. The whole made a very respectable force as they moved out toward the anticipated fight.

It was surmised that the enemy, which was in considerable force some three miles out, was making a feint to draw out our force from the town, when they would enter it by some other road. The 21st was then drawn in and each company posted at commanding points just outside the town where they could easily concentrate in case of a surprise at any given point. The raiding party was estimated by some as high as a thousand horsemen.

Nothing more was heard from them during the afternoon and at dark strong pickets were thrown out in every direction with the regiment lying on arms all night. All citizens were ordered to remain indoors under penalty of being shot if not complying. The night passes away silent as death, nothing occurring to break the stillness but the barking of multitudes of dogs which can be heard at great distance at the farmhouses.

June 14

I was on picket two hours in a cornfield where I could hear the slightest sound on two roads so that a surprise could not overtake us. Sunday morning found four companies of us bivouacked in a large cherry orchard a quarter of a mile northwest of the courthouse. We lie on arms all day with time being spent playing card and dominoes, reading dime novels and picking the ripe cherries. Sergeant John Wallace and Lem Whitney were sent out with a flag of truce on the Owingsville pike. They went fifteen miles and found no enemy but counted seven of the 14th Kentucky murdered by the side of the road and five badly wounded. They made extensive inquiries at the houses in the vicinity but could not gain any reliable information which direction the enemy came or went. They were told that no quarter was given. When a 14th Kentucky man was caught, he was instantly shot or bayoneted. Major Williams was shot but not killed. The 10th Kentucky came in from Richmond [Kentucky] in the evening.

June 15

We remain in the orchard all day. Two field pieces were posted on a hill near the Hinkston road where they command three pikes leading into town. Two new mounted regiments arrived during the day the 8th and 9th Michigan. Maysville is reported burnt by the raiders which shows the direction taken by the raiders. Several families have been ordered to leave town within twenty four hours for "Dixie" after being implicated in assisting and giving information to the raiders. The town again assumes it usual business appearance.

June 16

On picket at the Ticktown pike under Lieutenant Bean.[30] Our regiment moved into a locust tree grove near the courthouse. The 8th and 9th Michigan and parts of the 10th and 14th Kentucky have gone out to the mountains to intercept the raiders when they return from Maysville.

June 17

I pitched my tent alone. The rebs went right into the trap set for them and lost nearly all their horses and stolen plunder. Most of them escaped in the woods, but twenty five were caught and brought into town. They were confined in our old quarters in the courthouse hall where I am a guard tonight.

June 18

Twelve more prisoners were caught and brought in today. They excite great curiosity among our boys; they are a very rough and ragged set but nearly all look wide awake, daring and determined. One of them insolently defied the guard, a Company K man, and insisted on going outside the bounds set for them; he was shot dead. The act was endorsed by the officers and these prisoner are consequently very quiet and tractable.

Received news that Lee's army is moving north into Maryland and that General Hooker has broken up his Falmouth camp where it has been for more than six months. This indicates an offensive move on the part of the rebels and a defensive move by General Hooker.

June 19

The 21st has been relieved of picket duty for the present by the cavalry and we are detailed to work on fortifications. I am on prison guard tonight.

June 20

Court-martial was held at the courthouse to try the Company K man for shooting the prisoner, but he was exonerated of all blame.

June 21

Sunday morning inspection at nine. Soldiers who attend church must go under guard of an officer, so strict are the orders that the provost guard will arrest them if not complying. Rev. Mr. Tompkins spoke to the regiment at dress parade.

June 22

Our prisoners were sent to Lexington; the hall being vacated, the New England Minstrels held a concert before a crowded house.

June 23

I was on guard at headquarters. Attended a large political meeting at the hall and heard Bramlette,[31] Governor elect. Another minstrel concert in the evening. The battery left for Hickman's Bridge tonight.

June 24

Colonel Hawkes is sick. The Rev. Tompkins spoke and offered prayer at dress parade.

June 25

A general inspection took place under Lieutenant Colonel King[32] of the 35th Mass.

June 26

Received news that Lee's army was north of the Potomac and advancing into Pennsylvania.

June 27

I went out with Cole beyond the picket post on the Paris dirt road to Mr. Fergerson's farmhouse; purchase supplies of butter and eggs, talk politics and return to camp much pleased with our visit. Henry's attempt to get a furlough is unsuccessful as no more furloughs are to be granted.

June 28

Heavy thundershower. Lee's army is moving on Harrisburg having occupied Carlisle, York, Chambersburg and other important places in Pennsylvania. This is turning the tables on us with a vengeance.

June 29

[No entry]

June 30

Regular monthly inspection and muster in under Captain Davis. A lieutenant of the 14th Kentucky, who was wounded in the late battle, died and was buried this afternoon under military honors; the 21st acted as escort and fired a salute over the grave; a large number of young ladies scattered flowers over the grave.

July 1

Nine men were detailed from the 21st for picket duty. John Wallace was detailed for provost.

July 2

The regiment drilled one hour in the manual. A guerrilla band destroyed a train of cars on the Frankfort and Louisville Railroad last night.

July 3

John Morgan[33] is advancing with a large force into the state from Cumberland Gap.

July 4

The citizens of Mount Sterling held a picnic on the Maysville pike celebrating the glorious Fourth. Henry has gone to Sharpsburg to spend the Sabbath.

July 5

I was on guard at headquarters. Flying rumors about Morgan's raid during the day and at seven in the evening orders arrived for the regiment to make all haste and march to Lexington to intercept Morgan. After great haste and excitement in which many citizens join, we start a little past midnight saying good bye to large numbers of the good people whose interest in the regiment had kept them up till the late hour. Great fears are felt for Mount Sterling as the people have taken a very pronounced stand for the Union and now they are left to the tender mercies or bloodthirsty vengeance of the hordes which sweep down from the eastern mountains.

July 6

With regret we turn our backs on the Arcadian life which we have led during the past three months. I presume few of our soldiers found a more charming holiday experience sandwiched between the severities of the Civil War than did the 21st while at Mount Sterling. The activity of the treacherous guerrillas of this portion of the state furnished us with enough of peril and danger to dispel the tedium, while our ambition to make a good impression upon the people was a stimulus which perfected our military bearing.

While our comrades engaged in deadly struggles at Gettysburg and Vicksburg, we were taking life easy in the beautiful groves of Mount Sterling;

yet I believe our service was beneficial, directly, in protecting friends of the Union and developing a powerful Union sentiment when it had well nigh been crushed out.

Indirectly, by our contact with all classes of people, they found in the New England soldiers the representatives of that force which had dominated and educated the nation in its best ideals, not that our regiment was composed of model men, but their spirit in the main was representative of those ideals.

With a singular lack of judgment Colonel Hawkes led us off at a rattling pace in the midsummer's night, forgetful in the excitement of the occasion that we had become softened and comparatively enervated by our quiet life. In ordinary marching halts for rest are made as often as every mile or at the most in every two miles. In our almost double-quick pace we go more then three miles with all our heavy trappings before a halt is called.

In our utter exhaustion we throw away our knapsack and overcoat in a sort of reckless despair: mutterings loud and deep to express our indignation and lack of discipline. By sunrise we reach Winchester where a halt for a few hours is made. Starting off again at the same rapid pace, the boys, with grim humor, declare that the Colonel's horse must have been wound up too tight.

Before noon the evil effect of such marching is made apparent. Hardly a corporal's guard remains with the leader—the entire regiment having fallen out by the wayside exhausted and footsore. Many have been sunstruck and left at farmhouses along the route. Like the mists before the morning sun, the 21st Mass Regimental Volunteers have faded out of existence. Any well ordered guerrilla band of fifty men could easily have scooped us all up as they had swept down the Winchester pike.

Before the middle of the afternoon my feet were covered with several large blisters, and I limp on a few miles alone and at last give out entirely; a baggage wagon came along and picked me up. I was jolted into Lexington, arriving there at midnight.

July 7

Before morning the straggling 21st had found itself gathered by the side of the Lexington and Danville Railroad under the guns of Fort Clay, a strong fortification commanding the railroad approaches to the city, as well as the great pike from Danville. Barricades have been erected on all the roads leading southward from the city. We find that the 48th Pennsylvania of the 9th Corps is the only regiment beside our own here in the city.

July 8

It is learned that Morgan has ignored us, and passing by to the westward, he is pushing toward Louisville on a daring raid to secure horses and plunder. Lexington being his home, he doubtless thought it not best to invite a battle here. Knowing the scarcity of troops in the state, his safety depends upon his swift movement.

The news of the surrender of Vicksburg is received and at noon thirty heavy guns at Fort Clay send out their glad salute in a deafening roar over our heads. News also that General Lee has been repulsed in Pennsylvania after heavy fighting and is retreating into Virginia.

July 9

Our camp in the beautiful suburbs of Lexington is in sight of the leafy canopy of the still more beautiful cemetery. Towering high above it is the imposing Henry Clay Monument surmounted by his colossal statue. Adjutant Parker and brother Henry arrived from Mount Sterling and joined the regiment. A picket was detailed from our regiment It is reported that General Lee has been cornered on the old Antietam ground.

July 10

I was on camp guard. Lieutenant Valentine arrived from Massachusetts. Morgan has crossed the Ohio into Indiana and is sweeping into the interior of that state.

July 11

Received a pass and visited the city; including the Henry Clay Monument. Henry is officer of the guard today.

July 12

I was on camp guard. The boys have had great sport with a blind violinist and singer, getting up an impromptu "shake down." The 12th Rhode Island, a nine months regiment, passed northward on the cars enroute for home. Inspection by Colonel DeCourcy.[34]

July 13

Went into the city on a pass. A battery went through here bound for Cincinnati.

July 14

News of the great anti draft riot in New York in which many have already been killed: "Foes without and foes within." This is a big job we have on our hands but we must spit on our hands and take a new "bolt."

July 15

News of the capture of Morris Island by our troops off the South Carolina coast and of fighting off Charleston. General Lee has escaped into Virginia.

July 16

Left our old campground and moved into the old convalescent campground a mile further west (southwest of the city) near the cemetery and on the Frankfort pike. Our camp is in a beautiful grove of lofty maple and whitewood with a fine aristocratic looking mansion in the center of extensive grounds - tastefully laid out with great profusion of flowers and shrubbery. I was on guard at headquarters. Received news of the capture of Port Hudson with 17,000 prisoners. Signed the payrolls and received two months pay.

July 17

Cole and I went into the city on passes.

July 18

The draft in Ashby has been completed and the draft officer, G.L. Hitchcock [George Loring Hitchcock George's father], has not been mobbed. The draft riot in New York has been subdued.

July 19

Attended Presbyterian church and apparently a wealthy one: rich toilets, melodious music, grand equipages and dull preaching critical visitor.

July 20

The wife of Major Richardson arrived via Mount Sterling.

July 21

I went into the city and bought boards for a bunk so I now have my tent arranged in a fine comfortable manner. Morgan lost two thousand men in Indiana and is now working his way back through Ohio.

July 22

Sergeant John Wallace has gone to Camp Chase in Columbus [Ohio] with a squad of men in charge of rebel prisoners.

July 23

I was on guard.

July 24

Went into the city visiting stores attempting the onerous task of exchanging greenbacks for reading matter. Colonel Hawkes went to Cincinnati.

July 25

Religious services were held in camp by a volunteer preacher of the Christian Commission; distributed tracts and religious reading of which we stand in great need as the camp is overrun with novels and reading trash.

July 26

I was on guard.

July 27

Mrs. Hawkes and Henry's wife arrived here from Templeton, Massachusetts.

July 28

I called on the Massachusetts ladies at the Broadway Hotel. Another raiding band of guerrillas under Pegram[35] have crossed the Kentucky River, fourteen miles below here aiming toward Paris—evidently intending to cut our railroad communications. The 21st was sent over to Fort Clay in case the enemy comes here.

July 29

We laid on arms all night and day but at night we are ordered back to camp and immediately to embark on the cars for Paris. Arriving at the depot, these orders are countermanded and we return to camp.

July 30

It was learned that Pegram attacked our garrison at Paris but retreated without injuring the railroad. They returned by way of Winchester and Mount Sterling burning our old quarters the courthouse. I was on guard at the gate near the railroad.

July 31

Regimental monthly inspection and company drill—the first one for three months.

August 1

Troops have been coming in from the south all day; very hot. The Rev. Tompkins from Mount Sterling visited the regiment. Sid Heywood has returned to the regiment from the quartermasters dept.

August 2

While on guard at noon, I was drenched to the skin by a heavy thundershower. Four hundred prisoners were captured and brought in from Lancaster. The regiment was detailed for work tomorrow.

August 3

One large squad was sent out to Saundersville, a rebel hole seven miles southwest to guard the polls at election.[36] Sixty men were sent to Louisville with the rebel prisoners.

August 4

The guards returned from Louisville and Saundersville. Visited the city on a pass.

August 5

Another detail from the regiment went to Louisville as guard for rebel prisoners.

August 6

I was on guard in a large peach orchard adjoining the mansion. The trees are loaded with the ripe, luscious fruit and as it is but a few rods from our camp, on a sequestered place it offers a great temptation to the boys. The negro slaves are instructed to furnish a generous supply to the guard.

National thanksgiving today over the great victories of Gettysburg, Vicksburg and Port Hudson. In camp it is recognized by omitting all drills and dress parade. I find much time for reading; many of our boys are busy with cards. The 60th Illinois passed through the city for Hickman's Bridge (or Camp Nelson).

August 7

Sergeant Major Lewis and a squad of men have gone out in the direction of Winchester, scouting rebels. Sergeant Chamberlin[37] with another squad went toward Camp Nelson. Charles Wyman of Ashby, who is employed at Captain Hall's[38] headquarters at Camp Nelson, called on me on his return from Cincinnati. With his innocent looking haversack slung over his shoulder and a small bundle of "personal effects" no one would suspect that he was loaded down with $50,000 which he was carrying out to Captain Hall for government uses. With the secret known only to a few, he passes back and forth among reckless men who could and would easily have relieved him of the treasure if they had known.

August 8

General Burnside passed through Lexington. Henry and Mary, his wife, are boarding at a family by the name of Hougland a short distance off on the Frankfort pike. By invitation I dined with them, sitting down in a civilized fashion to a table and tablecloth for the first time for a year. Of the family of five members, four were deaf and dumb; one daughter, a young lady of about twenty three years, was the only one who had the use of five senses yes, six senses for the sixth sense of conversation with hands and fingers was carried on with great ease and rapidity. The general air of refinement and politeness distinguished the whole family and the occasion was a thoroughly enjoyable one to me. The young lady was very vivacious and with the utmost good nature held her rebellious views in spite of the presence of two of Uncle Sam's servants.

August 9

Sabbath. I attended the Presbyterian church. Jonas Davis[39] and I called on Mary in the evening. Quite a number of ladies were present at dress parade.

August 10

General Burnside was in town; evidently preparing for active work as troops have been passing constantly southward over the Lexington and Danville Railroad. Colonel Hawkes drilled us in battalion drill the first time since we left Newport News. Evidently it was done for the edification of the Massachusetts ladies who watched evolutions with interest.

August 11

General De Courcy, who is in command of the department, visited our camp and the anticipated orders to march were forthcoming at dress parade.

August 12

Off for Camp Nelson! I had to guard the peach orchard in the forenoon which I regretfully leave at noon. We pack up and march away from our beautiful grove.

After some delay it was decided to have us go by rail as far as Nicholasville. So in the perfect sunny afternoon we glide out of this fine southern city past the great park (Ashland), the country seat of Henry Clay's family; we pass great orchards of luscious peaches tantalizing the beholder

Sergeant Jonas R. Davis

Davis entered the military from Templeton, Massachusetts, on August 23, 1861 and served as a sergeant in Company A, 21st Massachusetts. He was promoted to first lieutenant on June 6, 1863.

along through this American Eden, "the blue grass region" which yields bountiful harvests. The timberland can hardly be called forests for the great trees of beach, maple, oak and walnut cluster not too closely together, and in place of any undergrowth the rich pasturage grows luxuriant beneath the trees. No wonder the "horse" finds its natural home in such surroundings, but it is a wonder that "Bourbon Whiskey" and the "bloody code" can find their seat in this paradise.

The cars quickly bear us out of these and into scenes of different aspect. We find ourselves in the rusty dilapidated town of Nicholasville, a place of some three of four thousand inhabitants. Unload and after some delay, loafing about the streets until dark, we march off through the deep fine dust over a broad pike southward about five miles and at ten o'clock camp down in an open field by the roadside.

August 13

After a sound sleep under the starry canopy of heaven, we get our coffee, brush off the thick dust and march briskly three miles into Camp Nelson[40] with drums beating and colors flying. I was much surprised to find it so large and busy a place: a military post of great importance as a base of supplies for the armies operating in the southern part of Kentucky and East Tennessee. The camps lie along the great stage road for East Tennessee via the Cumberland Gap about a mile from the Kentucky River where Hickman's Bridge crosses it. The country in the vicinity of the river becomes very rugged and precipitous while pine, spruce and other evergreen trees begin to appear.

As we enter the place, we pass Captain Hall's headquarters. As quartermaster of the post, his staff of clerks and orderlies occupy numerous tents overlooking the camp; then we pass large corrals of mules and teams and beyond these are various camps of hospitals and troops rendezvousing here. We go into camp in the edge of a piece of woods that is mostly pine on a slope facing another, on which lies a large convalescent camp and between the two runs the stage road.

The day is occupied in laying out and pitching our camp in the most approved style. Before night we are notified that we are to receive a visit from General Burnside; we, therefore, brush up and prepare ourselves with unusual care for the reception of our favorite commander. Soon the great cavalcade composing the staffs of Burnside and Hall could be seen approaching from a distant hill and the 21st, drawn out in dress parade, give these favorite officers an enthusiastic reception. After congratulatory words from them the dress parade is finished and the men crowd around them to greet them with a shake of the hand.

General Boyle[41] is commander of the post and General Fry[42] is the present commander of the department, and both are stationed here. A person given to punning says that if a *general boil* and a *general fry*, the result in a *burned side* and we shall have a *captain haul* over the whole business. This is the fact that Captain Hall, although a subordinate in rank, is in reality the mainspring which runs the whole business, while General Boyle duties are of less importance.

August 14

I have fixed up a bunk and put my tent in cozy style. I keep my butter and milk in a hole in the ground cool and fresh. Cole has been detailed as has others for General Burnside's private secretary. Details have also been made for regimental headquarter guard which has been established in a cottage a quarter of a mile away. Colonel Hawkes has been appointed Assistant Inspector General for Camp Nelson.

During the day we learned of our proximity to Boone Cave[43] not a half mile away; so after dress parade a few of us armed with candles and matches wandered off through the woods till we arrived at the top of a rocky precipice hundreds of feet in height over which we look down into the rapidly rolling river. Climbing down over the rocks with difficulty and clinging to the branches and twigs growing out of the clefts, we find the entrance which is so low that we crawl several yards on hands and knees.

At last we enter a lofty chamber; here we light our candles and start on our exploring tour. This first room or hall is large enough for a regiment to be drawn up in line! Out of this are several openings, some of which we explore until we come to a terminus, driving out multitude of bats. At last the main passage is reached along which we grope, sometimes entering large chambers then through small ones where the outlet or inlet is just big enough to squeeze through. In nearly every part we find stalactite formed into fantastic and beautiful shapes. Sometimes we had to climb up over rocks twenty or thirty feet or crawl on hands and knees through some small aperture over thick slime. Without any guide and after going on in this way for perhaps a half a mile, our courage begins to fail us.

The strangeness of the situation was almost terrifying and we turn back. It was conjectured that we were then groping along several rods directly underneath the various camps, full of life and activity while here was the death like stillness of a tomb. Our chattering and jollification was somewhat forced "whistling to keep up our courage." Then what if these immense roofs of rock, held up by what, we knew not, should fall? Imagination gave haste to our retreating footsteps when down we would fall in the slimy path and candles would be extinguished. With half feigned and half real fear, we would scream out to our retreating comrades for help. Such a place must be the natural home for snakes and all manner of reptiles so that our thoughts were not altogether free from anxiety.

At last we crawl out into the pure warm air of the summer night and feel an inexpressible relief as we leave the clammy damp dead air of the cave. The cave is said to have been explored for a distance of five miles and must run many miles in all it various passages. Here is said that Daniel Boone found a safe retreat from the Indians and I can well believe he could easily defend himself from any number provided he was well supplied with food and ammunition. Returned to camp saturated with mud and tired.

August 15

The great drawback to Camp Nelson is the scarcity of water nearly all water has to be brought in barrels with army wagons for a distance of three miles while the horses and mules are driven to the river to drink. I was detailed with three others to guard the most important spring three miles from camp. Our duties were to keep horses, mules and their drivers from stirring up the mud so as to keep its water clear.

I learn that the 9th Corps has returned from Vicksburg and our old brigade is encamped at Covington.

August 16

Weather cloudy. We were not relieved from our post at the spring until four in the afternoon. Were much interested in seeing General Burnside leave Camp Nelson with his staff and a large bodyguard starting for East Tennessee two hundred miles away over bridge less rivers and lofty rugged mountain ranges. A very long wagon train supplied with food and material necessary for carrying out the great enterprise of opening up East Tennessee followed him. Charles Wyman called to see me this evening.

August 17

I was on guard at the new hospital building. Major Richardson has been appointed Provost Marshal and Captain Parker, Assistant Quartermaster of the post.

August 18

The wives of Colonel Hawkes, Major Richardson and Lieutenant Hitchcock arrived from Lexington and found quarters at the cottage. A member of the Christian Commission held religious services with the regiment at dress parade. I went down to the river in the afternoon about a mile from camp. At this place the river runs through a narrow gorge with steep rocky bluffs on either side.

August 19

Frank Peckham[44] has been detailed as ordnance sergeant and Lem Whitney detailed as clerk at General Fry's headquarters.

August 20

I was on guard at headquarter's stables. Henry Cobly of 36th Mass called to see me. In the afternoon, the body of General Nelson,[45] who was shot in some quarrel at Louisville, arrived here enroute for internment at Camp Dick Robinson. It was escorted with military honors through camp by a detachment of the 1st Division of the 9th Corps, marching to slow and solemn music of the 48th Penn Band to the headquarter tents of General Fry by whom the procession was led. The 21st was paraded in line at "Attention" at Fry's headquarters and the body remained over night.

August 21

General Fry and staff accompanied the remains of General Nelson to Camp Dick Robinson. Several of our boys joined the regiment from Lexington.

August 22

General Ferrero, who returned from Vicksburg, was in camp with Captain Hall. Ansel Orcutt[46] joined us from Portsmouth Grove, Rhode Island, hospital.

August 23

Sunday. Attended preaching services at General Fry's headquarters. Colonel Hawkes returned to the regiment. Quarters inspected by the post surgeon.

August 24

I was detailed with twelve others under Captain Parker, Company B, to go to Louisville as guard for forty rebel prisoners. Marched to Nicholasville through a fine clay dust, ankle deep and under a scorching sun. Rode in cars to Lexington and at dusk, amid a heavy thundershower, delivered our prisoners to "No 3" jail for the night and found lodgings at the "Soldiers House" next to the Broadway Hotel. This place was the former residence of some rebel and was confiscated for use of soldiers passing through town.

August 25

Stroll about the city awhile in the forenoon and then get our prisoners, and embark on the cars at two in the afternoon. Arrive at Frankfort late in the afternoon. Saw the public buildings the arsenal and State House, a very fine structure and then cross the Kentucky River which is very broad at this point. The 2nd Maryland Regiment is performing guard duty here. Blockhouses for the protection of the railroad at important points have been built after Morgan's raiders passed through here. As we pass through the beautiful country we watch the many places made familiar by war's operations.

At dusk we arrive at Louisville and for more than a mile our train moves at horse trot pace across the city through broad straight streets. On either side the signs over the brightly lighted stores indicates either that we are passing through the "German quarter" or that Louisville must be an imported European city. Reaching the depot, we disembark with our rebel companions many of whom we feel quite well acquainted with. March another mile and surrender our charge to the military prison in the southwestern part of the city.

Then cross the street a short distance away and find lodgings in the Soldiers' Home. This "home" is truly named: conducted in every way to insure the comfort of its guests—built and designed for this explicit purpose. Entering the yard by the sentinel, we pass pretty beds of plants and flowers and report at the office. We are shown into the large reading room furnished with a well filled library and other conveniences and told to make ourselves thoroughly at home.

These luxuries are highly appreciated and the short evening passes all too quickly when we are directed to the great dormitories on the second floor provided with bunks to accommodate several hundred soldiers. Here everything is kept with most scrupulous neatness. Lie down to rest between clean white sheets with pillows for the head, luxuries I have not enjoyed for more than a year.

For awhile our jolly squad enjoys a great frolic over our unusual good fortune. One boy with pretended ignorance of the use of a pillow imagines it is intended for a series of gymnastic exercises. Another one carefully packs away his dusty clothes between the sheets and crawls under the bed to sleep on the floor, while another rests his weary feet on the pillow and hangs his head off the foot of the bed. A quiet, impromptu scuffle between others who propose to see how many comrades they can rob of their sheet and blankets drive sleep from our eyes until the late hours. At last sleep over takes me and after an undisturbed and refreshing rest I awake to find the bright sunny day well begun.

August 26

After our morning duties and coffee, I look out and find we are within stone's throw of the great depot of the Nashville and Southern Railroad on Broadway. The street or avenue is the most superb of any I have ever seen. A hundred feet wide, with sidewalks a rod [5 1/2 yards] in width, running straight and level as far as the eye can reach, lined on each side with great old shade trees the entire length. For a most part, this is the "elite avenue" of the city with its elegant mansions on either side.

Captain Parker kindly allows us to have the day for sightseeing, so I spend the forenoon in visiting the locomotive works of the Nashville and Southern Railroad and then go down to the banks of the Ohio River to watch the great river steamboats as they come plowing up from New Orleans and down from Pittsburgh and Cincinnati. I strolled about the streets visiting several large flour mills in operation and tobacco warehouses probably the largest in the world. Market Street was a scene of busy activity. At equal distances are built very long market houses where all kinds of produce are offered for sale. I saw here the largest peaches I had ever seen. It is the height of the peach season and Louisville the greatest market for them, as the immense quantities piled up in crates at the express offices, testified.

At night, after satisfying a ravenous appetite, I spent the evening in reading and retired early, ready to sleep after such a day of sightseeing.

August 27

Left the "Home" at five, marched down past the Galt House to the depot where we took our return trip to Camp Nelson. Arrived at Nicholasville at 1:30 p.m. where we find very extensive preparations for building the Tennessee Railroad over the mountain which is being pushed rapidly as a military necessity. We had a very tedious tramp through clods of dust back to Camp Nelson where we arrive at six in the evening after a most enjoyable excursion.

August 28

Colonel Hawkes and Lieutentants Lawrence and Sampson with 6 sergeants have gone to Massachusetts for conscripts. Mrs. Hawkes returned home two days ago in response to a telegram informing her of the serious illness of their little daughter, Mary. I have been putting in more improvements to my tent.

August 29

I was on guard at the "prisoners' pen" which consists of two large hospital tents inclosed by an imaginary line several rods square. This is thickly guarded by the detail from the 21st. Sam Adams,[47] from Orange, Mass. who deserted from the regiment at Newport News more their a year ago, returned to the regiment after enlisting in a Pennsylvania regiment; becoming sick of that regiment, he voluntarily returned to his first "love"(?). Allen,[48] the 9th Corps mail agent, has been to see us.

Standing on my beat in the evening the scene is one that impresses me. It is a mild serene night, lighted by the full moon, and from my elevated position of the slope, I look across the valley and see the white tents of the 21st Mass and 49th Kentucky on the outskirts of the tall pine grove spread out on the hills beyond—all dotted by the numerous campfires; further away in the background up in the pines on the crest of the hill are the great headquarter tents of General Fry forming a camp of considerable size by itself. Away to the left are the extensive corrals and cavalry camps. Turning halfway round to the right, away down through the gorges and narrow defiles, the deep sullen roar of the swift, rolling Kentucky River resounds. Back of me lie the thickly packed camp of hospital tents. The witchery of the calm, beautiful night steals my thoughts and sends them "wool gathering."

What will be the next move on this part of the great chessboard of war? Will its results send me back to peaceful pursuits in my happy northern home before winter? Or am I to follow those who have already been swallowed up in the great wilderness beyond that sullen roaring river? Who knows how soon the answer maybe: "Shot on picket," "Died in hospital," "Wounded and prisoner." Thus the lone soldier finds companionship with his thoughts.

August 30

I don't forget my anniversary days. I left Massachusetts for the seat of war one year ago today: a year crowded with thrilling and severe experiences but none which I regret for the part I have taken in them.

August 31

Monthly regimental inspection and muster in under Captain Davis. Lieutenant Valentine is acting adjutant. I called on Henry's wife in the evening and made the acquaintance of Mrs. Richardson.

September 1

Government issued to the regiment: blouses, socks, shirts, blankets and knapsacks. I am on guard at regimental headquarters. Allen returned to Company A for duty. Jonas Davis is acting sergeant major.

September 2

Learned that Mary Hawkes died a week ago. Captain Hall visited the regiment at dress parade; only three commissioned officers were in line owing to the large number of details.

September 3

Long line of darkies[49] escorted into camp and reported at General Fry's headquarters for work on the railroad. I wrote to John Mayo of the 33d Mass.

September 4

On guard at quartermaster's tents. Two squads detailed from the regiment to go to Louisville with prisoners. Think we must be thinning out the rebellious natives from Kentucky. Out of the regulation number of thirty commissioned officers for the regiment, only one appeared in line at dress parade.

September 5

Our sutler has been filling up his stock from Cincinnati. Learn that General Burnside has reached Kingston, Tennessee and thinks that part of the state is free from any large force of the enemy.

September 6

On guard again at quartermaster's tents. Charles Wyman called to see us. And now orders have come for the 9th Corps to march. The regiment was inspected by the medical director of the 9th Corps.

September 7

Another regimental inspection by the inspector general. Received letter from John Mayo, Bristoe Station, Virginia, where his regiment is guarding the Alexandra and Orange RR. Another squad went to Louisville with prisoners.

September 8

I am on guard at the prison quarters. The camp is excited over the report that we are to leave our comfortable quarters and follow General Burnside.

September 9

The report was verified and we are ordered to join our old brigade which has already gone forward. The 51st New York arrived and reported to General Fry for duty superseding the 21st Mass. Asa Franklin Van Buren Piper[50] and I called on Henry and wife in the evening.

September 10

Guard was mounted as usual. Captain Hall has been doing his level best to have our marching orders rescinded. Our officers say that it was understood by Gen. Burnside that the 21st should remain here through winter, but General Potter,[51] wishing to favor his old regiment, has succeeded in effecting the change. Communication by telegraph has been sent to Burnside for his decision, which is awaited with anxiety by the regiment which is very human and when it has a good thing would like to keep it. Reports that Chattanooga, Morris Island and Cumberland Gap have been captured. Called on Henry and wife again.

September 11

I was detailed for guard at prison quarters but was relieved by a guard from the 51st NY early in the day which signifies that the question has been decided in favor of the 51st NY. We have no reason for complaint for the very pleasant summer duties in Kentucky; the remainder of the day is occupied in preparations for the march of two hundred miles away from civilization over the mountains via Cumberland Gap. Lem and I took a parting look at the big cave.

*   *   *

Eight

The East Tennessee Campaign

With the Virginia and Tennessee Railroad providing an unbroken connection for the Confederacy between Maj. Gen. Braxton Bragg's army in the west and General Lee's army in the east, East Tennessee was an important strategic region. Although barriers of nature essentially isolated the area from the North, many of the region's leaders and a majority its people supported the Federal government.

In early June 1863, General Burnside sent two divisions of the IX Corps to reinforce Maj. Gen. Ulysses S. Grant's army in Mississippi, where Grant was engaged in besieging Vicksburg. The 21st Massachusetts remained at Mount Sterling, Kentucky. These divisions returned to Kentucky (the First Division on August 12 and Second Division on August 20) depleted and exhausted. The Union army's recruitment policy, however, called for the addition of new regiments, and thus the divisions remained understrength.

On August 16, 1863, Burnside left Camp Nelson, an 800-acre depot located five miles south of Nicholasville, Kentucky, on the long-postponed invasion of East Tennessee. His army consisted of 15,000 men of the recently constituted XXIII Corps, led by Maj. Gen. George L. Hartsuff. The IX Corps would follow later. The army, due the area's miserable road network, divided into five columns fanned out across a front of more than a hundred miles.

The Federals crossed the Cumberland Mountains by seldom frequented roads and by some that were deemed impassable by a large army. Soldiers climbed the rugged terrain with an indomitable persistence and courage. Horses and mules were tested to their utmost. The objective was to cross the mountains into East Tennessee, surprise the Confederates and capture Knoxville (thereby gaining possession of the entire region). Supplying the troops and securing lines of communications were tremendous obstacles to the campaign's success.

Major General Simon Bolivar Buckner, who had assumed command of the Confederate Department of East Tennessee on May 12, 1863, was ordered by Gen. Braxton Bragg to evacuate Knoxville before Burnside's troops arrived. On September 2, 1863, Col. John W. Foster's brigade of Federal cavalry occupied Knoxville without any resistance. General Burnside received an enthusiastic welcome from the 5,000 residents of Knoxville when he arrived the next day. The army had marched more than 200 miles in two weeks, and Knoxville was now firmly in Federal hands.

On September 9, Brig. Gen. John W. Frazer surrendered the Cumberland Gap to Burnside without firing a shot. This important and easily defensible pass was one of the region's critical communication links. General Frazer and 2,000 Confederate soldiers (including the 55th Georgia and the 62nd and 64th North Carolina regiments) were taken prisoner.

Burnside notified President Lincoln the following day that he wished to retire to private life now that East Tennessee was occupied. Lincoln, however, insisted that he needed the general until the region was fully secured, and thus denied the general's request. Burnside dispersed his troops along a 170-mile front from Charleston, Virginia, to Carter's Depot, Tennessee, in order to guard the East Tennessee and Georgia Railroad and the East Tennessee and Virginia Railroad. Anticipating a Confederate movement into the region, Burnside directed the IX Corps to proceed to East Tennessee as soon as possible, and he ordered all his troops back to Knoxville and Loudon on September 18. The 21st Massachusetts left Camp Nelson for East Tennessee on September 12, passed through Cumberland Gap and engaged a Confederate force at Blue Springs on October 10. Hitchcock's regiment finally arrived at Knoxville five days later after having marched 185 miles.

Several important departmental command changes took place in mid-October. On the 18th, Maj. Gen. Ulysses S. Grant assumed command of the Military Division of the Mississippi, a large area composed of three departments: Ohio, Cumberland and Tennessee. General Burnside retained command at Knoxville, Maj. Gen. William T. Sherman assumed command of the Department of the Tennessee, and Maj. Gen. George Thomas, who relieved Maj. Gen. William S. Rosecrans, was placed in command of the Department of the Cumberland.

The Confederates were also active during this time, using their advantage of interior lines to shift troops west from Virginia. General Lee sent Maj. Gen. James Longstreet's Corps with the divisions of Lafayette McLaws and John

Hood to reinforce General Bragg in September 1863. The addition of these troops enabled the Confederates to defeat Maj. Gen. William S. Rosecrans and his Army of the Cumberland at Chickamauga on September 18-20. After Bragg squandered his opportunity to retake Chattanooga, Longstreet's 17,000-man force, including Maj. Gen. Joseph Wheeler's cavalry, was detached by Bragg on November 4 to engage and defeat Burnside's army and reopen direct rail communications with southwest Virginia. Eight days later, Longstreet's Corps approached Loudon. His troops were exhausted and hungry, and expected rations and supplies were not forthcoming. As Longstreet's Confederates approached, Capt. Orlando M. Poe, Chief Engineer, Department of the Ohio, fortified the heights on the south side of the Tennessee River opposite Knoxville. Poe reinforced and enlarged the defensive forts and earthworks around Knoxville's eastern, northern and western perimeters, while the Tennessee River protected the southern side of the city. Fort Loudon (renamed Fort Sanders in honor of the mortally wounded William P. Sanders), was located in the northwestern angle of the Knoxville perimeter. Its parapets were thirteen feet high and sloped forty-five degrees, and a ditch, which was six to eight feet deep and eight to twelve feet across, surrounded the fort.

When Burnside sent 5,000 troops toward Loudon to confront and to delay the Confederate thrust, Longstreet crossed the Tennessee River and headed for Lenoir's Station, eight miles northeast of Loudon. When Longstreet arrived on November 15, the Union troops were gone. "Old Pete" hastened toward Campbell's Station, intending to defeat the Union troops piecemeal. Following parallel routes, Longstreet's and Burnside's troops raced for Campbell's Station, a strategic hamlet 15 miles southwest of Knoxville, where the Concord Road from the south intersected the Kingston Road to Knoxville. If Longstreet took Campbell's Station, he would cut Burnside off from his Knoxville fortifications and compel him to fight unprotected by his strong earthworks. Union Col. John F. Hartranft's division of the IX Corps (including the 21st Massachusetts) with Col. James Biddle's cavalry were the first Federals to arrive at Campbell's Station. The troops secured all the roads and allowed the retreating Union troops to pass through by 11:00 a.m.on a rainy November 16. The Federals formed a stout battle line formed with Hartranft's division on the left, Ferrero's division of the IX Corps on right, and Brig. Gen. Julius White's division of the XXIII Corps in the center.

As the Union line was forming Longstreet approached and ordered attacks against both Union flanks. Major General Lafayette McLaws' Division launched a hard-hitting assault and Burnside's right front buckled for a time before rallying to hold its ground. Brigadier General Micah Jenkins, a Longstreet favorite, maneuvered his division ineffectively as it deployed and

*was unable to turn the Union left. Burnside took advantage of Jenkins'
lackluster performance to withdraw his three divisions on the Kingston Road
three quarters of a mile and redeployed them on a ridge. The Union force
withdrew after dark and retired into the defenses at Knoxville. Brigadier
General Robert B. Potter, commander of the IX Corps, reported that Hartranft's
energy and prudence were responsible for the successful retreat. Brigadier
General William Sanders, with fewer than one thousand men, met Longstreet's
troops two miles from Knoxville and stalled the Confederate advance for hours.
Sanders was mortally wounded in the effort, but the additional time enabled
Engineer Poe to complete and strengthen the Knoxville fortifications. At Fort
Sanders, the ditches were widened, trees fellingand wires stretched from stump
to stump. On November 17, Longstreet arrived and a quasi-siege of Knoxville
began.*

*At 6:00 a.m. on the 29th of November, under cover of fog and with frost
covering the earthworks, three brigades of Lafayette McLaws' Division (William
Wofford's Georgia Brigade, Benjamin Humphrey's Mississippi Brigade and
Goode Bryan's Georgians) assaulted Fort Sanders. Without means to cross the
ditch or scale the icy parapet, the attack was doomed. Within twenty minutes the
assault was over. The Confederates lost 129 killed, 458 wounded and 226
missing, while the Union lost but five killed and eight wounded. "I know of no
instance in history where a storming party was so nearly annihilated," boasted
Captain Poe. Within an hour after the failed assault on Fort Sanders, Longstreet
was notified by President Davis that Bragg had been defeated at Missionary
Ridge on November 25 and that he should abandon Knoxville and rejoin
Bragg's army. After consulting for three days with his senior officers and
realizing that his tenuous supply situation prevented a march across the
mountains to join Bragg in northwest Georgia, Longstreet decided to retreat up
the East Tennessee and Virginia Railroad toward Bristol, Virginia. Meanwhile,
by December 4, General Sherman with a 25,000-man relief force sent by
General Grant from Chattanooga had closed within two-days march of
Knoxville. On the following day, Burnside's pickets discovered that the
Longstreet's army had retired. Sherman arrived at Knoxville on December 6.*

*On December 11, Maj. Gen. John G. Foster assumed command of the
Army of the Ohio, and General Burnside left Knoxville three days later.
Confederate casualties in General Longstreet's Corps during the Knoxville
Campaign (from November 14 to December 4) were: 198 killed, 850 wounded
and 1,296 captured. Total Union casualties for troops commanded by Burnside
during the Knoxville Campaign (November 17 to December 4) were: 92 killed,*

*394 wounded and 207 captured. The 21st Massachusetts lost four killed, 11
wounded and two captured during this period.*

*   *   *

September 12, 1863

The morning was bright and we were up at five; waited until eight when the
2nd Maryland and the 48th Pennsylvania came along and we joined them,
taking up the line of march. Instead of joining the old 2nd Brigade, which had
been cemented by ties of blood and long service, we are now in the 1st Brigade,
2nd Division with Colonel Sigfried[1] of the 48th Penn commanding the brigade.

The wilderness, which we have imagined, opens up to us a fine farming
region after leaving the rugged region in the vicinity of the Kentucky River.
Arrive at Camp Dick Robinson in the afternoon and go into camp nine miles
from Camp Nelson. Soon after we had pitched our shelters, a deluging shower
poured down upon us with heavy thunder which did not ease till after dark. In
the evening we received our pay.

September 13

Cloudy but good marching weather. Broke camp at six and marched all day.
Passed through Lancaster and camped near Crab Orchard, nineteen miles from
Camp Robinson.

September 14

In the morning marched through the village of Crab Orchard, a typical
southern town which has the reputation of being in constant broils and
bloodshed. We marched four miles and camped in a rough field a mile beyond
Crab Orchard. Found the 2nd Brigade encamped across the road so the division
is once more united after a separation of nearly six months. Henry has been
detailed as aide de camp for Brigade Commander Sigfried and looks down upon
his fellow 21st comrades from his serene height on horseback. Some men were
always in luck. My first battle of South Mountain was one year ago.

September 15

Did not march today. Regiment inspected by Captain Davis. Five days
rations were issued, which we have to distribute on our clothing ,haversacks and
knapsacks—all being over loaded.

September 16

Roused at five and started at eight. Found easy marching for eleven miles; halted two hours for dinner. The company cooks prepare coffee three times daily which is highly appreciated. Camp for the night two miles from Mt. Vernon. The country begins to appear more hilly.

September 17

Passed through Mt. Vernon, a small dirty village around which are built fortifications. It seems hardly possible that so miserable looking place needs protection; we are therefore compelled to believe they are thrown up for protection of the outside world from such a godforsaken hole. So we hurry through it and find the country growing more mountainous and wild.

Just before noon we met the captured garrison of Cumberland Gap twenty five hundred in number: a sorry looking set ragged and dirty. General Frazer,[2] the rebel officer who was commanding at the time of capture, followed the line some distance in the rear and appeared quite crestfallen and dejected. All were under a strong guard, enroute for Louisville to board at government expense.

Late in the afternoon we toiled up the steep rough sides of Wildcat Mountain. Stopping for a short rest on the summit, we survey a scene of wilderness: forests sweeping away in all directions as unbroken as any that our early pioneers ever saw. As we descend on the southeast sides, the blue outline of the Cumberland is discerned away in the far east. Here are the scenes of Zollicoffer's[3] battle of a year ago where lofty trees were felled across the road, doubtless effectually blockading the pathway for a time but now the passage is cleared.

After a fifteen mile march we go into camp at dark near the banks of the Rock Castle River. The rugged beauty of the scenery is enjoyed and appreciated by us although it makes our march very difficult and tedious.

September 18

Since the night was stormy, the traveling was not improved. After crossing the river, we began the ascent of Rock Castle Mountain. Although the road was not rough, it was one straight, long, steep inclined plane from base to summit of more than a mile.

The remainder of our march of eight miles was over quite level road and through dense forests one of the most lonely routes I ever saw. We passed but one cabin in all the route until we arrive at London where we go into camp.

Here we receive rations of fresh meat which are cooked for us during the evening. The 11th N.H. is stationed here a lone outpost in the mountains.

September 19

The night was very chilly, warning us of the approach of fall frosts. Marched fourteen miles through a more open and inhabited country than yesterday. Camped fourteen miles from Barboursville and forty miles from Cumberland Gap. We are now in the heart of the wilderness about a hundred miles from any railroad and each day getting further away from the paternal care of Uncle Sam.

September 20

This morning opened mild. Passed through Barboursville and encamped a mile and a half beyond it near the banks of the Cumberland River where three days rations were dealt out. In the evening I saw a signal rocket fired from a distant mountain top doubtless a friendly one.

September 21

Left our camp at seven and followed the course of the river, finding easy and level traveling although shut in by lofty mountains. The scenery is grand and romantic. The river twists about like a huge serpent, and although we march fourteen miles, it is ascertained that we are only seven miles from our last nights camp. Reaching the famous Cumberland Ford of which we have heard much since we came into Kentucky, we strip off shoes and stockings, roll up pants, wade across and camp on the opposite bank.

September 22

Colonel Griffin[4] of the 6th N.H. takes command of the brigade. Take up the line of march and toil up over Log Mountain. After our halt for dinner, we move ahead and suddenly come out of the mountains which have shut us in so long and stand face to face with the Gibraltar of the South, five miles away. We get our first view of Cumberland Gap from a most striking point. Stretching away northward and southward like a Cyclopean wall, the Cumberland range shuts out the vision of the promised land beyond: unbroken, except at the one point which we know to be the "Gap."

The forest has been cleared entirely for miles along the sides of the range in the neighborhood of the Gap, and we see in their place lines of fortifications zigzagging tier above tier to the summit. We are impressed with the apparent insurmountable defense which the enemy has made and are not a little amused to know that General Burnside slipped around through another way and rapped on the back door. With a part of his force standing where we now do, he was able to step in without any trouble and send General Frazer and his Johnnies north.

Plodding wearily up its steep rocky sides, at four o'clock we find ourselves standing in the Gap. Looking backward to the north, the eye takes in a scene of unbroken solitude and forests—wild in the extreme. Turning our faces southward, the contrast is very remarkable. Looking into East Tennessee, the landscape is dotted with habitations, fertile fields and great cultivated tracts. Two remarkable objects right here in the highest part of the Gap by the side of the road are the centers of interest. One is a large spring of the purest and coldest water bubbling up from the rocks where the weary and thirsting pilgrims refreshed themselves. The other, only a few yards from it, was a great square rock, the cornerstone of three great states: Virginia, Kentucky and Tennessee.

Many of us availed ourselves of the opportunity to stand upon the mystic spot, the central point whose boundaries were washed by the Atlantic, the Mississippi, the Ohio and the Potomac. Our imagination was equal to the stretch. After planting the colors of the 21st on the rock and giving three hearty cheers for the Union which by this act symbolized restoration, the regiment descend a few rods into Tennessee and camped near the buildings occupied by our government for garrison and commissary stores. Marched fourteen miles.

September 23

Broke camp at seven and march into a very different appearing country from what we have seen for several days open and cultivated land in all directions. The Cumberland range is the natural boundary which divides not only states but marks a different character in the people it separates. We feel a new inspiration as we press forward into the promised land. Our march was in the direction of Morristown, a station on the Virginia and East Tennessee Railroad, forty seven miles from the Gap.

Approaching the village of Tazewell, the desolations of war are apparent: field after field with crops of corn and other grain are standing choked and overgrown with weeds for need of a tiller, and the emaciated swine so poor that they have to lean against the trees for support. Passing through the main street, we see only the naked ruins of the brick walls standing as nearly every house had been burnt. It was said that the inhabitants were a thrifty Union loving people and thus they received the vengeance of the rebels. Encamp just outside the town, thirteen miles from last nights bivouac.

September 24

Left camp at seven and march all the forenoon; arriving at the banks of the Clinch River, we halt for dinner and in the afternoon find quite a task in crossing the ford. The stream was unusually deep and the current strong; we therefore found much difficulty in keeping our footing; many a man was upset and received a cold bath. Most of the way over the broad stream, the water was more than three feet in depth. The fun which those who made the crossing successfully was at the expense of the poor dripping ones. Encamp on the opposite bank eight miles from yesterday's camp and spent the remainder of the day in a general washing of clothes and bodies by the entire brigade.

It was a novel sight to see the thousands of men filling the stream, bathing and lining the banks washing clothes. Our wagon trains containing supplies (excepting a few belonging to the brigade) have gone forward to Knoxville by a different route. As we shall have to climb the Clinch Mountains, five days rations are dealt out to each man thereby lightening the loads of the favored mules.

September 25

The morning opens clear and at six we were on the march. For a time our route lay through a charming valley quite thickly dotted with large, rambling, well to do farmhouses and out buildings. The thrifty appearance of the well cultivated fields remind us of our northern houses. The long climb of the mountain from the northwest side was accomplished with ease until we neared the summit; we encounter rocks, piled promiscuously along the road, threatening destruction to the patient mules which slowly pick their way along over these obstacles dragging the heavy army wagons.

Arriving at the summit, we halt and careful preparations are made for the more trying ordeal of the descent. A large part of the 21st is detailed (myself included) to assist the teams. The glorious prospect spreads out before us in all directions entrancing the beholder by its beauty. Away up in one of the loftiest ranges of the many which extend across the East Tennessee region, we look down into the far and famed country—a section famous for its mild and even temperature, great fertility, constant verdure, pure water and great abundance.

It is a wonderful area in resources but undeveloped because of the great natural obstacles which have hitherto deterred the enterprising railroad builders except one artery, the East Tennessee and Virginia Railroad running parallel through the valley.

Isolated in the very heart of the United States, we are struck by the almost primeval character of the country and its people. Away in the far distant east, the Great Smoky Mountains are discerned. This is the continuation of the Virginia Blue Ridge and is the dividing line between North Carolina and Tennessee. Although standing out in bold relief are many prominent peaks, they are only distinguished as a pile of ethereal blue. While in the intervening space, the eye detects several distinct ranges of lesser altitude—the whole appearing like vast waves of the ocean. Far down below us winds the broad Holston River like a silver ribbon, in and out among the mountains toward the southwest. For the most part the valley appears to be open and well cultivated; however, few houses or hamlets can be distinguished.

The strategic importance of this great undertaking dawns upon us more clearly as we look down where we know the railroad lies and realize that if WE can hold the area, our part in the scrimmage is important. Preparations for the descent include clogging and chaining the wheels of the army wagons, fastening long ropes to the ambulance wagons with which to hold them back, and transferring the sick to the backs of horses and mules.

The first half mile of descent is exceedingly slow and perilous; probably no teams were ever sent over a worse path jagged rocks and huge round boulders completely filled the way. At one point a long unbroken steep with a layer of rock some three rods in length at a forty five degrees incline, teams were kept from destruction only with the utmost efforts; one team was overturned and dashed to pieces and one mule instantly killed.

At last the difficult task was accomplished and at noon our part of the force is safe at the base of the mountain where we halt for coffee in a romantic glen beside a musical little brook tinkling down among the rocks. While eating our lunch and lolling around on the grass under the cool shade, we look back up the rugged heights which we have just overcome and see the white tops of other teams, far up thousands of feet running the same gauntlet which we have passed through.

Continuing our march in the afternoon, we pass some great health resort - springs about which are extensive brick buildings. The fine clay dust arose in a constant and thick cloud so dense and enveloping us so completely that we could not see two rods away. We are covered with it: clothes, faces, hair, and would easily have been taken for "graybacks." At night we reached the Holston River and prepare to cross. The stream is about a third of a mile wide and three to five feet in depth. Every man undresses and, fastening clothes and equipments to his gun, throws them over the shoulder and wades in. Fortunately the current is not strong; as each man reaches the bank, he dresses and goes into camp which is on the bank of the stream. We march thirteen miles today.

September 26

The brigade was roused and put in motion by Aide de Camp Hitchcock, and after a march of seven miles reach Morristown, a place of considerable size where there are the shops for manufacturing rolling stock of the Virginia and East Tennessee Railroad. After a halt for dinner, our march is continued following the railroad southwesterly. At night we go into camp at Mossy Spring, a small station on the railroad after a march of nineteen miles along a level route. After we had pitched camp, the 18th Kentucky passed us going toward Knoxville. The dusty roads have become well nigh intolerable.

September 27

Left camp at six and after marching three hours and pass through New Market, we make a halt of several hours at noon near the railroad; meanwhile a brigade of mounted infantry passed us comprised of the 60th Illinois, 71st Indiana and a full battery. By the middle of the afternoon we reached Strawberry Plains, where the railroad bridge over the Holston River has been destroyed. A line of plank laid singly across the deep stream was all we had to cross on. As the operation required considerable care for the brigade to file over singly, we were delayed over an hour while the teams went several miles further down and crossed at a ford. Went into camp at sunset. We met several deserters from Bragg's army going to their homes. Marched eighteen miles.

September 28

Continued our march all the forenoon and at noon arrive near the barracks and buildings known as "the Confederate conscript camp of instruction." Halt for dinner, after which continue our march some three miles further and go into camp in sight of Knoxville near the north bank of the Holston. The great march has been accomplished and the troops are in good condition: have marched two hundred and five miles. The exceptionally fine weather conduced much to the success of the march although the dust has kept us very dirty. James Carruth, who was detailed as hostler for one of Burnside's staff officers and came over the mountains ahead of us, came up to our camp to see the boys.

September 29

Major Richardson and Captain Clark arrived in camp direct from Camp Nelson. I cleaned my gun and equipments and washed in the Holston River. At night General Burnside rode out to see how his boys bore the long march. We received him enthusiastically. Half rations were dealt out tonight for the first time, and we begin to realize that our situation may become unpleasant for being so far from our base of supplies.

September 30

I procured a pass and visited the city; passed by the home of Parson Brownlow,[5] whose radical Unionism did so much to influence this section to stand by our country. The city is built on two or three hills and presents a very dilapidated appearance. Unlike most southern cities and villages which are usually built of brick, Knoxville is a wooden city and many buildings unpainted. At present the place has the appearance of a military beehive and few citizens are seen. Monthly regimental inspection by Major Richardson. Called on Henry at brigade headquarters.

October 1

Our regimental sutler arrived last night and today his goods are the attraction for the boys. Rations of soft bread were given out. Reports that the enemy has captured three loads of mail between here and Cumberland Gap.

October 2

Afternoon company drill was begun. Several promotions were announced at dress parade: Ed Lewis of Company A to 1st Lieutenant, H.S. Hitchcock of Company A to 1st Lieutenant of Company I, Lawrence to 1st Lieutenant of Company A, Parker to Captain of Company A. I saw a black bear which was captured in the Smoky Mountains.

October 3

A part of the 1st Division has been ordered to march back to Tazewell.

October 4

Active operations for us opened today. At nine in the morning we are ordered to leave our camp standing and proceed to the depot [East Tennessee and Virginia Railroad[6]] where the brigade embarked and were hurried northeasterly. After riding several hours, we arrive at Bull's Gap, sixty miles from Knoxville, where we disembark and bivouac in a very rough field near the station. The night was cold and windy so that I catch but a couple hours of sleep; most of the time is spent on the windward side of a big campfire. A large force of rebels have entered the state from Virginia and do not intend to allow us to remain unmolested in this important position.

October 5

Marched through the Gap and five miles beyond where we halt near Lick Creek. Company A, which has dwindled down to half a dozen men, build a shelter of rails covered with brush, which we all share in common. With a large rail fire on the open side, we succeed in keeping comfortable. Having received a ration of meat, the evening was spent in cooking. The rebel force is only five miles from us so we anticipate a brush with them very soon.

October 6

Lemuel and I were sent out on picket and were on a post with a 48th Penn. corporal. As the enemy's outposts are now within two miles of us, our watching was no sinecure silence and vigilance of the strictest sort all through the night. It appears that our force is inadequate to meet the enemy; we are therefore awaiting the expected arrival of General Wilcox, who is coming over the mountains with several thousand Indiana troops.

October 7

We were relieved from the picket line by the 8th and 9th Michigan Regiments. Rations are all gone and none expected immediately we forage the country.

October 8

Foraging parties brought in flour in small quantities captured from the neighboring farmers. Several prisoners were captured and brought into camp with their horses and wagons at night. Dress parade was held at night.

October 9

Another day of waiting and toward night the situation began to assume a different aspect. The long looked for reinforcements "hove" in sight direct from Cumberland Gap. They were welcomed with hearty cheers. About the same time our wagon train with our tents and supplies arrived from Knoxville. In anticipation of the advance against the enemy tomorrow, we were inspected by companies in arms.

October 10

At seven we are on the road moving northward toward Blue Springs. The western troops were moved past the 9th Corps as they were composed of cavalry and mounted infantry regiments. Our division brings up the rear protecting the several batteries of Burnside's army. Generals Burnside, Willcox, Potter and Ferrero are all present, and as they have proven themselves brave fighters in the past, their boys have full confidence in the result.

After a march of four miles or more, the enemy is found just beyond the small village of Blue Springs. The infantry was halted while the mounted men attempted to dislodge them but were not successful. At noon we were double quicked through the village and our division divided up and sent forward to support the various batteries which found fine positions on the various hills and fired their deadly missiles for several hours into the enemy, but they had the cover of dense woods and held us at bay until late in the afternoon.

In the meanwhile, the 21st Massachusetts laid in the rear of Lieutenant Benjamin's[7] Battery somewhat sheltered, although the minies whistled about us through the trees and shells exploded in uncomfortable proximity. Only a few were wounded in all the time which we were under fire. At last General Burnside decided to give them a taste of his old 9th Corps and sent the 1st Division which swept forward into the woods which had concealed the foe all the day. The rattle of musketry and cheers of our boys soon told us that the field was won and the enemy forced to retire.

Night closed the conflict with considerable loss on both sides but the prestige of winning the first battle in the campaign gave our troops great confidence. [At the Battle of Blue Springs the Confederates lost 66 men killed and wounded and 150 taken prisoner and the Union lost 100 men killed and wounded.]

October 11

We laid on arms all night but the enemy had found our force too forcible and quietly stole away before morning and by daylight we were up and prepared to follow them. General Shackleford's[8] cavalry was given the lead and by nine we were all in hot pursuit.

When we consider that the enemy as well as a large part of our own force were mounted and that the enemy was quite anxious to get away from the fighting veterans of the 9th Corps, it can be understood that the chase was one that tried our endurance to the utmost. For six hours we hardly halt for a rest and much of the time we went on double quick speed.

The day was fine and our spirits were good. Passing by farmhouses, we were continually informed by the happy Unionists that the rebels were only four or five miles ahead of us "going right smart" and "reckoned they wouldn't stop befo' they struck the Potomac." Occasionally we passed a fallen horse, which proved that the race was severe even for horses. At three in the afternoon our boys go racing through the streets of Greenville, the home of Andy Johnson, much to the bewilderment of the good people, who were coming out of church - this being the Sabbath. When dusky night drops her mantle over us, thoroughly exhausted , we go into camp a short distance beyond Rheatown and give up the chase. The distance traveled was estimated at thirty three miles.

October 12

Orders came at six for us to resume pursuit but General Burnside decided it was not best to get further away from Knoxville, so these were countermanded and the army rests for the day. A very large mail arrived at night; the first one received since we came over the mountains.

October 13

We began our return tramp for Knoxville following in the wake of the wagon train. Passed through Greenville at noon and go into camp by the middle of the afternoon making a tramp of eighteen miles. Several of the Company A boys, myself included, found very comfortable quarters in a barn on a huge pile of chaff.

October 14

A portion of the 1st Division was taken on board the cars during the night and sent to Knoxville. Colonel Hawkes and Captain Sampson joined us in the morning having just returned from Massachusetts via Cumberland Gap. Took up the march at seven and went as far as Bull's Gap Junction where we pitch camp at noon. The day was cloudy and raw; hardly had our fires going to cook our coffee, when General Burnside came in from the front and ordered us to continue our march. We were interested in seeing the method of reversing locomotives by the triangle instead of the more familiar turntable. March twenty miles and camp near the village of Russellville.

October 15

March through Russellville, a dirty looking place full of rebellious citizens, and nine miles further to Morristown where transportation awaited us. We gladly accepted the situation and rode into Knoxville where we arrive late in the afternoon. Although we have become inured to the hardship of long marching and have reduced it to something of a science, the iron horse is a welcome assistant.

Reaching our old camp ground, we find ourselves (Company A boys) in a sad plight: All our tents which we were ordered to leave standing were lost probably stolen. To add to our troubles, the rain began to fall. Dr. Cutter[9] kindly robbed himself of the large fly of his hospital tent which afforded shelter from the rain from above, but as it fell in torrents all night, we laid in a running stream of cold water until morning. Found a letter for me from W. Lamb,[10] who is stationed at Rodman's Point, North Carolina.

October 16

I arose at daylight feeling quite demoralized. After the past two weeks of wear and tear, an involuntary shower bath is not particularly exhilarating, and I have to confess to an attack of the blues. A change of company commanders returns Captain Barker[11] to Company B and Captain Parker to Company A. Before night Company A discovered a vacant chamber in a neighboring dwelling house, which we appropriate and find a most acceptable substitute to the bed of soft mud which has been our lot.

October 17

Cleaned up gun and equipments for inspection.

October 18

Sunday morning inspection. I went into the city on a pass.

October 19

I was detailed to go out with Sergeant May to hunt up a rebel spy who was supposed to have joined one of the new Kentucky regiments encamped on the fairgrounds three miles out. After looking through the camps of several regiments, we alighted on the company where the spy had been, but he had evidently "smelt the cat" and disappeared. After some further quest, we give it up and return to the city, reporting to General Burnside's headquarters, and then we return to camp at dusk.

October 20

And now it is in the opposite direction in which we look for trouble. The 1st Division has been sent southward toward Chattanooga while orders for us to march tomorrow have been issued. Distant heavy cannonading has been going on in the direction of Loudon southwesterly. We anticipate lively times if the force returns which we have driven into Virginia and the new enemy from Bragg's[12] army attempt to pinch us. The guerrilla bands can easily cut off our communications with Kentucky. The old 2nd Brigade arrived from Kentucky.

October 21

We were drummed up at four with orders to move at six. Waited until eight when these were countermanded and we were set to work pitching tents again. Learned that the firing of yesterday was a conflict between General Wolford's[13] cavalry and the advance guard of a detachment from Bragg's army.

October 22

With the instinct born of experience the Company A boys, having secured a lot of boards, set to work in spite of the immediate prospect of moving to erect some fine comfortable quarters. By noon we had them completed and I had sat down under my own "vine and fig tree" to enjoy the fruit of my labor and eat my dinner. After fifteen minutes of this repose, orders to march at two arrive. We march to the depot and loaf about the place until eight o'clock in the evening, when we pack into freight cars and move southward. Although only twenty eight miles southwest of Knoxville, the train did not reach there until half past one in the morning, being obliged to move forward with great caution for fear of obstructions by a lurking foe.

October 23

We tumble out of the cars at Loudon; the rebels had destroyed the bridge when Burnside first came into the state. It was a large structure over which the railroad crossed the Tennessee River. The river at this point is broad and deep and the massive stone piers stand high out of the water as monuments to mark the severed link which has bound the Confederacy together. But this we do not see until morning.

Dropping down by the side of the railroad track in the pitchy darkness, sleep quickly draws oblivion over us until early dawn when a heavy thundershower awakens most of us; we stand or squat with our rubber blankets tightly hugged, receiving the pelting deluge. One figure lying prone and still is revealed to our disconsolate boys completely wrapped in a rubber blanket. Colonel Hawkes quietly draws away a corner of the blanket and reveals the peaceful features of Captain Davis wrapped in unconscious slumber. Of course such blissful repose in the midst of so much discomfort could not be permitted and the edge of the blanket was placed so as to receive and conduct a small Niagara down the spinal column of our popular officer. Up jumps the thoroughly awakened man with his favorite swear word, "Gosh."

The shower settles into a cold dismal northeast storm, and the brigade remains hugging the struggling fires until the middle of the afternoon. Despairing of receiving orders, the men take the law into their own hands and break up into small bands and "took to the woods" for shelter. Company A formed a squad by itself and made a shelter of rails over which we laid our rubber blankets. We build a huge fire of hardwood rails which are piled against a great oak tree. Under this comfortable shelter our twelve comrades crawl and make the gathering night cheery with our songs and laughter. The names of these who chummed together through so many stirring scenes were: Orderly Sergeant Jonas Davis, Corporal Albert Osgood nee "Brick top," Charley Wilder, Wilbur Potter, Sam Adams, Jack Reynolds, Charley Blackmer,[14] Marcus Gould[15] nee "Jule," Lem Whitney, Frank Peckham, Asa Franklin VanBuren Piper and George A. Hitchcock.

As we turn in for sleep, we take turns watching the fire as it eats into the heart of the tree in case it should fall in a wrong direction and crush the sleepers, but morning finds us unharmed.

October 24

The 2nd Brigade with Generals Burnside and Potter came down from Knoxville.

While exploring the woods, we came upon a deserted camp of log huts which were appropriated by the 2nd Maryland boys and the 21st Mass. Company A secures a hut for its exclusive use. One drawback to our comfort is in the necessity of assuming offensive operations against the common foe (fleas), which claim a prior right to our shanty. Cannonading is heard a short distance away down the river which indicates our proximity to the enemy.

October 25

General Burnside pitched his headquarter tents about twenty rods from our shanty, and as there are several Company A boys detailed as hostlers and clerks with his staff, we have received calls from them. Indications point strongly to the probability that a strong detachment from Bragg's army is determined to force us out of East Tennessee. We shall see.

October 26

I called upon Henry at division headquarters. Learn of an order just issued by the War Department for the reenlistment of volunteers into veteran regiments with a bounty of $452.

October 27

The day was spent reorganizing camp; so Company A leaves its log shanty and gets back into line again.

October 28

We were drummed up at four and the army struck camp and marched down to the banks of the Tennessee River [at Loudon] near the pontoon bridge. We learn that the enemy is attempting to flank us for the purpose of getting possession of Knoxville. The only Union force on the south side of the river is mounted infantry which was withdrawn during the forenoon to the north side. The infantry meanwhile lies in long lines of battle prepared to defend the pontoon and protect the retreating horsemen.

We learned that a locomotive and several freight cars had fallen into Union possession on the south side which had been very useful until now. We were not long in realizing that we were to be treated to a grand spectacle as the distant sound of a whistle was heard. From our point of observation we could see the railroad track for nearly a mile beyond the river, uninterrupted clear up to the first pier of the destroyed bridge. From this point down to the surface of the river was a distance of perhaps seventy five feet. The rumble of the approaching train sent a thrill through the army as it realized its fate. Soon it came rushing into sight. With almost breathless interest we watched to see the engineer as he slackened the speed enough to jump off, but at the same time turning on full steam. This was about a quarter of a mile from the yawning chasm. On came the doomed train increasing in speed until with a terrific bound the entire train was hurled down into the river. The engine boilers exploded with a deafening roar throwing clouds of spray and steam far out on the river and immediately the whole train disappeared beneath the water, indicating the great depth.

By ten o'clock the troops were all across and the 21st went to the farther end of the bridge—filing singly; each man took a plank to the north bank, depositing it by the side of an awaiting train. Just before the final loosing of the pontoon, several panic stricken darkies rushed down from the further side and begged to be allowed to cross which was granted. As they reached our bank, gratitude and happiness shone from each particular pore off their black faces for their deliverance. Then the further end was unloosed and the current swing the line around to our side where they were dragged ashore to await transportation.

About an hour after the bridge had been taken up and we had been anxiously watching the distant heights, a horseman was distinctly seen to ride out more than a mile away, halt, watch us for a few moments and then gallop back out of sight. Nervously we laid on arms along the banks of the river in full sight and easy range of a battery fire which was confidently expected each moment all through the afternoon.

Although wondering why the army was not withdrawn out of range, it was surmised that possibly General Burnside wished to give the enemy an exaggerated impression of the size of his army by spreading it out over the surrounding hills. About five in the afternoon a rebel officer rode out and down to the opposite bank bearing a flag of truce, requesting communication. An officer of our division answered the call by crossing to meet him. Whatever the communication was, we never knew. At dark the division moved back out of range of rebel artillery and camped for the night in blissful ignorance of hostile movements.

October 29

At light we rouse up and face toward Knoxville. The morning is clear and mild and the mud is very deep from the heavy rains of last week. As our backs are toward the foe, we can't help surmising that a heavy force is closing in upon us. After a toilsome march of six miles, we pitch camp near Lenoir's Mills, a station on the East Tennessee and Virginia Railroad, twenty three miles from Knoxville.

The 1st Division encamp on the northwest side of the railroad and the 2nd Division on the southeast.

October 30

The Holston River runs parallel with the railroad, a quarter of a mile in the rear of our camps. General Burnside and staff went up to Knoxville, and at dark we hear cannonading up the river. Piper and Adams were detailed to assist in laying the pontoons opposite our camps; it is therefore inferred that our retreat was for the purpose of securing a stronger position for resisting the heavy force moving against us.

I was detailed to guard regimental headquarters at night which closes down upon us with a heavy rain and intensely dark. When I go on my beat at nine, all fires are out and silence reigns supreme. Watching is out of the question, so my five senses are concentrated in the one of listening. After becoming accustomed to the suspicious sounds in the vicinity and of the scout and picket firing in the distance, I satisfy myself that my body is actually present and that my faithful old "Enfield" is tightly grasped beneath my rubber for I cannot discern the faintest outline of either; the rain is pelting in torrents.

I assure myself that I cannot be court martialed for deserting my post in the presence of the enemy, and then take a rapid flight (mentally). With one bound I have crossed the Holston, Clinch, Cumberland, Allegheny, Blue Ridge and many other lofty ranges and deep rivers, and once more I am in my quiet boyhood home nestling among the hills of New England. I contrast the two scenes. There: father, mother, brother and sister gathered in the peaceful home far away from any thoroughfare where a soldier's uniform is ever seen or any memory of wars desolating hand only as found in the pages of the closely scanned "Journal." To this circle the reality is no more than the story of the Revolutionary War, only enhanced by the knowledge that two of their number are in the midst of it.

Here (the scene with mental vision also): the blackness of night, the bivouac exposed to the inclemency of approaching winter, shut in by natures great barriers, by Lee's formidable army in Virginia and Longstreet with his well known fighting Corps pressing upon us and Bragg's army backing them up, living on half rations and tents lost "Halt! Who comes there?" "Corporal of the guard with the second relief." "Advance!" And the big nineteen year old baby lies down to dream out the home pictures for four hours when the task is again taken up.

October 31

Regimental monthly inspection. Company A squad is feasting today. In addition to our half rations we have a sheep which the foragers brought in. The enemy tried to cross the river nine miles above and cut us off from Knoxville but was repulsed. Henry came down to see me and brought a letter from home.

November 1

Heavy frost last night. I was the only member of Company A in line for inspection—all the others being sick or detailed for service elsewhere. About noon Jonas [Davis] hands me a written order detailing me to division provost guard. I pack up and report at once to headquarters of General Sigfried. Find quarters with a young Scotchman, member of the 7th Rhode Island and a native of Glasgow who enlisted from New Bedford, Mass.

November 2

I have assumed an extra duty—hostler for staff officer Hitchcock.

November 3

Rode my horse down to Lenoir's Station and got him shod at the division wagon camp. Reports of General Lee's defeat between Bull Run and Alexandria.

November 4

Captain Davis has been appointed provost marshall on the 2nd Division staff. The enemy has become quiet and our army seems to be taking breath.

November 5

Half rations continue to be dealt out to the army, but I receive an extra half ration as hostler, with the one furnished to provost guard.

November 6

I was on guard at headquarters; the night was very cold.

November 7

Charley Blackmer came over here as hostler for division surgeon. Willcox's brigade has been driven back from Greenville and the 3rd Brigade of the 1st Division has been ordered up to help them; they left here during the night. I received a letter during the night.

November 8

Another very cold night. Went over to the company and had my descriptive list made out. The provost guard was inspected by Lieutenant Dillenback[16].

November 9

Clothing and supply train is looked for tonight; flour was dealt out as our ration for today.

November 10

I was on guard at the big corn pile which feeds all the horses and mules belonging to the division. Corps commissary arrived with long supply trains, just over from "Kaintuck." A welcome sight to our eyes, but they look rough and worn for their long journey. Our division received orders to march tomorrow.

November 11

A large detachment of the 2nd Division laid the pontoon bridge in the rear of their camps.

November 12

I was on guard at the forage pile near Corps commissary tent; stood guard four consecutive hours in the night. I received my blanket which was left in Camp Nelson. It was forwarded to me in the officers baggage.

November 13

A wagon train from Kentucky came in tonight loaded with clothing. Burnside's army is being inspected by Grant's inspector general.

November 14

Stormy. While lying under our shelter early in the morning planning how to fortify our tent from future storms, Henry thrusts his head into the tent and said: "Make all possible haste and pack up after which come to headquarters and help us for Longstreet, who has been very quietly massing his forces for the past few days, has thrown a heavy force across the river during the night and is hurrying to overwhelm us."

Within fifteen minutes we hear the long roll beating from the camps in every direction; tents going down like magic and a large force went out on the double quick to destroy the pontoons. The planks are thrown into the river and the boats smashed in pieces by the axes of the pioneer corps. As these sounds reach our ears, the excitement is intense. It takes but a few minutes to get the headquarter tents and baggage packed, loaded and on the move toward Knoxville.

For the first time since I joined the regiment, I am separated when it is preparing for battle, for I am guarding division headquarter train. We hurry along at double quick, passing long lines of troops, all facing toward Knoxville and away from the enemy. After marching a couple of miles near the railroad, a whistle from an approaching train is heard and a locomotive with one car dashes past from Knoxville toward the enemy with tremendous speed and on the platform stands General Burnside with a stern determined look on his face.

The army is once more heading in the right direction, toward the enemy. It was inspiring to see how quickly confidence was restored through the army by the sight of that man on that train moving in that direction. We hurry on toward Knoxville and soon leave the army behind; the proceeding seems strange enough and I feel very much out of place. We march all day and at night quite late the wagons are parked in a large level field. During the night the weather changed; the wind arose and a hurricane passed over the camp tearing down tents and scattering camp fires.

November 15

Soon after daylight we move forward with the wagon train. News came in during the night that the enemy was slowly pushing back our army, which took advantage of the ground giving battle to the enemy until nearly flanked; then it would fall back in good order until a new vantage ground was taken, and the operation repeated . Colonel Hartranft has assumed command of the division.

This is the Sabbath, and we march down through the streets of Knoxville just as the people are coming out of church from afternoon service. While moving down the street, the report is received that the army is fighting desperately and the dull heavy reverberations of artillery confirm the report. There is also sharp and rapid cannonading going on across the river in the southeast about four miles away, showing that the attempt is being made to get around the army and into the city.

November 16

The day is dark, damp and chilly. Fearing the possibility to drawing the fire from the enemy's artillery and an attempt to capture our wagon train, we leave the city which is "set on a hill and cannot be hid," and move out half a mile on the Tazewell road northerly where we remain all day and night. Our entire force under General Willcox came in from Bull's Gap and took positions on the north side of the city. We learn of the Battle of Campbell's Station [thirteen miles from Knoxville] which was a general engagement fought yesterday afternoon. The 9th Corps has arrived just outside the city.

November 17

The day continues dark and chilly. The past twenty four hours have been full of activity and strange experiences. Our corps arrived in the city in the morning and from our position under the hills, we see the troops massing in strong lines on the heights which lie on the north and west sides of the city, forming a semicircle around it with the Holston River as a base on the southeast side.

After moving from place to place behind the hills so as to get our train out of sight of the enemy, by the middle of the afternoon all the provost guards are sent back to their respective regiments. I find the 21st on a prominent hill overlooking the city at its back and taking in a wide sweep of hills on the west—a mile distant along which I discern the enemy busy as swarming bees at work felling trees, digging and fortifying.

Down in the intervening space partly covered with woods, I see the flashing of the skirmishers guns of both armies. Every bummer, negro and detailed man are set to work, and the whole army is digging with a will for we all understand that this means a siege. The position occupied by the 21st is the most convenient of approach to the city and has the widest sweep of vision toward the hostile lines so that it is used by the generals for observation; a corps or division staff officer is kept constantly posted here.

Every man of our brigade, both officers and privates, are set to work at dark with pick and shovel throwing up fortifications. By midnight the 21st has a very respectable shelter already begun when we were ordered to go out on our left and support a battery; we again set to work to throw up protection for its gunners (afterward called Fort Byington). In every direction, the stillness of the night was broken by the sounds of pick and shovel. Buildings and fences are torn down; everything obstructing the line of vision or hindrance to a line of battle was removed.

During the pauses, the sounds of axes and falling trees from the distant hills in our front told us that our challenge was accepted by the enemy. After day light we caught a little rest; part of the Company A boys found an undisturbed spot in the kitchen of a house just back of our earthwork. In the afternoon we were kept under arms in the trenches in expectation of an assault.

At dark I was detailed with half the regiment to go out on the skirmish line. We move out, down the hill in the darkness to a point a quarter of a mile in front where the old relief is stationed. Not a whisper is allowed and the strictest care is used to reach the various posts without arousing the vigilant enemy, who is posted only a few rods beyond. Here we stand all night, suffering severely from the cold, in an open field where the chill wintry wind sweeps down from the northwest. Perfectly still we must keep, no stamping or thrashing to keep the blood in circulation. Occasionally we hear the low voices of the "Johnnies" in front of us.

November 19

At daylight the skirmishers concealed themselves behind hillocks, trees or buildings and watched for opportunity to "pepper" away at any moving thing in our front. As a rule it was difficult to find anything to fire at and our imagination could hardly help us to believe that every tree or building in front protected the gray clothed enemy, but the rapid crack of musketry with the accompanying smoke and ominous whack of bullets against the buildings was warning enough for us to keep undercover but at the same time to watch our chances as well.

I, with half a dozen others, found protection behind a barn where we took turns in peering out on the two sides; the movement usually attracted a shot from the rebels when we would instantly return it. During the pleasant forenoon the rebel line of skirmishers was pushed forward, driving ours back several rods, but we rallied behind a large brick house and effectually stopped them. During the remainder of the day we kept up so constant a fire and no further attempt was made to force us back.

The city is completely invested, and it is supposed that the bulk of Longstreet's Virginian army is encircling the city in a line of not less than five miles in length. On the south side of the Holston River, General Wolford's cavalry and mounted infantry are attending to their wants. The problem is how long will Longstreet dare to remain here with Sherman's army between him and Bragg while Lee's army is several hundred miles away in Virginia with broken connections. On our side, the supplies of food for man and beast are very low but our fighting spirit is very good, so it is a question of endurance.

November 20

At dark we were relieved and all night and day I laid in the trenches. At dark the enemy opened fire, sending a few shells over our heads into the city with what effect we do not know. New fortifications are continually going up and a formidable continuous line already confronts the enemy. Confidence is therefore felt of resisting greater battalions. After darkness has settled upon us, the skirmish lines in our front were illuminated by the burning of several houses which stood between the lines. This was done by our men to keep the enemy from securing them. A detail of men is kept in all such places; the buildings are packed with inflammable material and when the enemy attempts to occupy them, they are ordered to light the torch and retreat. This accounts for the evenings illumination.

I was detailed to go on the skirmish line as relief near one of the burning buildings. When relieving the old picket, we creep stealthily along behind fences and buildings until we reach the vicinity by our respective posts; we crawl out on the open field on hands and knees under the friendly shelter of darkness to the rough rifle pits formed of piles of fence rails. From two to six men are at each post according to the importance of the position, and about five rods apart, while the enemy's line at some points comes almost as near us in front.

Rain poured all night and all day incessantly. Our condition may be better described than understood. A pool of water settled all around and in our rifle pit; this protection is so low we have to hug the ground to be shielded from the rebel bullets, and still we must be constantly watching affairs in our front. Occasionally changing position to rest our sore limbs, a head or arm is exposed to the watchful rebel picket when whiz comes a minie; we are wet to the skin, not a wink of sleep for nearly thirty six hours. Darkness throwing its shield over us and new relief taking our places, but I return to the damp trenches to eat my half ration of bread; the weather has cleared away cold. Lying down in my wet clothes to make up my lost sleep under such conditions is hardly flattering.

November 22

The regiment was allowed to occupy some dwelling houses in the rear of the fortifications if half the reserve force was constantly present in the trenchers. Quarter rations only were issued today which indicates the extremity to which our army is being pressed. A few shells from the enemy were fired into the city which our batteries returned. Another house on the picket line was burned tonight. I went on skirmish line again. This time in a very exposed place where the rebels can get a bead on us from three directions.

Sam Adams and I occupy a pit hardly large enough for two to stand upright. Therefore, we take turns during the night enlarging it; while one watches, the other digs—loosening the clay soil with the bayonet and throwing it out with the hands. It was very slow tedious work, but by daylight we had an excavation large enough to conceal our whole bodies beneath the surface. The dirt was thrown up in front on the top of which we stick up little pine boughs thickly together through which we can watch the rebels.

November 23

The picket firing was very vigorous through the day; rebel sharpshooters apparently did great execution firing up to our fortifications; one troublesome fellow was posted behind a tree a dozen rods on our left, and by careful watching I noticed that his head came in sight every time he fired. Two or three times I attempted to bring him down, but once when I drew a bead on him, he was evidently watching for me.

Either an unusual movement of the mask of twigs or the bright sunlight exposed my head: Flash! Zip!—a duck of the head and a twig fell into the pit, cut off exactly in the range of my head. A smarting sensation on the top of my head as if a bullet had gone through my scalp, and I clap my hand to my head instinctively. All this was done in an instant and Adams cries, "My God! Hitchcock, you're shot." It takes several moments to convince me that I am unharmed; the concussion of the ball as it whizzed through my hair caused a smarting sensation which lasted several minutes. It was a very close call, and the instantaneous action as I saw the flash was all that saved my life.

Toward night the firing from the rebel skirmish line increased to an incessant rattle, but without much apparent harm, except a member of Company I [Ransom Bailey], who was shot in the arm. At dark the firing suddenly ceased as well as the sounds of the axes which had been heard very constantly in their fortifications. For an hour or more this portentous stillness lasted while Adams and I watched with straining eyes and loudly beating hearts for the attack which we felt sure was to come.

The time for placing the new relief had passed when Captain Sampson came out to us and whispered: "The enemy is preparing to charge in line of battle on our breast works; stand firm and as soon as you see their lines, give them two volleys squarely and then fall back." With guns full cocked and pointing squarely in front, we had only a few minutes of the terrible suspense after he had passed on to the next post; suddenly, the wild rebel yell sounded sharply out on our right and almost simultaneously a long flash of light as they poured a heavy volley over us; for a moment we hugged the ground until the first volley passed over; then we raised our heads and saw a line of flashing fire from the woods on our left a dozen rods away. By the flash of their guns we saw that our pickets on our right had retreated; waiting a moment more until this second volley had died then the yell broke out again and headlong came the rebel line close upon us. Sam and I fired squarely into their ranks and jumped out of our pit, scudding down the slope as far as the railroad several rods in our rear with bullets whistling all around us.

The railroad here was raised a couple of feet above the surface of the ground, so we were safe from the bullets. This had been the "inside line" of pickets but now it was entirely abandoned. Creeping along behind the railroad some distance, we get among the extensive railroad shops and mills just as they burst out in flames. These stood between the picket line and our fortifications. We find them all deserted; dodging about to keep away from the glare of the conflagration so as to not be marks for the rebel bullets, we at last reach the fortifications and find every one prepared and expecting to receive the assaulting columns.

In meanwhile their lines had halted under protection of the railroad. By this time every building dwelling houses and shops near the railroad was in flames. The fire soon caught the arsenal buildings where ammunition was stored including a large numbers of shells. Explosion followed explosion and fragments of timbers, iron and bricks were thrown high into the air with showers of sparks, all furnishing a grand and awful pyrotechnic display that makes the surrounding blackness grim indeed. The most sublime spectacle of all was the burning of the saltpeter stores which sent a clear blue flame a hundred feet high lighting the country with a weird light.

The troops were all on the qui vive for the expected attack. Burnside stood near us looking through his night glass for a long time with his staff. More than thirty houses were burned, aside from the arsenal, railroad shops and flour mills. The 48th Pennsylvania was sent out which forced back the rebel line beyond the houses which they had temporarily occupied. Several rebel prisoners were taken, who proved to be the Palmetto Guards of South Carolina. No further assault was attempted; evidently the big bonfire disconcerted their plans.

November 24

Another night of watching in the trenches broken by short naps while lying on arms; before daylight the 21st Mass and 48th Penn are ordered to move out to the front - beyond the depot to the right of the burnt buildings. Beyond this area was an open tract of ground where our line of battle was formed. We now understand that our duty is to force back the rebel line to its original position.

Several houses were filled with sharpshooters who immediately opened fire on us. Day was just dawning as we swept forward among the buildings and leaping over fences behind which were concealed large numbers of the enemy who gave us a destructive fire; several of our boys fell, but we soon had the satisfaction of seeing the rebels skedaddle pell mell, leaving everything knapsacks, blankets, haversacks and rations so sudden was our attack. Several prisoners were taken, but we do not stop; away we rush after the flying rebels, over the Kentucky branch of the railroad, and a quarter of a mile beyond, we were ordered to halt right under the guns of the enemy's line.

We were again withdrawn to the line of the railroad under a sweeping fire from the enemy, but lying down we had the protection of the railroad embankment of two or three feet in height. We at once open a brisk fire until every "Johnnie" was back in the picket holes of their original line. But our brave men now realized that they were bottled up right under the works of the enemy with their line of rifle pits only a few rods away. Although protected from the enemy's artillery by the railroad, a large rifle pit filled with rebs a short distance on our right troubled us for a while. By giving them our undivided attention we were able to silence them.

After remaining in this position several hours, orders were received to withdraw the brigade. Our officers were in a quandary to know the safest way to execute the order; two ways only were open for us to retreat: One was to run the gauntlet of the concentrated fire of the rebel fortifications and rifle pits up a steep bank to the protection of a house whence we could withdraw in comparative safety; the other was to crawl flat on the stomach more than twenty rods behind the shelter of the railroad sleeper and rail to a basin from whence was an other outlet.

After a long hesitation no one being quite ready to set the example and offer his body as a mark for the watchful enemy, Major Richardson leaped up and with a few bounds cleared the space followed by a shower of bullets; he reached the shelter in safety as all the shots were too low. Soon a second man followed and safely reached shelter, but the bullets intended for him struck a poor fellow of the 48th Penn, who lay partly concealed behind a stump. He was hit in the head, rolled over in plain sight of us all and died.

Most of the 21st then chose the safer way which was very fatiguing. If anyone is desirous of learning what the task was, let him try stomach crawling in the slimy southern mud for the long distance which we traversed. I was not a handsome looking soldier as I plodded up into our fortification with my mud saturated clothing, but I was joyfully greeted by Brother Henry who had been anxiously looking for me.

Our little German cook[17] was shot while he lay concealed in a handcar which stood on the track. He lay groaning all day and after dark was brought in by two comrades and died later.

November 25

I was aroused up before light and detailed with others to reinforce the picket of the 2nd Brigade. Traveled over the same ground we charge over yesterday morning. From our rifle pit we saw a rebel officer ride out on a mild white horse and very coolly reconnoiter. Several "lightning despatches" from our rifles sent him flying back into the woods out of sight. Later in the day, musketry and cannonading was heard across the river on the opposite side of the city where General Wolford is holding the enemy in check. Ripley[18] was killed by a rebel sharpshooter while standing in the breastworks in the afternoon.

At night we were relieved from picket and set to work digging rifle pits further in advance which took us very near the rebel line. Through the cold, dim, starlit night we ply the pick and shovel until near daylight, working very carefully and silently, knowing that if discovered by the rebel picket our lives wouldn't be worth a "brass farthing." We dug one pit in the front yard and another in the garden of a very tasty modern built house, ruthlessly tearing down choice shrubbery and vines. Costly furniture was strewn all about the grounds. As a memento of the nights work, I took a fine map of North America which I found lying in the wet grass and afterward sent it home.

November 26

We returned to quarters before daylight. Thanksgiving Day in Massachusetts: the contrast is very sharply drawn between the great New England feast day and our present condition. The food supplies are so nearly exhausted that mules and horses are being killed in order that their rations of corn may go to the human animals. Our own ration for the day consisted of roast beef and only one meal—no side dishes, no bread and potatoes or anything else. And for this we were indebted to the rebels. A heifer inside their picket line wandered out between the two lines when a Union bullet brought her down, and three brave fellows dragged her inside our line. Surely we have cause for thanksgiving and we didn't fail to thank the discomfited Johnnies. Our cook, "Jule," confiscated a lot of barley which he burnt and made into coffee for us.

I went into the city in the afternoon and called at division headquarters on the acquaintances which I made while I was with the provost guard. Tonight all the troops are ordered to be in marching order and at their posts as it has been ascertained that the enemy will attempt to break through our lines.

November 27

We stood in the trenches all night and nearly all day awaiting the expected attack, but it did not come. The enemy has evidently been feeling for the weak points in our picket line so we feel quite certain we shall yet receive them. During the night as one of our videttes was standing in front of his rifle pit in the shadow of a large tree, he heard the rustle of leaves close by him; watching closely he discovered the form of a man slowly crawling up within a rod. As the man had not discovered the presence of the vidette, he continued to move nearer until within arm's length. Our man suddenly whispered to him that he was covered and to crawl silently into the rifle pit from whence he was taken as a spy to headquarters.

November 28

My turn comes to go on the picket line so before daylight finds me in the rifle pit near the ruins of a brick mansion. A drenching rain poured all day long soaking through my rubber and woolen blanket, and I am wet to the skin. It is near nine in the evening; the enemy's firing suddenly increased until a regular volley from an advancing line was heard a quarter of a mile down the line in front of the 1st Division accompanied by the wild rebel yell. After a few minutes the firing diminished and we knew nothing of its result. We wait another hour anxiously watching, lying in the mud, when another volley and another yell nearer than before many of the bullets spattering about us.

The firing gradually ceased, but now our batteries on the hills have discovered something worth firing at through the pitchy darkness; suddenly one opens its thunderous fire, then another and another until all the hills on this side of the city are ablaze with the lurid sheets of flame. Shot and shell go screaming uncomfortably low over our heads. We are satisfied that the enemy is massing its forces on the picket lines under cover of the darkness, preparatory to making a grand attack. The thunder of the big guns, the scream and whir of shells, accompanied by the occasional rattle of the rebel's musketry and their wild yell, all tend to stir us up to the highest pitch of expectancy almost painful by its tension.

November 29

About two o'clock in the morning my turn to go out as vidette arrives. It was not a specially pleasurable task to step out of the comparative shelter of the picket post and stand alone in the darkness face to face with the enemy, momentarily expecting a volley, but the need was imperative to give quick warning of any stealthy approach. So I stand peering into the darkness exposed to the pelting rain from above and "hail" from the front for half an hour when I was startled by the yell and a volley just the other side of the house a few rods on my left. The bullets flew past me and immediately the picket posts were abandoned to the left. The men rushing up to ours said that the enemy came upon them from the rear, expecting to capture them. This showed that all the lower part of the line had been abandoned or captured. We were then withdrawn back across the creek—the enemy immediately following and occupying our pits.

We begin at once to throw up a new line of pits. Just before daylight another charge was made on my right as the new relief was approaching. Sergeant Cummings, who was posting the picket, was killed and others wounded. We yield our places and hasten back into the breastworks and pour down a cup of hot barley coffee. In meanwhile, the chill gray dawn was creeping in and shutting the night of suffering out, but it ushered in the grand assault upon Fort Sanders, half a mile south. We were at once summoned to arms. The enemy's siege guns and artillery all open fire and their messengers of death came crashing through the buildings, many reaching far into the city.

Then the long gray lines could be dimly discerned through the fog and increasing dawn, sweeping up the hill toward Fort Sanders. We had only to wait and watch and listen to the unending yells of the brave fellows and incessant musketry. As the fort was the key to our position, we were prepared to make a counter charge in case the enemy were successful; by daylight the desperate contest was over and our brave boys still hold the "key," and down past us through the street come pouring a long stream of the captured graybacks.

The facts are at last ascertained. Longstreet took the flower of the rebel army and threw them against the fort filled with two or three veteran regiments and Captain Benjamin's battery. The first obstacle which threw them in inextricable confusion was a telegraph wire which General Burnside had ordered run along a foot from the ground fastened to stumps; undistinguished in the gray dawn, the front line tripped over it while the on coming lines tumbled over them in great heaps in the ditch. Then our boys tossed lighted hand grenades over the parapets among them causing great slaughter and the rout became complete. Then while the remnant were fleeing down the hill, the 2nd Brigade charged among them and captured several hundred.

An armistice was granted by General Burnside to enable the enemy to carry away its dead. So throughout the day a lively conversation was carried on between the picket lines until the signal gun at five proclaimed hostilities again opened.

November 30

Couriers from Sherman's army have succeeded in getting into the city and given the welcome news that large reinforcements are near at hand for us. Our quarter ration of wheat bran does not give much sustenance but hope makes a good stimulant to wash it down. I went on picket at the brick house by the railroad.

December 1

Off picket at daylight and on again at night. Surely this is a good deal of a good thing, but I am one of the healthy ones and have to do double duty. We are all hopeful that the end of the siege is not far off which makes it easier to endure. General Burnside issued orders to the troops, praising them for their fortitude and giving accounts of a great victory by Grant's army at Chattanooga - the news came through the lines by the couriers.

Before going on the picket line I accepted an invitation to dine with Henry, who boards at a citizen's house a quarter of a mile away in the city. It was a good square meal and highly relished, but I could not help thinking the citizens ought to divide with the starving soldiers. Henry presented me with a fine heavy cavalry overcoat, most acceptable with the approach of the wintry weather. "The friend in need is the friend indeed."

December 2

Our picket post is at the brick springhouse, the rendezvous of the officers of the pickets; although the nearest post to the rebel line, I had a much easier day than usual in less watching and more opportunity to exercise my limbs. Our boys have held conversation with the Johnnies throughout the day. Each side agreed to withhold firing until due notice is given. Although not in strict line of military discipline, it has made the hostile lines quite "chummy." We learn that the 6th South Carolina Regiment is picketing in front of us; they fought us a year ago at Fredericksburg.

December 3

We were held in the trenches through the night anticipating an attack. Our artillery kept up a desultory firing. It is rumored that the enemy is being withdrawn.

December 4

There was no firing on the picket line and only one shot from the rebel artillery during the day—evidently sent to warn us not to be too inquisitive about their movements. Much amusement from the contraband conversation was created for our starving boys, who are determined to have fun even out of their misery.

A young heifer had been coaxed by some tricky reb up toward their own line and then shot, hoping thus to secure a feast. It was a poor shot; the heifer, frightened, turned tail and ran into our lines and Harper[19] gave her a finishing shot and dragged her into our rifle pit in plain sight of the discomfited "Johnnies." Then began a series of altercations, entreaties and persuasions from them that we give up their rightful booty, which point could not be distinctly seen. But when they proposed to trade, they struck the Yankee in his weak spot. Negotiations at once opened and a small piece of the beef was exchanged for some rebel newspapers.

The joyful intelligence was brought down to our lines that General Sherman has fought a battle at Loudon, breaking the enemies lines and forcing them northward. Large reinforcements have arrived below the city, while General Sherman has arrived at General Burnside's headquarters. A large body of rebel prisoners has already been brought in.

During the night watching was kept up as strictly as ever. Toward morning a staff officer of our division came down to our post and said it was believed that the enemy's picket line had been abandoned; he requested someone to volunteer to go over and ascertain. We had heard their conversations and had seen them replenishing their fires at three o'clock so that no one responded with alacrity to the possible chance of capture.

The man on duty as vidette was Corporal Harrington,[20] and he was ordered to undertake the task. With a solemn face he gave up his watch and other valuables, and leaving messages to his friends, he went out into the darkness. After an absence of some twenty minutes he again appeared and reported that he crawled on hands and knees as far as the creek; then crossing over, wormed himself carefully up to the nearest pit; hearing no sound, he grew bolder and with a leap bounded over into the empty pit. He then examined others and found all empty. The news was immediately carried to headquarters.

December 5

Before day had fairly dawned, General Wolford's boys went galloping out on the Jacksonboro road to worry the retreating enemy. We at last breathe freely and dare to stand out on the breastworks without fear of rebel sharpshooters; so we revel in the freedom.

Later in the day our picket line was abandoned—the scene of three long weeks of intense and painful watching. Our brigade was sent out to reconnoiter among the deserted rebel works. We met scores of ragged miserable looking rebel prisoners, nearly all seemed glad to have fallen into Union hands.

After a tedious tramp through mud and rough woodland, over hill and dale, we returned to Knoxville from another side. No force was found but the preparations for siege were quite formidable. Marched ten miles. Signed the payrolls after we returned.

December 6

Wrote letters home and received pay from Uncle Sam. Toward night we were favored with a call from Generals Sherman and Burnside with their staffs, who came up to view the enemy's vacated works from our fortifications. General Sherman is a smart, energetic appearing man but rather plain and unmilitary in his undress military suit: slouch hat and civilian's overcoat, heavy sandy whiskers and tall.

December 7

At four in the morning, orders came to march at seven with three days rations, which being interpreted meant, one days rations to last three days. As we marched out of the city northward, the army passed by the home of Parson Brownlow where we saw his family standing in front watching the passing troops. They seemed gratified to hear the hearty cheering of our men for the sturdy old loyalist (who was not there). Among the group was a rebel officer, the brother of the parson's wife, who is held as a prisoner of war.

From a commanding eminence on the road we see it filled with troops for miles. The entire 9th and 23d Corps are on the move to drive the invaders out of the state. Sherman's men remain in the city. The day is fine and the change of duties is very acceptable to us. After a brisk march of twelve miles we halt for the night.

December 8

No signs of an early start in the morning, so I tramped off among the mountains foraging. We secure a quantity of meal and dried peaches and get back to camp in time to take up the march at ten. The enemy is discovered to be a dozen miles away, and we hear that Sherman is moving up on the opposite side of the Holston River while we are on the road to Bean's Station. March eight miles.

December 9

Took up the line of march at half past seven. Our route lay along a valley between two ranges of mountains running in a northeasterly direction with a width of two or three miles from summit to summit. The lofty Clinch range is on our left. Fires are burning in the woods all along on the sides of the mountains, doubtless as signals for the benefit of the enemy. Our supply of rations is exhausted and we get down to parched corn: "Isn't that a dainty dish to set before a sovereign people like we." At noon we go into camp near the village of Rutledge after a march of thirteen miles.

December 10

Laid in our bivouac all day. The boys have instituted general foraging parties by permission of officers, which return to camp from time to time laden with pigs, turkeys and chickens. The gambling instinct is brought out in the raffling out the prizes. A hearty welcome to John Wallace was given, who arrived from Cumberland Gap. He came with the first squad which has arrived since the siege started; he had to wait there all the while. He says that large mails are waiting for us at the Gap. We received two days rations of corn meal at night.

December 11

There was no movement of troops today. General Foster[21] has arrived from the north and assumed command of this department with headquarters at Knoxville. Although foragers scour the country, breadstuffs cannot be found in any quantities as the region has been thoroughly cleaned out, yet many manage to conceal theirs by burial.

December 12

A train came in from the Gap last night. Our sutler came with it and says he has three loads of stuff at the Gap for us. A large detail was made for a provost guard to protect citizens from the ravages of the troops. Hunger makes a brute of a man and therefore is somewhat excusable.

December 13

Regimental inspection of arms and equipments at ten o'clock. The boys foraged a large lot of eatables for the company, consisting of chickens, biscuit, beans, dried apple and peach, cabbage and pork.

December 14

Change of weather during the night to very chilly and cold. Received orders at midnight to march at seven, which were countermanded before we started. We received for the first time for a long while a half ration of sugar and coffee which was a great luxury. The mails have arrived and I received a large bundle of papers and letters.

December 15

Received orders to be ready to march at a moments notice; so we struck tents and laid in line of battle all day. It has been learned that the enemy has received reinforcements from Virginia and is pushing us back—fighting at Bean's Station. Under cover of darkness we file out on the road and take a backward track over one of the roughest roads I ever knew; fording several streams and plunging on in the darkness. The order of companies and regiments was broken up: all hands pushing and jostling each other like a flock of sheep. After some six miles of this sort of travel, we halt, rejoin our units and build large fires of rails; then we lie on arms during the remainder of the night.

December 16

At nine in the morning we again move backward; continue for about six miles and are then ordered to about face and drawn out in line of battle. Thus far we had heard or seen nothing of the enemy, but are told that they are pressing our cavalry so closely that the cavalry have united with our infantry and are skirmishing as they retreat.

December 17

Our division is drawn out in one long line of battle extending clear across the valley and throw up a barricade of rails, which will prevent a cavalry charge. Our cavalry dismounts and their horses are taken to the rear. They then form another line a few rods in front of us and lie down flat. All being in readiness for the reception of the enemy; their line of skirmishers were soon seen advancing out of the woods far up on the sides of the mountain on our left.

Our line of cavalry falls back in our rear while our line of skirmishers is thrown out. Captain Benjamin's battery from an elevated ground just back of us opens fire on the advancing line; they take shelter in the cover of the woods again. Night soon steals on and no general attack is attempted. General Granger[22] arrived with the 4th Corps from Mississippi via Chattanooga so we now feel able to hold our ground. During the afternoon heavy and incessant cannonade was heard across the river doubtless from some portion of Sherman's force.

Rations were dealt out at dark and rain began falling so I sat up most of the night cooking. Before morning the weather cleared up cold.

December 18

As the enemy does not show itself in the morning, the 21st is ordered out to relieve the skirmishers. We find them advanced two miles from the main body of the army, and the enemy's line a mile further. Brother Henry and another staff officer were sent out to place the foremost pickets while the main line of the regiment is deployed in a lone thin line with its base resting at a large farm house.

We form a barricade of rails, but before it is finished we are ordered to fall back a mile nearer the main army at dusk. A straight unbroken line now runs from summit to summit across the valley. Company A was posted by itself beyond a small creek where we all settle down to a strict watch all night long. No disturbance takes place, but the intensity of our watch in this lonely place, where the silence is profound, is most wearing.

*   *   *

Bivouac of Co. A, 21st Massachusetts in the woods at Loudon, Tennessee, by George A. Hitchcock

Nine

Winter in the Mountains

A small Union force, including the 21st Massachusetts, trailed Longstreet's Corps as far as Rutledge, thirty miles northeast of Knoxville, but it was deemed inadvisable to attack the larger body of Confederates. Longstreet's troops remained in East Tennessee until the following spring, causing considerable annoyance to Union troops by threatening their supply lines. The Southerners experienced extreme hardship during the winter in their camps around Russellville and Morristown, with only shelter tents for protection, inadequate clothing and a critical shortage of food. The weather was bitterly cold—the worst winter in decades.

By December 27, 1863, two-thirds of the 21st Massachusetts, including George Hitchcock, had reenlisted for three additional years of service. On January 6, 1864, the reenlisted soldiers received orders to march back to Camp Nelson and proceed by train to Covington, Kentucky in preparation for their return to Massachusetts and a thirty-day reenlistment furlough. The regiment left Blain's Cross Roads on January 7 with 200 Confederate prisoners, starting their miserable trek back without sufficient food and clothing while having to endure severe winter conditions. The veteran Bay Staters arrived at Camp Nelson during the early evening of January 18. The men reached Cincinnati by train eleven days later on January 29, and arrived at Worcester, Massachusetts, on the evening of the 31st. A throng of civilians turned out to greet them the following morning.

On January 28, 1864, the United States Senate and House of Representatives approved a resolution thanking Maj. Gen. Ambrose Burnside, and his officers and men "for their gallantry, good conduct, and soldier-like endurance." There were only four joint resolutions approved by Congress during the war that thanked an individual for great service to the nation.

*   *   *

December 19, 1863

Our lonely watch was uneventful and lasted throughout the day. Doubtless the enemy is satisfied that our position and force is too strong to assume the offensive. We were relieved at night and find the regiment in regular camp on the edge of a forest which shelters it from the north and west winds. We proceed to pitch tents and make ourselves comfortable for the night. The regimental sutler has received a large stock of goods—I buy a pair of boots. My shoes are worn out andthe approaching winter makes this a necessity for me.

December 20

The weather is growing very cold; the muddy roads have frozen hard and rough. We are in the neighborhood of Blains Cross Roads. Regimental inspection by an officer of the brigade staff. I was detailed for picket duty at five at night. The nights are very long.

December 21

Laid on picket all day with Lem Whitney for my comrade and Charley Wilder for corporal. When we return to camp at dusk, we find a cheery place with large fires burning and the boys much interested in two large loads of sutler's goods which have just arrived. Our knapsacks came with the same train.

December 22

Mended clothes. All detailed men have been ordered to report to their regiments. I was again detailed for picket duty.

December 23

The day was cold and cloudy. At daylight our picket line was deployed across the valley, each man about a rod from his next, and in this way the line extended from ridge to ridge. We were then ordered to advance in a straight line. Sweeping up through the mountain sides and valley we could thus discover any traces of the enemy or lair of guerrillas which infest these fastnesses.

My position in the line kept me well up on the side of the Clinch range. I found a very rough passage and at times almost impassable—up steep pitches, then down into a ravine, then winding around some precipice and through long tangles of underbrush. Through all this wild tramp the greatest difficulty was experienced in keeping in sight and pace of my right guide; occasionally losing sight of him for a few minutes, then by calling I would find and keep along with him. While passing through one dense thicket, I lost sight of my guiding man (Bailey), and when I at last closed in with the line, Bailey[1] was gone and never seen by the regiment afterwards.

After traveling about six miles in this manner, we halt and feeling certain that the enemy has been withdrawn; we rest awhile and then return to camp by the main road. Passing several farmhouses, our conversation with the owners develops very loyal sentiments; however, some over did the thing, and ten to one if they hadn't already repeated the same lesson with variations to the men in gray. The "doggoned" yanks could find their hidden corn and tater piles just as quickly as the Johnnies, and it was well to keep in with both sides. But one old man, who we saw standing in front of his house, showed the mettle of a typical loyal East Tennessean. He exclaimed with great indignation, "Kill every mother's son of them, my rascally tory neighbors. I have four sons fighting them and if government would take me I would go too."

December 24

It was very cold last night. Cannonading was heard in the direction of Morristown. An order was read at dress parade giving notice of and calling for the reenlistment of veterans.

December 25

Celebrated Christmas by eating goose which had been kindly loaned by some obliging rebel. Charley Blackmer and Jack Reynolds joined the regiment from Knoxville. I went over and called on the boys of the provost guard at division headquarters. At night was detailed for picket; my post is on the summit of a high hill overlooking the entire picket line and camps.

December 26

Rained hard all day. Made a shelter of a "fly" which kept us "decently uncomfortable" until relieved at night. On returning to camp we find the boys in a state of great enthusiasm over the idea of reenlisting as veterans. Dr. Cutter was making a speech upon a large stump, presenting the advantages of the new call and stimulating the patriotism of the boys. It is presumed that the promise of a thirty day furlough right in the dead of winter (going home to Massachusetts and receiving a large bounty) had its influence in bringing more than three fourths of the regiment to reenlist for three more years. But the government knew the importance of holding these veteran regiments, and the spirit of patriotism was surely at the bottom of the enthusiasm. Of course I joined the new recruits.

December 27

The report of the reenlistment of our regiment was sent to the corps headquarters and we understand that the 21st Mass is the first one to respond to the call from East Tennessee, although a Michigan regiment is nearly even with us.

December 28

Sam Gould[2] and Reuben Mann,[3] who have resisted the appeal to reenlist until today, have now joined the ranks.

December 29

The reenlisted of the 21st Mass and 48th Penn were sworn into the new service by a regular army officer; we are in for another three years of service unless the rebellion is crushed sooner. I went on picket on the advanced line in the woods.

December 30

Colonel Hawkes has received orders to report his 21st regiment to Governor Andrews in Massachusetts, and we are to leave here as soon as we can get ourselves ready. We are to go by way of the Gap with four days rations. We do not anticipate as easy a march as we found on coming out.

December 31

Commenced to rain at night. The regiment was mustered in for pay and those who have refused to reenlist are to join the 36th Mass. I went on picket at night at the "side hill post" which lies in an exposed position. I did not catch any sleep during the night so I watched out the old year and ushered in the new.

January 1, 1864

One year ago found me doing picket duty in Virginia, looking southward across the Rappahannock and over the bloody field of Fredericksburg—keeping watch over the foe. This morning finds me at the same duty in East Tennessee, looking in the opposite direction for the foe.

During the night the wind changed, snow began to fall and before daylight the weather became intensely cold, turning the snow to sleet; but when morning broke, the sun came out shining clear in a bitter cold sky. All the pickets kept busy bringing rails for an enormous fires; we were enabled to roast one side while the other froze or by constant change of position we are kept from becoming baked ice. It tries the mettle of the veterans, but as our rations begin to come in more regularly we are able to defy the elements. Mercury fell to several degrees below zero. When we return to camp at night, we drew rations of hardtack, sugar and coffee.

January 2

Cloudy and very cold, no thawing all day and all nature frozen stiff. Henry has returned to the regiment and has been assigned to Company A as its commander. One hundred and seventy rebel prisoners were sent up from Knoxville to whom the 21st will act as escort over the mountains to Camp Nelson. Half the regiment is detailed to guard them; consequently, no picket detail was made. Much interest is taken in our new allies the graybacks; most of them are very ragged and barefoot.

January 3

The weather moderates at night and rain began to fall. I have been guarding prisoners. Asa Piper, the only Company A man who refused to reenlist, was detailed as teamster and left us today. Captain Clark brought orders from Knoxville for us to draw pay at Camp Nelson.

January 4

Put this down in your diary! Two ears of corn to each man was the only ration for us today. Our stomachs rebel at this wholesale robbery of the poor mule. As we sit gazing in awe and wonder at these emblems of a peaceful bucolic life, we are puzzled to know why the little boy in the reading book called for "only three grains of corn mother."[4] Perhaps his teeth were poor and he couldn't chew any more. But our rebel friends do not exhibit any unusual surprise at the "hog's food" and seem well contented to fare as we do.

January 5

This is a mild winter's day which I spent very quietly. I assist Henry at building his eleventh hour chimney and pitching his tent. The veteran soldier learns to fulfill his plans for comfort regardless of prospected changes. We are all anxiously awaiting the order for marching, and our bright anticipations bear us up far above the present hardships and our thoughts are far away from this isolated region.

January 6

I am again detailed to guard the rebel prisoners. In conversation with one of them, I found that he belonged to Longstreet's army and fought us at Fredericksburg [Antietam]—directly opposite our regiment at Burnside bridge. He has since been in the Battle of Chancellorsville and most of the battles around Chattanooga. The long anticipated order came at night for us to march tomorrow morning.

January 7

We are up early and packed but do not start until afternoon. Snow began to fall early in the day. All our extra clothing and shoes we distributed among our rebel friends and at two in the afternoon file out of camp with them between two lines of our boys. In high spirits we bade farewell to our old comrades, and passing the division and Corps headquarters, we cheered our Generals who saluted us; then setting our faces "northward" struck out into a blinding snow storm and left our army behind.

After passing by Blains Cross Roads, we march some seven miles and encamp on the opposite side of the Clinch range. We have some curious feelings as we realize we are now cut off from our army and have no knowledge of the whereabouts of the enemy. Company A made a fine shelter of rails and our fly pieces outside. Sam Gould returned to the company so I bunk with him. In fine spirits we sit up quite late and enjoy ourselves around the enormous campfires while the snow fell fast all night long.

January 8

At daylight the clouds cleared away and we push forward in the deep soft snow which began to melt early in the day. By the middle of the forenoon, we passed the headquarters of General Willcox, who commands the new Indiana Brigade which is posted along the road toward the Gap. General Willcox warned Colonel Hawkes to keep a strict watch for guerrillas, who are very troublesome in this region. By sunset we reached the banks of Clinch River [Walker's Ford] and were put across in a ferryboat, straggling into camp a mile beyond—twenty miles from our last camp. As the sun disappears the air grows cold.

January 9

The day is fair and cold. The prisoners now march in the rear of the regiment and today I march as guard with them. Passed through the lonely village of Tazewell [Tennessee] and encamp a mile south of the Powell River after a march of seventeen miles. Reuben Mann overtook the regiment at night and informs us that the 8th Michigan Infantry is only a few miles behind us and also bound for home on their veteran's furlough. As the sun sinks out of sight the air grows bitter cold, and as there is a scarcity of rails in the vicinity, a vacant log house is demolished and soon we have an immense roaring fires going.

The prisoners were permitted to go out and hunt up rails which were discovered and quickly transferred to camp. These men give us no trouble and nearly all seem quite contented to be with us and share our comfort. I stood guard four hours during the night by one of the rebel camp fires. Few of them find much sleep or rest in the biting cold, so thinly clad are they that only by constant motion can they keep from freezing.

January 10

I caught only one hour sleep just before daylight by the big log fires of our own camp. When daylight dawns, we are conscious that we have passed through the coldest night of the winter. The frost works on the hair and beards of the men and gives us all a most venerable look. We are off at light and with light hearts and brisk walking soon warm up. A short walk brings us to the Powell River over which we cross on a large new bridge guarded by block houses and a fort on the north side. Guerrillas are hovering around so that our men dare not leave the command for any distance.

Arrived at Cumberland Gap at noon where we find a sutler and began filling our lean haversacks. Company A has a fund on account of commuted rations which is now brought into use for purchasing supplies, and we feast on a limited scale. Boots and shoes find quick sales with the half clad, half shod rebels who happen to have the "simon pure" gold and silver as well as stacks of confederate scrip.

Reaching the famous cornerstone, we once more cast a look back over the country which has been the scene of so much of hardship and privation during the past few months. Then turn forward into an unbroken wilderness of forest, mountains and snow. Pushing forward, we reach Log Mountain where we encamp for the night after a march of sixteen miles. Here we found a supply train toiling up the sides of the mountain which was an inclined plain of glare ice. We drew rations of hardtack, sowbelly, coffee and sugar: full rations for the first time in over THREE MONTHS!

January 11

Weather mild and snow melting. I guarded prisoners. The 8th Michigan passed us; being unincumbered with prisoners, they get over the ground faster. Congratulations were passed between the two regiments. Left camp at near noon, marched seven miles to Cumberland Ford where we cross on a pontoon and encamp on the side of a mountain overlooking the river. We met two long wagon trains carrying supplies into Tennessee. My post, guarding prisoners during the night, was by a large stump which I set on fire and as it made so comfortable a position for me I remained by it all night. When off duty—I went to sleep, rolled into the fire and burnt my overcoat and blanket quite badly before I realized my situation.

January 12

Waited for our wagon train to overtake us and did not get started until noon. Marched through Flat Creek and camped for the night about eight miles from our last camp. We again draw rations of hardtack and meat from a supply train which we met. We met three long wagon trains and large droves of cattle going over the mountains which impresses us with the magnitude of the undertaking of keeping a large army so far away from railroad lines of communication.

January 13

Started before light and marched eight miles to Barboursville [Kentucky] where we halted to buy shoes of which nearly everyone stands in great need. My boots proved a poor bargain, having burst about the toes and so afford no protection from the snow, water or dirt and simply keeping my bare feet from the broken stone of the pike. I was allowed to carry the company kettle in the rear of the regiment, thereby favoring my sore feet in traveling.

January 14

Started at light and marched all day, camping at Camp Pitman. Passed through London; was on prisoners guard until night.

January 15

The day was dark and cold. Started before light on the Richmond road, but my feet being so sore I was obliged to give up at last and was piled into an old rickety cart which Dr. Cutter had pressed into service from some farmer. Crossed the Rock Castle River in a large ferryboat. Passed several large fine looking farmhouses which indicate that we are approaching the end of the wilderness. We went into camp [near Big Hill] after a march of fifteen miles on a side hill in deep snow. I am twenty years old today.

January 16

A beautiful day. Our soft beds of snow we found somewhat settled in the morning; the warmth of our bodies melted holes so that we laid below the snow level. At nine we commenced the ascent of Rock Castle Mountain and all day we kept our course along the ridge of mountains, known as the "Hog's Back," overlooking the surrounding country. At night as we near our journey's end some signs of cultivation begin to appear and at last we descend Big Hill, a very long and steep mountain, and encamp in the valley near the camp of the 47th Kentucky. I made a bed of fence rails on which I essayed to sleep.

January 17

Started before light in a drizzling rainstorm on the Richmond pike which we soon left and took a very poor circuitous route. The smooth hard pikes were very hurtful for our worn out feet so that the change to the soft muddy dirt road was a relief. Rain fell incessantly through the day. Toward night we struck the Lancaster pike and camped ten miles from Lancaster, making a march of about fourteen miles. I rode most of the way in an army wagon, my feet being very sore and swollen. Threw away my stockings as they gathered more grit and sand than they kept out. Many of the boys are in a like condition.

January 18

Another stormy day. Started before light and reached Lancaster at ten in the morning. Pushed on to Camp Dick Robinson reaching there at noon and halt for coffee. Took up the line of march early in the afternoon. The men kept giving out along the march so severe was the tax on sore feet. As I was unable to keep up with the main body and the wagons were all filled, I received permission to "straggle." As I neared the Kentucky River, my feet became very painful, and it was only with the greatest difficulty that I drag them along through the soft "pudding" mud which covers the pebbly bottom of the pike.

During the evening I struggle into Camp Nelson in an utterly demoralized condition, having covered twenty five miles since morning. The good father of the 21st, Captain Hall, who is still in command of this important base, was bustling about caring for the poor fellows as they came straggling in. He had opened a large new building and sent in great loads of clean straw, quantities of hot coffee, soft bread and meat. The boys were loud in their praises for this friend.

Our rebel friends, in whom we had become quite interested by our mutual hardships and contact, were turned over to the provost marshal and sent to the military prison.

January 19

After a most comfortable nights rest, I awake to find a deep snow on the ground, the sky clear and cold. The detailed boys of the 21st, who were left here, came in to see us. Clothing was given out and I drew a new suit throughout. Bought a very respectable dinner at a saloon in order to celebrate the fact that "Ain't I glad to get off the wilderness." Feel pretty thoroughly used up.

January 20

Captain Hall, who was bound to do the handsome thing for the 21st, furnished United States transfer wagons for transporting the entire regiment to Nicholasville where we were quartered in the courthouse several hours. At three in the afternoon we embark in the cars for Covington, arriving there at midnight. After some delay we found quarters in barracks outside the city, a mile from Cincinnati.

January 21

Cold and drizzling rain all day. Our officers set to work immediately making out the discharge papers and muster in rolls for the regiment. Received a visit from Charles Hayward [an old friend from Ashby], who is engaged in business in Cincinnati. I went into Covington with him. Dr. Cutter is examining the regiment man by man; the sound ones are to be allowed to reenlist.

January 22

The 6th N.H., another veteran regiment, is here and was paid off today. The 50th Penn came in tonight.

January 23

Clothing and shoes were issued tonight. The 100th Penn came in tonight.

January 24

Our barracks were filled to overflowing so the 100th Penn was sent over to Cincinnati for quarters. Cole and I went over to the Eleventh Street Hospital to find Lem Whitney, who is sick; we could not gain admission. I again signed enlistment papers.

January 25

Succeed in gaining admission to see Lem Whitney; find him suffering excruciating pain from a lame leg. The 6th N.H. Regiment left tonight bound for home.

January 26

Today reveals a terrible disappointment for me. After all that I have endured in the frightful march over the mountains with the bright hope sustaining me of the home furlough, I am told I must turn about and tramp back without the regiment into the wilds of East Tennessee. The facts of the case are these: Although a recruit in the 21st and having served less than two years, the legal age of a "veteran," we were allowed to reenlist in East Tennessee with the full understanding of all the corps and department commanders that recruits to Massachusetts skeleton regiments (July 1862 call) were to be allowed the special privileges (granted to no other state) enjoyed by veterans of two years and over. The government plainly held out these inducements and on these conditions I enlisted.

Colonel Hawkes accepts the dictum of the higher officers, who either know nothing of this special order or who are jealous of Governor Andrew's influence with the government; instead of telegraphing directly to Governor Andrew to know the truth, Colonel Hawkes allows himself to become their dupe and ourselves the victims of his inefficiency.

As a palliative, Major Richardson was sent to Lexington today to endeavor to secure furloughs for us so we may go home with the regiment. It is unnecessary to say that our indignation knows no bounds, but as there are not more than half a dozen who are affected by the decision, our feelings have no weight with anyone. The regiment was mustered into the new service today and tonight the 48th Penn arrived from Tennessee.

January 27

Major Richardson returned from Lexington unsuccessful and had orders for us to return to Lexington and report to department headquarters. The ugly fact that we must "about face" and leave our old chums and companions with whom we have fought and endured all manner of hardships, just as they are about to enter into the privileges and pleasures to which we are justly entitled, is aggravated by the fact that any efficient commander knowing that a great injustice was being done would dare to break through the petty rules of red tape and give us our rights.

The 21st was paid off in the afternoon and many of the boys scattered off into Cincinnati to get rid of the pocket burning greenbacks, leaving the barracks at night nearly deserted. This was a relief to the ears of those who remained for the crowded condition of the barracks during the past few days have made our quarters a noisy bedlam. But few of the boys returned during the night so a turbulent time is apprehended when the drunken crowd returns in the morning.

While I was returning from the spring during the evening, I was suddenly taken sick and fainted away. I had nearly reached the barracks·when I fell and became unconscious. After a few minutes I revived and dragged myself into the barracks and by morning I was better.

January 28

During the forenoon I went into Covington and drew two months pay; crossed the Ohio into Cincinnati and called at the business of R.A. Holden;[5] then I rode out to Mt. Auburn (two miles) with Charles Houghton and dined with Mrs. Hayward at the residence of Mr. Holden. On my return I made a few purchases including a nice thick rubber blanket.

January 29

At five in the morning I packed up and went down to the depot to meet the train for Lexington but was too late; so I went over to Cincinnati, got a shave and bath, and returned to Covington in time for the two o'clock train. I arrived in Lexington at seven in the evening and found lodgings at the Soldiers Home on Broadway.

January 30

I went out in the morning to Fort Clay where I found the members of the regiment, who had been rejected for reenlistment, situated very comfortably in barracks clean and warm. When Dr. Cutter examined the regiment, he found quite a large number of men whose dissolute habits had brought on loathsome diseases, and he very wisely cut them off from the privileges of reenlistment. These are the comrades with whom my lot is cast and the stigma of disgrace as well as the association I must endure with them surely "when it rains, it pours."

January 31

Sabbath day; I attended the Presbyterian church in the morning and Methodist in the evening. Wrote letters home and ate roast turkey for supper.

February 1

I was detailed with nine others to report to the provost marshal in the city. We were instructed to make ourselves scrupulously neat for the Commander of the Post, Colonel William S. King of the 35th Massachusetts, was ambitious to show the citizens of Lexington how much finer and more soldierly his Massachusetts boys could appear than the average western soldiers who were about town. I was posted at the market and had orders to preserve order in streets in that vicinity. The 18th Kentucky Regiment passed through on the cars.

February 2

Saw Captain Hall on board the train bound for Cincinnati. More of the 21st boys came down from Cincinnati just recovering from the effects of a spree.

February 3

I went on guard today; my post was in front of Colonel King's Headquarters, a fine residence on East High Street the most fashionable street of the city, on which is the home of rebel John Morgan. My principal duties were to walk back and forth with stately martial tread and salute all passing officers. This is what the war worn veteran dubs as "parlor soldiering" and looks upon with ill concealed contempt. But it isn't so bad as marching back over the mountains and I am content to remain until my regiment returns. One of the 21st "left behinds" was shot in the head while on guard down at the market. He was engaged in stopping a row when a policeman, firing into the crowd, hit him. It is not supposed to be a serious wound.

February 4

A disagreeable squally day. I attended an entertainment in the evening at Melodeon Hall. The 116th Indiana passed through the city.

February 5

This morning the 117th Indiana passed through for home. These are Willcox's six months troops whose term of service has expired.

February 6

Snow began to fall in the afternoon. I was on guard on Mulberry Street above the market. I found a drunken man who was making considerable disturbance and arrested him. Took him to the provost marshal and from there down to Number Four Jail.

February 7

Sabbath. Cloudy and cold. Attended Presbyterian Church. Descriptive lists arrived for the Company I boys.

February 8

We boys got up a petition and sent it to Governor Andrew with the approval of Colonel King; praying to be allowed to remain with the 21st Regiment instead of being transferred to the 36th Mass.

February 9

I was on guard at Colonel King's house. He came out on the front steps at evening and told me that he had received orders to send us all home to join our old regiment! How about the two years' recruits now? We have just learned that communication has been cut off from Knoxville. The rebels have sent a raiding party around to the north of it capturing our trains.

February 10

Our forces have fallen back from Blaines Cross Roads into Knoxville.

February 11

A beautiful day, warm and spring like. Freeman Cole and I walked out a few miles on the Georgetown pike and visited a hemp factory. In the evening I went with Sam Gould two miles out on the Frankfort pike, and we called at a fine farmhouse where he had previously scraped an acquaintance. The pikes about Lexington are the grandest drives in the world: very broad, smooth as a floor with easy grades, and macadamized rock covered with a fine white clay.

February 12

I was on guard at a large wholesale whiskey storehouse which, being filled with confiscated liquor, has been closed and held by government. It is on Water Street nearly opposite the police station. A grand banquet to the Kentucky veterans was given by the Soldiers Aid Society in the Masonic Hall to which all the soldiers stationed in the city were invited; I enjoyed the banquet very much. The tables were spread with every delicacy in a beautiful hall the post band furnishing music for the occasion.

February 13

I took another walk out on the Louisville Railroad for three miles - nutting; found many butternuts. Do not wonder now why such quantities of "butternut" clothing abounds in Kentucky. The 129th Ohio passed through the city for home.

February 14

Sunday. Attended Presbyterian Church in the morning and Methodist in the evening. Several long freight trains passed through for Camp Nelson tonight.

February 15

I am on guard at Colonel King's house. Our quarters were changed to the headquarters building where we have coal and gas to burn. Our descriptive lists came today and requisition made for clothing. Three men who have been detailed at Newbern two years joined us today.

February 16

This morning while I was on guard at three, the wind took a sudden turn to the cold corner and blew very piercing. I went out from very warm quarters without extra clothing and think I must have taken a severe cold, as I feel strangely about my bones. We pack the stoves with wood and keep them red hot, but the intense cold is not driven out of the barracks. Our requisition for clothing has been denied for want of the signature of a commissioned officer (all in Massachusetts); red tape stands between us and comfort. Our boys, who have not the loftiest ideas of patriotism, are growing mutinous under this repeated injustice. The Kentucky soldier accept the kicks and slights with becoming humility. Attended a concert of the Allegheny Bell Ringers tonight at the Melodeon.

February 17

Weather continues very cold. When the old guard was taken off, the new detail refused to do any further duties until clothing was furnished them. This means mutiny and is indefensible, but not without excuse. I am down sick with a cold and severe headache. Sergeant Fox[6] was taken to the hospital.

February 18

Three cheers for Captain Hall. He learned of the difficulty with the 21st boys; came up from Camp Nelson and (cutting red tape all to shreds) furnished us with the much needed clothing. Here is a "shoulder strap" who is worthy to wear them, and if the boys had the power, they would make him commanding general of the armies.

*   *   *

U.S. General Hospital #2
Transylvania College, Lexington, Kentucky in February 1864
(Lexington-Fayette County Historic Commission)

Ten

Hospital Life

George Hitchcock recovered from "remittent bilious fever" and "dropsy" (edema) at the general hospital in Lexington, Kentucky, and spent additional time recuperating on a medical furlough in Ashby.

On February 29, 1864, President Lincoln signed a bill that revived the rank of lieutenant general and nominated Ulysses S. Grant for this position. The United States Senate confirmed the appointment on March 2, with an annual pay of $8,640. On March 8, Grant arrived by train in Washington with his 13-year-old son Fred. After checking into the Willard's Hotel, the new lieutenant general walked two blocks to the White House, where in the Blue Room he met President Lincoln for the first time. Grant returned to the executive mansion the following day to receive his commission as lieutenant general and assume his responsibilities as general-in-chief.

On March 10, Grant met with Maj. Gen. George G. Meade at Brandy Station. Grant retained Meade as commander of the Army of the Potomac and appointed Maj. Gen. William T. Sherman commander of the Military Division of the Mississippi. The Illinois general planned a spring campaign involving the simultaneous advancement on several fronts against the South's two principal field armies: Gen. Joseph E. Johnston's Army of Tennessee, which was defending Atlanta from its position in North Georgia, and Gen. Robert E. Lee's Army of Northern Virginia, defending Richmond while dug in along the Rapidan River.

After traveling west for discussions with Sherman and after deciding to accompany the Army of the Potomac, Grant established his headquarters on

March 26 at Culpeper, Virginia. A critical decision was made in April that would have a direct effect on tens of thousands of lives—including George Hitchcock's. On April 17, Grant halted all exchange of prisoners until the Confederates: (1) agreed to release a sufficient number of officers and men as were captured and paroled at Vicksburg and Port Hudson, and (2) accepted that no distinction whatsoever will be made in the exchange between white and colored prisoners in the military service of the United States.

On the 4th of May Grant and the Army of the Potomac crossed the Rapidan and plunged into the thickets of the Wilderness, where Lee's army attacked and brought him to battle. Three days later, Sherman's troops advanced toward Rocky Face Ridge, Georgia, the first barrier on the long road to Atlanta.

*   *   *

February 19, 1864

In the morning the orderly sergeant in charge of the barracks advised me to be carried to the hospital. He thought I was sicker than I knew and needed care. I had never been sick a bed a day in my life and had a horror of army hospitals in general. As I felt sure I had only a severe cold which would soon be better, I objected. But I soon found out by others that it was feared I was coming down with the smallpox which is quite prevalent.

I consented to go and was carried in an ambulance to the General Hospital on the north side of Lexington. This was in the spacious buildings known as the Transylvania University, the well known seat of learning of Kentucky where Henry Clay and many other prominent men received their education.

The main building is beautifully situated in a large park on elevated grounds overlooking the city and facing the south. The large buildings situated some distance back from the main building, which had been used as dormitories and boarding houses, are now occupied and used by surgeons, nurses, cooks and for special cases, as smallpox hospitals and convalescents. The main building is filled with sick soldiers and I was carried into "Ward One," known as the College Hall—a very large high airy hall now filled with seventy five iron hospital cots which are all occupied.

Everything is kept in perfect order and neatness with several nurses having charge of certain number of patients. My opinions in regard to army hospitals changed somewhat, but I began to feel very sick during the day and didn't take much interest in anything. However, I was satisfied that I had not any smallpox or should have been carried to another place. Before night a high fever had set in.

February 20 through March 2

[No entries]

March 3

For two weeks my diary must necessarily be a blank. I suppose I have been very sick with fever and some of the time was rather "loony," but today the doctor says my fever has left me. Got off my bed for the first time and with the help of my good kind nurse drew on my pants and sat up long enough to write home, giving an account of myself. My nurse is a man of about thirty years, a sergeant in some western regiment: a very quiet, calm fellow—cheery and faithful, one whom I love to watch as he goes about his duties so ready to respond to the constant calls both day and night and always an encouraging word for his various patients. This is the first sickness of my life when I have been confined to my bed, and the doctor calls it "remittent bilious fever." I am very weak and continue to have returns of the fever.

March 4

The payrolls for the 21st boys remaining here arrived and are being signed.

March 5

I was mustered in for pay with the rest.

March 6

I saw a patient, who has been sick in the second cot from mine, breathe his last. Rather hard lives for us who are weak and sick to have to see these sights.

March 7

Signed the payrolls. Tonight brought me a great treat—letters from home. Among these was a printed order which my parents received from Governor Andrew in response to their request to know why this unjust treatment had been permitted to the recruits of July 1862. It is a publication issued from the War Department at Washington explicitly stating that in order to keep up the old fighting regiments of Massachusetts to effective numbers, Governor Andrew was authorized to solicit recruits with the inducements that they should be entitled to all the privileges and standing as those who originally enlisted. Although having served less than two years, they could reenlist just the same as the veterans, but this was "applicable to no other state but Massachusetts."

This order was countersigned by Governor Andrew with instructions to commanders of regiments to govern themselves accordingly. This fully puts the poor private in the right and leaves the enlisting officers of our regiment responsible for a great injustice done. Although impossible to correct the mistake in full, it relieves me and the rest to know that we shall not be sent back to the 36th Mass. We are still members of the brave old 21st.

March 8

I received a call from Sam Gould, who I was heartily glad to see. His comforting jolly words encouraged me much. I was allowed to step out of doors for the first time just for a minute. I found that my descriptive list has been sent on to Massachusetts by mistake, which means that I was left in Lexington by mistake; I therefore cannot draw my pay without it. O dear! How long and weary are these days!

March 8 through March 11

[No entries]

March 12

Another break in my diary. I am unable to sit up but a few moments at a time, and although suffering no pain, I am intensely weak. The surgeon says I have the dropsy. Our ward is very full; seven new admissions arrived tonight.

March 13

Sunday. The weather changed to very cold. Our hospital chaplain held services in our ward at ten o'clock—very precious and comforting to me. More sick ones arrived tonight. Frank Burpee[1] came to see me. The boys don't forget their sick comrade. Frank is one of the victims of the mistaken officers.

March 14

Clark[2] and Cole called to see me. They say I am considered a very sick man. They also brought letter from home and one from Lem Whitney, who is in the hospital at Covington. Several admissions to our ward include one with small pox who was kept down stairs. I managed to get down stairs to dinner for the first time today. Find my appetite growing keen.

March 15

Snow fell in the afternoon. I considered myself lucky in securing a can of oysters which was highly relished. I witnessed the death of another man in our ward tonight.

March 16

A careless ambulance driver brought a man into our ward whose face was broken out with smallpox. His condition was at once discovered, and he was carried down stairs out into the cold air. It is said that the effect of the cold killed him, for he died in a few minutes. I called on Sibley,[3] who is a patient in Ward Five—one of the smaller rooms in the building.

March 17

St. Patrick's Day. I am not feeling as well today, although the bloat in my feet is not as full as it has been. My feet and limbs have been swollen almost out of shape some of the time extending as far up as the body.

March 18

Newspapers say that General Burnside has been assigned to the Command of the Department of the South. I have made application to have my descriptive list forwarded to me here from Massachusetts so that I may be able to draw pay.

March 19

Witnessed another death tonight. These sights seem very sad to us as we think that no loving friends can be with them to say a last good bye.

March 20

Sunday services were again held at ten in our ward. Feel very sick again, having taken more cold, but still keep up hope

March 21

Received precious letters from every member of the home family with bundles of papers, pamphlets and money. My sickness has not made me the only sufferer. My poor mother evinces an anxiety which means mental suffering that only a mother can know. I learn that Henry has been appointed a recruiting officer for the 21st with office in Worcester, Massachusetts.

March 22

Sam Gould was in to see me today and says that a captain is in town collecting all the detailed men and absentees of the 9th Corps. Our squad expects to leave here soon. They were paid today.

March 23

I feel decidedly better; the swelling of my limbs has gone down so much that I can get a pair of shoes on my feet.

March 24

The swelling continues to go down, though my feet are quite sore. I have traveled around the hospital a good deal today.

March 25

Snowed in the night. The boys expect to leave Lexington on Monday. Burnside's 9th Corps is to be taken from this department and transferred to the Army of the Potomac. Received news of a rebel raid into this state.

March 26

The 9th Corps will rendezvous at Annapolis, Maryland and the 21st Mass has gone there. One of the female cooks connected with the hospital died tonight.

March 27

Received letters from home. Cole and Burpee came to see me, bringing up my knapsack. It is reported that this hospital department is to be transferred to Camp Dennison, Ohio.

March 28

Received a pass and went down town. Our squad left tonight at six. News has been received of a fight at Paducah, Kentucky and the place burnt by the rebels; the commander, General Thompson,[4] was killed.

March 29

Sam Gould brought my rubber blanket to me. He goes away tomorrow. My time was employed in sewing, reading and writing.

March 30

[No entry]

March 31

I do not feel as well. The copperheads of southern Illinois are rising and five thousand troops have been called for. The core of the 9th Corps is expected to pass through here tomorrow enroute for Annapolis.

April 1

I am taking books from the hospital library; have been reading the *Life of Martin Luther* and the *Life of General Havelock*.[5]

April 2

Today have read Exposition of the Knights of the Golden Circle[6] and *Travels in Egypt and Palestine*. I have made application for a furlough, but there is little prospect of receiving one for there are so many ahead of me and only a few are granted each week. The furloughs all have to be sent for signature—first to Louisville and then to Cincinnati and back.

April 3

Sunday service as usual. The days drag wearily by.

April 4

I received a pass and went into the city and over to Fort Clay which made me very tired. Quite early this morning the bells of the city sounded the alarm of fire, and the monotony of hospital life was broken by the sight of a burning dwelling not far from here. It was entirely destroyed. My quarters were changed and I have gone into the convalescent ward—the windows open toward the city, facing the great pillars of the front portico.

April 5

I learned that my furlough has been forwarded for signature. At noon an alarm of fire sounded and again at night the last one a very heavy one.

April 6

I was examined by Dr. Meacham, the Head Surgeon of the hospital. Others have been examined and sent away. New arrivals of sick; the hospital is overflowing. I had a sick turn this afternoon caused by taking cold.

April 7

Sergeants Fox and Irish[7] were sent away to join the regiment. While lying on my cot, I was startled and agreeably surprised to hear the surgeon's orderly call my name and tell me to walk down to the office and receive my furlough which has been duly signed. I had made no calculations upon receiving one so that the announcement was a delightful surprise, and a home visit is yet to be a reality. Although I am feeling better, I am not to start until Monday—today being Thursday. How can I wait four days?

April 8

More than thirty patients were brought in tonight who were laid about on the floors of the corridors and every available space for lack of suitable room. Two full regiments of cavalry passed through the city and encamped just outside.

April 9

Over a hundred convalescents were transferred to the barracks today. I secured my furlough and transportation papers at the post quartermasters and am now ready for my journey.

April 10

Sunday. I walked out about Lexington, taking farewell looks at scenes of interest which I may never see again. I packed my knapsack and prepared for an early start in the morning.

April 11

Laid down early to sleep, but excitement drove it from me, and after a restless night I arose at four and hurried away to the station, preferring to get away on the early train rather than wait till the half past five train. Before I had gone half way, my boasted strength had left me, but by resting on the sidewalks in the cool air of early morning, I succeeded in reaching the station nearly a mile away in time for the train.

After a delightful ride for five hours through a magnificent country, I come in sight of the circle of hills and bluffs which surround the city of Covington; these are fortified and manned for the protection of Cincinnati, which lies on the opposite bank of the Ohio. Arrived at Covington at eleven and crossed immediately to Cincinnati, stopping at the Soldiers Home on East Third Street.

In the afternoon I went out to secure transportation home. After a long tramp I found the post headquarters where I received an order for transportation, signed by the post commander. I then went out two or three squares further and found the post quartermasters where I receive a package containing more orders. I proceed to the general ticket office of the Eastern Railroad where I secure tickets for seven different railroads sufficient to land me in Fitchburg, Massachusetts.

Red tape is appeased and I am at liberty to hunt up my old companion, Charles Haywood [former resident of Ashby], and we make a tour of the city in horsecars. Bade him farewell; in the evening; I linger about the dreary waiting room of the Soldiers Home until eleven o'clock at night when I appropriate a luxurious seat in a passenger car of the Little Miami Railroad and rolled out of the city bound for my long journey of twelve hundred miles.

April 12

Riding all night brought me before light to Columbus where a change of cars is made and during the forenoon pass through Galion, Crestline and many other places, arriving at Cleveland in the afternoon. Change cars again and go by the lake shore route, riding a long distance in view of Lake Erie: through the cities of Erie, Penn; Dunkirk and Buffalo, New York, where at dark a third change of cars puts me on the New York Central Railroad. And now begins a very severe headache which absorbs all my attention and keeps me awake throughout the night. The endless rattle, rattle, rattle of the trains becomes torture to my brain.

April 13

I raise my head at daylight and find the country very chilly. Off in the distant southeast, I see the snowcapped Catskills. Pass through Schenectady and arrive at Albany in the morning at nine. Bought a breakfast in the station and crossed the Hudson on a ferryboat. Take a southeasterly course passing through the wild mountains of the Berkshires; at noon I am in Springfield, Massachusetts. The dull pain in my head is not as severe, but my interest in the varied scenes about me is lessened. Change cars and proceed on the Western Railroad to Worcester.

Snow lies all around us. Arriving at Worcester at two in the afternoon, I have two hours to wait; so stretching my limbs, I walk up on to Main Street in a purposeless way. As I turned around the corner not half a dozen rods from the station, I walked squarely against my father and brother Henry, neither of whom supposed I was within a thousand miles of them as I had written nothing of my expected trip. Words are inadequate, but my father was not ashamed to be demonstrative. At four I went to Fitchburg with father; had a sleigh ride home in the evening and at nine surprised my mother as I stepped into the dear old home.

April 14 through May 5

[No daily entries during this span]

Was so thoroughly prostrated that I did not leave the house for two days and on the 15th was suffering such severe pain in my head that Dr. Emerson[8] was called. I found relief and the following three weeks passed all too quickly in delightful intercourse with friends.

*   *   *

"The surmising is that our new leader, Grant, means business."

Eleven

Grant's Campaign

On March 18, 1864, after a reenlistment furlough, veteran soldiers of the 21st Massachusetts left Worcester for Annapolis and joined a reorganized IX Corps commanded by Maj. Gen. Ambrose E. Burnside. The corps acted as the army's reserve, reporting directly to General Grant until May 24, when it was assigned to George Meade's Army of the Potomac. The 27,000-man corps included 3,500 black soldiers in Brig. Gen. Edward Ferrero's division—the first colored troops to serve in the Army of the Potomac. The 21st Massachusetts, assigned to Col. Daniel Leasure's brigade in Brig. Gen. Thomas G. Stevenson's division, passed in review in Washington with the balance of the IX Corps before President Lincoln and General Burnside on April 25. The corps marched southwest and reached Bealeton Station, Virginia, on April 30. On May 5, Burnside's corps crossed the Rapidan River at Germanna Ford and joined with the Army of the Potomac, most of which had crossed the previous day. On May 6, while the Battle of the Wilderness was raging, George Hitchcock left his home in Ashby, Massachusetts, to rejoin his regiment south of the Rapidan.

General Grant accompanied Meade's Army of the Potomac in the field and made the army's strategic decisions. He planned to utilize his unlimited supplies and manpower to prevent Lee from employing the Confederacy's interior position to rapidly redeploy manpower elsewhere. Instead of Richmond, Grant viewed his objective as Lee's army, with which he sought to stay in constant contact. Through the use of protracted combat, Grant intended to bleed Lee through steady attrition.

Lee's three corps of 65,000 men faced Grant's army of 120,000 Union troops just below the Rapidan River in the Battle of the Wilderness on May 5-6. Grant planned to march rapidly through the Wilderness and gain the open countryside beyond Spotsylvania Court House, but Lee attacked the Union army in the tangled thickets. A bloody two-day battle ensued. The larger Union army was neutralized by the densely wooded area, as was its superior strength in artillery. Grant suffered 18,000 casualties during the battle, while the losses for Lee's army are estimated at about 9,000 men. Both sides suffered heavy losses in general officers, and Lee lost the service of James Longstreet, who was critically wounded by friendly fire at the height of the battle.

The 21st Massachusetts Regiment was engaged on May 6. When Longstreet's troops in their slashing counterattack successfully turned the flank of Frank's brigade and rolled up Greshom Mott's division, precipitating a Union fighting retreat and redeployment along the Brock Road facing west, Maj. Gen. Winfield S. Hancock ordered Leasure's brigade to reconnoiter and to determine if any Confederates were forming for an attack. The brigade swept down the line across and opposite the front of Hancock's II Corps without serious opposition from the Confederates. During action in the Wilderness, the regiment suffered 18 casualties, including eight soldiers who were captured and later imprisoned at Andersonville.

During the afternoon on May 7, Union supply wagons moved to the rear, but rather than heading north, they turned south. This was the first time in Virginia that the Army of the Potomac continued an offensive after its initial battle. Grant moved Meade's army past Lee's right flank and was determined to reach Spotsylvania Court House first, positioning the Union army between Lee's army and Richmond. Determined Confederate troops, however, reached Laurel Hill first, checked the attacks of Maj. Gen. G. K. Warren's II Corps, and secured Spotsylvania Court House. Lee was able to use the watershed between the Po and Ny rivers as a bulwark for a twelve-day defense against Union onslaughts on May 10, 12 and 18.

On May 10, VI Corps Union-soldiers, led by Col. Emory Upton, briefly forced their way into the "Mule Shoe," a U-shaped salient bulging from the Confederate lines. On May 12, Hancock's II Corps succeeded in penetrating the salient, resulting in the fiercest and most deadly hand-to-hand fighting of the war. Eighteen hours of continuous fury ensued in violent rain squalls for an area known as the Bloody Angle. In the end, the Confederate line pulled back and then held. It is ironic that the day before Grant's message to Washington stated that he "propose to fight it out on this line, if it takes all summer."

During the Spotsylvania campaign between May 8 and 20, the casualties were more than 18,000 for the Union army and more than 10,000 for the

Confederates. The 21st Massachusetts Regiment was engaged at Spotsylvania on May 10, 12 and 18, suffering loses of 39 men, including two soldiers who were captured and later imprisoned at Andersonville. On May 10, General Stevenson was killed by a Confederate sharpshooter. The IX Corps lost an inspired and capable leader. Lemuel Whitney, who had joined and served in the Union army with George Hitchcock, was wounded in the arm on May 10 in a fruitless attack on Confederate entrenched positions.

The Union campaign in the Wilderness and at Spotsylvania, between May 5 and May 21, was a strategic defeat for the Confederacy, because Lee's army was unable to prevent the Union army from penetrating further into Virginia and from bludgeoning its way closer to Richmond. The Union forces had suffered tremendous casualties, but in this war of attrition the Confederate loses were irreplaceable, especially the experienced officers.

Frustrated by the impossibility of penetrating the Confederate defenses at Spotsylvania, Grant initiated another jug-handled flanking movement twenty-five miles southeast toward Hanover Junction. Lee left Spotsylvania and entrenched along the North Anna River covering the vital railroad junction before the Union army arrived on May 23. After crossing the North Anna River and failing to breach the Confederate defenses, Grant recrossed the river on May 26-27 and moved twenty miles southeast, again turning Lee's right flank. The Union army crossed the Pamunkey River at Nelson's Bridge and Hanovertown on May 27-28 and closed on Totopotomoy Creek, where Lee's army again confronted the Union forces. In the movement from the North Anna River, the 21st Massachusetts Regiment took a circuitous route, while Lee's army marched half the distance.

The exhausted soldiers crossed the Pamunkey River at Hanovertown on May 29 during the early morning hours and continued for two miles before halting. Later that night, George Hitchcock rejoined the regiment.

On May 31, after the armies skirmished along the Totopotomoy Creek for three days, Brig. Gen. Alfred T. A. Torbert's cavalry division (Sheridan's Cavalry Corps) drove back a smaller force of Fitzhugh Lee's cavalry and seized the road junction at Old Cold Harbor. Both sides called up infantry, and on June 1, there was savage fighting in front of Old Cold Harbor. In the morning Sheridan's cavalry, fighting dismounted, repulsed Confederate infantry intent on recovering the key road intersection. In the afternoon soldiers of the VI and XVIII corps carried the fight to the Confederates. After the Union troops were initially successful, counterattacking Confederates closed the breach in their line. During the night of June 1-2, both armies maneuvered and redeployed, facing each other across six-mile-long parallel-lines of earthen fortifications stretching from Topopotomoy Creek to the Chickahominy River.

There had been relentless and ceaseless warfare for four weeks. The casualties were enormous: 44,000 for the Union army and 25,000 for the Confederates. Grant attempted to maneuver Lee into open-field combat where superior Union manpower and firepower could destroy the Confederate army, but Lee's tactical skill, coupled with friction within the Federal command structure, thwarted Grant's initiatives, and the Union army was confronted by an entrenched defense at every new location. The conflict had become a war of attrition.

∗   ∗   ∗

Comments in 1890:

The furlough on which I visited home was called a "sick furlough" because it was granted by order of an army surgeon. It was of the utmost value to me at this time to complete the recovery of an illness which was induced by the terrible strain upon my constitution in the march over the mountains upon half or quarter rations. When therefore the end drew nigh, I was feeling better than I had been for a long time, and although the partings from home friends were painful, I was enthusiastic to get back into the ranks of the 21st and have a part in the glory which we could begin to see was coming through a perfected Army of the Potomac.

May 6, 1864

I learned that General Burnside, commanding his reorganized 9th Corps, had joined this army under the command of General Grant. Henry, having completed the duties in Worcester as recruiting officer, met me in Boston and arrangements were made for us to return to the front together. He then returned to Templeton, engaging to meet me at Worcester on the morrow enroute.

I look up my old friend, Charles H. Wood [former resident of Ashby and son of the Rev. Charles W. Wood], who was employed in Cotrell's bookstore on Cornhill; after tea we took a stroll out to Dorchester Heights where General Washington turned his guns on the British. The view of Boston and the harbor was magnificent by this early summer twilight as we watched the harbor lights coming out one by one and the great city by gas light.

Private George A. Hitchcock

This photograph of Hitchcock was taken on May 2, 1864, while on medical leave. Hitchcock left his home in Ashby, Massachusetts on May 6, while the battle of the Wilderness was raging just below the Rapidan River, in order to rejoin his regiment. He linked up with his comrades on May 29, just a few days before the debacle of Cold Harbor.

May 7

Spent the night with Mr. Severance on Charles Street near Beacon and during the forenoon went out on the "Mill Dam" toward which are now some of the finest avenues of the city. As the time for departure drew on, I went down to get my knapsack which had been deposited in a store on Exchange Street. I became puzzled by the labyrinth of "cow paths," which so many others have been before, and I was unable to find the right place. Fearing I should miss the train and thereby lose my traveling companion, I gave up my knapsack and went on to Worcester in the evening.

I met my brother, who realized (better than I) the importance of that knapsack full of necessary articles right from home. He therefore advised me to return to Boston and get it, giving me the right directions.

Thereby, I must forego the pleasure of my brother's company as he must proceed directly to Washington. I returned to Boston at half past ten Saturday night, arriving there at midnight and found fine lodging at the Soldier's Home, 76 Kingston Street. News of heavy fighting in Grant's Army is received in the papers.

May 8

Sunday; rode our to Mt Auburn in the afternoon and by invitation attended a Sunday school concert by the Old Colony Mission on Beach Street, hearing pretty singing by the children and a short speech by Reverend J.P. Bixby.

May 9

Found my knapsack and at half past two in the afternoon left Boston on the Norwich Express, arriving there at sunset. Having two hours to wait for the steamboat train for New London, I walked about the city; got supper and listened to some fine music by a band; at quarter past nine, I boarded the train and reached Allyn's Point at ten o'clock. Embarked on board the steamer, "City of Boston," and after enjoying the calm beautiful starlight night for an hour on deck, I turned in at eleven to my berth.

May 10

Up at daylight and with the enthusiasm of youth, I go out on deck to take in the view; find we were approaching the city of New York. Landed at Jersey City, took breakfast and at seven, started for Philadelphia where we arrive at quarter past eleven. Rode across the city through broad level streets in horsecars and at noon boarded the train. Took dinner in the novelty of a dining room on wheels which occupied two thirds of an ordinary passenger car. Arrive in Baltimore at five and "on to Washington" which we reach at seven in the evening. Before leaving the track, I found Dr. Hitchcock and Henry A. Goodrich, who had been sent out by the town of Fitchburg to look after the wounded men from the Battle of the Wilderness. I found quarters for the night in the "Soldier's Rest."

May 11

At nine in the morning I gladly left the "Rest" (?) with a battalion of soldiers who were returning to their various regiments at the front. Boarded a train which was standing in the street in front of the Capitol. Rode across Long Bridge out to Alexandria—from thence to Camp Distribution near Arlington Heights, four miles from Alexandria. We were furnished quarters to await transportation to our regiments.

May 12

I was detailed for fatigue duty with a lot of others and went out to work on the road near Fort Runyon. The day was hot and there were numerous complaints by the chronic growlers, who doubtless supposed they ought to be transported immediately on beds of roses to their regiments, instead of handling the pick and shovel and building roads for Uncle Sam. With blistered hands I worked until near noon when a heavy shower drove us back to camp. The place is called Camp Convalescent and is a large village of barracks. At night I drew a new canteen, haversack and shirts.

May 13

At half past four in the morning we are ordered up and marched to the ordnance department where I drew gun and equipments. When the regiment left me in Covington, I had to give up the trusty old Enfield rifle which had been my close companion day and night through all the active months since I first joined the army. This old rifle was one with which I was loth to part on account of associations. It had a handsome burl walnut stock of which I was proud and I had cut into it the initial H, so that I was able at any time to pick it out of the stack even in the darkest night. Even the bright new gun could not make its place good in my estimation.

Then in the midst of a heavy rainstorm, which tested the qualities of my excellent new rubber blanket, several hundred of us started out for Alexandria. This is the first time for five months that I have marched fully equipped.

Plodded on through a deep slimy, sticky, clay mud to Alexandria, a severe test to the vacation soldiers who had become softened by the home coddlings. After various ignominious falls and uncouth demonstrations on this slippery, "sacred Virginia soil," we brought up at a levee, willing to sit down anywhere in the mud; each foot brought up clay enough to build a good sized chimney. I had been rather vain of my "spick and span" clean army blue but repeated embraces with "mother earth" made me a rebel gray, and I confess I didn't look near as pretty at the end of the march as at the start.

At noon we embark on the steamer "Swan" and sail down the Potomac. Six miles below Alexandria, we pass Fort Washington on the Maryland bank at a bend which commands the river six miles below. Our course becoming due south where the river broadens toward the sea and we see the low Maryland shores on the left and the more hilly, ragged shore on the right. We met a steamer whose decks were covered with wounded men just returning from the bloody battlefields of Wilderness. We gave them rousing cheers as we passed them, but the only response, the waving of a few hats, was a sad mute testimony of the cruelty of war.

As we near our landing place—Belle Plain, ammunition is dealt out in bountiful supply. After filling cartridge boxes, the balance is deposited in knapsacks and haversacks. Some men recklessly throw their surplus into the water forgetting that the time may not be far away when they will be glad to have it. My extra supply is consigned to my haversack which later on became watersoaked and gave my hardtack a peculiar saltpeterish taste.

Landing at Belle Plain on the Potomac Creek at a long wharf, I see various other vessels moored among which was a large steamer belonging to the Sanitary Commission which is doing its deed of mercy. Here we witness a pandemonium of sounds. This is the temporary landing place for the supplies of the Great Army of the Potomac, at a narrow, winding cut in the line of bluffs. Along the shore are packed long lines of army wagons going in opposite directions. Thousands of struggling, wounded soldiers moving down to the boats. Officers, quartermasters, commissaries and wagon masters dashing back and forth through the thickest of the crowd; mule drivers making the air blue with curses and the musical voices of multitudes of mules calling for supper.

Then, away back over the hills comes the sound of the evening "retreat" from various camps. If this is the **base** of supplies, I think I prefer the **tenor**. Crowding our way up the narrow defile, the genuine indications of war are brought to our notice as we encounter a long line of rebel graybacks, which prove to be the captured officers of General Johnston's command which was taken in a body in the Wilderness. Generals Johnston [Johnson[1]] and Stuart [Steuart[2]] were among the number. Our company finds a rough piece of ground not far away where we bivouac for the night.

May 14

In the morning we find a better place about a mile further inland where tents are pitched and we go into regular camp. About noon a large squad was detailed from our battalion (myself among the number) and sent down toward the landing where we come insight of a large natural basin a quarter of a mile in diameter which was filled with a great mass of rebel prisoners over nine thousand of General Johnston's command. These are being held for transportation to northern prisons. We are placed on guard. While standing on guard, a long line of our wounded men came in from the front. They report that a heavy battle took place on Monday which the 9th Corps was engaged. [Spotsylvania Campaign in Virginia from May 8-20, 1864]

May 15

A very long wagon train came in from the front filled with wounded and a continual stream of men on foot comes pouring in—wounded in all sorts of ways. The indications are that desperate fighting is still in store for us; the surmising is that our new leader, [Ulysses S.] Grant, means business as this last terrible slaughter indicates. New troops are constantly arriving from the north and passing us for the front; tonight Corcoran's Legion arrived from Fairfax.

May 16

I am on guard again over the Johnnie rebs. Three thousand were sent away and six hundred were brought in from the front. A long train of captured artillery arrived. Grant has ordered all the "parlor" soldiers around Washington to be sent to the front; consequently, a number of heavy artillery regiments arrived enroute for the army: each man loaded down with two or three woolen blankets, overcoats and knapsacks stuffed to their utmost capacity. They were wearing paper collars, white gloves, shining brasses and spotless clothing. "Cleanliness may be next to Godliness" but the veteran soldiers realize the rude awakening which must come to these fellows as they start in on their first campaign, and no small amount of chaffing is given them by the rough looking boys who have seen two years of hard service.

At night a band belonging to a German regiment from Philadelphia played patriotic air to our rebel visitors. Such tunes as "We'll hang Jeff Davis," "Down with the traitors" and "Red, White and Blue" were played with an unction that brought out howls and groans from the seething cauldron of graybacks. If no worse insults are given to them by our boys, they have no right to complain for the grand, inspiring music may stir their hearts to realize the crime they are engaged in.

May 17

Toward night I learned that a battalion of returning furloughed men like ourselves had arrived from Alexandria. Thinking I might find Henry, I hunted them up. They were engaged at dress parade, and I was fortunate in finding Henry with whom I had a few moments talk. I planned to see him tomorrow. I read in a Baltimore paper the account of the battle at Spotsylvania.

May 18

Somewhere about midnight while sleeping soundly, I was aroused with the startling report that Mosby[3] with two hundred guerrillas was within two miles of our camp, preparing to dash in and rescue our great body of prisoners. For a few minutes we were in a quiver of excitement, standing in line in the intense darkness expecting soon to hear the cracking of rifles. Soon, however, the assurance that our thousands were abundantly able to cope with this sort of an attack allowed us to lie down again and sleep till daylight without a suspicious sound to again disturb us.

But in the morning our battalion was ordered to proceed to White Oak Church where we were divided into three companies and sent in three different directions. Ours moved off some three miles in a southeasterly direction. Here we again divide into squads of a dozen men each and deployed a quarter of a mile apart. Our squad finds itself, after a march of eight miles, in the fields not more than three miles from the Landing. We halt for night establishing a picket.

Among our number are several Indians who belong to a company of sharpshooters composed entirely of Indians of the Iroquois tribe from northern Wisconsin. During the evening while around our campfire, we watched our Indian friends with much interest. They held themselves aloof from our squad, talking to each other in their own language in a low tone and occasionally breaking out in some wild song, peculiar and weird. Instead of standing in military style with gun to shoulder when on duty, they seemed to be allowed entire freedom of action and would go creeping off in perfect silence into the darkness apparently enjoying themselves in the duty which was evidently sport for them. We pale faces regard them with decided respect—willing to yield them preeminence in this sort of calling.

May 19

Lieutenant Sawyer,[4] from the 21st Mass, passed by us from the front—going to Washington with a squad of wounded men. He informs me that Lem Whitney has been wounded. In the afternoon we were relieved and marched to White Oak Church, a modest plain little building near some woods. Here we joined the rest of our battalion and proceeded to Fredericksburg.

By sunset we reached the great barren uplands which a year and a half ago were covered with the camps of the Army of the Potomac. It was with some difficulty that I discovered the site of our old Falmouth camping ground on account of the undergrowth of brush that had sprung up hiding old landmarks. Thrilling memories came over me as we passed over the familiar sites and descended the steep banks of the Rappahannock, recalling the gloom which hung like a pall over the army when we last came over the ground returning from the slaughter at Fredericksburg. At nine o'clock in the evening we crossed the river on a pontoon bridge and encamped in the city after a march of eight miles.

May 20

The morning was very warm. I undertook an investigation of the city for which I had an exceeding curiosity. The circumstances under which I first saw Fredericksburg were such that I saw it only in the midst of the awful carnage and then the long weeks which followed when I saw it only from a distance and in possession of the enemy. The sad effects of the war upon this once beautiful city are seen on every hand. I should think half the buildings were in ruins from the terrible bombardment received at that time.

Then, being the center of later operations, most of the inhabitants have left and now it is almost solely occupied by the Union Army as one vast hospital. Every available shelter, churches and warehouses are filled with the wounded from the Wilderness and Spotsylvania. The very few houses occupied by citizens were thrown open for the shelter of our wounded and the rebellious inmates ordered to assist in their care.

After a long hunt I found the 9th Corps hospitals established in a church. The pews had been previously removed and the floors from basement to galleries were covered with wounded men wounds in every particular part of the body. Some laid very quietly while others were crazy with agonies endured, a sight most sickening. Many who were not severely wounded were assisting as nurses, dressing wounds and helping the helpless. I found Lem Whitney acting in this capacity, caring for a poor fellow whose leg was amputated. As fast as the men died, they were laid side by side in the church yard where I see long rows of silent dead awaiting the "dead cart," which was constantly coming and going. In the afternoon I was detailed to go out on the old battle ground and help raise hospital tents. At night a train of army wagons came in from the front bringing its freight of wounded from last nights battlefield. While they were unloading, two were taken out who had died during the journey. Among the number were several wounded rebels who received the same tender care as our own men.

As I lie down to sleep I cannot shut out the scenes of suffering which I have witnessed during the last twelve hours. It would be impossible to find anything to surpass it in form of intense bodily suffering. Much comment is heard concerning the new order of things which General Grant has inaugurated of forcing a battle each day regardless of the terrible slaughter.

May 21

Soon after midnight our battalion was roused by the beating of the long roll. In less than five minutes we were in line of battle prepared to resist an attack when it was found that we had been "done" by some frightened officers who had heard the report of small arms down in the city, which they supposed signified an attack from guerrillas but was afterward ascertained to be the result of a drunken row.

At about nine, army wagons began moving out on the Bowling Green Road guarded by a large force of cavalry and infantry. All day long for ten hours this immense procession kept moving on the longest I ever saw. Later in the day cannonading was heard a few miles out in the direction they have taken. Considerable anxiety was felt that if a large rebel force had attacked them, the opportunity to seriously cripple our army might be the results.

May 22

Our battalion moved camp a short distance out of the city on the Bowling Green Road. I was detailed as safe guard at a dwelling house near camp where the inmates gratefully furnished me my dinner and supper for the protection rendered. Two steamers have just arrived via the river; also a train of cars from Aqua Creek, the first since General Burnside was here over a year ago. We learn today that General Grant has taken the immense supplies which we saw yesterday and with his great army has broken loose from all connections with

Washington—moving and no one knows where. Evidently he doesn't propose to advertise his movements for the benefit of the rebel government. Such audacity must doubtless throw our martinet officers into fits. The appearances indicate that "popular opinion" has made and unmade commanders of the Army of the Potomac for the last time and that Government has decided to let the present commander "run the shop."

May 23

I visited the battle ground and went over the identical ground where we fought and charged in that awful butchery of eighteen months ago. In the afternoon I visited the 9th Corps hospitals and saw our 21st boys again. The wounded are being removed very rapidly; the severest cases are sent by the water route and the others by rail to Aquia Creek.

May 24

The monotony of the day was broken by the arrival of a lot of refugees, who with all their earthly possessions on their heads and backs, were bound north. The Union army has penetrated a section toward Richmond, which has not been open before so the negroes are swift to avail themselves of the new found liberty. A schooner laden with supplies came up the river. Distant rumbling of cannon indicates the direction of the army. At night I went on camp guard in a heavy thundershower. Learned that our army is in the vicinity of Hanover Court House.

May 25

Heard more cannonading during the forenoon. Preparations for evacuating the city are being completed so I presume we shall not be needed here much longer. At night a detail from our camp was summoned to carry the wounded on board the boats; so in the midst of a furious gale and shower I went prepared for a night job. On reaching the hospitals we found other details at work ahead of us; therefore, didn't have to stay very late. I carried several poor fellows on to the boat; each trip was half a mile in length, which brought out the perspiration.

May 26

A very hot day. I laid under my tent most of the day. A detail of one hundred men from our battalion is to leave here tomorrow place and purpose unknown. I am one of the chosen ones. At night I walked up across the city two miles nearly opposite Falmouth and found Lieutenant Sawyer returning after dark. I found the streets dark and deserted and but few of the houses lighted. The effect was very somber and gloomy as occasionally I passed some place where some soldiers were too low to admit or remove. The city seemed like some vast charnel house which I shall be glad to leave.

May 27

The night was very stormy. Roused up at three and at eight started for Bowling Green as guard for a train of medical supplies in company with a squadron of cavalry. Our road runs parallel with the river for several miles so we went over the old battle ground of Franklin's Corps[5] of December 1862.

For a long distance where the river bends, the southern slope is broad and even half a mile back from the river when the land rises abruptly. This was an advantageous position for the enemy to resist the attack of Franklin, especially as the attack was not backed up with any spirit by the commander. The entire route lay through a rich and delightful country, highly cultivated where are the finest tobacco plantations of the South.

At one time during the day we met a small cavalcade among which was a woman whom we were told was "Pauline of the Potomac," a celebrated spy employed formerly in McClellan's service [erroneous information—possibly Pauline Cushman, a former Union spy who had escaped execution and was traveling to Washington from Kentucky].

In the middle of the afternoon while some of the cavalry attached to our command were straggling in the fields half a mile away, they were fired at by horsemen, who instantly galloped out of sight. A squad of skirmishers was deployed and sent into the wood, but as it was thought afterward that the party consisted of only one man—the owner of the house where the cavalry were depredating; the skirmishers were withdrawn and we continued our journey.

Arrived at Bowling Green at five o'clock and bivouacked twenty two miles from Fredericksburg. The village consists of only half a dozen houses surrounding a large smooth lawn. The army passed through here yesterday morning and the temporary base of supplies is at Port Royal. The junction of the two roads to Richmond and Port Royal is close by our camp, consequently there was continual passing all the time we remained here.

May 28

In the morning a large party of negroes passed our camp "bound for freedom," and after we took up our line of march, we were constantly meeting squads of them who were taking their first opportunity to escape from slavery. It was a very interesting and hopeful sight in connection with the cruelties of war to see the joyful faces of these poor darkies as they realized the great change which was coming to their condition.

We cross the Virginia Central Railroad and the Mattapony River and begin to keep a vigilant watch; news has come to us at noon that the portion of the cavalry which left us at the Mattapony was shortly afterward taken by a band of guerrillas. Passed through Milford and Morris Stations, the latter was a complete ruin passenger and freight depots, engine houses and wood sheds were all smoldering and smoking ruins. A short distance beyond we pass a steam mill in flames, showing that the destroyers were not far ahead of us. Hundreds of dead horses lie all along the road as they were shot down and no one seems to be left in these parts to bury them. For twenty miles we pass the loathsome carcasses as they poison the air! Sometimes a dozen or more are seen lying in sight of each other indicating the places where the opposing forces made a stand.

During our march late in the afternoon, our commander became alarmed and took us off the main road through fields and by roads several miles out of the way, coming back again to the main road near Hanover Court House. We were hurried along at double quick to keep up with the cavalry which was riding at a trot. At last the limit of endurance is reached and the infantry begin to straggle until the line becomes stretched out over a mile in length; the commander rides back and drives the men along at the point of his sword. We continue at this rapid rate until late into the evening when at last the lieutenant commanding the infantry exclaims, "colonel may go to the devil with his bodyguard if he chooses, but I am going to take the responsibility to hold these men together and keep them in fighting trim in the event of an attack from guerrillas." His conduct certainly seemed reasonable, but the cavalry had soon left us and our hundred men were plodding along through the darkness alone with no definite idea of the proximity of friends or foes.

In pursuing our lonely way through the silent night near the edge of some woods, we are startled by hearing a voice ahead speak out sharp and clear, "Halt!" The order was obeyed instantly; then for a minute in the pitchy darkness all was silent as the grave, except the almost audible knocking of our hearts, as visions of guerrillas, ambuscades, Libby Prison and starvation rose quickly before our minds. Again the order comes, "Advance one man and give the countersign."

This sends our lieutenant forward; we have reached the cavalry outpost of the Army of the Potomac. Although without the countersign, an explanation of the situation permits us to pass and we are greatly relieved. Another mile of walking brings us to our infantry pickets; we drop down from sheer weariness by the side of the road on the damp ground in sight of the campfires of the main army a couple of miles away; soon I am lost is sleep after a march of more than thirty miles.

May 29

At daylight we start along hoping to find the colonel under whose command we were but do not find him. After a march of a mile and a half to the little village of Mangohick, we halt and get our coffee near the camp of General Wilson's[6] cavalry. This is the rear guard of the army which pushes every straggler and hanger on before them. We take up our march, and being inside the lines, we pursue our way quite leisurely. By noon we had reached Pippin Tree Ford on the North Anna River [Pamunkey River] where we overtake the wagon trains which were halted temporarily of the south side. Shortly after crossing the river our party separate, each man turning to hunt up his regiment as best he can.

I felt as lonely as a country boy in a great city plodding along on my own hook. I found a division of colored troops belonging to the 9th Corps[7] on the north bank of the Totopotomoy Creek, crossed on a pontoon bridge and passed a large camp of negro refugees. I now take my course toward the sound of the artillery and infantry firing which is incessant in a southwesterly direction. I saw General Hancock[8] at the head of his Corps which was marching to take a new position. Two miles further on and I come upon great bodies of troops working like beavers throwing up entrenchments. I now begin to realize that I am pretty nearly at the front, for I see only a short distance in front a strong line of skirmishers engaging the enemy. Constant inquiry reveals to me that I am in the midst of not less than three Corps.

My quest for the 21st among the hundreds of thousands was no easy task as they lay massed together, but not far from a typical southern farmhouse I found troops of the 9th Corps who told me that the 21st was not far off. What a busy noisy scene: the clatter of picks and shovels, the tramp of cavalry, the ringing orders from brigade officers and the hum of voices of the tired troops as they were gathered around campfires for their evening coffee and hardtack. It was sunset and brigade bands far and near were taking up the "Retreat," a thousand drums rolling out the various parts, the click of axes and crashing of falling trees and last but surely not least, the incessant rattle of musketry and occasional roar of artillery. All these gave me a thrilling and impressive sense of the active campaign in which the Army of the Potomac is engaged.

Wending my way in and out among the troops with the oft repeated question, "What regiment?" I at last received the answer, "21st Mass," and found myself at once in the presence of the familiar faces and my old comrades of Company A. Many of the well known faces have dropped out by death and wounds, or as prisoners since this fearful campaign has begun; and many new ones have been added as recruits that it doesn't seem quite like the old crowd with which I had campaigned so long. But I was quickly surrounded by the crowd of inquiring friends, and I experience satisfaction in at last getting back into my place among the old comrades, even though the aspect is foreboding and the retrospect is frightful. I was rejoiced to receive from Colonel Hawkes a package of home letters of which I had been deprived nearly a month.

I was considered FRESH (after my seventy mile forced march) and better prepared for a night on the skirmish line than the rest of the company; so in less than an hour after I had joined the regiment, I was out on the skirmish line some twenty rods in front of the breast works. It was nine o'clock and dark—only the flashing of the musketry lighted up the scene. Here our "First Relief" was deployed and kept step to the constant reports of the firing and whizzing of bullets, and I was once more a full fledged member of the Union Army.

May 30

At daylight the army was again in motion, and although ready to move, it was four or five hours before the 21st took up the line of march, awaiting the moving of other commands. At nine we marched half a mile, halting in the road near Bethesda Church where Generals Grant[9] and Meade[10] had their headquarters. Here we saw their staff officers sitting about under the trees in the pews which had been taken out of the church. At noon we move forward a short distance and again at various times during the afternoon, moving and halting but making little progress: evidently feeling the way to secure a good point of attack.

The skirmish line was active with occasional volleys of musketry, indicating attacks from one side or the other. And thus the day wore slowly away until five o'clock when Generals Burnside and Crittenden rode up to our brigade and ordered it forward in line of battle. General Crittenden[11] is the present commander of our division. We move forward behind the skirmishers, each brigade of the 9th Corps taking position under a brisk fire from the enemy. We are now not more than four miles [actually closer to 12 miles] from Richmond but with the rebel army vigilant, active and determined and planted between us and the city. It now seems to be a battle of giants in which human beings are but pygmies.

By sunset we have halted [Shady Grove Road] and the entire line of this part of the Union army seems to have become transformed to diggers. I was detailed with a large squad to go back to the Pioneer Brigade and get picks and shovels. Returning after dark, we passed through the camp of the Indian sharpshooters. As they were seen by the dim light of their small campfires in the midst of some tall pines behind low breast works, the picture brings vividly to mind the schoolboy studies of the early history of our country. We all work busily until far into the night, throwing up entrenchments. I lie down in the trench prepared to get a short nap but was soon disturbed by an attack from the enemy in our front; they evidently intended to force back our picket line, but the attack was repulsed.

May 31

By morning, very respectable breastworks had been thrown up, although the work had been done under difficulties; continual firing and whiz of bullets made us willing to keep our heads down. The country appears quite level in our vicinity with scattering forests which afforded opportunity for the movement of troops on either side without being discovered. Sometime before noon our line of skirmishers were pushed forward but were driven back. Then the 1st Brigade was sent out, and they were repulsed with losses.

Word was brought in that Corporal Lander[12] had been shot on the skirmish line. Dr. Oliver[13] and two assistants climbed over the breastworks and soon returned bearing on a stretcher the dead body of brave Lander. He was shot through the heart while going from one post to another, performing the duties belonging to him. The spot where he fell was in plain sight of the rebel lines which made it perilous for anyone to go after the body, but one of the pickets jumped out of his rifle pit, ran and grabbed the body by the heels, dragging it back to his hole. I went out at night on picket and was stationed at the same post where Lander was killed; consequently I am close by the Johnnies and do not feel at all lonesome.

June 1

The day opens hot. At light our skirmish line was advanced a dozen rods where we throw up a rail shelter. This point is not quite so exposed to the fire of the rebel sharpshooters, but we are right underneath the rebel post so are able to pass the compliments of the day. The line which we vacated was occupied at one by the 3d Division, which throw up very strong breastworks of logs.

Early in the afternoon the rattle of musketry opened with a vengeance some distance away on our right. Then the artillery opened a rapid fire, signifying a general engagement in that part of our line. Just after we had been relieved at dusk and were returning to the main line, the rebels advanced in line of battle toward us. Captain Howe, who had charge of the retiring picket, immediately formed us in line of battle behind the new entrenchments occupied by the 103d New York. We had not long to wait in the gathering darkness; the enemy notified us of their approach through the thick woods by a long sheet of flame from a thousand muskets and the familiar rebel yell. They were only a few yards away, but from our strong protection we were unharmed and Captain Howe rose up quickly after their volley and gave us the order, "Fire!" Our aim was sure and the volley effective for they immediately fell back out of sight.

We returned to the regiment which had just returned from digging and had received a fire from the right, wounding several and killing Warren Clark. Jack Reynolds was mortally wounded by a shell fired from one of our guns; the shell burst right over our regiment and a piece as large as my hand had torn open his bowels, showing a ghastly wound. Poor Jack was carried back to our wagon train where he died before morning and so another of my old Company A comrades was taken from us.

*   *   *

Twelve

Captured at Cold Harbor

The Second Brigade of Thomas L. Crittenden's division, to which the 21st Massachusetts belonged, underwent a series of command changes during May and early June. Lieutenant Colonel Gilbert Robinson replaced Col. Daniel Leasure on May 14, and was himself replaced on the last day of the month by Col. Joseph M. Sudsburg. The confused state of affairs is evident by the fact that George Hitchcock believed that Colonel Leasure was still in command of the brigade on June 2. Colonel Sudsburg was replaced on June 4.

On June 2, 1864, Ambrose Burnside's IX Corps was positioned on the far right of the Union army line. The left of Burnside's line was formed near Bethesda Church, three miles northwest of Cold Harbor and adjacent to Warren's V Corps. Since a one-mile gap existed to the left of the V Corps, General Meade ordered Warren to extend his troops to the left, closing the interval between himself and Maj. Gen. William F. "Baldy" Smith's XVIII Corps. General Burnside was ordered by General Meade to "move simultaneously with General Warren so as to keep massed in rear of his right," thus consolidating the Union line and preventing any flanking movements by the Confederates. Confederate troops from Maj. Gen. Robert E. Rodes' and Maj. Gen. Henry Heth's divisions attacked the V and IX Corps during this redeployment, when Maj. Gen. Thomas L. Crittenden (who had succeeded General Stevenson as commander of the First Division of the IX Corps), prematurely recalled his pickets. Rodes' Division went into action on the right of Heth's Division. The Second Brigade of Crittenden's division, which was in the rear during the redeployment, was attacked by General Heth's troops.

Assistant Adjutant General Charles J. Mills, Crittenden's division, wrote to his mother:

> *Our Corps was on the extreme right, and the movement therefore should have been prompt and speedy, and the pickets not drawn in till we were well started. Instead of this they were drawn in before our rear had left, and we hadn't got more than half a mile, when the enemy came, right in our rear and we had a pretty sharp thing for about an hour; our Second Brigade [21st Massachusetts, 100th Pennsylvania and 3d Maryland regiments] got badly cut up.*

Colonel Elisha Marshall, commander of the Provisional Brigade (later the Third Brigade) in Crittenden's division and the only officer in the division to submit a report, noted that before any troops could be put into position the Confederates advanced rapidly upon the pickets, taking many prisoners. Marshall continued: "The enemy rapidly drove in our pickets, and owing to the fact that there was a gap between the Ninth [Burnside] and Fifth [Warren] Corps on the left of the Second Brigade, the enemy flanked our lines, and consequently caused the retirement of the Second Brigade."

Lieutenant Colonel George P. Hawkes, 21st Massachusetts, wrote in his diary that the regiment "remained until 4 p.m. [the movement by the IX Corps commenced about one in the afternoon according to Colonel Marshall] when the 9th Corps was to change position in order to unite on the right and rear of Warren's Corps. The rebels took advantage of our movement and made an attack on our rear. We had the hardest shower here I ever seen."

In his memoirs, Confederate Lt. Gen. Jubal A. Early stated that in the afternoon on June 2:

> *Rodes' Division moved forward, along the road from Hundley's Corner toward Old Church, and drove the enemy from his entrenchments, now occupied with heavy skirmish lines, and forced back his left towards Bethesda Church, where there was a heavy force. Gordon swung round so as to keep pace with Rodes, and Heth co-operated, following Rodes and taking position on his left flank In this movement there was some heavy fighting and several hundred prisoners were taken by us.*

Major General Henry Heth offered a slightly different version of the event: "Near Bethesda church I struck the IX and V Federal Army Corps. General Early was on my right." According to Heth, he told Early "that the enemy was withdrawing from my front, and that I had already given orders to attack. We drove the enemy to the entrenchments he had thrown up near Bethesda church." Heth also recalled that his men, and not Rodes' had led the way: "But

*as Rodes failed to advance, my right flank became fearfully exposed and I gave
orders to my brigade commanders to fall back."*

Although the bloody little affair barely warranted mention in the official
records, the 21st Massachusetts Regiment suffered 47 casualties that afternoon:
13 killed, 21 wounded and 13 captured. One of those taken prisoner was
George Hitchcock.

*   *   *

June 2

All the earlier part of the day was unusually quiet for us who had become
accustomed to rattle and rumble and roar. The oppressive stillness was in the
atmosphere as well upon the army like that which precedes a thunderstorm. The
heat being oppressive and the thinning out of our ranks so many familiar faces
conduced to make us unusually silent. But the spell was broken in the afternoon
by orders for us to move out of our breastworks by filing right and crawling on
hands and knees. This we did until we reached a point where it seemed as if we
could retreat without discovery. In this way the whole 9th Corps had been
withdrawn from their entrenchments and was rapidly and silently moving back
to be put in some new position.

When a half a mile away from our old position, our division halted for our
skirmish line to be brought in. While waiting for them, a heavy thunderstorm
broke over us. Simultaneously with the crack and roar of heaven's artillery came
the same sound from the enemy's line which had followed us, and as the minie
balls whizzed about us, we realized we were attacked in the rear. The place
where we were halting was on a large open plain with a chain of hills covered
with woods lying back and beyond, a quarter of a mile distant.[1]

Out of these woods came the long lines of graybacks advancing to attack
us. In less time than it takes to write it, the whole Corps had "about faced" and
was swinging into lines of battle and began charging toward the enemy and the
woods. As we advanced, a withering fire met us from our right front, while a
long line of graybacks were seen hurrying around toward our left with evident
intention to flank our brigade: for our brigade commander, either through
drunkenness or cowardice, had failed to keep his line back and joined to the rest
of the division.

At last it was halted on the open field near a point where the ground sloped
away in front. Here the brigade laid down and poured volley after volley into the
enemy close in our front. But soon the flanking force opened on our left and

swept us with a destructive fire. Our brigade was now receiving the concentrated fire from three directions, and although we had given as good as we received, the knowledge that we were virtually without a leader served to weaken the unity of spirit.[2] Men were being mowed down like grass, and having no protection from the deadly fire, it is not strange that our line melted away.

A part of the 48th Penn first retreated; the contagion spread and our 21st, which I had never before known to do so, broke—the men running like frightened sheep. Colonel Hawkes and a few of our officers tried to hold them back and for a few minutes a small body held together around the colors. But at last Colonel Hawkes jumped up and said, "Come on boys," and away we all fled. It was a rout. With a field swept as was this, it was "Every man for himself and the devil take the hindermost." Where our men went I knew not. Some dodged behind fences—all took to the first shelter offered. I was unfortunate in having two large boils (the result of my sickness); both were on my legs and one on the cords under my knee. This made locomotion difficult and painful so that I couldn't keep up with the rest. Seeing some of the men leap over a fence, I supposed this was our rallying point so I dropped into a rifle pit a few rods away, expecting to be able to join the rest when the line was reorganized. The hole where I lay was hardly more than a foot in depth shaped and like a grave, but it was sufficient to hide me, although half filled with water from the deluging rain which had just fallen. I hugged the ground and listened to the pandemonium of sounds. I realized what it was to be between the lines in the midst of a great baffle.

The artillery playing from all the heights around seemed to be directing its fire to the spot where I lay. Shell after shell in rapid succession exploded over and around me, tearing up the ground and covering me with dirt. Volleys of musketry from all directions swept over me. Once when there came a lull, I raised my head to ascertain the situation when "thud," "thud" came two bullets, striking within a foot of my head. This gave me the uncomfortable feeling that I was watched.

I know not how long I laid here; minutes seemed hours. As dusk began to settle down, I wondered why our lines did not charge as the musketry had ceased suddenly. I was conscious of hearing the murmur of many voices and knew that an advance was in progress, but from which direction I could not distinguish. The sounds grew more distinct and I heard the orders from the various commanders, preparing their men for the charge. Then I raised my head to look toward our line, when to my horror I found the sounds came from the opposite direction and long lines of graybacks were sweeping across the plain right over my living grave. To run away now appeared to me to be the height of folly for they were within a couple of rods of me; so I rose up and at once received the order from one of the officers to "Surrender!" which I did by pointing to my gun which laid half buried in the mud and water. Thus, I became a prisoner of war.

It is foolish to "cry over spilt milk" or to say what might have been done. With a private soldier as I was, the opportunities to know or judge of the various movements on a bafflefield is impossible, and the danger in becoming separated from my command was only fully realized after I was captured. Running the gauntlet alone at any time after our regiment broke seemed to me to be instant death. I quickly realized the terrible misfortune which had come to me, and it was with anguish that I kept saying to myself, "why didn't I keep up a little longer with the boys and be saved." The officer who ordered me to surrender I learned afterward was a colonel of a North Carolina regiment. (The brigade was commanded by Brigadier General Stephen D. Ramseur [Colonel William R. Cox] and was composed of the 2nd North Carolina Regiment led by Colonel William R. Cox, 4th North Carolina Regiment led by Colonel Bryan Grimes, 14th North Carolina Regiment led by Colonel R. Tyler Benneff, and 30th North Carolina Regiment led by Colonel Francis M. Parker. They were in Major General Robert E. Rodes' Division in the 2nd Corps under Lieutenant General Richard S. Ewell.)[3] This colonel immediately detailed a man from the ranks to take me to the rear.

As I passed through their ranks, one or two insulting salutations greeted me which I took no notice, but as the whole affair took place while their line was in motion, they were too busy to notice me. As soon as I was divested of my equipments, I was hurried to their rear over the ground we had just passed in our advance. Here I saw rebels busy in disrobing our dead and wounded. This was not a time for remonstrance, although I felt indignant for the rebel line was just uttering their yell as they charged against our boys and a thick storm of "minies" rattled all about; messages from home they seemed to me as I was rapidly hurried back out of range of our fire.

Darkness and a drizzling rain had settled down upon us as we tramped through the woods. All through the woods the rebel forces were massed and were being hurled against our lines, as the incessant raffle and thunder indicated. The narrow road was crowded with batteries hurrying up to the front or to new positions. Ammunition trains and ambulances were all drawn by mules. An opposite stream of ambulances was pressing back to the rear laden with wounded accompanied by crowds of "skedaddlers" and prisoners. As I went back over the breastworks which I had helped to build and seeing now from a new standpoint, I felt as if defeat had surely come to our army and despondency made the gloomy situation all the more terrible. I thought that I was now about to face the horrors which rumor had already made familiar to me.

After tramping a mile, I was delivered into the charge of a provost guard which had already received about a hundred prisoners—mostly from my own brigade as I soon ascertained. A rebel officer seeing my fine rubber blanket came up and ordered me to hand it over to him. I appealed to my guard to save it for me, but he declined to interfere. Pushing forward through mud and darkness, hardly a word passed between fellow prisoners; each one was too fully occupied with the gloomy thoughts of our present uncomfortable situation and of our very dark future prospects. We dragged along for three miles and were turned into an open field like a drove of cattle; we laid down in the wet ground and passed the night.[4]

June 3

When morning broke, I raise my head and look over the field to find it covered with bluecoats. Many had been brought in during the night so that our company must have numbered a thousand or more. I soon find Jim Miller[5] and nine others of our regiment—all of whom were taken to a log hut where they found shelter.[6] Charley Wilder was wounded and taken prisoner but was carried past our procession last night—probably into some hospital in Richmond so we have lost track of him.[7]

A sorry looking set of fellows we were but it was a comfort to see the familiar faces of our 21st boys. Clothes all soaking wet as well as all the remaining food in my haversack. The morning dark and cloudy; many of our number wounded with limbs or heads bound up; we stood or sat around in the mud watching the new order of things Not many rebels were seen near us excepting the strong guard which surround the field. Soon the roar of artillery and rattle of musketry announced that the two lines were hotly engaged some two or three miles away [Battle of Cold Harbor].

But starting out early a long string of "fresh fish" we were, nearly half a mile in length. Taking at first a northeasterly direction, we passed directly by the headquarters of General Robert E. Lee at Mechanicsville, a crossroads village. Although we were moving away from our lines, the sounds of baffle increased as the day advanced and the faint hope was felt that perhaps our lines were pressing back the enemy and we might yet be released through necessity—futile hope. Striking the Fredericksburg and Richmond Railroad on the northerly side of the city, we follow along its track and cross Chickahominy Swamp at Meadow Bridge; here we passed the old works of General McClellan, thrown up during his Peninsula Campaign two years ago, showing how near our army came to Richmond. After a march of ten miles in a roundabout way, we reached the outside fortifications of the city—four miles west of the city.

Here our crowd of prisoners were searched by a provost guard, and after a halt of four hours, went on; the sounds of the artillery firing still continued but were fainter and our hopes were correspondingly low. We passed through the suburbs of the city which nature had endowed with surpassing beauty but stern war had forced the enemy to sweep away the groves and foliage until a large portion of the surrounding country was a desolate waste. We arrive in sight of the spires and turrets of the long looked-for and fought-for city as the hot afternoon sun shone out upon it. We look at it across a great barren plain unobstructed by fence, tree, bush or anything which could hide or shelter a man. Across this plain which ran around the city apparently, we could see the black muzzles of many heavy guns a mile beyond. Such formidable fortifications seemed insurmountable and were well calculated to hold back our army if it should succeed in getting so near the city. But we pass by them finding them "manned" by boys and officered by a few "kid glove" fellows who were doubtless "too nice" to come into any closer contact with the vile northern mudsills.

Approaching the city from the northwest, almost the first buildings of any importance which we see are the State Almshouse and the Capitol building of the Southern Confederacy. We march directly by and watch with great interest the rebel stars and bars which floated above as the symbol of this atrocious rebellion while at the same moment we could hear the deep rumble of the cannon which signifies death, destruction and bitter anguish all over our fair land. We have little time for moralizing as we trudge down through the crowded streets. Our party was evidently an unusually large one judging by the hilarious sport which the thronging populace indulged in at our expense. The boasted chivalry of the South was shown by all manner of hootings, jeers and ridicule heaped upon our poor hungry, tired, dusty, defenseless procession. Occasionally one of our number had the spirit to give a good retort, but for the most part we were content to watch the faces and surroundings of this long sought for city. Many of the business houses flaunted the sign, "Fresh arrival of blockade goods," which indicated the chief source of their supply and maintenance.

After crossing the city we arrived at our destination: the great tobacco warehouse called Pemberton Prison—now used for receiving Union prisoners.

This was situated on Cary Street, directly opposite another large tobacco warehouse used for the same purpose, called Libby Prison—both overlooking the James River. Here six hundred of us were stowed away in three great low damp dirty rooms. The privies at the end of each room were open all the time, having no doors and emitting an abominable stench, almost suffocating. So this is the falling of the curtain, the closing of the book of our part in the great drama for the present at least.

Notice was served on us that any one caught looking out of the windows, either sitting in or leaning out, would be instantly shot. A young Kentuckian was shot yesterday because he was standing too near a window; no warning was given him but a bullet lodged in his shoulder. This is a warning we are all careful to heed. As the day waned, we had laid ourselves out in some sort of order on the floors in long lines; each floor full of prisoners was summoned to go down stairs where the rebel lieutenant in charge with several assistants searched each man separately. All extra clothing, knapsacks, haversacks, canteens, money, pocket knives and valuables were taken from us.

I was allowed to keep an old case knife; also my little, water soaked, pocket Testament they vouchsafe to return to me as something which they surely could have no use for, but for which I was most grateful. My pocket diary was closely inspected, but I suspect the chirography was too deep for them to unravel and so I was permitted to retain that. The wearisome examination and robbery was not ended until midnight, and after making the gratuitous statement that all money and valuables would be returned to us when we were exchanged, the rebel officer allowed us to turn in for the night.

*   *   *

Georgia Railroads and the Campaign for Atlanta

1864

TENNESSEE

Knoxville
Kingston
Campbell's Station
Loudon
Sweetwater
Athens
Charleston

Chattanooga

Cleveland

NORTH CAROLINA
GEORGIA

Spartanburg
Greenville

Ringold
Dalton **Battles for Atlanta** *May-September*

SHERMAN
Rome
Resaca
Cassville

Kennesaw Mt.
Allatoona
Marietta
Dallas

JOHNSTON / HOOD
Atlanta
East Point
Jonesboro
Madison

Athens

Columbia

From Camp Lawton, Hitchcock is shipped to Florence, S.C.

GEORGIA RAILROADS
1. Western & Atlantic
2. Atlanta & West Point
3. Macon & Western
4. Georgia
5. Georgia Central
6. Southwestern
7. Savannah & Gulf

Griffin

SHERMAN
La Grange

Augusta

"March to the Sea" *Begins November 16*

Milledgeville

William J. Hardee retreats into S.C.

Griswoldville
Macon
Millen

Auburn
Columbus
Dublin
Swainsboro
Statesboro

Prior to Sherman's March, Hitchcock is transferred on Nov. 2 to Camp Lawton, near Millen, Ga.

ANDERSONVILLE
George Hitchcock imprisoned here

HARDEE

Savannah
Occupied December 21

N

Americus
Cuthbert

GEORGIA

Dorchester

Douglas

Albany
Dothan
Blakely
Moultrie
Brunswick

Marianna
Bainbridge
Thomasville
Valdosta

FLORIDA

Atlantic Ocean

Tallahassee
30 MILES
Lake City
Jacksonville

ALABAMA

Mark A. Moore

Thirteen

Prisoner of War

*While George Hitchcock was headed toward Richmond as a prisoner of
war during the predawn hours of June 3, Union troops began a full-scale
frontal assault against the strongly entrenched Confederate lines at Cold
Harbor. The attack was cut to pieces almost as quickly as it began, and many of
the Southerners later stated that they were not even aware a serious
coup-de-main had been attempted. Union casualties were appalling. More than
5,000 men were killed and wounded in less than thirty minutes, and another
2,000 more would be listed under one of those categories before the dreadful
day ended.*

*The battles Lee and Grant waged while moving across the Virginia
countryside locked in a deadly grasp generated thousands of prisoners of war.
A recent Union proclamation created a special set of problems for these
unfortunates. From late July 1862 to November 1863, captured soldiers were
either exchanged or paroled on their oath of honor not to bear arms against
their captives. Irresolvable disagreement over the exchange system led in late
October 1863 to the cessation of prisoner exchanges. In December 1863, there
were more than 13,000 Union prisoners in Richmond: 6,300 confined on Belle
Island, a small island in the James River, with the others imprisoned in tobacco
warehouses known as Libby, Crew's, Pemberton's, Smith's and Scott's.
Brigadier General John H. Winder, who had graduated from the United State
Military Academy at West Point in 1820, was responsible for the supervision of
the prisons in Richmond.*

Since there was a limited number of prison guards, the people of Richmond were apprehensive about an uprising by the Union captives. General Lee realized that the prisoners in Richmond posed a problem to the Confederacy. They added to the acute shortage of food and clothing, increased the cost of food for civilians, overburdened the limited transportation system and endangered the city from attacks by Union raiders. As a result, he recommended that prisoners be sent to "some point or points in the deep south" where there was little chance of attack and where wood was cheap and provisions abundant. In late December, Andersonville, Georgia, was selected as the best site for a stockade to accommodate 10,000 prisoners.

Two events hastened the removal of prisoners from Richmond to Andersonville. On February 9, 1864, 109 officers escaped from Libby by digging a 57-foot tunnel to a shed near the prison.. The escape was remarkably successful for only forty-eight of the escapees were recaptured. The mass breakout was followed on February 28 to March 3 by a Union raid on the capital by Brig. Gen. H. Judson Kilpatrick and Col. Ulric Dahlgren. The two officers each led a column of horsemen with the avowed objective of liberating prisoners and creating as much havoc as possible. It is also possible that the raiders intended to set fire to the city and assassinate President Jefferson Davis and members of his cabinet. The event itself was not successful. Dahlgren was killed outside the city and the failure of the two columns to unite doomed the expedition to failure.

On February 17, The Richmond Dispatch pleaded for the removal of the prisoners. The first group of captives sent south, 200 men in four boxcars, left Richmond on February 18 and arrived at Andersonville on February 24. Four hundred prisoners a day were sent to Georgia for the next few months. Between May 5 and June 4, more than 8,000 Union prisoners of war, captured in the Wilderness, at Spotsylvania, North Anna, Totopotomoy Creek, Bethesda Church and Cold Harbor, passed through Richmond en route to Georgia. By the end of June, there were 26,367 prisoners at Andersonville, including George Hitchcock, in a stockade designed to hold only 10,000 men.

*   *   *

June 4, 1864

We were divided into messes of twenty men each and drew our first ration. Some of our number had been without food for three days. I had eaten nothing for twenty-four hours. We are given a piece of very coarse corn bread and a concoction called bean soup—composed of a gill [quarter of a pint] of muddy water, a couple of beans and a dozen bean-bugs floating on the top. But we eat it with a relish.

June 5

We were joyfully surprised with the information that we could send letters home and in a short time our room had the appearance of a crowded country writing school minus desks. I wrote to Colonel Hawkes and home but was careful to write nothing that I thought might endanger it being sent through the rebel lines. I drew the same kind of rations as yesterday. Begin to feel the need of outdoor air.

June 6

I catch glimpses of green fields stretching away beyond the James River southward and the sight is most inviting and tantalizing. The chief occupations in our crowded room today has been "skirmishing" for lice, reading Testaments and sleeping, but the hours are tedious and long. Our letters were sent down the river in a flag-of-truce boat.

June 7

The rebel lieutenant in command called the roll at half past seven. He expressed surprise that so many of the Yanks knew how to write; said he noticed the best penmen came from the New England states. I read my Testament and a sketch of Colonel James Gardiner[1] of the English Army, both of which served to keep my courage up. A lot of wounded rebel soldiers were carried past our prison. At night each man was called by name and marched across the street into Libby Prison where we spend the night.

June 8

A large crowd of prisoners was sent away to Georgia from our Pemberton quarters, and we were returned to them again. This time I was placed on the fourth floor. Feel very hungry.

June 9

We were aroused at three in the morning, took one days ration of corn bread and bacon, left our quarters under guard and turned our faces westward, marching down the long street past the great Tredegar Iron Works where most of the cannons and war materials are made; we cross the James River on a passenger bridge. Our interest while crossing was centered in the little island a short distance down the river called Belle Isle where a large number of our Union prisoners have been confined and suffered during the past two years.

At the village of Manchester across the river, a large number of us are packed away in old rickety freight cars—fifty men to each car. The day is hot and sultry and the doors are not allowed to be opened but a crack so the air inside is very stifling. Move away on the Richmond and Danville Railroad in a southwesterly direction, but as the rebel guard fill up the only opening at the doors, I can get no idea of the country through which we passed. At Burkeville Junction [Burke's Station] where the Lynchburg and Petersburg Railroad crosses, I caught sight of large stores and munitions awaiting transportation to Richmond. Reached and crossed the Roanoke River at dark.

June 10

Spent a sleepless night in the stifling car. Reached Danville at eleven o'clock in the forenoon where we disembark and march a short distance to the military prison—a more comfortable and cleanlier place than those we left at Richmond. We are now one hundred and fifty miles from Richmond near the North Carolina line. Drew rations and at dark we are again packed into cars smaller than those of yesterday but fifty to a car just the same. For quite a long distance our train moves very slowly over a new made road throughout the night.[2]

June 11

Just before daylight quite a scare among the occupants of our car was caused by the caving in of the top. It was a very dilapidated rotten affair and the weight of the guards, who were on the top, crushed it in. This crippled out the sides of the car, and the only way we kept them from falling over was by all hands holding them in place and supporting the roof with our arms and hands for several miles until we reached Greensboro. Those in charge of the train took no notice of the accident until we arrived at Greensboro where all changed cars, and we find better accommodations on a smoother road. The beautiful town was almost completely hid under the dense foliage of immense shade trees.

At noon our train passed through Salisbury where there is a military prison containing Union prisoners. Rain began to fall and continued through the afternoon and our train moves very slowly. At five we have reached Charlotte, North Carolina, one hundred and twenty miles south of Danville, Virginia. Here we are turned out like sheep into a rough wet field where we bivouac for the night and receive the usual ration. Laid down feeling very hungry and tired.

June 12

An east storm soaked us to the skin so we were cold and very uncomfortable. While remaining here through the day, Union prisoners were brought in and others were sent southward. Brisk trading was carried on all day between guards and prisoners, who had been fortunate in concealing money and valuables from the rebel robbers. The prices in Confederate money were at the rate of ten dollars per loaf of bread, three dollars per dozen for biscuit and onions at fifty cents apiece. We hogs had rooted up the ground until it had become very muddy so we moved to a drier spot to pass the night.

June 13

The day opened cold, rainy and cheerless. Left Charlotte at four in the morning for Columbia, South Carolina, crossing the Catawba River—a wide deep river. Passed through Winnsborough in the afternoon and arrived in the evening at Columbia, the capital of South Carolina—one hundred and ten miles from Charlotte. Our train was "switched off" two miles below the city where a ration of four round sea biscuits and a piece of pork was given to each prisoner. We were kept in the cars which remained stationary all night.

June 14

Continued cold and rainy. Started at four in the morning on the Branchville Railroad—found it very rough, hard riding [South Carolina Railroad from Columbia to Branchville and then to Augusta]. Rode nearly all day through a swampy country thinly inhabited. Crossed several small rivers reaching Augusta, Georgia, during the night after crossing the broad Savannah River. Rode a hundred and forty miles during the day.

June 15

A very agreeable change in the weather—the day opening warm and bright. We were kept very closely in the cars while remaining at Augusta until one in the afternoon when all were ordered out to get rations. I used my eyes for all they were worth while off the train. Saw quite a thrifty looking place and considerable building going on; the carpenters all appeared to be negroes, who hammered, sawed and planed in time to continual singing. Embarked on another train on the Georgia Central Railroad, which proved to be the smoothest road I have seen yet. Passed through very level, swampy country.

June 16

The day was cloudy. I slept soundly through the night and at four in the morning crossed the Ocmulgee River and arrived at Macon, a thriving city, one hundred and sixty miles from Augusta. Our route during the forenoon lay through immense swamps where trestle work was required for miles to carry the railroad. The thick heavy foliage, the towering pines adorned with pendant mosses and clinging parasites told us of the tropical region which we have now entered. Some of our number near the door saw a "copperhead," a deadly poisonous snake by the side of the train; that is the fit emblem of the cowardly northern sympathizer of the rebellion. At noon our train drew near our destination: Andersonville, Sumter County, Georgia—sixty miles due south from Macon in the southwestern part of the state placed in the midst of a level wilderness of pines.

*   *   *

The main gate at Andersonville, as drawn by George A. Hitchcock

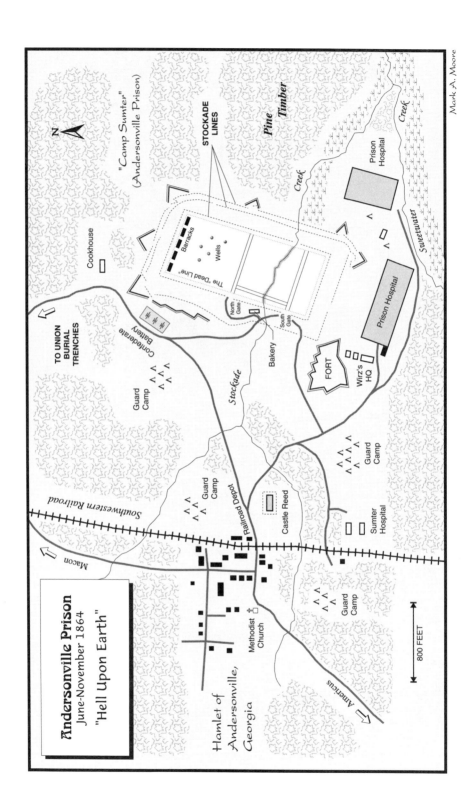

Mark A. Moore

Andersonville Prison
June-November 1864
"Hell Upon Earth"

Hamlet of
Andersonville,
Georgia

"Camp Sumter"
(Andersonville Prison)

STOCKADE
LINES

Pine Timber

Prison Hospital

Cookhouse

Barracks

Wells

The "Dead Line"

North Gate

South Gate

Bakery

Prison Hospital

FORT

Wirz's HQ

Confederate Battery

TO UNION BURIAL TRENCHES

Guard Camp

Stockade

Guard Camp

Sumter Hospital

Guard Camp

Railroad Depot

Castle Reed

Guard Camp

Southwestern Railroad

Macon

Methodist Church

Americus

800 FEET

Creek

Sweetwater Creek

N

"The teeth drop out—the jaws become set and a
general rotting process is the last stage"

Fourteen

Andersonville, Georgia

Andersonville was the largest military prison, North or South, established during the Civil War. It was officially called Camp Sumter. Located adjacent to the Southwestern Railroad—ten miles northeast of Americus and more than fifty miles southwest of Macon. Andersonville was populated by about twenty people when it was selected as a site for a prison. The hamlet included a railroad depot, church, store, cotton warehouse and a dozen dilapidated houses. The United States Post Office Department changed the name of the railroad depot from Anderson to Andersonville in 1856 to avoid confusion with Anderson, South Carolina.

The prison stockade was still not complete when the first Federal prisoners arrived in February 1864, and thus two pieces of artillery were deployed to guard its one open side. The stockade was completed by the third week of March. It covered more than 16 acres with a 17' log palisade in the shape of a parallelogram—780 feet by 1,010 feet. The ground sloped toward the center of the compound, where a shallow creek ran from west to east. Sentry boxes, called "pigeon-roosts," were located on platforms along the outside of the stockade. In late March a three-foot-high railing was constructed about 19 feet from the palisade. This warning line, better known as the "deadline," marked the point beyond which no prisoner was allowed to cross upon threat of death. Despite the abundance of timber in the vicinity of the camp, there were no buildings constructed inside the prison pen. A bakery was completed in May and located outside the stockade on the bank of the stream running through the prison. There were two entrances to Andersonville on the west side of the stockade—the North Gate and the South Gate. Earthen forts were constructed around the exterior to quell any prison riots and to defend against any mass attacks.

Lieutenant Colonel Alexander W. Persons of the 55th Georgia Regiment was replaced as post commander by Brig. Gen. John H. Winder on June 17, 1864, and served until October 9, when Col. George Gibbs assumed and held command until May 1865. Captain Hartmann Heinrich (Henry) Wirz, born in Zurich, Switzerland, was in command of the interior of the prison from March 27, 1864 to May 7, 1865, except for a convalescent furlough during August.

For administrative reasons the prisoners were divided into detachments, which made it easier to issue rations and maintain discipline. Each detachment, which numbered 270 men, was divided into three squads with a Union sergeant assigned to each. When rations were issued once a day, the sergeant distributed the ration to the three messes of his squad, and a sergeant of each mess distributed the rations to about 30 men.

When the time the prison opened in February until May 17, 1864, prison guards were assigned from regular Confederate units: 55th, 56th and 57th Georgia regiments, Leon Florida Artillery and the 26th Alabama. The prisoners were cognizant of this and the relationship between captor and captive was largely based on mutual respect. In May, however, this relationship deteriorated when the guards were replaced by the newly-formed 1st, 2d, 3d and 4th Georgia Reserves. Composed of young boys and older men, the reserves were poorly drilled, disorganized and inexperienced.

While the changing of the guard created some problems, the prisoners faced a more direct threat to their health from the lack of fresh water and the buildup of sewage. Although the creek originally provided clean drinking water, the prisoners had no choice but to use it for bathing as well as a latrine (called sinks by the soldiers). The slow moving stream also carried the waste from the Confederate camps outside the stockade as well as the bakery. East of the stockade the creek drained into a swamp caused by blockage from fallen timber, which generated a horrible odor and provided a breeding ground for mosquitoes and other vermin.

According to Confederate records, 45,613 Union soldiers passed through Andersonville. On August 8, 1864, there were 33,114 prisoners in the stockade—the largest number on any one day. Between February 1864 and May 1865, 12,912 prisoners died from disease, poor sanitation, malnutrition, overcrowding and exposure to the weather. During the course of just one day, August 23, 1864, 127 prisoners died—the largest number of recorded deaths over a 24 hour period. Diarrhea and dysentery accounted for fifty-nine percent of the deaths at Andersonville, while scurvy was the other major medical problem.

From May 22 through November 1864, a general hospital was located on three acres near the southeast corner of the stockade. Bed-less tents accommodated 2,000 patients in an area that the prisoners regarded as simply a stopping point between the stockade and the burial ground. Seventy-six percent of the hospital patients died. On June 30, thirteen doctors cared for 26,000 prisoners, and by August, with more than 33,000 prisoners behind Andersonville's walls, only four doctors were on duty. The others and half of the 24 hospital staff were on sick leave or "leave of indulgence." The excessive number of prisoners compelled the Confederates to enlarge the prison, and on July 1, the captives were redistributed into an enlarged stockade of more than 26 acres (the length of the palisade was expanded to 1,620 feet).

The Confederate guards also suffered ill effects from being stationed at Andersonville. In July and August, inspection reports noted that 66.4% of the Southern soldiers reported sick, with a mortality rate of 2.3%. In late July, a Confederate inspector general noted that of an aggregate force of 3,600 men: 647 were on sick report, 452 were without arms, 227 were on leave, 385 were absent without leave, 297 were on detached service and 48 were in the guardhouse. The remaining 1,544 officers and men were divided into three shifts to guard 30,000 prisoners.

Although there was gross mismanagement at Andersonville, the problems were almost unmanageable; Confederate leaders were unable to relieve the situation. They lived with the fear of small groups of prisoners escaping, fear of a general prison uprising, fear of escaping prisoners burning the neighboring towns and fear of Union raiders from Sherman's army. With but limited manpower available, the Confederates concentrated on reinforcing their defensive barriers rather than improving the sanitation facilities. In August they constructed a second barrier 90 to 150 feet beyond the main stockade to prevent prisoners from escaping and to provide resistance against attacks. The earthen forts surrounding the stockade were reinforced and a third stockade line, which was designed to provide a covered way for marching troops between fortifications, was started but never completed. Most of the prisoners were transferred to other locations by October and at the end of November 1864, there were only 1,359 prisoners remaining behind Andersonville's walls.

Former Andersonville guard George Glover, who was 15 years old during his tenure at Camp Sumter, wrote in 1908: "The people of Americus, ten miles away, were in constant dread—a terror which only the people who lived during those days of weeks and months can fully realize. They believed that should the prisoners make a dash and escape the stockade, Americus would be their first point of attack and the town would be burned." On August 13, 1864, Brig. Gen. John Winder reported on the status of the camp: "We have now here 33,000 prisoners of war, and more arriving almost daily. We are crowded to excess, and the mortality is very great—amounting to 633 in seven days. I think no more prisoners should be sent here if it can be avoided. I do beg that you press everything for the prison at Millen so that we may relieve this prison."

During the first week in October 1864, General Winder moved his headquarters from Andersonville to Camp Lawton near Millen, Georgia, then to Augusta, and finally to Columbia, South Carolina. Winder was named commissary general of all prisons east of the Mississippi River on November 21. He died suddenly of a heart attack on February 6, 1865, one day after his arrival to inspect the Florence stockade in South Carolina. Although Winder was criticized as a tyrant in the Southern press and vilified as the "inhuman fiend of Andersonville prison" in the North, he performed an impossible task with limited supplies and manpower. If he had survived the war, Winder probably would have been charged with war crimes for his treatment of Union prisoners.

The man most closely associated with Andersonville's horrors, Henry Wirz, "the demon of Andersonville," was executed on November 10, 1865, for war crimes. When prejudices nourished by a long war were greatly aggravated by the assassination of President Lincoln, Wirz's death was encouraged by vindictive politicians, an unbridled press and a nation seeking revenge. He was the only Confederate official put to death after the war.

*   *   *

Comments in 1890:

At first but little could be seen which indicated any presence of the great body of men known to be here: a few rough-board sheds for railroad purposes and a few scattering camps of rebel soldiers. Soon, however, we were made conscious of the presence of the ruling genius of the place. As the weary, cramped and homesick prisoners tumbled out of the cars, they were met by Captain Wirz,[1] a grizzly, dirty looking Dutchman whose head was adorned with a snarly mass of long, unkempt, wiry, gray hair surmounted by a shapeless, gray, military cap—much too small for his head. His face, what could be seen above a thick and tangled beard, was drawn out of human shape or appearance by scowls and wrinkles, presenting generally a very wolfish appearance. As he rode up and down the line on his white horse cursing the "damned Yankees,"

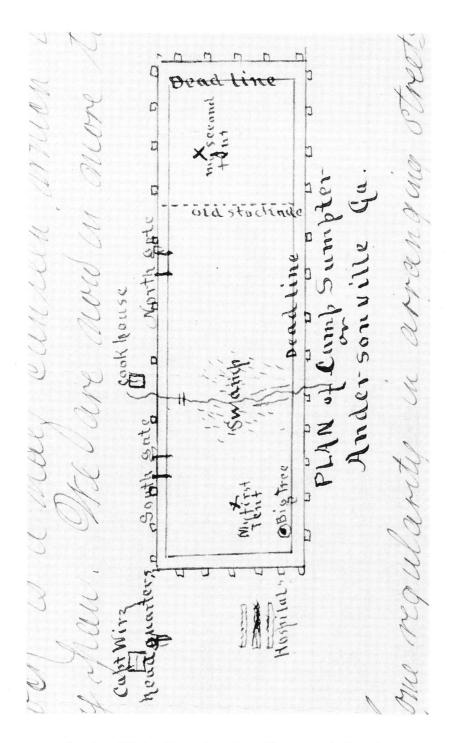

Location of Hitchcock's tents in Andersonville, as drawn by the author.

occasionally striking a prisoner with the slave driver whip in his hand, he appeared the incarnation of evil, the devil in human form.

June 16, 1864 [continued]

Our column of prisoners move a quarter of a mile up to the headquarters of Captain Wirz, a rough board shanty on a slight elevation which overlooks the prison pen. The huge stockade is seen sometime before we were able to discover its contents. Great pine logs planted upright in the ground standing twenty feet high fitting close together. Along the top at regular intervals were built little platforms for sentries. The prison pen is planted in the heart of a great pine forest with just space enough cleared to command the pen by the guard camps outside: one vast level circle of gloomy pine surrounding us on all sides. As we approach the place, a cloud of smoke hangs over all, rising from innumerable fires, through which we discern a dense black moving mass of humanity that reminding me of a great disturbed ant hill.

Our column stands in line for an hour or more while the blundering and ignorant rebel sergeants go through the ranks and attempt to enroll our names. We enter through the great double gates which shut us in from the world, and for the first time we are made to realize what are the horrors of the place of which rumor had already whispered to us. As we move slowly along through the pressing crowd of our fellow prisoners who are seeking for familiar faces, we see squalor and filth on every side. A terrible stench rises from the excrement which cannot be disposed of. One of the first remarkable features which I notice is the universal dusky, Afric hue of the faces of our men, excepting only those who have recently entered. This was caused by leaning over the lintel fires which each man must do in order to cook his ration with the pitch pine sticks. As soap is unknown here, the blackness soon becomes a permanent affair. We are assured that we shall look the same after a week or two; then I try to get away from the crowd; I work my way off toward the right among the lintel blanket shelters but do not succeed in finding a clear spot; crowds are everywhere.

Someone tells me I had better sit down where the first chance offers, and this I do for if I had waited until dark, I am assured that I could not find even room to stretch out. I squat in a lintel space with Jim Miller; he goes to hunt up the boys of the 21st, who were lost in the Battle of Spotsylvania.

Found Bailey and at last the mystery of his disappearance was explained, when on December 23d he was with the regiment advancing on skirmish line. He tells a story of hardship which makes the heart ache. While pushing through a dense thicket of underbrush, two Tennessee guerrillas suddenly pounced upon him and hurried him forward on a lonely path up over the mountains out of the way of our outposts and forced him to march ninety miles to Bristol, Virginia, from thence to Richmond where he was imprisoned in Belle Isle through the winter. Early in the spring he was brought down here when the stockade was first opened. He is troubled with scurvy and complains of the cold nights for he has worn out all his clothing; his only covering is a pair of worn out cotton drawers. His face and naked body are black as a negro from the smoke and his gaunt, bony body is fearful to look upon. A look of dull apathy was unbroken while he talked with us. He directed us to the spot where we found Osgood, Potter, and ten others of the 21st. OH, what a sorry looking set of fellows, so poor and emaciated, though prisoners but one month. The remainder of the day was passed in listening to their stories of the horrors which seem to be our inevitable lot.

We went back to our spot sadly out of spirits. Jim says, "I wish I was dead" and I—well I am glad my friends don't know how I am situated. When we lie down on our bed of sand, we are cautioned to "freeze" to our ration bags or we may lose them before morning; so we fasten them to our blouses and try to sleep. Jim wakes me at ten o'clock and we find rain falling. Sleep is banished for the rest of the night and morning finds us drenched to the skin.

June 17

We found three men who had just arrived from Sherman's army among whose assets was one woolen blanket. A partnership was formed composed of the following: William H. H. Martin,[2] 51st Ohio Regiment; George Middy,[3] 51st Ohio Regiment; Henry Clark,[4] 72nd Indiana Regiment; James Miller, 21st Mass Regiment; and George A. Hitchcock, 21st Mass Regiment. Two woolen blankets were sewed together and then several hours were required before sticks were found which supported our shelter. When at last it was up, we found that the only way in which we could all lie down under it was to lie "spoon fashion," all on one side; when one wanted to turn over, all had to go over with him. We were literally packed like sardines. By daylight we agreed to take turns walking around camp while the remainder found room to sit under the shelter.

There are now over twenty thousand prisoners[5] here and new ones arriving every day. The stench which pervades every portion of the camp is well nigh unendurable, but we are assured that we shall become accustomed to it in a few days. Great numbers are dying everyday, many of them from scurvy on account of the universal use of the flabby, greasy bacon-sides, which go by the name of sowbelly. At night we drew our first ration of rice and sowbelly. The rice was half-cooked and half a pint only. Our water supply comes from a small sluggish brook which flows through the center of the camp. The camps of the rebel guard are situated along its banks above us while just outside the stockade the cookhouse also contributes its share to the filth which flows into camp. The thousands of dippers constantly stirring up the muddy water near its entrance to camp sends the filthy mixture down upon hundreds of bathers and this is our only chance for cleanliness.

June 18

We are formed into the 83d detachment: each detachment is supposed to contain 270 men but death thins out the ranks fast. The 270 men are subdivided into three squads of 90 each. The only organization in camp allowed is the one man appointed from each squad to draw the rations for his 90 men. Each morning a rebel sergeant counts us up to see that none are missing. This morning when our roll is called, several could not be readily found so Captain Wirz tells us we shall have no rations until we find them. This seems like hunting for a needle in a hay mow, but hunger makes us keen and after awhile all are accounted for. The greatest interest centers in the man who draws our rations. So when late in the afternoon the wagons bring in the rations, all hands are out, watching our sergeant with greedy eyes.

The dreary monotony of the forest circling our camp outside finds its opposite in the ever moving crowd inside. A space of two or three acres through the heart of our camp along the bank to the brook is a treacherous impassable swamp where no one can go without sinking in out of sight. Here all the refuse matter settles and each morning a close inspection reveals a living, moving mass of corruption and worms, "born and bred" in a night, which the vertical rays of a torrid sun dry up by day and send out a deadly miasma. This is enough in itself to account for the terrible mortality which increases each day.

Several prisoners from Sigel's[6] West Virginia army came in today, many of whom had been wounded, and instead of being taken to hospitals, they were turned in here with wounds undressed and no opportunities to care for them. While outside after wood under guard, thirty-six prisoners escaped by over powering their guard, driving them along with them. Our rations today were corn bread (two inches square) and sowbelly

June 19

Very hot; heavy shower in the afternoon. A lot of prisoners from Sherman's[7] and Butler's[8] armies came in. Miller and Dyer of Company K are sick with diarrhea. I found Walter Lamb of the 25th Mass, who was taken prisoner June 1st at Drury's Bluff. Two men were shot by the sentry who was trying to kill another prisoner crossing the "dead-line." This dead-line is a small rail nailed to upright posts about three feet high, running around the entire camp inside the stockade—about twenty feet from it. Not a soul is ever allowed to cross it for any purpose whatever. The object is to keep our men from getting near the logs where they might easily dig and overthrow the guards and make a grand break for liberty. If a man through ignorance or otherwise even reaches across this for anything that may have been dropped or leans against it, he immediately becomes the target for the two or three sentries nearest him.

A prisoner was killed near by our shelter last night by falling into a well, either purposely or otherwise. These wells are being dug in all parts of camp, but as they have to be sunk so deep before water can be reached and only sticks and tin plates are used to dig with, it is only attempted by the most persevering ones. We have the rumor that Grant has got into Petersburg, Virginia.

June 20

Very hot until afternoon when rain began and continued incessantly several hours. Dyer is better and I am down with the same disorder. The sight of so many forms of suffering accompanied with my own illness makes my spirits pretty low.

June 21

Hot as ever and the usual shower in the afternoon. Another man shot on the dead-line today. The guard is composed of Georgia home guards, either old men or very young boys ignorant and cruel, unlike the average fighting rebel who has learned some spark of honor by contact with Union soldiers. These guards brought up under the blighting curse of slavery are so bigoted that they believe cruelty to be a part of their duty as soldiers. Over one hundred men died today, but their places were made good by a larger number who came in from Sherman's army.

June 22

Very hot! Rations of a pint of raw meal and a small piece of sowbelly. The tantalizing report of an exchange of prisoners to begin July 1st is supplemented by the additional fact that transports are enroute for Savannah to receive us. We long to believe it because the rebs tell us that the New York Herald says so.

June 23

Very hot. A lot of prisoners from Grant's army, taken at Petersburg, were brought in today. The Yankee propensity for trading is indulged in by the fortunate men who escaped the strict search which the Potomac boys underwent. A most aggravating display of eggs, biscuits, cucumbers, squashes, potatoes, beans and parsnips are seen for sale or trade. It is torture for the poor fellows who are dying by scores each day for want of these same luxuries. These are brought in by the rebel guards who are glad to exchange them for cash, pocket knives or military buttons. One of the unpleasant effects of the starving men is their brutish disposition. Men, who under any other circumstance would not be induced to quarrel, are continually falling into bickering and fights. Today there have been several knockdowns where clubs, razors and fists were freely used.

June 24

Very warm. Our ration for yesterday was mush and sowbelly. Today we only had raw meal and salt. We do not venture out from under our shelter for long, because the sun is scorching.

June 25

Very hot. Rations of raw meal and meat; but as I have no wood to cook with, I eat them raw. Am surprised to find how quickly hunger will force me to adopt a dog's life. "What to eat" is the supreme interest to every man in this place. All else is of second interest. I had a good wash in the creek but no soap. Rows are on the increase; all the devilish spirit seems to come to the front. First, a few loud words; then a rush of several men at each other and a sound of murderous whacks; when the crowd dissolves, bloody faces or blackened eyes show us how companions in misery can treat each other.

June 26

Prisoners from General Steele's[9] army came in. I washed my pants in the creek. Am feeling quite weak from diarrhea and am consequently "down in the mouth." This is the Sabbath but how unlike our quiet peaceful New England sabbaths! Poor starved men of all nationalities: men of no principle, bounty jumpers, "Dead Rabbits" from New York and "Plug Uglies" from Baltimore watching their opportunity to prey upon the sick and weak. Men crazy from their misery and men dying in all parts of the camp—all combine to make it a scene of horror which all will remember to their dying day. Shall I ever get out of this? And yet I know a good God has us under His keeping and I will trust him though the cloud is very dark.

June 27

Rumors of heavy fighting with Sherman's army. Prisoners from Grant's army came in. Two prisoners were brought in, who tunneled out ten days ago and had traveled over a hundred miles. They had lived on sweet potatoes chiefly, taken from plantations along their route. When near the Florida line, they were over taken by the bloodhounds and so they returned to camp refreshed with pure air and a change of diet. This tunneling has become so popular with our boys that the trained pack of bloodhounds are a necessity. Each morning we hear their deep baying as they make a circuit of the stockade followed by their mounted keeper. Whenever they strike a trail, they break into a fierce howl and the sounds gradually die away as they disappear in the woods. Several men were shot on the dead line-today.

June 28

Hot; heavy thunder shower in the evening. Six hundred prisoners from Grant's army came in—taken near Petersburg. Among them we found the familiar faces of Winn,[10] Stephens[11] and Tyler[12] of the 21st. Thirty Indian sharpshooters from northern Michigan were also among the number. I learn that poor Company A came out of the fight with only two men who were not either killed or wounded. I learn also that brother Henry has joined the regiment and is acting adjutant.

June 29

A soldier from Ohio, who laid sick with fever within arms length of me, died during the night. He was a large powerful framed man, full of vigor and health but death claimed him all the same. Showers in the afternoon; our ration today consisted of two quarts of meal. We don't dare ask any questions, but think it highly probable they have decided to fatten us to stock the pork market for the rebel army.

It has been discovered that the outlaws in camp, taking advantage of the lack of any discipline, have organized themselves into a league styled the "Raiders" for the purpose of robbery. This is partly the cause of so many rows; they take advantage by overawing any who resisted them. In this way matters have come to a terrible state during the past two days. Two men are known to be murdered by them. One of these was thrown into a deep well and his neck broken (I heard them during the night when the deed was done). Many have been knocked on the head and plundered; nearly all were known to have money, watches or other valuables. The rebel authorities have allowed the prisoners to form an organization of several hundred known as the "Police," who are armed with shillelaghs and are hunting down the devils. The afternoon has been one of great excitement as twenty or thirty of the raiders have already been secured and sent out.

June 30

Passed a sleepless night for the police and the raiders kept fighting all night long. The raiders realize that it is a fight to the death and they are desperate. The morning found the camp in the wildest excitement. Several were found concealed in one of the shanties under a pile of blankets and pine-boughs—buried with their booty. A persistent search was kept up all day, but at three in the afternoon the ring leader was unearthed from a shanty and only by the fiercest struggle could the police get him outside the stockade unharmed, so enraged were the prisoners. But Captain Wirz immediately ordered him back into camp—doubtless understanding what the result would be. As soon as he appeared, he was taken by the infuriated mob and from my standpoint saw a confused rush of men, the hurling of missiles and fifteen minutes later was told that his body was carried out mangled beyond recognition. We now feel a greater security for the ring must be effectually broken up. It is hinted that the remainder, who have been arrested, will be pardoned and sent back but that would hardly be safe with the present temper of the prisoners.

July 1

At noon an opening was made into the new stockade. The original one, inclosing about eighteen acres, had become so densely packed that when eight acres more were added to it, the crowd seemed as great as ever. Jim Miller and I left our western chums and went with our detachment into the new part. We found a member of the 34th Mass, Levi Shepard,[13] who had a rubber blanket, and we three go in together, using my woolen for a cover at night and a shelter by day while Shep's rubber is used to lie on. Jim has none but his share in the stock is a half canteen which is used as a fry-pan. We are now in more tolerable comfort. Some regularity in arranging streets was attempted, but as there was not half room enough, the streets were all taken up so that by night we are in as great a confusion as ever.

July 2

Very hot. The boys found occupation in securing pieces of the old stockade with which to make sticks for shelters and fuel. Many in the new part are digging up stumps and roots of the trees. I discovered an old acquaintance, a member of the 36th with whom I had tented at one time. He was captured near White House Landing while on his way to join his regiment on May 30th. Water is becoming very difficult to get and is very filthy. Owing to some mistake on the part of the rebel authorities, our squad drew double rations. Such good luck we are very careful to keep to ourselves for in the general demoralized state of our natures our honesty does not suffer us to return the extra ration.

July 3

Very hot. A general roll call through out camp. When our detachment answered, half a dozen members were missing who could not be accounted for so our rations were cut off for the day. "Virtue has its own reward" it is said, and so does vice for now our extra ration becomes very convenient.

July 4

Very hot. The glorious Fourth dawns upon this irrepressible community of free and enlightened patriots in captivity: free in spirit if not in body and enlightened as to the depth of human woe and cruelty. FEASTING is the order of the day. Of our pint of meal we had burnt meal for breakfast, mush for dinner and raw pork for supper.

A reorganization of detachments was made, owing to the rapidly thinned ranks by death. It is in this way that we had received more than our share of rations for the past few days, drawing dead-men's rations. Ours is now the 63d Detachment.

In place of the usual fireworks in the evening, our thirty thousand irrepressibles filled the night air with patriotic songs. "We will hang Jeff Davis to a sour-apple tree" was sung with great unction, but the chorus "Glory, glory, hallelujah!" rolled out gloriously from all parts of camp. Hardly had the sounds ceased when the "Star-Spangled Banner" was caught up and waved in a mighty chorus of song across the stockade into the EARS if not faces of the dastardly rebel hordes outside. For an hour or more, the enthusiasm of our boys kept the ball rolling. When the chorus "Down with the traitors" was being hurled into the ears of our captors, the cry was taken up, "Three cheers for Vicksburg and Gettysburg." Thus did the loyalty of our clipped wings find expression. Our impromptu celebration very aptly ended with GROANS for "Hog Winder" and "the Dutch Captain." The joyous notes of the inspiring songs died out in a wail of despair—most realistic and seeming to rise from the blackness of the world of woe. How many lives were going out and rebel hate becomes powerless to hurt.

July 5

Very hot but a strong breeze blows up from over the swamp. The report of a death by cholera creates hardly a ripple of interest, for death is busy in so many ways that cholera will have to fight for a chance, with scurvy, fever, diarrhea or dysentery. Rumor of the fall of Richmond on the 2nd.[14]

July 6

Very hot. More prisoners came in today. The camp is full of rumors of an exchange which is to begin tomorrow. I succeeded in securing an ax for a few moments with which I cut up some wood. My old case-knife has been my only wood chopper heretofore.

July 7

Very hot. Well, the day passed off with no exchange. Several "wood riots" and knockdowns have broken the monotony of the day. The "wood riot" is caused by a quarrel over the ownership of a stick of the precious wood which cannot be stowed away as can our rations, but by lying in a common pile it is not strange that proprietorship is often mistaken. The rebel quartermaster has issued axes to each detachment. This puts an end to the loaning of axes at fifty and seventy-five cents an hour which the bloodsuckers have been practicing.

July 8

Very warm. Several hundred prisoners from Grant's army and from James Island came in which made unusual commotion outside. One poor fellow of our squad died during the night. He had been sick with diarrhea and had no friends near him when he breathed his last. The sudden dropping away was doubtless owing to the great change of temperature from the hot day to a cold night. I found a largely attended prayer meeting near us in the evening. It was a most impressive sight to see the poor sick fellows crawl up to catch the words of earnest prayer which went up to our common Father. Men, who never had framed words into prayer, felt that a higher than human helper must be appealed to.

July 9

Very hot with shower in the afternoon. Another member of our squad died today. A large number of prisoners from Hunter's [15] West Virginia Army came in. They report that a large number of the 2nd Corps are on the way to this place. Andersonville seems to have become the general prison pen for all who are taken by the rebels.

July 10

Very hot with showers around us at night. More prisoners came in. The monotony of camp was broken by the parade of several camp-police having under guard three prisoners who had been stealing from their fellows. One side of their heads and faces were shaven bare, presenting a very comical appearance. This will make them marked men, and as if to make their punishment more adequate, the noisy unsympathetic crowd pelted them with stones and cudgels as they were hurried along, bearing on their backs the placard "Thief."

July 11

Another day of excitement. Seven hundred prisoners from Grant's army came in. Soon after noon timbers were brought into camp and a scaffold was erected near the south gate. At three in the afternoon the entire rebel garrison was paraded at conspicuous places in line of battle; their batteries, which are place on different sides so as to sweep the camp, were all manned. We all understood what was to be enacted; so when the hour of four o'clock arrived, every living soul, inside and out who could move, was watching for the entrance into camp of the six "raiders" who had been condemned to death. All the work, from the trial to the execution was performed by the Union soldiers, as the rebels would have none of the blame to rest on their heads. As the procession entered camp all was still as death. The condemned men climbed the scaffold, their spiritual wants were attended to by a Roman Catholic priest [Father Peter Whelan]. Meal-bags were then drawn over their heads and the ropes adjusted about their necks. Then, in the presence of more than forty thousand spectators, at a given signal the drop fell and five souls went struggling into eternity. The rope on the sixth man broke, and falling to the ground, he gave a bound and was away like a frightened deer overs tents, smashing in the frail shanties in his race of despair. He reached the swamp where he floundered about in the deep mire, begging most piteously for his life, but after a few moments he was retaken, brought again to the scaffold and this time launched into eternity. One man was from a Rhode Island regiment, one from New York, one from New Jersey, one from Pennsylvania and two were marines. There is now a feeling of greater security than there has been for a long time for all feel that the spirit of outlawry has now been effectually suppressed, but I hope never to witness another scene like this.[16]

July 12

Showers around us have cooled the air so that it is quite comfortable. Six hundred prisoners from Grant's army came in among them was Allen[17] of the 36th Mass from Baldwinville. I bathed in the muddy creek in the evening. Prayer meetings every pleasant evening and very largely attended; the poor fellows realize their need of a higher than human helper and their condition leads many to put their trust in the Lord.

July 13

Very warm but cloudy. An extra ration of rice was dealt out to all in camp but no salt to go with it. Two men were shot on the dead-line and a third was fired at. There are now one hundred and ten full detachments in camp, of two hundred and seventy men in each beside several thousand who are in the hospitals outside. These hospitals are nothing more than rough covered sheds—no bunks or beds or comforts of any kind.

July 14

Warm in the forenoon but cloudy in the afternoon. Several were shot on the dead-line during the day. These were newcomers who were ignorant of the deadly nature of the dead-line and who trespassed beyond it to secure either a green twig or something that had been thrown into the vacant space. No one who has not been in so crowded a place can realize the fascination of the clear space beyond the dead-line. It is also asserted that a thirty-day furlough is given to every sentry who kills his man on the dead-line.

The sergeants of the detachments were called to the gate and informed that "grape and canister" would be poured into camp without any further warning if large crowds collect or any unusual commotion occur. The rebel guard was ostentatiously paraded in view of camp and two guns fired. All indications point to a general fear on the part of the rebs of an "uprising" by the outraged prisoners. "A guilty conscience needs no accuser."

July 15

A few cripples and bummers from Sherman's army were sent in. It is stated that the rebs have suspicions of a tunnel of large dimensions being nearly ready through which a large body of men can quickly escape and overpower the guard. A search is being made to find it. A petition has been circulated for signatures to send to our government, praying for a speedy release. However, there is another party which will have something to say to that; meanwhile, death will do its share in the release of prisoners.

July 16

Two tunnels have been discovered; one tunnel runs fifty yards beyond the stockade and would have doubtless proved a great success if the place had not been betrayed by a 7th Maine fellow, who sold his brethren for an extra "mess of pottage." Jim Miller has gone in with Osgood so Shep and I have the tent to ourselves.

July 17

Last night was very chilly but today is warm. The 7th Maine traitor was hunted down by the police and put to torture; one side of his head was shaved and with the placard "Traitor" on his back, he was paraded throughout camp being most unmercifully beaten by the justly indignant prisoners. A most unwelcome change of rations—molasses in place of meat.

July 18

The night was so cool we slept with our tent folded about us. Another man killed on the dead-line; said to be done by the accidental discharge of the sentry's gun. Prisoners who came in today report that Montgomery, Alabama,18 has been burnt by a federal raiding party.

July 19

Very hot. Hog Winder has allowed six men to go to Washington to present the petition to Lincoln.[19] The men were chosen by a committee of twenty prisoners. Wonder if they will want to come back again. The raiding party is said to be moving in our direction with the intention of affecting our release.

July 20

The rebels have become thoroughly alarmed. Negroes have been pressed into service and are throwing up fortifications all around camp. Raw militia is being hurried in on the railroad. Two prisoners were discovered just as they were emerging from the outside end of a tunnel and shot; several others had already escaped. Webster,[20] who has been our detachment sergeant, was removed from the position and Mumford[21] appointed in his place.

July 21

The Johnnies have been very active outside and trains have been running all day and night. A few prisoners taken near Atlanta came in. Molasses instead of meat was again issued. It acts like poison on all who are troubled with diarrhea so there is a great amount of trading. Men exchanging it for anything eatable.

July 22

Three hundred prisoners from Grant came in who were captured on the 29th of June. Work on the fortifications continues but not so many troops came in today. Several tunnels partly dug were discovered. Sentry fired at a man near the dead-line but missed him.[22]

July 23

Cloudy and comfortable; rations of cornbread, sowbelly and salt. "Raiding" has been going on and several fights occurred but the police are vigilant.

July 24

Last night was very cold and the day very hot, which increases the mortality. Rations of rice and sowbelly. Today is the Sabbath.

July 25

Last night was the coldest of the season. I could not sleep and so laid awake listening to the coughs and groans from all directions. I have a canker in my throat which is painful. More tunnels were discovered by the rebs which shows how desperate our boys have become for it is no easy task to dig a hole several rods underground without shovel or pick with the danger of having the earth cave in behind you and bury alive all who may be inside. Rations of rice but no salt to go with it. With the one supreme, ever present thought of something to eat, I go up and down through camp and see watermelons, apples, eggs, doughnuts, berry pies and biscuits exhibited for sale, but no one has any money and the sight of them is torture.

July 26

Cloudy and rain. I have taken cold and my throat is quite sore. Rations are raw meal and sowbelly.

July 27

I have been a soldier two years. Four hundred men from Grant and Sherman came in today. Several of these were one hundred day men whose time had nearly expired; one of these while reaching under the dead-line after clear water was shot dead and his brains blown into the water. I traded off my pork ration for cayenne pepper with which I treated my throat; canker is very painful.

July 28

Hot. Shower in the afternoon. I have great difficulty to talk and eat on account of the canker in my throat. Seventeen hundred prisoners from Sherman came in. During which time the rebs fired a solid shot over our heads which lodged in the marsh just outside the stockade. It caused a big scare and the crowds which were greeting the new prisoners were instantly dispersed. The fortifications surrounding our camp are nearly completed.

July 29

Very hot; the usual shower in the afternoon. A line of white flags have been placed through camp, beyond which no crowds must collect or the poor, sick, defenseless prisoners will be treated to shot and shell. The satanic Winder will hardly dare carry out such a threat for the crowded condition of the camp makes its obedience an impossibility. Three hundred prisoners from Grant and Sherman came in. Webster and Laird[23] went outside to work on their parole of honor. Two men of the 11th Mass [J.M. Miller[24] and James Gaffney[25]] died near me. I have been digging roots for fuel, using my case-knife and hands.

July 30

Very hot. Our rebel sergeant has been trying to get Yankee shoemakers to go outside, promising extra rations for their help. Macon is reported captured by a raiding party. The coarse uncooked corn meal has again brought on diarrhea.

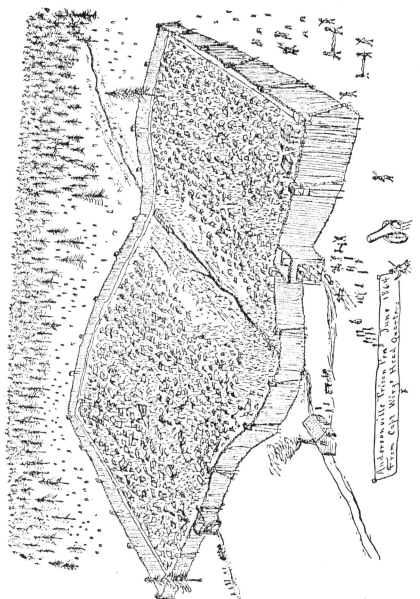

Facsimile of a sketch of Andersonville made on the spot by the author.

July 31

Very hot. The rebs have been chopping down trees all around camp to serve as a blockade against a charge of cavalry. Rumors of exchange and parole. I am suffering a severe headache and fever.

August 1

Very hot; rain last night. I was sick all night but am better this morning. This is what tries a fellows spunk, but I don't give up easy. A preacher from outside held services in camp and read the exchange report from a newspaper. Ambulances have been taking the sick out of camp all afternoon.

August 2

Very hot; a heavy thunder shower in the afternoon flooded camp soaking us all. I am weak and sick with diarrhea and have a cough. A lot of prisoners came in who report the interesting news that they were captured at Macon under General Stoneman[26] who was moving toward this place to attempt to release the prisoners. It is reported that he has been captured. The sick have been going out to the hospital all day.

August 3

Very hot. The removal of the sick has continued through the day, which causes much surmising as to the why and wherefore. The remainder of the captured from Macon came in today making about seven hundred in all.

August 4

Very hot. No sick were taken out; neither roll call or sick call took place. Prisoners from Sherman came in. One of my squad died near me this noon. A prayer meeting was held near by in the evening.

August 5

Very hot. All the sick of the first eight detachments were taken out. More prisoners from Sherman came in. I had a severe headache at night. We are continually tantalized and tormented with the sight of peaches, apples, chickens and soda water offered for sale at fabulous prices.

August 6

The day is very warm. The dread monotony of our miserable life is broken only by multitudes of rumors of exchange which serves to aggravate the credulous ones. Some and doubtless most of these rumors are started in camp, but it is suspected that the rebs encourage rumors in order to keep us from conspiring to escape. One man was killed on the dead-line and another was shot at in the evening.

August 7

Very warm. Several convalescents came in from the hospitals and report an awful condition of affairs there—no medicines, no proper care and nothing to relieve the dying. They prefer to be in camp where they can be near friends. Prisoners from Sherman came in. Exchange reports are on the wane. I am feeling better excepting an irritating cough.

August 8

A row of sheds inside camp at the west end are being erected for the sick. Rain all the afternoon.[27]

August 9

Very warm. The heaviest thunderstorm of the season occurred in the afternoon which flooded camp and undermined the stockade in several places so that it fell over, causing wild excitement among the authorities outside. The long roll was sounded and all the guard turned out. The batteries all manned and turned on us poor fellows who watched their alarm with much amusement. Four hundred prisoners from Sherman came in.

Poor old Boyer [Buchele[28]], a German from Ohio, died near me. He has been lying for several days almost within arm's length of me, perfectly helpless, exposed yesterday to the pelting rain. All night he laid moaning and calling for water while every draught given to him seemed to throw him into spasms. When at last he rolled over and his eyes became fixed with the glassy stare of death, we all felt relieved that rebel hate could harm him no more. This evening I went over and was cheered up with a good talk with Walter Lamb of the happy old school days in Templeton.

August 10

Heavy shower in the afternoon. The rebels worked like beavers all day putting the stockade in shape again. I drew half rations of bread, raw beans and meat but no wood to cook it with. I am feeling well but awful hungry. The wet weather is rapidly increasing the mortality.

August 11

Very warm; rain in the afternoon. The rancid bacon, flinty corn bread and "beans that are not all beans" make us dainty. The beans came to us cooked with all sorts of chaff, dirt and bean bugs, but it all fills us up and I suppose I ought not to complain. Prisoners came in from Sherman. The old stockade is all up again and negroes are at work erecting another one twenty rods outside the old one so that tunneling will be a more difficult matter than ever.

August 12

Rations of bread (half cooked), rice (quarter cooked) and meat (slightly warmed). It requires great self-restraint to reserve any of our ration for a second meal; receiving them at night our custom is to divide it equally: put one part out of sight at once and immediately eat up the other part. By lying down and attempting to sleep the night away, we feel justified in getting up early and finishing the remainder. More prisoners came in today from Sherman. Report of an exchange of officers who are confined at Macon.

August 13

Very hot and clear; beautiful moonlight evenings. Shep and I have two new neighbors; men from Iowa who have stretched their blankets with ours. They were captured in the rear of Johnson's[29] army while raiding. They were robbed of a large amount of money, their watches and clothing. It is pleasant to hear and see their cheery voices and words, like a breeze from God's land. The bank of the creek has been boarded up so that we can dip for water without stirring up the mud. Shower in the evening; our ration was better tonight.

August 14

Prisoners from Sherman today—report Atlanta taken by the Union forces.[30]

August 15

Very hot; cloudy in the afternoon. Headache at night. Rations smaller than ever.

August 16

Very hot with shower in the evening. Two years ago I was mustered into Uncle Sam's service to attempt to put down the rebellion. Today I find the tables turned and the rebels trying to put me down. It is hard to believe that any government can prosper which sanctions such cruel persecution of helpless men.

August 17

The very hot weather makes my head ache. I found a very welcome diversion in reading a book on temperance; the first reading I have seen since my capture except my precious little testament.[31]

August 18

Very hot. Our detachment had the misfortune to have a new rebel sergeant to call the roll. He was a very ignorant fellow and found much difficulty in reading our names. He skipped names which he could not easily make out, and the result was that rations were cut off. More prisoners from Sherman came in. I am "down sick" with diarrhea and headache.

August 19 through August 21

[No entries]

August 22

Tonight finds me able to write. I feel that I have passed through one of the severest experiences of my life and have been very near death's door. The weather has continued hot and my diarrhea took the form of dysentery. I was almost helpless and my head ached so that I was nearly crazy. On the 19th, I thought of my regiment as being mustered out of service, the date of its expiration of service. My sickness made me childish and my spirits went down to zero. Oh that the Pale Horse would not stare me in the face so hard and constantly. Yesterday I felt that my pluck had nearly vanished, and it seemed as if the only hold on life was the comfort derived from the precious words which I kept running in my mind, "My son, despise not thou the chastening of the Lord, nor faint when thou art rebuked of him: For whom the Lord loveth he chasteneth, and scourgeth every son whom he receiveth. If ye endure chastening, God dealeth with you as with sons. "[32] My constant prayer was for resignation and in agony of heart I asked God to spare me from dying in this awful place with no friends near. Yet Shep has been very kind, helping me all that was in his power. Today I feel that my prayers have been answered for I am really better. The mortality on these cold, wet nights is great. A hundred each day are carried out to be placed in the long trenches. A large prayer meeting was held on the flat in the evening, where men cried to their Maker out of sore hearts. Rations today—corn bread, beans and molasses. Why will they give us molasses?

August 23

Very hot all day and night.[33] Mosquitoes are very troublesome. Two members of the 34th Mass died near me—one was Baker.[34] Prisoners from Kilpatrick[35] came in.

August 24

Very hot. I am feeling much stronger. Shep went outside with a dead body. Although he remained only a few minutes, he seemed greatly refreshed. He said it seemed delightful to get a breath of pure air. Another man died quite near me tonight. Some prisoners were taken out of camp who were discovered to be commissioned officers. For reasons known to themselves they had chosen to be disguised as privates.

August 25

Very hot. Rations—raw beef and beans. A few prisoners came in.

August 26

The rousting hot weather is driving men to idiocy. Many have been sun struck and died. The effect of starvation combined with the fearful heat first makes us childish, then stupid and if death doesn't step in, the predominant effect upon many is to make them fools. Rations: bread, one morsel; sowbelly, one bit; salt, one atom; and molasses, plenty. Funeral services were held over a dead comrade near my tent, which seemed civilized; it is rarely the case that anything follows the death of one but to immediately hustle the body up to the main gate; guards are always in attendance to watch the bearers until the sad task is performed of laying it along side the last one in the long trenches and the living corpses are safely returned to camp.

August 27

Very warm but a good breeze which keeps the fine clay dust stirring and there's not a wisp of grass or any green thing in all the camp. The rebs report that heavy fighting took place on the 19th at Petersburg where Grant was defeated. Rumors are thick in camp of an exchange soon to take place. Showers occurred in the night.

August 28

The Macon Telegraph gives an account of a general exchange of all prisoners. To the credulous this brings light into the eye, but "hope deferred maketh the heart sick" and I shall not enthuse until I see the Stars and Stripes once more between me and this hell upon earth. Prisoners from Sherman came in.

August 29

More prisoners from Sherman came today and still there's room for more for this devil's mill demands much grist, as the almost constant stream of dead testifies.

August 30

Warm and clear. Last night was cold and uncomfortable. The heavy shower a day or two since washed out quite a bank of earth not far from the dead-line when out poured a large stream of pure cold water. It has flowed ever since, and thousands are being supplied from it with no diminution in its quantity. It has been named "Providence Spring,"[36] and surely he must be a fool who would doubt after such a manifestation of our Heavenly Father's watchful care.

August 31

Warm and cloudy. A third stockade is being erected outside the others for greater safety.

September 1

Last night was uncomfortably cold. Drew rations of Beef, Bread, Ham, Beans, and Salt while some detachments had Rice instead of Bread. Microscopes were not furnished us to see what we were eating so I use capital letters in order to make the ration seem as large as possible.

September 2

Another cold night but the days are not so fearfully hot. I find plenty of time to sit and count the days, weeks and months; and so I realize that I have been a prisoner three months. What an age it seems, since I saw the good old flag and heard from home.

September 3

Cloudy with northeast wind. A crowd of convalescents came in from the hospital and as many sick went out. During the afternoon an unusual commotion in camp was caused by the announcement of the arrival of a mail from the North. What anxious faces there were as the names were called of those who received letters, but I am used to disappointment so my heart did not break when I found I did not receive one. Lagara,[37] the cheery old Frenchman who was taken prisoner at the same time that I was, received a letter from his wife and generously read it to us greedy ones to whom it seemed like a breath from dear old home.

September 4

The day was mild. Wilbur Potter let me read a letter from Templeton in which I learn that Colonel Hawkes has resigned and gone home; also that Geo Potter had become a Christian. Although this was about all there was in it, no one can ever understand the pleasure I found (except those in the same situation) in reading this letter. As there was so little to be learned in these letters aside from private family affairs and as so many received none, it is believed that the rebs destroyed any which had anything not pleasing to them. Clark[38] of our squad died tonight and Dwinnell[39] of Company G went out to the hospital; I presume we shall never see him again as his strength is gone and he is very badly emaciated.

September 5

Hot again. Drew double rations of rice, molasses, bread and pork, but as soon as we found that a mistake had been made and Squad 3 had lost theirs, most of us divided with them.

September 6

The whole camp is wild with excitement over the prospect of an exchange for the first eighteen detachments are now under marching orders. No one understands its meaning, but there is a universal uplifting of heads by those who had already shut out hope.

September 7

Very hot. Ten detachments were taken out but part were sent back for want of transport; however, all went in the afternoon and ten are ordered to be in readiness to leave at night. Of course the universal topic is: "Where are we going?" While most are inclined to believe it is only an exchange from one prison pen to another, all are hopeful in the prospect of a change whatever it may be. I drew a pint of meal and pork. Holshoult [unmarked grave—not listed among Massachusetts soldiers and not listed in Atwater List of prisoners who died at Andersonville] of the 34th Mass, a noisy, profane fellow of our squad, died tonight. A sad death indeed for one who had no hope for anything better in another world.

September 8

Cloudy; mosquitoes troublesome. Several detachments went out during last night and a large number went tonight. My turn will not come until the last end. Rations of raw meal and beans.

September 9

All the sick have been moved into the sheds at the west end of camp. These sheds consist of simply a roof, no sides, under which are arranged long tiers of shelves on which are laid the sick, spread out like codfish to dry. Prisoners came in and many went away at night. Rations of bread and beans but no salt.

September 10

Rourke of our squad died tonight [unmarked grave—not on Atwater List] and I was detailed to carry him out. It was the first time I had been outside these horrid gates since my arrival three months ago. Although outside less than three minutes and then not further than inside the second stockade, the breath of fresh air gave me hope for a new lease of life. Rations: rice meal and molasses but no salt. Several detachments went out at night and this morning. Forty detachments have now gone and the camp looks quite deserted, though there are yet over twenty thousand here.

September 11

A beautiful harvest moon shines down upon us. I wonder if the dear friends at home look up at it and think I may be watching it also. Ten detachments left tonight. Nearly all of the 21st boys have now gone, Jim Miller among the number. How homesick it makes a fellow feel to see all his friends leaving him in such a place as this.

September 12

Alvin Graton[40] of Company C stopped with Shepard last night. Eighteen detachments go today.

September 13

A large number of "flankers" from our squad got out last night with those who went away; as a result our rations are larger tonight. These "flankers" are men who belong to the newer detachments and for the sake of getting away, slip into the ranks of those which are going out. If discovered, they are ordered back. Our detachment received orders tonight to be ready to go tomorrow.

September 14

Very hot. The train which left last night collided with a freight train six miles north. The result was that eight cars were thrown from the track and smashed—killing and wounding about sixty Northern "mudsills." The rebs did not take much notice, so trifling an affair, only to send all the uninjured back to camp and we do not leave today.[41]

September 15

Days hot and nights cold. Eleven hundred of our sick were sent away. At last the definite announcement is made that an exchange is to be made!! Two thousand of Sherman s men, who were taken in the battle at Chickamauga and have been prisoners longer than any others, are ordered to leave on a special exchange. The confusion incident on taking them out delays the drawing of our rations until far into the night. 0, how hungry we are! There was a heavy shower in the night.

September 16

Hot. A large number have been going out all day. Six hundred of yesterday's batch returned to camp for want of transportation.

September 17

Cloudy; much rain during the night. Seven hundred prisoners of the Sherman exchange left, several of them belonged to my detachment. It is very lonely and seems very drear to see so many deserted burrows and dens all over the camp.

September 18

Equinoctial storm. No prisoners went out and indications are that no more will be sent out at present; consequently, the hope that has buoyed us up in seeing the desertion of the place has gone out and faces are very long. Shep is sick with diarrhea.

September 19

Cloudy; rained all last night. Webster and Laird were sent back into camp, because two or three of their comrades ran away. They say that it is understood now that the prisoners have only been transferred to other prisons near Charleston and Savannah. Eleven hundred more of Sherman's exchange were sent out. In order to prevent flankers from getting out, the rolls were called and no man was quite bad enough to answer to another man s name and thereby shut out the rightful one from this last chance for life.

September 20

Cloudy; rain in the night. I discovered signs of scurvy in my mouth, having appeared around the gums of my diseased teeth. The gums swell up and turn to a dark purple. Where others have it and do not recover, this swelling spreads in a few days until the face and neck turn black as if the blood settled all over it; then the teeth drop out—the jaws become set and a general rotting process is the last stage. With others the disease shows itself first in the limbs, rendering them stiff and helpless. My general feeling is one of complete lassitude and low spirits. We drew no bread today.

September 21

Cloudy and rain. The nights are so very chilly and damp that great numbers are sick with colds. For a change the rebels gave us in place of bread or meal a lot of condemned sea biscuit stuff that was so moldy the guard outside had refused to touch it. Nevertheless, the little handful was an acceptable change from the meal or "grit" as we call it. With the hardtack we receive beans and molasses.

September 22

The sun shone out scorching hot at noon bringing a shower in the afternoon. The camp has been reorganized into new detachments of two hundred and forty men in each. These are divided into four squads of sixty men.

They number from 45 to 73 so that makes our present number of prisoners 6720. I am placed in detachment 72.

September 23

Shower in the afternoon. Brisk trading between the guards and prisoners. Almost the only article of commerce which the prisoners possess is military buttons which they gladly part with for sweet potatoes. The result is that most of our blouses are minus buttons. Quite a cortege of rebel officers, some of them of apparently high rank, rode around camp between the stockade and dead-line on a tour of inspection.[42] I think they must feel proud of the chivalric manner of treatment of defenseless prisoners by the accredited agents of the haughty South.

September 24

Showers throughout the day. I washed in the creek. Ration of raw meal. The Dutch Captain has been inspecting the delivery of rations and tells us we are entitled to more than we get. Mirabile dictu! What a kind paternal care is expressed by the remark! Kick a man when he is down and then tell him he ought not to be kicked.

September 25

The day is clear and mild. Last night was so cold we could not sleep. We begin to despair of getting away at all. So many disappointed hopes make the heart sick. Can we keep our courage much longer? This is the question we are constantly asking ourselves.

September 26

Roll call and all names which are not responded to are "docked" on rations. Prisoners who have lately come in from Sherman say that the "special exchange" was true, but that there has been no general exchange. We don't like to believe it for we had built high hopes on the belief that our turn was soon to come. The outcome of the general inspection the other day is that the chief quartermaster has been inspecting camp. That is too thin after all that has happened during the awful months that have past. Perhaps the rebs have begun to wake up to the fact that the civilized nations of the earth have something to say and that it is wise to be heeded.

September 27

When our roll was called, it was ascertained that several were absent who had "flanked" out with those who had been sent away so our detachment has been filled up with others. Our ration of beans is smaller than ever and the most filthy we have ever had: dirt, bugs, worms, chaff and pods being the principal ingredients. Hope the chief quartermaster will keep away in future if this is the result of his visit. The shout was raised, "Fall in!" Several more detachments were sent away. But as ours is near the last, I am left behind and we are again disheartened. More prisoners from Sherman came in.

September 28

Warm; more comfortable last night. Drew rations of meal, beef, beans, wood, pork, salt and molasses!!! They were dealt out by crumbs, drops, splinters and teaspoonfuls. Three and a half detachments went out today.

September 29

Someone has brought in a *History of the World* by Peter Parley. In its rounds through camp, I secured the book for an hour and enjoyed a rare treat. Drew small rations of meal, beef and beans.

September 30

Very warm and sultry. At roll call all the detachments were filled up. Drew rations of molasses in place of meat, a very poor substitute for these poor, starving skeletons. Some one gave me a taste of a sweet potato. What a delicious morsel. Presto! A teaspoonful of soft soap was given to each prisoner, but as we can't eat it, no one knows what to do with it.

October 1

Washed in the creek just to use up my ration of soap. I found several suspicious looking white spots about my body, but as the soap didn't hold out, I don't know as the bath left me looking much handsomer than before. Rations of bread and beans—the one great central thought: Rations, Rations, Rations. Another train load of prisoners left today.

October 2

Four months a prisoner and oh what long ones they have been. A few Sherman prisoners captured near Atlanta were brought in. Drew a splendid ration of beans. We know beans when we see them, which reveals the Yankee blood in our veins. If we haven't quite lost our reckoning, this is the Sabbath up in God's country, but there is nothing in these parts to remind us of the day.

October 3

Heavy showers. Several men went out on their parole of honor as teamsters and choppers.

October 4

It is very hard to sit day after day with nothing to occupy the mind; the harrowing query keeps coming up, "Must we die here?" Anything, anything to break the blank outlook. This is what breaks down the great strong men who lose hope. Another load of prisoners went away this evening among whom were Graton and Barker[43] of the 21st. Two shots were fired on the dead line.

October 5

I was detailed to "pack" or "tote" the sick and dead to and from the sheds for which I get an extra ration of bread, rice and molasses. My teeth and jaws are quite sore.

October 6

Cloudy and rain. My teeth ached so that I could not sleep. I trade away my ration of meal for beans which I eat as dry as possible to check the progress of scurvy. Rations today of bread, beans, bacon, beef and molasses, just enough to keep the lice and fleas lively. These are companions in our misery which "stick closer than brothers."

October 7

A cloudy and damp day. I had a suffering night from my teeth and gums. Shep is sick with fever and ague as are many others. It is reported that Sherman is fighting and his rear cut off.

October 8

Clear and cold—sudden change in the night. I lost another nights sleep from a toothache. How the poor fellows sink down by this exposure to the changing weather; their bloodless bodies have nothing to withstand it and multitudes go to their death every day from this cause alone.

October 9

Clear and cold—very chilly last night. We were all ordered to move over into the south end of this great deserted camp where we are put into as compact a space as possible, and are formed into detachments of five-hundred men each. Shep and I are in the 4th detachment. We dug a hole in the ground over which we spread our blanket for another cold night is expected, and we must work constantly to keep off the death chill. This is the Sabbath and we are in the pen, but there is no one to help us out of it even if scripture does say so.

October 10

Spent a night of suffering and sleeplessness. Coldest night of the season. The guards were very noisy all night. From their elevated posts they were exposed to the freezing wind, so they made night hideous by all sorts of shouting and catcalls. The usual regulation sentry night call, "Post number one and all's well" with the long drawn out "all" on a higher key was varied by all manner of ridiculous cries in their outlandish backwoods vernacular. There are now not more than twenty-five hundred men here. Shep and I mess with Sergeant Phelps[44] of Vermont and twenty others, most of them also from Vermont. My teeth ache all day; very severe and part of the time it was the "jumping" ache. Ten Dutchmen went out on their parole of honor for special service for the Dutch Captain—O that I were a Dutchman!

October 11

The day was mild. Spent a more comfortable night. The sick at the sheds are receiving hardtack. What a delicacy that would now seem to me. Three hundred prisoners from Sherman came in; they were captured between Atlanta and Marietta.

October 12

My jaws are very sore. I lose much sleep for want of covering and shelter. Clothing is worn very thin and the single woolen blanket which has been used for our shelter from sun and rain through all the months has become very thin. With nothing between us and the damp cold ground but Shep's rubber, we curl up together, draw the woolen entirely over us and look like a pile of vegetables covered up in our hole. All the prisoners were kept in line all the forenoon while the rebel sergeants arranged the rolls and the quartermaster rearranged the camp into streets. A new dead-line was put up.

October 13

More rearranging and moving about. We now lie very compact, occupying about three acres of ground. According to my reckoning, I make a thousand men to occupy a third of an acre. I have been peddling coffee at the hospital sheds—made from burnt meal.

October 14

Cloudy and cool. Spent another night of suffering. Many are at work fixing up their tents, trying to have them comfortable. Many were admitted to the sheds. Street sutlers with sweet potatoes and biscuits are on the street.

October 15

Shep and I have been digging our grave deeper, over which we spread our blanket. Teeth ache all day and another sleepless night.

October 16

I was detailed to "pack" the dead—as the rebs say, when we carry the dead out of camp. I carried two men belonging to the 19th Massachusetts, one of whom had died in great agony apparently. His body and limbs had stiffened into the same shape which his contortions had left him when he died: legs drawn up, head drawn back, eyes rolled back and arms outstretched as if in defense. The fearful sight will never be effaced from my memory. We now lie down for the night to wear away the long hours. If they would only get wood by which we could keep fires, it would be a relief.

October 17

Frosty. Large details were made for men to go out after wood. Rations of beans and raw molasses or sorghum but no bread. I used up my molasses to make candy. Rained in the evening.

October 18

Cloudy but cleared away in the afternoon. I went outside the stockade for wood; the first time for four months and O how like a new life it seemed. Saw green grass and leaves, got a breath of fresh air, smelt good smells and my eyes drank in new sights. No one can appreciate it as we do who have been deprived of them so long. It gives me a new longing to live and with it a new torture in the hopeless aspect of our future. Shep and I have been writing home—sending for boxes but that 's all the good it will do. Several convalescents tried to escape from the hospital, but were captured by the bloodhounds.

October 19

Shep sick with diarrhea. Ration of rice and molasses.

October 20

Warmer last night. I went out again for wood so we have a fire to sit by this evening. Beans and beef for today's ration.

October 21

Pleasant day but cold night. Several from our mess went to the hospital—Webster among the number. Ration of rice and molasses in place of beans and beef.

October 22

Shep and I have fixed up blankets with Laird of Pennsylvania, by which arrangement we get an extra blanket for nights.

October 23

Very cold and heavy frost last night, for which cause could not sleep much. I went out again for wood.

October 24

Last night I had a comfortable rest, the first for a long while. We think we have our tent made quite comfortable. The chief sutler's shanty was overhauled by the Dutch Captain and his goods confiscated for the benefit of the sick in camp because of selling liquor.

October 25

Camp rumors of exchange of ten thousand men of the Potomac Army. If this be true, where are the men which have left here? No more details to go out for wood because some of the men attempted to escape. Salt is very scarce so the Dutchman has all salt to be confiscated which is offered for sale in camp. Teeth ache very severe this evening.

October 27

Stormy. Our tent was flooded. I am hoarse with a cold and generally used up on account of loss of sleep. Our ration is bread and rice—very small, barely enough to sustain life.

October 28

Hard toothache and poor nights rest. Washed in creek and mended shirt. I traded off my ration of beans for an excellent ration of rice. A mud shanty fell in near by breaking one man s back and badly crippling two others.

October 29

Very cold and heavy frost last night. Toothache very severe. Fixed up our tent so as to make it weather proof. Six prisoners came in.

October 30

Had about an hour's sleep last night. Shep has applied for admission to the hospital but was refused. The misery endured for the past week or two drives

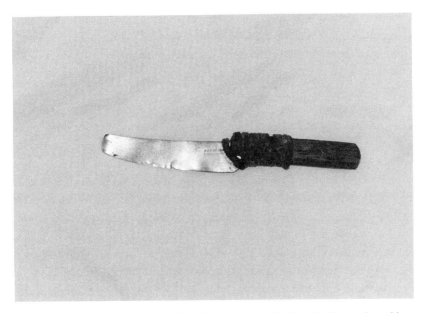

Confederate authorities at Libby Prison removed all valuables and cooking utensils from Union prisoners, which forced them to be creative. The author made this knife from a broken blade, two pieces of pine pins and leather strings. He used throughout his tenure as a prisoner for cutting wood, splitting soup bones and cooking. The nicks on the blade were caused by splitting soup bones into chips.

away all interest in what is going on in camp so my diary suffers. The whole camp is under orders to be ready to march.

October 31

Warm. The 1st, 2nd and part of the 3d detachments went away in the morning. No enthusiasm is raised as was the case last month, because we believe it is only an exchange of one prison for another and the rebs spread the report of exchange so that there will not be any attempt to escape while being transported. The rebel sergeants have been calling for carpenters to go out to work on their parole of honor. Rations of bread and rice cooked without a particle of salt.

November 1

The sheds at the west end have been emptied of the sick; part are returned to us and part carried outside to the hospital.

November 2

A cold northeaster began about midnight and rain poured incessantly for twelve hours. While most of the tents were flooded, ours was kept comparatively dry. What an appropriate day for our last in this "hell upon earth." In the morning while sitting "moping " as usual, orders came for us to be ready to start at eleven in the morning. Grim humor this—as if we should require time to pack our trunks. Yet we wait through the long hours of the day as we had waited for five long months with apathy and hardly the belief that we should go at all. We are told that transportation was not ready; so at dark, I drop to sleep and am sleeping soundly at ten o'clock at night when the summons came, and we are hustled up and out through the huge gates in pitchy darkness and a pelting rain. Between two strong lines of guard about half the remaining portion of Andersonville prisoners pass to the railroad station. We now feel assured that this prison pen is about to be abandoned and whatever the future may have in store for us, we are devoutly thankful to look back into the blackness, lighted from the outside of the stockade by a few dim fires of the rebel guard, and feel that we are permitted to get out of it alive while so many thousands of our comrades are now under the sod all around us. We also pass out from the domination of the Dutchman as we pack into freight cars—eighty-three men counted off to each car and move northward toward Macon.

*   *   *

Fifteen

Millen, Georgia

Camp Lawton was located five miles north of Millen, Georgia, at Magnolia Springs, near the Augusta Railroad. It was constructed during late summer of 1864 to accommodate the excess of Union prisoners at Andersonville. Lack of funds and the failure to impress labor delayed the occupation of the prison until early October. After being shuttled from Andersonville, the prisoners at Savannah were sent to Millen on October 10. All of the prisoners at Andersonville able to make the move were shipped to Millen along with their guards. Seven hundred sick prisoners were included in the relocation.

The stockade, one of the largest prisons in the world, measured 1,398 feet by 1,329 feet and enclosed forty-two acres. The stream running through the prison was large and there was no swamp as there had been at Andersonville. The ground was divided into thirty-two sections by streams sixteen feet wide; each area was designed for a thousand prisoners and then separated into ten subdivisions. The prisoners constructed huts from tree branches that were left within the stockade. Water flowed beneath the sinks, insuring adequate removal of excrement.

The cooking facilities were not completed, however, and the hospital and health supplies were only slightly improved from Andersonville. On November 8, 1864, Capt. D. W. Vowles, commander of the prison, reported 486 deaths among the 10,299 prisoners. He also stated that 285 prisoners were detailed to work at the post and 349 prisoners had enlisted in Confederate service. The popular term for these men was "Galvanized Yankees," although to be fair, some prisoners used enlistment as a means for escape.

The departure of William T. Sherman's army from Atlanta on November 16 and its rapid advance east across the state forced the abandonment of Camp Lawton. On November 22, General Winder reported that all the prisoners had been sent to Savannah. Although some prisoners were sent by rail to Blackshear and Thomasville in south Georgia, the majority of the Camp Lawton prisoners, including George Hitchcock, was transferred to Florence, South Carolina.

Sherman's March was wreaking havoc on a system that was already collapsing.

*   *   *

November 4, 1864

Packed like sardines and no change of position is possible. Eighty-three human breathers soon make the air of the shut up car very foul, but all through the night and the day in the one same sitting posture with the rain pelting against the car and nothing to eat, surely misery cannot much further go. We passed through Macon at daylight and turn on to the Charleston Railroad. Not the least idea can we gain of the country through which we pass. It is far into the night when we stop at Millen Station and are allowed to get out and stretch our aching limbs. As each car load is counted off, it is found that several have escaped during the journey while one of my own Mess was found dead in my car. He had been sick and the crowded condition of the car had killed him; one more victim to rebel cruelty. We are more than two hundred miles from Andersonville and none too far away either. March half a mile and come to the gates of another stockade [Camp Lawton], but we are kept outside until daylight.

November 4

The weather cleared during the night and the day opened very cold and windy. Suffered severely for lack of shelter and clothing. Have taken a cold. After arranging the shivering crowd into detachments as before, the rebs turned us into the pen where rations are issued to us: rice, meal, beef, beans and salt. Found the place a great contrast to Andersonville. Although about ten thousand of the old prisoners are here, the camp is laid out with some pretense of

Exterior view of the prison at Millen, Georgia.
Harper's Weekly

regularity and a considerable clear space covered with grass. There is a creek of good water running through camp and I camp down by its side, thinking if I could only keep warm I should be all right.

November 5

Drew two days rations; better in quality and quantity than at Andersonville. The men who arrived here first have made very comfortable winter quarters of logs. Several hundred, who thought they were going to be exchanged, in their disappointment and despair, have taken the oath of allegiance and gone into the rebel army. Poor soldiers they will make for a falling cause.

November 6

Chilly day. I didn't sleep much on account of the cold. Laird and I went outside for wood.

November 7

Warmer last night. I found Lamb and Graton. Our 9th Division moved across the creek on the slope nearer the rest of the prisoners where we make a temporary shelter. A Savannah newspaper has notice of an exchange of ten thousand to begin next week so the exchange stories continue to be the favorite topic. Quite a flurry was caused in the afternoon by the discovery of the executioner of the six raiders last summer by some of the old gang. They had prepared to mob him and kill him in the confusion, but he got away and ran like a hound for the gate where the guard let him go out unharmed.

November 8

Light rain. I got a comfortable nights rest. This is the Presidential election day in the North, and as the rebel authorities appear to have great interest in it, the prisoners propose to show them what we can do. They evidently think they have reduced our spirits by starvation to that state whereby we will all be anxious to have peace declared by recognizing the Southern Confederacy, and this they expect to be accomplished if McClellan is elected. Early in the day many stump speeches were made and vigorous campaigning done in behalf of both candidates. Considerable blatant talk was indulged in by the hoodlum class who always vote the democratic ticket. Betting away rations but as usual those who talk least can do more; when we organized a polling booth, great efforts were made to overawe the doubtful voters. At night the result showed that out of a vote of over 9000, Honest Old Abe received a majority of 975. Many of the old Potomac boys vote for McClellan because they still remain loyal to him, yet believe in seeing the war pushed until the rebellion is overthrown. Others in their weakness and misery are made to believe that our Government has heartlessly abandoned us. Therefore, I am highly satisfied with the result, and much chaffing of the rebel guard is indulged in over their disappointment.

November 9

I went out twice today for wood. Saw General Cottrell [Gartrell],[1] commander of the rebel forces in this vicinity. There was great cheering outside among the rebs which the guard told us was caused by the news of a general exchange. If we could only be made to believe it, we would do the cheering for both sides.

November 10

Rain in the morning but cold and windy at night. A rebel officer has been in camp looking up and taking the names of those most destitute of clothing, presumably to prepare our men for the coming winter.

November 11

Clear and cold. A recruiting officer has been in camp, enticing prisoners to enlist into the rebel army. Several went from our division. Pretty hard up must be the cause that accepts such service as that. The clothing inspector examined our division in the afternoon. For sale in abundance: roast chicken, boiled sweet potatoes, eggs, biscuits, butter, pumpkin and potato pies, rice and bean soups, soda cakes and molasses, but our experience is the same as the Ancient Mariner—"Food a everywhere, but not a morsel for us."

November 12

A chilly wind all day. We were deprived of our much needed two days rations on a very peculiar excuse. Several of the men, who had enlisted in the rebel army, could not be found at roll call and the authorities feared that they had been murdered by our boys, who are very indignant at their action; consequently, our rations are withheld until they are found. A prisoner nearly naked perished from the cold near me. All the remaining prisoners from Camp Sumter came in today.

November 13

A chilly wind and frosty night. Names of the sick, seventy-five from each division, were taken to the surgeon who examined and passed them out—being sent to be exchanged at Savannah. Shepard and Graton were examined and passed. They expect to go away tomorrow. Savannah papers have accounts of the meeting of the Commissioners and an agreement of exchange. What an inducement to be sick!

November 14

Coldest night of the fall. The camp was pleasantly surprised to receive a ration of sweet potato instead of meal—also hard soap. I wrote a letter to send home by Shepard if he should be fortunate enough to reach our lines.

November 15

Mild, but very frosty and cold last night. Shep and his crowd left last night. It did me good to see my old chum get out of this, but how my heart sunk as I felt that I must always be left behind. The sutlers and those having money bought the positions of nurses to attend to the sick on their homeward trips. A few Sherman prisoners came in today.

November 16

Very pleasant. Sweet potatoes were again issued. The sick did not leave today as the transports which were to take them at Savannah harbor ran aground; they were all returned inside the stockade. A train bearing exchanged rebels passed here for Augusta; also a train load of our sick from Andersonville arrived here.

November 17

Had a good nights rest. Drew a ration of rotten sweet potatoes and a small piece of meat. Wood cannot be had for no squads are allowed outside.

November 18

Warm with rain last night. A new sergeant, who could not read very well, called our roll and made such slow work of it that we could not get our rations until after dark. Three spoonfuls of rice are all that kept us through the day. Laird and I drew rations in a different mess tonight. Shep's crowd of sick left us today and the surgeons are examining for another load.

November 19

Storm came on at night. Another change of sergeants caused another day of starvation on a mouthful of beef. Another train load of sick left tonight.

November 20

More sick were examined and passed out. All the old Chickamauga and Belle Isle men were taken out for exchange. At midnight the cry arose: "Fall in, 1st and 2nd Divisions." They packed up and went out. We who are left can't understand the rush.

November 21

Storm all day. As soon as the 2nd Division had vacated its comfortable quarters, I with others arose at one o'clock in the night and occupied one of the fine shanties. We enjoyed it until dark of this day—when lo! we are ordered to pack up and leave. We start off in the rain in great wonderment as to the meaning of this haste. Rumors are rife that Sherman has something to do with it and our suspicions are confirmed when we reach the depot and see train after train hurrying down past us toward Savannah, laden with every description of household goods: furniture, countrymen and their families and negroes of all ages. Numberless trains of all sorts arrive and deposit their freight along the side of the railroad. We, meanwhile, have to stand waiting in a terrible freezing, biting wind for hours.

November 22

But at last near four o'clock in the morning, more dead than alive and chilled to the heart, we are packed on a train—sixty to a car and glide away on one of the smoothest railroads I ever passed over. Our three weeks imprisonment in Millen was in several ways beneficial to us: the change of sights and opportunity to breath pure air, pleasant surroundings and the knowledge that more humane counsels prevailed with those in authority. All these causes served to raise our well-nigh despairing spirits so that when we drew out of Millen in such a pitiable condition, our hearts had taken new courage. The belief that Sherman was not far off gave new courage for us to hold out a little longer. The country through which we passed was a monotonous level—almost entirely covered with great stretches of pine forests.

All day long our train moves in a southeasterly direction and at sunset we arrived at the suburbs of Savannah and pass through beautiful surroundings. Right through the heart of this fine handsome city to the farther side where at dark we disembark and find the weather bitterly cold. A flat open field by the side of the railroad with no shelter of any kind is our camping place for the night. No fuel is provided, no food for the past two days and many of us nearly naked. Too weak and bloodless to find any heat from within, we sink down on the cold ground—many to perish. Yankee wit comes to our aid. Probably no one would ever have thought of the thing except freezing men like ourselves. Two or three men would sit down on the ground hugging each other; then others would pack up against them, locking and interlacing arms and legs until a solid pile of humanity of twenty or more found mutual warmth from each others bodies.

November 23

When the morning dawned and the numerous stacks of human beings were unraveled, several of our number were found frozen stiff and ice a quarter of an inch in thickness formed. As we look about us we find we are within stone's throw of a large lumber yard where plenty of fuel could easily have been secured with which to keep life within us if the rebel guard had permitted. The death of our comrades we laid to their account and heartily curse our captors. During the day, however, a little wood was brought in and we hug the smoky fires. Two days rations of hardtack and a little thick syrup were issued to us.

November 24

The day was milder than yesterday. Beef and salt was given out. The kind hearted citizens of Savannah, who found out our condition, have been bringing in food and clothing all day. I have not the spunk or strength to secure anything, only those who are strongest succeed in the fierce tussle for them. Trains have been constantly arriving from the upper country, bringing in rebel troops, negroes and household goods. All are dumped along the side of the railroad track in the greatest confusion and panic. We look on with much satisfaction as we learn that Sherman is pushing right along triumphantly toward this place. A lot of our prisoners were taken away, going south on the Florida road. The sick were also taken away while those remaining were allowed to get wood from the lumber yard; the night closes upon us finding our condition more comfortable.

November 25

The day was clear. How the eyes brightened as we heard the faint but distinct rumble of heavy guns off to the northeast. The guard told us they were from our fleet off Charleston. What a welcome sound; it seemed as if it was the voice of friends calling to us. The kindhearted people of Savannah continued to bring in food and clothing all day. It is cheering to feel that we are near to those whose humanity overmasters their enmity. I secured some boiled rice which sustained me until the rations arrived at dark, which were hardtack and molasses. A train of cars came at nine in the evening when we were hastily hurried on board. Inquiry of a rebel officer who was directing the loading brought out the usual answer: "You are going to Charleston to be exchanged." In our great longing to believe it, many brightened up with hope while some said that it was the same old ruse to keep us from attempting escape. Yet the suspicious haste and evident disturbed manner of our captors caused a great amount of conjecture and surmising among us.

November 26

We rode all night through what seemed an interminable wilderness of rice swamps. It was here that my mind was made up to attempt to escape. I had secured a place near the door and believing that I could not be many miles inland from Beaufort, which I supposed to be held by our forces, I felt as if this might be my opportunity. Crowding up close to the door, I watched for my chance to jump. But mile after mile I could see only the tall grass standing out of the water; we were passing through the immense savannas of Georgia which surround the Charleston and Savannah Railroad. The outlook was dubious and before I could make up my mind for the decisive leap, sleep had overtaken me; when I next opened my eyes, it was daylight and by sunrise we were approaching the noted nest of the Palmetto rattlesnake, Charleston. Crossing the broad Cooper and Ashley rivers, our train enters the city and is brought to a halt on one of the broad streets in the upper part of the city. Very pretty and tasty dwelling houses lined the street with wide shady piazzas surrounding them. The day was fine and mild, and as we remain stationary all the forenoon, many spectators came to view the Andersonville pack. Not any of the sympathetic interest which the good people of Savannah had exhibited was here vouchsafed to us; only a cold curious stare greeted us. Soon after noon our train moves out of the city for about five miles; we are ordered to change cars, and as we turn northward, we realize that our exchange is "of cars only." Again we move through the same low level monotonous pine region up through central South Carolina until ten o'clock when we arrive at Florence, a junction with the Columbia and Wilmington Railroad—one hundred miles north of Charleston.

* * *

Sixteen

Florence, South Carolina

The Confederate military prison two miles from Florence, South Carolina, was under construction in September 1864 to hold prisoners sent to Charleston from Andersonville. While the stockade was being erected, the prisoners were restrained in an open field. Twenty-three acres were enclosed by by a palisade which measured 1,400' by 725', surrounded by a ditch five feet deep and seven feet wide that discouraged tunneling. Dirt was piled against the stockade to form a guard walk about three feet from the top of the wall. A small stream flowed through the prison, but unfortunately for the occupants, the miasmic Andersonville swamp was duplicated (six acres were swampy). The dead-line was ten to twelve feet from the stockade and was marked by a small ditch and in some places by a pole-fence. On each corner of the stockade a platform was erected for a piece of artillery. Six hundred blacks were utilized to construct the facility, and they were still hard at work on November 5.

There were 12,362 prisoners at Florence on October 12. Of these, 860 were hospitalized and 20 were paroled. Most of the prisoners were emaciated and covered with vermin. They had no blankets and very little clothing. A Confederate inspection, dated November 5, 1864, reported 11,424 prisoners: 599 were hospitalized and 90 were paroled. The prisoners were divided into detachments of 1,000 men and ten companies of 100 men each. Colonel George P. Harrison, Jr. was the commander of headquarters post at Florence. Lieutenant Colonel John F. Iverson, 5th Georgia Infantry, was commandant of the prison and in charge of the guards.

The hospital, which was located within the stockade and built with branches from trees, afforded some protection from direct sun but not the rain.

There was only one medical officer assigned on October 12. In November, although a rough frame-work was partially completed for a proposed 100-patient hospital, the sick prisoners were separated by a pole-fence within the stockade.

The prisoners received very little meat and subsisted primarily on sorghum syrup and meal. Since the Union soldiers at Florence had been imprisoned for some time, the mortality rate was high: twenty to fifty died each day from diarrhea, scurvy and other ailments. A total of 18,000 prisoners passed through the Florence prison. Since the prison records were destroyed, almost all of the approximately 2,800 who died were unidentified.

*   *   *

November 27, 1864

Bivouac by the side of the railroad until morning, when our names are registered and once more we are turned into the old familiar stockade. Here we meet all the old prisoners who had gone before us, crowded as badly as at Andersonville. The great prison pen in the form of a quadrangle with the entrance on the south, considerably narrower than Andersonville but running northward nearly a quarter of a mile. The location is low and swampy with a stream running sluggishly through. Laird and I spread our blankets together and at night draw a ration of meal and flour, which with a few chips we make a supper. Lie down on the cold, damp ground and although our hopes are dashed by this termination of the "exchange," I feel that the change of scenes and air have stimulated me so that I am by no means ready to say "die" yet.

November 28

After a cheerless, sleepless night, I get a breakfast of flour paste. Found all the old comrades of the 21st Massachusetts well; also Jim Miller and Middy, my Ohio friend. The camp is crowded badly and the rations are said to be smaller and poorer than ever. The sick are being paroled each day.

November 29

The night was milder. I bought some straw with a borrowed five dollar confederate scrip. Mended clothes which are in a miserable condition. The sleeves of my blouse and shirt are almost entirely gone, showing a pair of skeleton arms; the backs of both garments are worn thin as gauze, while my pants are worn entirely away from the knees down. My cap consists of simply two pieces of cloth sewed together. I was detailed to go outside for wood. Ration of a pint and a half of flour and a splinter of green gumwood. More prisoners from Mill en stockade came.

November 30

Had the chills last night thereby losing my sleep. Jim Miller was admitted to the hospital. I bathed in the creek. Rations of a pint and a half of meal with beans and salt. No more sick are sent away as the railroad is occupied in rushing troops down to intercept Sherman, whom appears to be pushing right into the heart of the Confederacy.

December 1

Winter has arrived and I still live. All the portion of the camp on one side of the creek was moved to the other, and then the entire camp made to move back again, each man being counted as he crossed the little bridge (a very original method of taking the census). A lot of "Galvanized Yanks," the turncoats who enlisted in the rebel army at Millen, were sent back into camp, as the rebels feared they would escape to our lines.

December 2

Six months a prisoner of war. Light rain last night. I traded away a dollar and a half "Confed" for a meal of sweet potatoes. Reports that General Foster has cut the railroad this side of Savannah; we were just a few days too soon in passing there.

December 3

Roll call and wood rations were omitted because of the large number of paroled sick returning to camp. It is difficult for us, however, to see the connection. I had succeeded in concealing a map of the seat of the war from the rebel searchers, which I traded away for a mess of sweet potatoes. Ration of a pint of meal and half a pint of grits.

December 4

We were again marched and counter marched across the creek in order to get a correct count—so much for the mathematical education of the chivalrous southerners. I copied a map of North and South Carolina. This is an occupation which finds much favor among the prisoners. Although much secrecy attends it, the purpose is very apparent. Rations—a pint of rice. A sick man was shot on the dead-line.

December 5

Frosty night but beautiful today. The sick have been passed out today. I drew a ration of a pint and a half of meal but no wood to cook it with.

December 6

Foggy in the morning but clear and cold at night. I heard preaching from a clergyman from Florence. Went out for wood. Rations of meal and grits and half a dozen spoonfuls of molasses. As molasses is not considered a necessary article of diet, the boys revived trade in order to dispose of the ration.

December 7

Chilly wind and some rain. The surgeons have taken out all the sick. Two hundred prisoners came in who belonged to Sherman's command and were captured near Milledgeville while raiding. This is the first authentic news we have yet had concerning Sherman's great movement toward the sea coast and was hailed with great interest.[1]

December 8

The day is very cloudy and chilly.

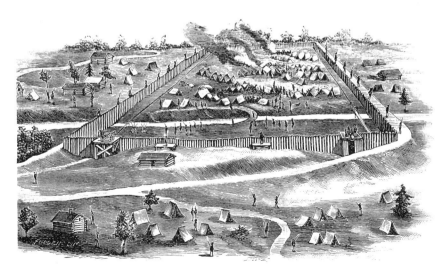

The only known rendition of the Confederate prison at Florence, SC
from Prisoners of War and Military Prisons (1890)

Seventeen

Release

Since November 25, 1864, Sherman's March had prevented the Confederacy from delivering prisoners to Savannah for the purpose of exchange. By this late date the logistical infrastructure of the Confederacy had been devasted. Many transportation lines were cut (or just plain worn out), and much of the space on those railroads still in operation was prempted by Confederate military authorities for movement of men and supplies. When the circumstances of war compelled the abandonment of further exchanges of Union prisoners at the Savannah River site, Lt. Col. John E. Mulford, United States Agent for Exchange of Prisoners, suggested the continuance of the exchange at Charleston Harbor. Lieutenant General William J. Hardee, Confederate commander at Charleston, consented to the change and Union authorities, Maj. Gen. John G. Foster and Rear Adm. John A. Dahlgren, agreed upon a truce for the exchange.

On December 4, Mulford arranged for a suspension of hostilities. Firing on the city and works in and about the harbor was suspended for the transferring of prisoners to Union ships. The agreement provided that no labor be performed by either party on works, forts, batteries or military defenses during this period. The truce did not affect the blockade of the port of Charleston by Union ships, and Union military and naval forces were not restricted from attacking, capturing or destroying any Confederate ships entering or leaving Charleston. Mulford stated on December 7 that 1,000 Union prisoners had already been received under this new arrangement, and he expected to finish the exchange in a week if the weather permitted. On

December 16, Mulford notified his superiors that the truce arranged with Confederate authorities at Charleston Harbor for the exchange of prisoners would terminate at 10:00 a.m. the following day, and that the status existing previous to this truce would be resumed by the respective belligerents.

*   *   *

My greatest flight of fancy could hardly reach the stupendous change in my condition which took place before I again took up the record. Three days later, under the dear old stars and stripes with a restful comfort that I had never known before, I recall the events.

December 8, 1864 [continued]

The remaining four thousand men in the camp, which included Laird and myself, were ordered to report at the dead-line near the main entrance for an examination by the rebel surgeons. We took along our shelters and everything which could be of use to us, because they would quickly have been appropriated by others if left behind. Drawn up in two ranks at open order, Laird and I were near the left of the line; the rebel surgeons walked along down the lines stopping here and there when some unusually pitiable looking prisoner was noticed. Some received sharp questioning and the usual professional examination and were then passed outside the gate to be paroled, but not one in a dozen were thus favored. Not much disappointment was manifested by any who were passed by—apathy was over us all. The disappointed hopes of the past month had taught us not to expect anything, so that when the doctor came along and passed me, I didn't mind it.

But he glanced back and evidently took in my dilapidated appearance, for he stepped back, asked my condition and examined me more closely: thumped my heart and my heart thumped back. Asked the name of my regiment and state. In answer to his question, "When does your term of service expire?" I answered that "it expired more than three months ago and I suppose my regiment has disbanded and gone home." He asked with some sarcasm: "Don't you want to reenlist and fight again?" I answered: "I'm fixed so I can never do any more fighting." With a smile he said: "You may go." Not crediting my own senses, I answered: "What did you say?" He repeated: "You may go." Forgetting everything in my bewilderment, even my old chum, I darted out of the gate. Dazed by my sudden fortune, I tried to think it was only another change of prisons to which I was subjected. While gathering my wits, I looked up and saw Laird following me. In our weakness and joy we clasped each other in our arms and cried like babes. Then we were called up to sign our parole papers which we understood forbade us to take up arms against the enemy for three months.

After this the gathering crowd of feeble-bodied, feeble-minded fellows were turned out into a large, level field where we remain all day and night with only a few guards to watch us. A ration of meal and sweet potatoes was given to us, and I devoured the potatoes, leaving the meal for tomorrow.

December 9

The day opened cloudy and cold; a bleak wintry wind chilling us—bloodless creatures—to the bone. The small fires were not sufficient to keep us warm while the smoke from them filled and blinded our eyes. Our names were called and each man drew a loaf of wheat bread. Soon after this, the sound of a whistle from the north started every man to his feet and away we all rushed for the cars.

Men, who at any other time would have been helpless, found strength in their limbs to carry them to the cars, but my own strength was gone when I attempted to climb into the rickety old cattle-car. With the help of others I was drawn into it and laid down thinking death was at last creeping over me: pain in all my joints, cold and shaking, and blind as a bat in daylight. In the gathering darkness the train [North Eastern Railroad] moved southward toward Charleston and all night we rode. I found some sleep but was conscious only of being very cold as I laid close to the slatted side of the car.

December 10

Cold and cloudy. By eight o'clock in the morning we had reached Charleston and disembarked in the lower portion of the city near the mouth of the Ashley River [Cooper River]. Passed through three or four streets which had received the fire of our blockading fleet, a demolished blackened mass of ruins: large storehouses with great ragged holes where shot and shell had torn through. The streets which had once been crowded with busy teams were now deserted and tufts of grass were growing up between the stones of the pavement.

At last we reached a wharf where we huddled together all day waiting for [exchange]—we hardly dared to think. A dense mist hung low over all, hiding like a curtain those points in the lower harbor which had become historic. The chill northeast wind blew in from the Atlantic. Near four in the afternoon the fog lifted and soon after, our interest was centered in a little rusty looking steamer rounding one of the wharves from the south and coming toward us. With quick beating hearts we watched it swing up to our wharf and the rebel officers on board ordered us to embark.

With its cargo of a thousand ragged wretches she turned seaward. "Are we ready to be exchanged?" This was the almost faithless query which many were constantly asking. So often deceived in the past, it would kill us, if now we were to believe and be disappointed! As we steamed down the harbor the keen December wind drove us to the sheltered side of the decks where, hugging our blankets, we watched the various points which were revealed through the mist: Castle Pinckney, Fort Moultrie and Sullivans Island. But all eyes were peering with intense gaze out into the thick haze. What were all these shivering skeletons trying to fathom? I glanced upward and saw the look of interest and sympathy upon the face of a rebel guard, who stood upon an upper deck looking down upon us. He knew what we were seeking. At last old ragged Fort Sumter came in view and as we passed close under its ruined battered walls, all eyes for a moment turned toward the historic pile.

Then the wheels of our boat ceased to revolve, and we were conscious of swinging around. Suddenly, the gaze of the prisoners, which had been confined to the southward, took in a sight which burst like a shock upon us. There, high before us only a few yards away, lay the majestic steamer, *City of New York*, from whose top mast waved the grand old Stars and Stripes and whose decks were covered with the old familiar boxes of hardtack and barrels of pork. Our eyes took in all the details but still were riveted on one object as in a dream—the dear old flag. The scene that followed beggars description. Men shouted and cheered, laughed like idiots, cried like babies, others danced or grasped each other and all acted like mad men. While the two vessels were being made fast to each other, our eyes would keep going back to the glorious flag.

No surer evidence of patriotic love was ever seen and no future events in my life can ever efface that wonderful scene. The *City of New York* was our flag of truce boat—stationed here from which prisoners from both sides were exchanged. Nothing could better show the paternal care of our government than the bounteous provision made for the comfort of all who passed over her decks. Gazing up on her decks our eyes were gladdened by the sight of ladies connected with the U.S. Sanitary Commission whose tender ministrations did so much for our battered armies. For six long months hardly once had I been privileged to see a woman. How comfortable looked the clean, bright, warmly clad officers and men who were moving about on her decks.

Before night had fallen we were all counted off and had stepped on our boat, breathing once more the blessed air of liberty, although at present a very chilly biting air. The official act of exchange was for a Union officer to stand on one side of the gangplank and a Confederate officer on the other side, each calling aloud the number of each prisoner as he passed over the plank. Once on our decks, we found ourselves in the presence of the quartermaster's stores where each man drew a new suit of clothing—entire with blankets. As fast as this was done, we passed to an inner cabin where guards were stationed and once more we were under espionage; but as the reason of it dawned upon us, our grateful hearts accepted the situation. We were required to strip off every vestige of clothing which was immediately taken by the point of the bayonet and tossed through an open door into the ocean. Only the contents of pockets or haversacks could we keep for relics. Anything that could harbor or conceal any vermin or disease was cast away.

We were then passed forward and found another vessel, *Star of the South*, joined to this, to which we passed and drew our first ration in God's country: hardtack, boiled salt pork, and hot coffee—the genuine, old fashioned, liberal supply which tasted like nothing we had seen for six months. After enjoying my supper in the warm cabin, I crawl off to the upper deck and find a warm cozy nook by the side of the smokestack, enveloped in a thick-warm-woolen shirt, pants, stockings, blouse, overcoat and blanket, with a clear, cold, starlit sky over me. I thank my Heavenly Father for my changed condition and drop to sleep.

December 11

The morning opens keen and cold. Rarely in a man's lifetime is there vouchsafed to him so great a change in physical surroundings. Waking late after a dreamless sleep, I get a late breakfast and receive an additional ration of onions which are eaten raw—this for the alleviation of scurvy. A bright, clear, sunlit day opens and a magnificent view of Charleston harbor is spread before us. Another load of our companions from Florence was brought down to the "flag of truce" boat for exchange, while another vessel lays at anchor not far off, laden with Union officers awaiting exchange. The ladies of the Sanitary Commission were busy all day attending to the wants of the sick. At night the steamer *United States* arrives and takes us all on board her spacious decks, and we sail away out of sight of the accursed Stars and Bars, the emblem of Hades in rebellion; never more to set eyes upon it only as a memento of a fallen cause. Laird and I still stick together and find a warm nook down in the hold near the prow where we spread our blankets and find rest for the night.

December 12

A fine day finds us out on the broad ocean. Although we dropped down the harbor last night, we did not weigh anchor until daylight. Watched with interest the gunboats composing our blockading fleet as we passed them. Facing northward the wintry air is very sharp so I do not remain on deck much of the day. Nurses find much to do in caring for the sick, many of whom are dying almost in sight of home. The heavy swell of the ocean toward night caused much seasickness. Doubtless the stomachs unaccustomed to nourishing and hearty food were peculiarly sensitive to the pitching and rolling. The evening was beautiful and cold with a full moon.

December 13

Cloudy with a bleak northeasterly wind. The sails of our vessel were furled during the night in anticipation of Hatteras gales. The captain's wife was the good angel of mercy, distributing supplies of vinegar, soap, pickles, towels and underclothing. At three in the afternoon we rounded Cape Hatteras. Saw the lighthouse and our blockading fleet off the inlet. At dark the clouds were heavy but no Hatteras gales have disturbed us yet.

December 14

Cloudy and light rain. Reached Hampton Roads at light and touched at Fortress Monroe for mails. A large fleet of vessels of all kinds and sizes lay at anchor here. After an hour's stop we proceed up the Chesapeake. At three o'clock in the afternoon we pass Point Lookout. Toward night we realize that we are nearing our destination so the boys become very jovial. I laid down to rest at dark and secure a good nap.

December 15

At midnight we are aroused and transferred to a light draft steamer, *Olas*, which lands us at the wharf of the Naval School Buildings at Annapolis, Maryland. Stepping out from our warm quarters, we encounter snow and ice and a keen winter's night. The change almost overcomes me as it does many others. I learn that thirty-three poor fellows have died during our three days voyage. Very hard to die so near home. Can the stain ever be wiped out which rests upon those persons whose refinement of cruelty has emptied the southern prisons of such wrecks of manhood? The demoniac spirit which permitted slavery has exhibited itself in its most hideous form by these awful past six months, and it seems surely as if I had truly stepped foot in God's country when I dragged my weak body up to the quarters provided in the College Green barracks.

At daylight a happy surprise was in store for me. I find the commandant of the post, who has charge of all the released prisoners, is no other than kindhearted, efficient Captain Davis of the 21st Massachusetts, who went out to war in my own Company A. The sympathetic, tenderhearted man, with eyes filled with tears when I made myself known to him, immediately takes me right into his house where I find his wife and little child, and I am accorded a warm welcome. The strangeness of being inside a pleasant home, sitting down to dinner at a table covered with a white cloth and eating in a civilized way, I do not get used to. It all seems like a romance or like a delightful dream from which I must soon awake. The great blank of the past six months of my life begins to fill up as the Captain and his wife tell me the news. News of the progress of the war, of the old 21st which had disbanded, of brother Henry who was shot through the lung at the Mine explosion before Petersburg last summer while trying to rally some colored troops; after lying near death's door for a long time, he had rallied and was now at home.

During the afternoon we were again ordered down to the great bathhouses where all undergo the luxury of warm baths. New clothing is furnished to all so that we may be completely free from vermin and disease. Colonel Tufts,[1] the agent appointed by Massachusetts to look after her boys, came through our barracks, found me and made inquiries as to my condition and needs (I think I am pretty well cared for). Another load of prisoners arrived at night which filled up all available space.

December 16

A cloudy day with freezing wintry air foretelling a snowstorm. I wrote my first letter home. Each state's troops were separated by themselves and mustered in for pay. I found Banks[2] and Tyler of the 21st, who have just arrived. After supper all the prisoners who came by the steamer *United States* were ordered to march to Camp Parole; we tramp out through Annapolis for two miles and a half, reaching there late in the evening. As each state is furnished with separate barracks, I am at last parted from my good friend Laird, who goes into the Pennsylvania barracks.

December 17

Cloudy and light rain with a heavy mist. I took cold last night and am not well today. Our quarters are light, clean and comfortable. Some Rhode Island fellows are in our barracks so I bunk with Church[3] of the 2nd Rhode Island. Wrote to Henry and was mustered in for "commutation of rations"—allowance of money for rations which I did not get while a prisoner of war. We drew three meals a day, having all we can eat, but are cautioned to be careful and not eat too much as many are hurt and often killed by the great tax on the enfeebled digestive organs. Rations of soup for dinner and sauerkraut for supper.

December 18

Cloudy and cold. I reported at the surgeon's headquarters and received medicine for cough and cold. I feel quite rusty and mean. The boat load of prisoners which followed us have now joined us at Camp Parole, and a large number have left to join their regiments. A chaplain of a Vermont regiment came in to see and talk with us—this being the Sabbath. In the evening services were held in the chapel.

December 19

A cold northeast storm all day. I found Orville Booth[4] of the 26th Mass, who was a prisoner in Richmond last fall. After his release he went home to Ashby on a furlough and has lately returned, so I learned news from home. At night receive orders for our commutation checks. More returned prisoners came up from the city and others were sent home on furloughs. Cleared up cold at night.

December 20

Cold and freezing wind during the day. I went over to the barracks of the duty men—those who are fit for duty—and found Orville Booth and Isaac March[5] (Ashby boys) and had a good talk and heard lots of news from home. Received commutation check. Many of the boys were able to get their's cashed and at once steered for the sutlers where they indulged in luxuries. I found Gethings and learned that Porter and Osgood were on their way home from Florence. Good!

December 21

Storm of snow and rain. At noon we were called to headquarters where we signed our muster and payrolls so I steer for the sutlers tent. I cough very hard and feel quite sick. Only part of the troops were paid off—two months pay.

December 22

Fair but very cold; freezing all day. More paroled prisoners came up from town. I have a very sore throat. We seem to be undergoing a system of general building up while awaiting the various red tape requirements after which furloughs will be furnished.

December 23

Clear and cold. Went over to headquarters the forenoon where my descriptive list was made out for my furlough.

December 24

Clear, mild and thawing. In the morning I was called to headquarters where I received my welcomed furlough; bought tickets to New York and received my two months pay—the balance to come later. Then a grand rush was made for the railroad station. When the train for Baltimore arrived, there were not half cars enough to accommodate our number. In their intense desire to get started for home, the crowding and jam was fearful. I became frightened, expecting to be crushed to death but managed to get free and saw the train move off with men hanging on to every inch of available space. Was thankful to get out unharmed but disappointed to again be left behind as is my usual lot. I found, however, that I could take the night boat from Annapolis, so I walked down to the city and boarded the steamer, *Star for Baltimore*, where I found comfortable quarters and a quiet ride—arriving at Baltimore at eleven in the evening.

December 25

Quite a company of us tramped about the silent, deserted streets until we found the Baltimore and Ohio depot but learned that no train would go out until morning. A kindhearted policemen, finding out our dilemma, took us in charge and managed to find comfortable quarters for us all. I, with several others, found a place to lie down on the floor of a kitchen in the rear of a lager-beer saloon, where a warm fire was kept burning all night, and we were comfortable. I caught an hour's nap at dawn; the generous saloon keeper sent us on our way with all the eggnog we could drink—free of charge.

Heard the early morning Christmas bells. At ten we left Baltimore and went on to Philadelphia, arriving at four in the afternoon; walked across the city to the Union Refreshment Saloon where a fine supper was furnished us and the kindest attention. At dark we cross the river on a ferryboat and took cars for New York. As the train was late in starting, we made the fastest time I ever knew—some of the way covering a mile in a minute; arrived in New York at ten. Were taken in charge by Colonel Howe, the New England agent caring for soldiers, who escorted us to fine quarters on Broadway at the New England Rooms. I crawled between white sheets—the first time for nearly eight months—and slept.

December 26

A drizzling rain all day. Got up at five in the morning and after breakfast went out into the city shopping. At two in the afternoon I sat down to a grand banquet given by patriotic New Yorkers to the soldiers who sere stopping at the New England Quarters. Speeches were made by Colonel Howe, E.C. Bailey of the *Boston Herald* and others. At night took passage on the steamer, *City of New York* of the Norwich line.

December 27

After supper went to bed and at midnight reached Allepus Point; by express train to Worcester—reaching there at four. As I went into the station I found Banks of Company K who had preceded me in coming from Annapolis. He was in a shocking condition. It was with much difficulty that I was able to learn that he was in the midst of the crowd which boarded the train at Camp Parole, Annapolis, from which I so narrowly escaped. His body was literally crushed in by the mad mob, and the once great strong burly fellow was apparently dying. He had been cared for and helped along so far and was now about to take the last stage to his home in Westminster. (I learned after reaching home that he died soon after he had been carried into his own home in the presence of his mother and sisters, but he was unable to tell them anything about it. I was, therefore, able to give them the particulars of the sad case.)

In the afternoon I continued my journey to Fitchburg, where I found many interested friends with whom I found a warm welcome. As father had not expected me so soon, I remained over night in Fitchburg.

December 28

And now comes the closing stage in my homeward journey. Dividing my time while in Fitchburg between Uncle Joseph and Dr. Alfred Hitchcock, the day quickly passed and at night my good father came for his wandering son, "who was lost and is found, who was dead and is alive again."

Reached home at seven in the evening and was clasped in the arms of my mother, who was the only person who had clung to the hope that I was still alive. All my friends had long given me up and mourned for me as dead. The last news of or from me was the letter I had written in Richmond just after my capture. No others which I had written were ever received until I arrived at Annapolis. The newspaper had reported me as "wounded and captured" after the Battle of Cold Harbor. Then the terrible reports of the mortality in Andersonville had confirmed the feeling that I should never again be heard from.

The excitement over all I had passed through during the journey home left me prostrate, and I was kept quiet for a few days but gradually recovered and soon felt that I was nearly as good as new.

December 29 and 30: [No entries]

December 31, 1864 [Saturday] and January 1, 1865 [Sunday]

The closing day of the eventful 1864 brought my brother Henry[6] and wife over from Templeton so that when the bright new years sun shone out on the peaceful Sabbath morning, it found us a reunited happy family. As the usual Thanksgiving day had been a sad one, no attempt had been made to celebrate it. The New Year's Sabbath was, therefore, made a most complete and appropriate one. After the public acknowledgments to Almighty God for the restored health of the wounded brother and released prisoner, we all sat down to the old fashioned New England feast of which I had so often dreamed and planned during the weary hours of captivity.

Last entries in the diary:

The brightening skies in our country's storm removed all thought of any need for any future services so that when the thirty-day furlough had expired, I received my discharge from Uncle Sam's service on the 26th day of January 1865 together with back pay and commutation pay in Boston. Truly such a generous and paternal Government deserved all the best services which her loyal subjects could give to her.

The 21st Massachusetts Regiment was mustered out of service on August 30, 1864, when discharge papers were made out for every member present or absent. I was absent and the discharge I found awaiting me. If I was technically out of the service, I was not so considered either by John Reb or Uncle Sam; so when the date of my furlough expired on January 26, 1865, another discharge paper was furnished me on which was indorsed the payment of bounty, back pay, commutation, subsistence furnished and transportation.[7]

*   *   *

Eighteen

Commentary on the Union Prisoners of War

During the Civil War, the United States housed approximately 220,000 prisoners and the Confederacy about 200,000 prisoners. Adjutant General Fred C. Ainsworth, Chief of the Records and Pension Office, reported in 1903 that "according to the best information now obtainable, from both Union and Confederate records, it appears that 211,411 Union soldiers were captured during the Civil War, of which number 16,668 were paroled on the field and 30,218 died while in captivity; and that 462,634 Confederate soldiers were captured during the war, of which number 247,769 were paroled on the field and 25,976 died while in captivity." This resulted in a mortality rate of 12 percent in the North and 15.5 percent in the South.

Historians agree that these figures are based on incomplete records and that the numbers for Union prisoners are undoubtedly too low. Several hundred Union prisoners died shortly after being exchanged, but their deaths were not included in the mortality figures.

* * *

Hitchcock's Comments In 1890:

A popular misconception exists concerning the Union prisoners of war: First, as to their value in determining the result of the war, and second, as to their ability to avoid capture.

Public sympathy for these unfortunate men has always been heartfelt and widespread, but just as in the John Brown episode before the war, many believed its importance was magnified beyond all reason and overlooked its real significance and far reaching influence; so in this, the treatment of the prisoners of 1864 by the Confederate government was a potent force in the overthrow of slavery.

First: In its direct effect, as in a game of checkers where one side is able to pen and hold enough of its opponents "hors de combat" [out of the fight], its victory is assured; so in the spring of 1864 while the South was drained completely of fighting material, the North with its unlimited supply was abundantly able to hold back its great army of captured rebels. Without any intention or desire on the part of the Union government, all exchange of prisoners was withheld many mouths and this kept a hundred thousand men of the best fighting material on both sides out of the arena of war.

How little the North ever felt the burden of caring for her captives—not so with the South. Every one of her men was needed, and her only claim of excuse for starving the Union prisoners—her total inability to procure food—would seem to testify to the great straits in which she was placed. Looking at it from this standpoint, our government could well afford to await the pleasure of the Confederates. This view was often discussed by the Union prisoners in Andersonville with great satisfaction. If we were not fighting in the ranks, we were holding back each his man from the other side.

But a wider and yet more far-reaching influence upon humanity was felt as the actual cause of the delay in exchange of prisoners became known. General Butler[1] could hardly have realized how great was the question which he was attempting to decide in the world's history when he insisted that, in the exchange of man for man, the negro must be considered an equal in the sight of law by the rebel government, as well as by the United States. Thus the grand struggle for human freedom went on, in which the Union prisoner was a factor, until the attention of the whole civilized world was drawn to the spectacle and "Andersonville" became the synonym—not alone of "fratricidal animosity" but was understood to be the result of the barbarism of slavery. Intelligent and humane persons, the world over and notably of the South, were educated to know the devilishness of human bondage. The forty thousand maltreated captives in Andersonville were, in this view of the case, accomplishing more in the grand results of Appomattox than perhaps they could have done by laying down their lives on the bloody battlefields all over the South.

Second: From various sources, both friendly and unfriendly, I have seen statements so misleading in regard to the way our prisoners were captured that to the dispassionate and unbiased mind there must often come the conviction that the prisoners as a class were not the bravest of the brave. For example: In the consideration of the pension bill for prisoners of war by the House of Representatives in Congress on April 21, 1890, Tarsney of Missouri is quoted as saying: "Many—**a large proportion**—were put in prison while evading their duty." The Honorable Mr. Cummings of New York also said: "many a man became a prisoner to escape fight, because he felt safer in prison than alongside his comrade in arms." These may be said to be "unfriendly" criticisms, which are despicable because they were given—not because they believe them—but for an ulterior purpose; namely, to please their constituency. With Tarsney, these utterances were doubly damning because he enforced his words with the assurance that he had been a Union soldier and a prisoner and knew where of he affirmed. It is true that every community has its blacklegs and every army its cowards and traitors, but if ever there was a self confessed Judas, this Tarsney surely is one. Their words are unworthy of notice only for the fact that they were uttered in the halls of Congress and as such have become a part of the history of the nation.[2]

A more worthy critic is found in the historian of the 21st Massachusetts Regiment, General Walcott of Cambridge. In commenting on this subject on the closing page of his book [*History of the Twenty-First Regiment Massachusetts Volunteers*, published in 1882], he used these words: "It is a good thing for an army when men dread to be taken prisoners more than to face the horrors of such battlefields as the summer of 1864 furnished so lavishly in Virginia. It is often so much safer to cling to cover, and surrender, than to run out from an untenable position under fire, that it is well to have the temptation lessened by a lively dread of the consequences of capture. I have heard more than one of the very best and bravest of our comrades say that fear of being sent to Andersonville had a very bracing influence on keeping them up to their work in those dreadful, never-ending days of bloody attrition against earth-works, when it seemed so often as if every real fighting man (and the army was by no means wholly composed of such men) must die before the end was reached."

Now General Walcott was not only a brave soldier but an astute lawyer. He was one whom I delighted to honor and for whom I had high admiration. These are reasons why his words will carry conviction to many minds which have no personal knowledge of the facts but does grave injustice to thousands who were so unfortunate as to fall into the hands of the enemy. Let us examine his statements: "It is a good thing when men prefer to face the horrors of the battlefields of 1864, than to be taken prisoners." Face what horrors? Why, the horrors of standing right up to the work of loading and firing into the enemy as fast as you can when they are making a fierce charge upon you—the moment which tries men's souls and the very moment when cowards and skulkers take to their heels for the rear out of harms way. The horrors of charging on a protected enemy when you see your comrades falling all about you, while you must push forward to secure the coveted position—how, in the name of common sense, can the enemy capture you unless you go where he is?

General Walcott stated that "it is often so much safer to cling to cover and surrender than run from an untenable position under fire." Is this the advice of a brave officer to his men to run from an untenable position for fear of capture? Who is to decide whether it be untenable, you or the enemy? If the commanding officer sees the wisdom of retreat and so orders it, I allow that the act of retreat under fire is as brave as in going forward. But the suggestion is absurd that when a body of soldiers is ordered to yield a position, a part of them deliberately disobey the order and lie, and they watch their retreating comrades, while they willingly welcome the advancing enemy and a "furlough in the South." The opposite is always true; cowards are the ones who will make the quickest time out of harms way. Military discipline had become so perfected in the summer of 1864 that men had learned to become almost automatous—to move as the rest did if they knew it was in obedience to orders. It was only in the earlier years of the war that men took the law into their own hands. Men had no clear knowledge of the movements or intentions of the enemy, and they understood only that the way of safety was with the rest of the command. I speak from the standpoint of a private in the ranks, not as the officer whose duty gives him the opportunity to know more of the situation.

General Walcott stated that "I have heard more than one of the best and bravest of our comrades say that fear of being sent to Andersonville kept them up to their work.." Kept them up to what work? Running away form the enemy for fear of being sent to Andersonville? Or daring the risk of capture to hold a seemingly untenable position. Why did not General Corse,[3] when ordered to "Hold the fort," become "brave" by yielding the untenable position through fear of Andersonville. General Walcott was a good officer, but he could not have been a good private and followed these suggestions.

Or if your take the General's words as a whole you become decidedly mixed in your understanding: "keeping up to the works," "running away from untenable positions," "bloody attrition," "clinging to cover"—I claim that these expressions as they are used, give one the impression that the "bloody attrition" of "keeping up to the work" was the best safeguard from capture, while the very opposite was true. The very large proportion of prisoners captured on the battlefield were those who "clung" not "to cover," but to a coveted position. Men, who having become separated from their commands because their commands had melted away in disorder, are forced to act for the moment on their own responsibility; they believed the wisest and bravest way was to "stick" to their position until the smoke of battle cleared or until it was clearly ascertained where they were to go.

The great routs of the First Bull Run and the 11th Corps at Chancellorsville were well nigh impossible in 1864, because the soldier had got over the foolish though natural habit of "dreading." And this is the one thing I desire to affirm, not for myself alone, but for the forty thousand or more like me, who, possibly not on account of undiluted bravery, but through recklessness it may be or momentary confusion, lost the opportunity to escape; and not one in a hundred found the element of fear the cause of capture. Large numbers were captured in whole commands by the act of surrender on the part of a superior officer.

General Walcott may have in mind some of the soldiers around Petersburg who were sent out—not led out—on some difficult task, and because they failed to execute the task, they were not ordered to retreat—their cowardly brigade commander dared not go to them but "clung to cover." I refer to a well known Pennsylvania officer of the 9th Corps.[4]

Of the number who were captured while straying away from commands on foraging expeditions with or without leave, I can have no idea, but I believe the number to be comparatively small and even these cannot be claimed to have been captured through fear; it was rather through the lack of fear that they permitted themselves to go beyond our lines to secure some coveted plunder.

I trust my friends may take especial pains to understand what I have tried to show: that although fear may and does have a place in every man's breast, it did not control the actions of the prisoners of war—only in very rare instances.

* * *

Appendix A

Historical Supplement

A memorandum from prisoner of war records at the National Archives notes that George A. Hitchcock, Company A, 21st Massachusetts Regiment, was captured at Cold Harbor on June 2, 1864, sent to Andersonville, Georgia, on June 8, 1864, and paroled at Charleston, South Carolina, on December 10, 1864. On December 22, 1864, he was furloughed for 30 days. The muster-out roll, dated December 15, 1864, New York, New York, lists Hitchcock a "prisoner of war since June 2, 1864; enrolled for unexpired time of regiment and entitled to be mustered out when inside our lines."[1] Hitchcock's individual muster-out roll, dated January 23, 1865, Boston, Massachusetts, stated that he was mustered-out on January 23, 1865. In the roster provided in *History of the Twenty-First Regiment*, by Charles F. Walcott (Boston, 1882), Hitchcock was listed as discharged on January 26, 1865.

The life of this literary-minded and intelligent young man was impacted by the ravages of war. He was unable to continue his education and all future employment was hampered by his debilitative health. Henry Hitchcock, George's brother, stated that "at the time of his release from imprisonment and discharge, George was a broken down man with a complication of ailments all of which were due to the exposure of army life and the confinement and privation and starvation while in prison."[2] Francis Wright, a resident of Ashby, noted that when he returned from military prisons, George "came to his father's at Ashby; he was then much emaciated and very feeble—he was a frightful sight."[3]

Although his poor health prevented him from seeking any strenuous work, he did find employment as a clerk at Baldwin's grocery store on Main Street in Fitchburg during April 1865. According to the proprietor, James Baldwin, "when he came to work for me, he plainly showed the effects of his long imprisonment at Andersonville. He lacked vigor and endurance and was generally debilitated in health, had a cough whenever he caught cold and seemed liable to go into a decline from consumption."[4]

After being employed at Baldwin's for less than two years, Hitchcock traveled to Cincinnati, Ohio, where he lived from 1867 to 1869. In Ohio, he boarded with Charles Hayward, his old school companion, served as a book publishing clerk, and taught a large class of black boys, most of whom were former slaves, at the Fowell Buxton Mission in Cincinnati. A fellow Sunday school teacher, Levi Goodale, mentioned that Hitchcock "was not in good health, although he was desirous of having his condition unnoticed."[5] According to Hayward, Hitchcock's hardships as a prisoner of war "had so completely undermined his constitution that any continued close confinement would result in his breaking down completely. He was finally obliged to leave the city on account of his health."[6] When he returned to Fitchburg, Hitchcock was rehired at Baldwin's grocery store and remained until April 1872. James Baldwin noted that "he was not so well and thought the work was too hard for him."

On October 6, 1868, George Hitchcock married Elisabeth Phelps Lowe in Fitchburg. They had two children: George Preston Hitchcock, who was born on June 30, 1870, and Annie Louise Hitchcock, who was born on October 15, 1873. In the early 1870's, George and Elisabeth lived with a friend, S. Austin Childs, and remained there most of the next three years. Childs was very concerned with Hitchcock's health and "thought he would not live many years—that he would die of consumption."[7]

Hitchcock's health, however, continued to slowly improve and by 1875 he was employed as a clerk with the United States & Canada Express Company at the railroad station in Fitchburg. He served for 30 years as a messenger for that company and the New York & Boston Dispatch Express Company. During his career he traveled more than a million miles on trains between Fitchburg and Boston. James Baldwin stated that he "often met him after his return from Boston on a trip as messenger, when he appeared to be all 'used up.'" Baldwin also noted that "he had always been a man of exemplary habits, strictly temperate, honest and industrious."

For most of his life Hitchcock was actively involved with Fitchburg's Calvinistic Congregational Church as teacher and superintendent of the Sunday school, treasurer, clerk and deacon of the church. He wrote the centennial history of the church, *A History of the Calvinistic Congregational Church and Society, Fitchburg, Massachusetts,* which was published in 1902.

Hitchcock was also an active member of the Grand Army of the Republic. He served as historian for the Edwin V. Sumner Post 19 and compiled hundreds of sketches of the war records of Fitchburg veterans. On September 15, 1876, during the tenth reunion of the 21st Massachusetts Regimental Association at Fitchburg, Hitchcock delivered a paper on the prison life of the regimental members at Andersonville which included several extracts from his diary. Charles F. Walcott, a former captain in the regiment, reviewed the "almost perfect daily diary " of Hitchcock's prison life at Andersonville and included a heavily edited version in his *History of the Twenty-First Massachusetts.* According to Walcott, Hitchcock "inserted a few general descriptions, but the record of his daily experiences is exactly as he made it from day to day."

Hitchcock's literary tendencies and patriotic fervor stimulated a deep commitment to the Fitchburg Historical Society after the former veteran's election as a member on March 19, 1900. Hitchcock served as vice president of the institution from 1907 until his death in 1915. While he was a member he wrote and presented numerous papers at society meetings, including the following: 1901—"First half-century of the Calvinistic Congregational Church"; 1904—"From Ashby to Andersonville, a historical reminiscence"; 1906—"A colonial patriot [Robert Kinsman], ancestor of an old Fitchburg family"; 1907—"Early Fitchburg homes" (presented the society with a bound volume of photographs of early homes in Fitchburg); 1911—"From hamlet to city"; and 1913—"Dr. Alfred Hitchcock."[8]

The old veteran spent a number of years unsuccessfully seeking a Federal pension. From 1873 to 1912 Hitchcock was immersed in dealings with the Federal bureaucracy. The lack of medical information—all his doctors were dead and no record of his examinations surfaced—was fatal to his application. In reply to the Commissioner of Pensions in Washington D.C., on August 29, 1881, George noted that "the only medical examination I received at the date of my discharge was by a surgeon of the Rebel army in the Florence stockade (South Carolina) on December 8, 1864, regarding the exchange of all sick prisoners of war." Unfortunately for the young Massachusetts private, Hitchcock did not return to the military after his final furlough and was discharged without any examination. After more than four decades of fighting the government his application for an invalid pension under the act of May 11, 1912, was approved—one year before his death. This time consuming frustration resulted in his bitterness toward Congressmen John C. Tarsney and Amos J. Cummings in 1890 as noted in his "Commentary on the Union Prisoners of War."

George Hitchcock refused to succumb to the frail health that plagued him for so many years. He was a survivor. Few would have predicted that the emaciated soldier discharged in 1865 would outlive his brother, who died in 1897, and his future wife, who passed away on February 6, 1905. In remembrance to Elizabeth, George wrote that "her domestic traits, her love of simplicity and her quiet life, all combined to endear her to the many friends she made all her life by her thoughtfulness and gentleness, and by all will she be remembered most tenderly."[9]

The Hitchcock's children followed widely divergent paths in life. George Preston Hitchcock graduated from Amherst College in 1892 and served in several educational positions: english and science teacher at Ansonia, Connecticut, High School from 1892 to 1893; chemistry teacher at Fitchburg High School from 1893 to 1896, and principal from 1896 to 1903; director of the high school department at Pratt Institute in Brooklyn, New York, from 1903 to 1905; and headmaster at Brookline, Massachusetts, High School from 1905 to 1913. He earned a law degree in 1910, became vice chairman of the faculty at Pratt Institute from 1913 to 1918, and was employed by Nichols Copper Company in New York City from 1918 to 1936. George P. Hitchcock died on May 15, 1957, at New Rochelle, New York. He was survived "by his widow, Carrie; a son, Richard of Babylon, Long Island; a daughter, Mrs. Alexander Drysdale of Pelham Manor, New York; and three grandchildren and three great-grandchildren."[10]

Annie Louise Hitchcock never married, and spent her life living and working in Fitchburg as a bank clerk. George Hitchcock lived with his daughter for the last three years of his life.

Time was catching up to the war's veterans. By the beginning of World War I newspapers around the country were mourning their passing. On November 4, 1915, its was the *Fitchburg Daily Sentinel's* turn. "Another War Veteran Gone—Death of George A. Hitchcock, Soldier in Civil War and Respected Citizen" read the headline to the obiturary. "George Alfred Hitchcock, a resident of Fitchburg for over 40 years, a deacon of the C. C. church and a veteran of the Civil War, died Wednesday evening [November 3, 1915] at his home at 46 Arlington street, aged 71 years, 9 months and 19 days."

*   *   *

"Bones, bones, only a bunch of bones. `Hullo, Hitchcock!' it exclaimed."

Appendix B

"From Ashby to Andersonville"

Presented at the Fitchburg Historical Society on October 17, 1904

George Hitchcock described his personal experiences in U. S. Grant's Overland Campaign in May of 1864, including his capture and imprisonment at Andersonville. This paper and an account of the meeting were published on the front page of the Fitchburg Daily Sentinel *on October 18, 1904.*

*   *   *

The month of April, 1864, was one of preparation. For three long years the Union army had struggle and fought with a brave foe, yet Richmond seemed as secure as ever, the head and brain of the Confederacy.

Grant at Culpeper court house laid his plans and organized the armies of the various sections of the South for united action.

For nearly two years I had campaigned with my regiment up and down the mountains and valleys of Maryland, Virginia, Kentucky and East Tennessee, and after a 200 mile, midwinter march over the mountains, had succumbed to a fever which laid me up in the general hospital at Lexington, Kentucky, for three months. One morning early in April as I was lying on my cot, I was agreeable startled as having received a thirty day furlough.

The following month was therefore one of preparation for me as well as for the commanding general. On the 30th of April, President Lincoln wrote the following letter to General Grant: "Not expecting to see you again before the spring campaign opens, I wish to express, in this way, my entire satisfaction with what you have done up to this time, so far as I understand it. The particulars of your plans I neither know, or seek to know. You are vigilant and self-reliant; and, pleased with this, I wish not to obtrude any constraints or restraints upon you. While I am very anxious that any great disaster, or the capture of our men in great numbers, shall be avoided, I know these points are less likely to escape your attention than they would be mine. If there is anything wanting which is within my power to give, do not fail to let me know it. And now with a brave Army and a just cause, may God sustain you. Yours very truly, A. LINCOLN."

Thus for the first time a free hand had been bestowed upon the field commander, while all former ones had been checked after veritable failure. One week later the campaign opened at the Wilderness. Within a month 55,000 men, or nearly half his army, had been lost, of which 9,000 were made prisoners of war. This in the army of the Potomac alone, exclusive of all the others which were under his control.

Is it strange that the Northern growlers dubbed him "The Butcher," or that Burnside's defenders of the Fredericksburg slaughter claimed that if you would fight a fearless foe, somebodies going to get hurt? The disgusted Confederate officers who could not see any military science in Grant's methods had to recognize later that it was his bull-dog grip which throttled the rebellion.

On the very morning that this bloody work began at the Wilderness, I left my home in Ashby, renewed in health and strength to join my regiment at the front. Arriving in Washington, the prosaic work began with me at once. All the large force of heavy artillery regiments which had guarded the capital since the beginning of the war had been sent to the front and the government depended largely upon just such transients as myself for work of defense, so next morning found me with a large number of new recruits and returning convalescents, with blistering hands, digging on fortifications and building roads. The new recruits (grumbling as usual), claimed they enlisted to fight—not to dig. They had not long to wait for this satisfaction. Twenty-four hours later we were sailing down the Potomac when we received our first supply of ammunition—the biggest I had ever received. They filled our cartridge boxes, while the surplus went into pockets and haversacks. Again the kickers complained of the heavy load and recklessly threw the surplus overboard. Not all my own supply was serviceable to the end, for the extra supply in my haversack became watersoaked a few days later, while lying in damp trenches and drenched in thunder showers. This lent a pungent, saltpeterish taste to my rations.

Passing a boat load of wounded from the Wilderness, en route for Washington, we gave them hearty cheers, but the salute was only feebly responded to by a few waving hands, while the decks were covered with the great silent sheet of torn and mutilated humanity.

Landing at Belle Plain, the great base of supplies for our army, we were again detained for service. The battle of Spotsylvania had just been fought and several thousand rebel prisoners were held here awaiting transportation to Northern prisons. We were therefore detailed to guard these. At midnight of the 18th of May I was startled from a sound slumber by the long roll beaten to warn us of an attack by Mosby's guerrilla band, which had made an attempt to stampede our guard and release the prisoners. They found the guard too strong however, but next morning I was sent with a strong party to reconnoiter in various directions, several miles out, but found no trace of the enemy.

We then pushed on to Fredericksburg. Here we were again held for service. For one whole week I was on duty in this vast charnel house. All the wounded from Wilderness and Spotsylvania, only a few miles distant, were brought here and churches, halls, stores and dwelling-houses were pressed into service. Very few citizens remained, but those who did were obliged to aid in the care of the stricken ones. I found plenty to do, erecting hospital tents, and carrying those who could be moved to the steamers, when they were taken to Washington. In seeking out members of my regiment, I found in one large church whence the pews had been removed, the floors from basement to galleries and steeple converted with suffering ones, wounds in every part of the body. Some were lying very still, while others were crazed with agony. Many who were not severely wounded were aiding in the care of others. Here I found my old tent-mate, Whitney, who had been wounded, but not severely, and was acting in capacity of a nurse. Men were dying and being laid in long rows in the church yard, where army wagons were continually coming and going for their gruesome freight.

Away, up from beyond the distant hills toward the south came rolling the deep sullen boom of cannon proclaiming the continuance of this deadly work. As this city was the first and only rendezvous for all the wounded, it is doubtful if there could have been found from all the battlefields of the war a more dreadful aftermath of suffering, confined in one place. I think also, it may be said of the "scary" feeling which one experiences on approaching a battlefield that it impresses one in inverse proportion to the distance separating us. The appalling sights about me aided the imagination as I listened to the distant roar and thought of apparent recklessness with which human life was being sacrificed

The evening before I left the city I went out alone across the great slaughter-field over which eighteen months earlier I had charged with my regiment upon Marye's Heights when Burnside commanded the Army of the Potomac. Returning through the dark and silent streets, a silence broken here and there by sounds of groans issuing from dimly lighted houses where lay the grievously wounded. There is always a peculiar sense of loneliness in wandering through unlighted city streets at night, add to this these sounds and only here and there the silent sentry moving upon his beat; it was indeed a relief to depart early next morning on a bright warm day, a member of quite a large escort (both cavalry and infantry) for a wagon train. In a southeasterly direction down along the bank of the Rappahannock, past the boyhood home of Washington, past Bowling Green where, over the same road eleven months later, the assassin Booth fled to his death. Grant pushing slowly on toward Richmond, and Lee as resolutely crowding him to the eastward, we were continually meeting bands of negroes of all ages with all their earthly possessions joyously moving northward for the Union army was now in a section hitherto held by the rebels.

We entered the war zone not far from Hanover Court House and began to encounter the putrefying carcasses of the cavalry horses shot during the Sheridan raid two weeks earlier. The sound of artillery firing seemingly nearer, but as mile after mile we marched, we came upon no signs of the near approach to a great army. Grant had indeed cut himself loose from all connection with his base. The commander of our escort began to grow nervous. The men were warned to stick close to the main body and no foraging was permitted. Some of our comrades who had visited distant plantations had not returned and we had been notified that Mosby was hovering around. As night approached the situation grew interesting. The commander urged on the men at double quick step. With his mounted escort this was an easier task than with the infantry. After a mile or more of such a pace the men began to fall out and the line "evaporated." Finally the lieutenant in command of the infantry exclaimed, "colonel may go to the devil if he likes but I am going to halt and collect my scattered men for I am sure we can put up a better fight with Mosby than in our present condition." We were passing through a thickly wooded and quite deserted country, the few white people seen we dared not trust to inquire of for our army's proximity, while the blacks were few and far between. Only the foul and tainted air proclaimed our nearness to the line of march. How easily Mosby could ambush our small party. The darkness of a mid-summer night had shut us in. Very silently we shuffled along, taking care to keep equipments from rattling.

As we were entering some very dark woods where no outline or form was discernible, suddenly the shout rang out, "Halt!" And we did halt. For a few moments the only sound heard was the heart-beat of each individual soldier. Visions of Libby and starvation arose. But after a pause—seemingly unnecessarily long—again came the command, "Advance and give the countersign." Our lieutenant goes forward and puts his head in the lion's mouth—figuratively speaking. But having no countersign, a few moment's conversation in a low tone and he returned to inform us that we had at last reached the cavalry outpost of the Army of the Potomac and we breathe freely once more. One mile further on we pass inside the infantry picket line and see the light of great camp fires two miles beyond, but we drop by the roadside thoroughly exhausted with our 65 mile tramp of the past two days and instantly drop to sleep.

The point where we overtook the army was about twenty miles northeast of Richmond and next morning our lieutenant dismissed his command, each man to hunt up his own regiment, a duty more easily said than done.

With the various corps continually changing position, if by inquiry I learned the location of the 9th Corps two or three miles ahead in a certain place; on reaching there I found it had gone, so it was tramp, tramp all day, but always toward the sound of musketry firing.

Toward night I came upon immense bodies of men in bivouac, preparing for evening coffee. Up and down I walked constantly asking, "What corps?" "What division?"

What a busy noisy scene the clatter of picks and shovels, the tramp of cavalry, the ringing orders from brigade officers, the hum of voices of the tired troops as they were gathered around their fires, munching hard tack! It was sunset and brigade bands far and near were sounding out the evening "retreat calls." A thousand drums rolling out the various parts in direct discord, the click of axes and crash of falling trees, the incessant rattle of musketry and occasional roar of artillery, all these gave me a thrilling sense of the active campaign. At last the answer to my oft repeated query "21st Mass," and I was in the midst of familiar faces and "at Home."

Five months had passed since I had been separated from my regiment. It was my first absence from it but how changed. Since then it had been recruited to full ranks in Massachusetts and now after three weeks of daily fighting the old familiar faces seemed few. "Killed, wounded or prisoner," was the answer to my inquiry. How hungry I was, and how good the army coffee tasted. I was busily asking and answering when, before half an hour had passed, the call came "Hitchcock you are detailed for the skirmish line." "What! so soon?" "You are fresh fish and the rest of us have had it every night for a month." After a seventy mile forced march, after watching for guerrillas, building roads, caring for wounded and all sorts of guard duty, I was hardly "fresh fish." Yet the worn, pinched faces of my comrades shut out all thought of murmur and under the friendly shelter of darkness I went out hardly twenty rods to the front where there was an incessant flashing of skirmish firing with the attendant whizzing of the minnie ball.

Here I was a last, up against the adamantine wall of the Army of Northern Virginia. Back there in Fredericksburg I might feel appalled, but here on the outer most front line with the two great armies only a few rods away on either side, with nerves tense and senses quickened by the feeling of responsibility, there was no room for fear. I was at my post of duty on the firing line and that was enough. My instructions were that I must not fire unless attacked and all the cracking of sharpshooters or nervous sentinels had no interest for me. I could not help the thought that not many had experienced so many phases of army life in so short a time as I. If I had the prescience to include the experiences of the next few days, it would have seemed overwhelming.

Very early next morning, May 30, the whole army was on the move, but little progress was made—marching to new portions seemed to be the order of the day and the 9th Corps was placed on the right of the main army near Bethesda Church. We were now on the Cold Harbor field, part of the army occupying the same advanced ground held by McClellan two years earlier. The next two days were occupied by Grant in crowding back Lee. But he would not be crowded. In taking our position we passed by the little country church standing alone in the edge of the woods. This was occupied, for the day, by Grant, as his headquarters. As it was near the noon hour we saw many of his staff officers seated outside under the trees, upon the pews taken from the church—some eating their lunch, others hurrying in and out with orders. I could but think, as I passed the door, how the thought of the whole civilized world rested with expectancy upon that man just within.

As the day waned the army was transformed to a gang of diggers and we worked until far into the night, raising a very safe line of breast works; then lying down to sleep. But half an hour had hardly elapsed when an attack from the enemy started us up to defend the advanced position and so this night passed. The next two days were hot and the same tactics were repeated only we held our same line of fortifications without material advance. A large detail of the corps was continually crowding its picket line right up into the enemy's.

I was on one particularly dangerous post at the apex of our line where the enemy was on three sides of it. Our protection was logs and a hole dug into the ground. Several of our 21st boys had been shot here. While hugging the ground, peering through the crevices, I noticed the deadly work of one rebel sharpshooter sheltered behind a tree, when a very peculiar incident attracted my gaze. The field in front was dotted over with many little dwarf shrubs. One of these I discovered to have changed position although I scarcely discovered perceptible motion. For half an hour this continued until suddenly a shot flashed out from it, the rebel sharpshooter dropped and up sprang one of Burnside's Indian sharpshooters (from Northern Wisconsin) and fled in safety back into our lines. By this ruse under shelter of the bush he had got his victim in range of his deadly rifle.

At dusk this advanced position was abandoned and while our picket detail of several hundred were skulking back through the dense underbrush to our main line, we heard behind us the crackling of twigs and suddenly the familiar rebel yell rang out as a long line of gray came charging out upon us. Dropping down behind the shelter of some felled trees we prepared to meet the onset. Their line halted and a blinding sheet of flame greeted us unscathed. Then at the command of Captain Sampson we rose up and fired square into the enemy's ranks when they prudently retired. A few rods farther back we retire and drop exhausted; I find my old tent mate, Jack Reynolds, writhing in mortal agony with his side torn open by an exploding shell which had also sent Warren of Company K to his last bivouac.

The morning of June 2nd dawned hot and sultry. The day advanced without the accustomed racket. It must be remembered that the soldier in the ranks knows less of general army movements at such times than those far away who read the papers. Occasional rumors of plans come to us. Butler had joined our army with his army of the James six miles farther down. Collisions had continually taken place which at any other stage of the war would have been honored by the name of battles. That our army had made no real progress during the past three days was evident to all. A feeling of depression was upon us all. As the afternoon advanced the skies were overcast with thunder clouds and our sweltering boys in the trenches were ordered to crawl on hands and knees to the right, hold equipments so that they might not rattle. Half a mile we may have gone in this manner; a strange sight it would have been if one could have looked on it from the trees above. To the experienced soldier this movement was made with much trepidation. It was the enemy's opportunity which he quickly discovered.

The whole 9th Corps was thus withdrawn from the enemy's front to a point a little to the north of Bethesda Church. We were marching to the rear, spread out on a broad open field, when out from the woods behind us belched the fire of the rebel artillery, sweeping murderously through our ranks. Quickly swinging into battle lines, we charged back on the gray ranks which were advancing out of the woods; the battle was on. The line we had just vacated left an opening which the enemy was quick to occupy and our line of battle was flanked by them. Simultaneous with the breaking of the storm of earth's artillery, heaven's artillery let loose, and a typical Southern downpour broke from the skies. Halting in an exposed position, we poured our fire into the enemy which was rushing to get into our rear. The field was swept with a leaden fire, lines were breaking here and there, our boys went down like grain cut by a sickle, and finally the command to retreat was given, but too late for many of us. The enemy swept up between us and the main body. Some had succeeded in scaling a Virginia fence and escaped; others took shelter behind a log shanty, while I leaped into a rifle-pit to escape the pitiless storm. I had not long to wait before the on-rushing line of gray had reached me. "Throw down your gun and surrender!" a command which I answered by pointing to my rifle which lay half covered in the pool of water of the rifle pit. My active military career had ended.

A brigade of North Carolina regiments under General Rodes, Ramseur's Division, Ewell's Corps, were my captors. A man from the ranks was immediately detailed to take me to the rear and in the deepening twilight I was hurried back over the ground where we had just been fighting and saw the rebel soldiery busy disrobing our dead and dying comrades. A little further on a rebel battery was taking position in the edge of the woods when one of the officers ordered me to give up my brand new rubber blanket. As the rain was pouring in torrents, I naturally demurred, but not for long, for his hand went down to his holster, out came a revolver, and off came my blanket. Further on new arrivals of Union prisoners were added until several hundred were gathered. All this time the roar was deafening. A few years ago I stood on this battlefield when a farmer, who had lived near by during and ever since the war, pointed out a ravine which he said was literally filled with dead men and horses of Union batteries which was the result of that terrific fire, when darkness ended the horror.

Just before being turned into a field for a night bivouac, I discerned in the darkness the forms of men carrying past me a wounded Union soldier. Inquiry revealed the fact that another of my former tent mates, Charley Wilder of Worcester, was being taken to die in Libby prison.

Next morning breaks and our company—bedraggled and soaked to the skin with an all-night downpour—looks around and discovers many familiar faces of comrades who had met the common misfortune. Up from across Chickahominy Swamp came clear, the sounds of the awful struggle and carnage which constituted the culmination of the Battle of Cold Harbor. This was virtually ended early on the morning of June 3 and Grant retired, foiled, as had been McClellan and Burnside before him, but he was frank to acknowledge that this was the one battle he never ought to have fought. And now for me it was "on to Richmond" with a vengeance. After marching westward two or three miles we pass by General Lee's headquarters at Mechanicsville House and then crossing the Fredericksburg railroad, enter the outer fortifications where a preliminary fleecing of Union prisoners took place. Overcoats and knapsacks disappeared; then onward until we enter through another line of fortifications beyond which was a great clean swept field, beyond this, a mile away, we see scores of blackmouthed cannon which could have swept off Grant's whole army if he had chosen to take this for assault.

Into the city, over Capitol hill, past the rebel capitol building, on whose steps and balconies we saw distinguished looking men whose names would doubtless be quickly recognized if we had known them; down through the streets crowded with people curious to see the unusually long line of Union blue. The failure of the Union arms made them unusually jubilant and sarcastic as we pass on and down toward the James River and at last enter the great tobacco warehouse known as Pemberton prison, directly opposite Libby prison. Three strenuous weeks had now rounded me up here "hors de combat."

A sort of vague nightmare rumor had been floating around during the past month of some dreadful place in the distant South where our boys were being carried and shut up to die like the flies which taste the poison paper. Nothing definite, only a place called Camp Sumter in Southern Georgia. Andersonville prison-pen was not then known. When Grant planned his great campaign in April, the Confederate government met these plans with the project of storing up its captives in this secluded place and all the wasted victims of Libby and Belle Isle were removed there. The black record of Libby had therefore passed into history at this time for these prisons were used only as temporary store houses for prisoners to await transportation to the great central southern prison.

This visit of a week in Richmond was not one of unalloyed pleasure, yet it prepared me for a future which needed preparation as the days lengthened into weeks and months. The first night every new arrival was ordered to strip off every shred of clothing and examined for hidden money or valuables. All money, jackknives, cooking utensils or extra clothing was taken away, and when returning to quarters, each man was in light marching order. They vouchsafed to return to me my army diary and pocket Testament. My army blanket was the one article of vital need which was spared to me. From Pemberton I was hustled across the street to Libby where I remained but one day, finding it much the same as the former place, both overrun with vermin and stench from sinks opening directly into our rooms whose doors were never closed. Not a head ever dared expose itself at the windows, for a rebel bullet was ever ready for such a mark and only the day before my arrival one man was shot in my room. From here I wrote my last letter to reach home—all later ones were never received—and for this reason my friends gave me up as dead, when the terrible rumors of mortality in Andersonville spread over the North.

On the 9th of June the journey to Andersonville began, which occupied just one week. A long line of rickety box cars packed with Union prisoners rolled slowly out of Richmond, down through the heart of the Confederacy, by way of Danville, Virginia, Greensboro and Salisbury, North Carolina, Columbia, South Carolina, and Augusta and Macon, Georgia. The journey was made without more incident than any other cattle train, for in all respects we were treated like cattle, receiving our light rations of half cooked corn-fodder occasionally, only we could talk. Nearing our destination toward noon of the 16th of June, those of us sitting near the half open door saw a repulsive looking dirty brown serpent stretched, lazily sunning on the embankment by the side of the railroad, which our rebel guard told us was a copperhead—one of the most deadly poisonous serpents known—when one of our number innocently replied, "Why! I thought a copperhead was a Northern rebel."

Arriving at our destination we were very curious to witness our surroundings, a very flat country with a cleared space around the railroad station, while beyond in all directions stretched tall pine forests; a few rough board shanties recently erected for commissary stores and but few natives in sight. A kind of out-of-the-world feeling possessed us, coming as we had, directly from the heart-center of the nation. As we bundled out of the cars we had not long to wait before realizing that the lid was being raised and we were treated to a sight of the chief demon of the nether regions; Captain Wirz came riding up through the crowd, storming and cursing the "damned Yanks," striking with his plantation whip any who happened in his pathway. It was my first knowledge of the character which later helped to make the place a world-wide horror. We were taken to his headquarters, a quarter of a mile distant where we were obliged to stand an hour while being registered by uncouth, ignorant, rebel sergeants. Just before we reached this place on a slight eminence, we came in sight of a huge stockade consisting of pine logs set upright, fitting close together 20 feet in height, along the top of which were perched sentry-boxes in which were those murderous Georgian home guards, who shot the starving fellows who wandered beyond the dead-line. When we halted in front of Wirz's little board shanty, I turn and look. Now the lid was off and I was gazing into Hades—like a disturbed monster anthill, I saw a huge moving mass of black through a dim, low-lying haze of smoke which rose from countless pine wood fires all over the camp, which gave a realism to the hellish picture.

In a space of eighteen acres, of which two acres were an impassable swamp, nearly thirty thousand men were packed without any semblance of order or system. Given a keeper like Wirz, a typical old slave driver, and this pack of humanity turned indiscriminately and purposely unorganized, and the result could be nothing else.

When at last we enter, and the huge gates close behind us; it was well that the veil was not lifted for me to see the five months which were to drag so slowly by before I could again go out, or to see the long silent procession of fourteen thousand [12,912 Union prisoners died between February 24, 1864 and May 4, 1865] of my comrades carried out and laid like cord wood in the trenches near at hand.

We move slowly along through the dense pack of emaciated, half-naked humanity blackened by hovering over the pitch-pine smoke of the little fires, the requisite for cooking each individual larder, each one anxiously watching for familiar faces. It was this great on-coming procession from every battlefield of the South, which interested us most. All through my imprisonment, like a breeze from "God's country," I long to escape from the crowd and sit down and rest after long standing; but it was a difficult task. When I succeeded, I became conscious of the searching gaze riveted upon me of a tall gaunt, black man, whose only covering was a worn out pair of cotton drawers nearly as black as his skin. Bones, bones, only a bunch of bones. "Hullo, Hitchcock!" it exclaimed.

Let us go back seven months to a point of time when our army was chasing Longstreet up through the mountain wilderness of East Tennessee. One chill cloudy day in December, my regiment had been deployed in a long skirmish line extending across the Clinch valley. I was toiling far up the mountain side, over rocks, through tangled under brush and forest. It was a wild, rough tramp of several miles in which we encountered no enemy but we had evidently not swept the country clean. As my part of the line was passing through a difficult place where great rocks and rugged precipices forced me to make a wide detour to the left, I became separated from my right hand comrade, Bailey of Company I. It was only for a few minutes when again closing in at the requisite distance of about twenty feet, he had disappeared. I joined to the next man above as the line kept moving forward and Bailey was never seen again. It was an eight day mystery and then he was forgotten. We knew him too well to believe he had deserted in that lonely region and assumed that he had fallen among the rocks and been injured and died; but a later search did not reveal him.

When my questioning gaze searched for recognition in those blackened features, I could scarce believe my eyes when he said, "Don't you know Bailey?" The great tall six footer then sat down by my side and told a thrilling tale. How that when passing through a ravine after losing sight of me, two guerrillas sprang out from the bushes; taking away his gun, they forced him to run on; when the summit was gained, they were beyond our reach. Then a long, tedious tramp into the enemy's lines and from Bristol, Tennessee, he was taken by rail to Richmond, where he passed the winter at Castle Thunder and Belle Isle. When Andersonville was open, he was among its first occupants. His clothing all worn and gone, suffering constantly from cold, the scurvy already fast taking away his life. With a dull apathetic look he talked on and I realized that one of the 21st stalwart and faithful men was fast nearing his end. Within a month he was laid away in the long trench. Here, too, we find the missing foragers of our Fredericksburg march a month ago, which proved that our dangers on that march to join the army were more real than imaginary.

The remainder of the day was spent in seeking out our old 21st comrades—Charley Goodrich among the number—and a worn, discouraged lot they were. Almost the first feature of our prison life was the intolerable stench pervading every corner of the pen, arising from the refuse of the thousands of diseased and dying men who were unable to go down to the swamp. This feature remained unremittingly to the end.

The oft repeated query—"What did they give you to eat and how did you spend your time?"—might be answered by giving a recital of an average day's occupation which was repeated with monotonous regularity by the many incidentals arising where thirty thousand human beings were kept so closely together.

Our day most naturally began late in the afternoon when the eagerly-watched-for ration teams were drawn into camp drawn by mules, all the work done by Union prisoners under guard. Bags of coarse white meal hulls and crushed cob, and sides of beef, varied occasionally by sides of rancid "sowbelly," cow-peas, new molasses and rice, but never more than two kinds daily. After the first months the number of prisoners became so large that these supplies were furnished uncooked and a ration of pine wood about the size of a policeman's "billy" must suffice each man for his daily cooking.

Like impatient cattle we watched the process of distribution, first to detachments of 270 which was then divided into three parts for 90 men and then to the squads of 30 when each member crowded around the distributor or sergeant and jealously watched for an equitable division. A beef shin-bone with every shed of meat cleaned from it was considered equivalent to the little slice of clear meat because of the juices in the cells of the bone, and many a bone have I chipped to pieces with my old broken case-knife to extract the luscious contents.

After distribution, which often was not completed until dark, the most famished would immediately devour their own and then greedily watch others in preparation. My usual custom was to halve mine, eat one part and bury the remainder in the ground. Then take down from the stick-supports my woolen blanket which had been our shelter from the sun, wrap it around us, lying on the rubber blanket of my comrade, pass the night listening to coughs and groans of the sick and the droning call of the guard, "Post number one and all's well." If the weather was stormy we kept the rubber over and the woolen under us.

In the morning an hour or two was spent in waiting our chance to bathe at the brook where thousands were stirring up the black muddy water in washing. After this a stroll up to the gate to see the long line of dead awaiting burial if perchance we might discover a familiar face. Then returning to quarters when the rebel sergeants came in to call the rolls. When this was completed, the remainder of our ration was devoured, and as the sun began to pour down its vertical rays upon us, we sat under our shelter examining clothing for vermin, reading my little Testament, writing up my diary, planning the fancy dinners we would get when we got away, and dozing away the hours until afternoon, when the whistle of the distant locomotive notified us that a new influx of prisoners was coming; my comrade and I took turns in going to the gate to watch for them. It was never safe to leave our few belongings alone for thieves were ever on the watch for such an opportunity. As the day waned the camp was on "qui vive" for the coming of the ration wagons again.

Although the Union soldier seems to have preempted the claim to know the tortures of starvation better than others, it is a Confederate officer who has most accurately delineated them. George Cary Eggleston says, "Hunger to starving men is wholly unrelated to the desire for food as that is commonly understood and felt. It is a great agony of the whole body and of the soul as well. It is unimaginable, all-pervading pain inflicted when the strength to endure pain is utterly gone. It is a great despairing cry of a wasting body—a cry of flesh and blood, marrow, nerves, bones and faculties for strength with which to exist and to endure existence. It is a horror which, once suffered, leaves an impression that is never erased from the memory."[1]

The tragedies of the dead-line, stamping out the raiders, listening to the weird baying of bloodhounds on the trail of escaping prisoners, the miraculous Providence spring, our Fourth of July concert, comrades nursing each other in sickness or closing their eyes in death, the final joyous release when close by old battered Fort Sumter's walls I stepped under the folds of Old Glory after more than six months of imprisonment, all these, and more, might furnish texts for whole chapters, but this must suffice to give a vivid contrast between Ashby and Andersonville.

George A. Hitchcock

Company A, 21st Massachusetts Regiment

October, 1904

*   *   *

"The whole matter was a sudden and impulsive outbreak, incited by bad liquor with which the soldiers had been supplied from some source unknown to their officers. . ."

Appendix C

The Incident at the Railroad Depot
March 30, 1863, in Columbus, Ohio

1. *Daily Ohio State Journal*, Columbus, Ohio, March 31, 1863:

An Unfortunate Affair: Riotous Proceedings—Soldiers Attack the Provost Guard—They are Fired Upon—Serious and Fatal Results

We regret to be called upon to announce the occurrence of a serious affray in our streets yesterday that led to fatal results to some of the parties concerned.

During the afternoon, three immense trains of cars, having on board a large portion of a brigade of troops appertaining to Gen. Burnside's command, en route for Kentucky, arrived at our depot. In view of preventing straggling, a small force of the Provost Guard was stationed near the depot. After the trains had stopped, a considerable number of soldiers left the cars and were making their way up into the city. As they emerged from the depot they were halted by the guard; to which the soldiers (being somewhat heated with drink) offered some slight resistance and much abuse. They were, however, turned back by the guard and quietly forced to return to the depot. There the soldiers heaped upon the guard the most vile abuse. The soldiers being reinforced by a large number of their comrades from the cars began to make demonstrations of violence, hurling stones, sticks, and mud at the guard. The soldiers were without arms; but being so greatly superior in numbers, and had become so violent in their demonstrations that Captain Skyles, commander of the guard, sent a reinforcement of some 25 men to their support, and also ordered a much larger detachment to move within supporting distance. Excited by drink and irritated by the firmness of the guard, the soldiers made a rush upon them, striking, beating, and maltreating the guard in a brutal manner. Lieut. Sullivan, of the guard, who had twice thrown up the pistol of one of the guard who threatened to fire, was struck and seized by several of the soldiers, who threw him, and were beating him when one of the guard struck the men upon the Lieutenant with the butt of his musket. This released the Lieutenant, and the soldiers thereupon made a rush for the alley east of High Street, with the view of flanking the guard. But they found a force of the guard posted there also. But now grown desperate, and being still further reinforced by several hundreds of their comrades, they made a rush upon the guard, who, thus overwhelmed by numbers, were forced back before the pressure. At this juncture the order was given to "fire." The guard at this opened fire, but firing almost entirely over the heads of the mob, for such now the soldiers had become. Sergeant Clough, however, cooler than the others, drew his revolver, and ordered the soldiers to fall back. They paid no heed to the order, but were rushing upon him, when he fired three successive shots, and every shot brought its man. Others of the guard now began to apply the bayonet and one of the soldiers received a severe bayonet thrust. Intimidated by the firmness of Sergeant Clough, who stood there like a hero, with determination stamped on every line of his countenance, the soldiers halted in their mad career.

At this moment orders came from Captain Skyles, commander of the guard, to cease firing. At the same time officers began to arrive from the depot and ordered the soldiers to the cars, which were then, at the suggestion of Captain Skyles, about to start from the depot. The soldiers, seeing that matters were becoming decidedly serious for them, soon after returned to the cars and were immediately carried off by the moving trains. One of the soldiers was taken up as dead. Two others remain, severely wounded. They were sent to the hospital and everything was done for them that possibly could be. Two of them are mortally wounded; the third will probably recover.

The whole matter was a sudden and impulsive outbreak, incited by bad liquor with which the soldiers had been supplied from some source unknown to their officers, who did all that was possible to quell the disturbance; which occurred so suddenly that no means could have been taken to prevent it.

Too much praise cannot be awarded to Capt. Skyles, the commander of the guard, for his prompt and consistent course in the premises. While the order to fire was not inopportune, the order to cease firing, given by Capt. Skyles, was most discreet and timely; for had it been continued, it would doubtless have brought out the whole force of the solders, with their arms, and the results must have been most serious and lamentable.

The whole conduct of the guard was highly commendable. They calmly encountered the abuse and insult, and even observed order when assailed by missiles from the hands of the soldiers; and only fired when ordered, at the last extremity, to do so. One of the guard was severely hurt by a stone thrown at him, and several were struck by blows from the fists of their assailants. Sergeant Clough's coolness and intrepidity in the face of the mob were admirable.

The whole affair was a most unfortunate one. The soldiers were spoken of by their officers as excellent men, orderly and well disposed. The mischief lay in the fact that liquor had been smuggled into the cars and the soldiers had unduly partaken of the mischief working spirit of rum. We are glad to learn the Captain Skyles has closed the rum shops of the city for the present, in order that no more mischief of like kind may be manufactured within.

2. *Daily Ohio Statesman*, Columbus, Ohio, March 31, 1863:

Unfortunate Military Conflict—Three Men Shot

An unfortunate affair occurred at the depot yesterday afternoon. Freight cars, conveying some twelve or fifteen hundred Massachusetts and Pennsylvania infantry and a battery, part of Gen. Burnside's old army corps, arrived from the East and stopped for a short time at the depot. As some of these soldiers manifested a disposition to straggle off into the city, a small detachment of the Provost Guard stationed here was posted across High Street, near the depot, to prevent this.

A small party of the soldiers excited by liquor and partly perhaps from some other cause, attempted to break through the guard and make their way into the city. Finding themselves opposed, they attacked the guard with clubs and stones, and drove them back. The mob soon swelled to a hundred and fifty unarmed soldiers, who made use of such missiles as they could pick up in the street. The guard was reinforced by detachments sent up from Captain Skyles's headquarters on West Broad Street.

A most determined attempt to break through the guard was made in the alley east of High Street. Missiles were thrown, which struck and slightly wounded several of the Provost guard. The latter fired several shots at their assailants, wounding three of them, one of whom was said to be mortally wounded, but at the last accounts we heard of him, he was still living.

The soldiers, with the exception of the wounded and a very few stragglers, were soon placed on board the cars, which started off on their way to Cincinnati.

3. *Columbus Gazette* (published weekly), Columbus, Ohio, April 3, 1863

Riot

On Monday afternoon, while a portion of the troops of the Ninth Army Corps, en route from the East to the West, were halting at the Depot, receiving the edibles provided by the citizens of Columbus, some of their number who had managed somehow to get some whisky, attempted to pass or break through the guard placed at the different streets, and finding that they could not do it, commenced using insulting and obscene language, and finally threw stones, billets of wood, etc., at them, whereupon the guard, having borne the insults with patience thus far, and patience ceasing to be a virtue, fired blank cartridges at them, which failed to produce any good results, and the storm of boulders and wood growing thicker and thicker, the guard fired but not with blank cartridges, for one of the insurgents fell mortally, while others were severely wounded. This settled the matter, the crowd dispersed, and the soldiers returned to the train which immediately moved off. The Colonel of the regiment justified the proceeding, and remained to attend to the wants of the wounded. We hear it rumored that one of the soldiers has since died, and that another is in a precarious condition.

Whisky was the cause of the difficulty, but how it was obtained is a mystery, as it could not be had at the saloons near the depot. Just so long as our soldiers are allowed the use of liquor, or others are allowed to sell it to them, just so long will the community be afflicted with such discreditable affairs as that of Monday last. And it is not confined merely to the private or common soldiers. Night after night, soldiers who wear straps on their shoulders, embellished with the different insignias of their positions, have been seen in our saloons, making night hideous with their demoniac yells; but in the daytime they are brushed and primped up, looking for all the world as if they had just emanated from a bandbox. And our people welcome them into society. Bah! Is the officer better than the Private? We can't see it.

Appendix D

Union Soldiers Mentioned
by Hitchcock in his Diary

Samuel B. Adams entered the military from Templeton, Massachusetts, on August 23, 1861 and served in Company A, 21st Massachusetts. He reenlisted on January 1, 1864.

Harrison Aldrich entered the military from Williamsville, Vermont, on August 23, 1861 and served as a sergeant in Company K, 21st Massachusetts. He was promoted to second lieutenant on March 3, 1862, first lieutenant on July 18, 1862 and captain on December 18, 1862. He resigned on April 25, 1863.

Courtland A. Allen entered the military from Gardner (Baldwinville), Massachusetts, on July 27, 1862 and served as a sergeant in Company D, 36th Massachusetts Regiment. During the Spotsylvania campaign on May 12, 1864, he was wounded in the hand and captured going to the rear. He was imprisoned at Andersonville. While being removed from Andersonville, he and five others jumped from the railroad train and escaped into the swamps. They remained for several weeks, subsisting on roots and berries, found a dug-out and made their way down the Altamaha River to the blockading squadron—six weeks after their escape.

Henry N. Allen entered the military from Templeton, Massachusetts, on August 23, 1861 and served in Company A, 21st Massachusetts. He was discharged with a disability on August 19, 1864.

Ransom Bailey entered the military from Lenox, Massachusetts, on August 23, 1861 and served in Company I, 21st Massachusetts. He was captured near Blains Cross

Road, Tennessee, on December 23, 1863, and he was imprisoned at Andersonville where he died of scorbutus on August 23, 1864 (grave #6,624).

Erastus E. Baker entered the military from Oxford, Massachusetts, on August 2, 1862 and served in Company C, 34th Massachusetts Regiment. He died at Andersonville of diarrhea on August 23, 1864 (grave #6785).

George S. Ball entered the military from Upton, Massachusetts, on November 11, 1861 and served as chaplain of the 21st Massachusetts. He resigned on December 3, 1862.

Prentice J. Banks entered the military from Alstead, New Hampshire, on August 23, 1861 and served in Company K, 21st Massachusetts. He was captured at the battle near Bethesda Church on June 2, 1864 and imprisoned at Andersonville. He died on February 11, 1865 at home.

Daniel E. Barker entered the military from Chesterfield, Massachusetts, on August 23, 1861 and served as a corporal in Company H, 21st Massachusetts. He was captured at the battle near Bethesda Church on June 2, 1864 and imprisoned at Andersonville.

George T. Barker entered the military from Boston, Massachusetts, on August 23, 1861 and served as first sergeant, Company B, 21st Massachusetts. He was promoted to first lieutenant on October 2, 1862 and captain on April 26, 1863. His military service expired on August 30, 1864.

George H. Bean entered the military from Biddeford, Maine, on August 23, 1861 and served as a sergeant in Company H, 21st Massachusetts. He was promoted to first lieutenant on April 26, 1863. His military service expired on August 30, 1864.

Charles A. Blackmer entered the military from Templeton, Massachusetts, on August 23, 1861 and served in Company A, 21st Massachusetts. He reenlisted on January 1, 1864. He died of wounds received during a battle in front of Petersburg on June 16, 1864.

Orville Booth entered the military from Ashby, Massachusetts, on September 8, 1861 and served as a corporal in Company B, 26th Massachusetts Regiment. He was taken prisoner on September 19, 1864, at Winchester, Virginia. He was discharged on August 26, 1865.

Joel J. Brooks entered the military from Gardner, Massachusetts, in May 1861 and served in Company F, 2nd Massachusetts Regiment. He was wounded in the hand at Antietam on September 17, 1862 but was not disabled, He was promoted to sergeant on

September 24, 1862. He was wounded and taken prisoner at Gettysburg while fighting in the meadow on July 3, 1863. He was discharged on May 28, 1864.

John J. Buchele served in Company E, 126th Ohio Regiment. He was captured at the Battle of the Wilderness on May 6, 1864 and imprisoned at Andersonville where he died of diarrhea on August 9, 1864 (grave #5138).

Francis Burpee entered the military from Sterling, Massachusetts, on August 8, 1862 and served in Company E, 21st Massachusetts. His military service expired on August 30, 1864.

James Cane entered the military from New Canaan, New Hampshire, on August 23, 1861 and served in Company B, 21st Massachusetts. He was captured at the battle near Bethesda Church on June 2, 1864 and was imprisoned at Andersonville.

James A. Carruth entered the military from Phillipston, Massachusetts, on August 23, 1861 and served in Company A, 21st Massachusetts. He transferred to Company F, 56th Massachusetts Regiment on March 18, 1863. After his reenlistment on March 18, 1864, he transferred to Company K, 36th Massachusetts Regiment and was separated from the military on June 8, 1865.

Moses A. Chamberlin entered the military from Templeton, Massachusetts, on September 25, 1862 and served as a corporal in Company A, 21st Massachusetts. He transferred to Company K, 36th Massachusetts Regiment and then to Company A, 56th Massachusetts Regiment. He was discharged on July 12, 1865.

Benjamin J. Church entered the military from Warwick, Rhode Island, on June 5, 1861 and served in Company A, 2nd Rhode Island Regiment.

Eliab R. Churchill entered the military from Ashby, Massachusetts, on August 5, 1862 and served as a corporal in Company E, 33d Massachusetts Regiment. He was killed on October 29, 1863 at Wauhatchie, Tennessee (Lookout Valley).

Joseph W. Clapp entered the military from Gardner, Massachusetts, on August 23, 1861 and served in Company A, 21st Massachusetts. He was discharged with a disability on October 17, 1862.

Elon Clark, a resident of Tennessee, entered the military on January 20, 1862 and served in Company K, 51st Illinois Regiment. He was captured during the Atlanta campaign and died at Andersonville of diarrhea on September 4, 1864 (grave #7760).

Francis E. Clark entered the military from Colrain, Massachusetts, on August 23, 1861 and served in Company C, 21st Massachusetts. He was captured at the Battle of the Wilderness on May 6, 1864 and was imprisoned at Andersonville. His military service expired on July 12, 1865.

J. Warren Clark entered the military from Petersham, Massachusetts, on August 12, 1862 and served in Company K, 21st Massachusetts. He was killed near Shady Grove Road at the Battle of Cold Harbor on June 1, 1864.

Samuel Clark (George Clark in the Atwater List) entered the military on March 9, 1864 and served in Company D, 60th Ohio Regiment. He died of fever remittent at Andersonville on September 5, 1864 (grave #7919).

William H. Clark entered the military from Pittsfield, Massachusetts, on August 23, 1861 and served as first sergeant of Company I, 21st Massachusetts. He was promoted to first lieutenant on March 15, 1862 and captain on October 30, 1862. On August 16, 1864, he died from wounds suffered during the Battle of the Crater.

William Henry Clark entered the military on December 23, 1863 and served in Company I, 72d Indiana Regiment. He was imprisoned at Andersonville and died at Wilmington. North Carolina, on March 12, 1865.

Henry Cobleigh entered the military from Templeton, Massachusetts, on July 24, 1862 and served as a musician in Company D, 36th Massachusetts Regiment. His military service expired on June 8, 1865.

Freeman Cole entered the military from Mendon, Massachusetts, on August 1, 1862 and served in Company A, 21st Massachusetts. His military service expired on August 23, 1864.

Joseph H. Collins entered the military from Athol, Massachusetts, on August 23, 1861 and served as sergeant in Company A, 21st Massachusetts. On January 3, 1863, he died of wounds received during the Battle of Fredericksburg while carrying the colors.

George A. Corey entered the military from Blackstone, Massachusetts, on August 23, 1861 and served as a corporal in Company G, 21st Massachusetts. He was captured at the battle near Bethesda Church on June 2, 1864 and was imprisoned at Andersonville.

Israel Cummings entered the military from Fitchburg, Massachusetts, on August 23, 1861 and served as a sergeant in Company D, 21st Massachusetts. He was wounded during the siege of Knoxville on November 29, 1863 and died on December 2, 1863.

Christopher A. Curtis entered the military from West Boylston, Massachusetts, on August 23, 1861 and served as a sergeant in Company E, 21st Massachusetts. He reenlisted on September 24, 1864 as a supernumerary.

Calvin Cutter entered the military from Warren, Massachusetts, on August 23, 1861 and served as surgeon in the 21st Massachusetts. He resigned on May 17, 1864.

Daniel Dailey entered the military from Ashby, Massachusetts, on August 23, 1861 and served in Company G, 21st Massachusetts. He was killed at the Battle of Antietam on September 17, 1862.

Albert H. Davis, who was born in Ashby, Massachusetts, entered the military from New Ipswich, New Hampshire, on November 28, 1861 and served in Company K, 6th New Hampshire Regiment. He was killed on December 13, 1862 at Fredericksburg (When the regiment was halfway across the field in front of Marye's Heights, a shell exploded in the midst of Company K).

Charles W. Davis entered the military from Templeton, Massachusetts, on August 21, 1861 and served as first lieutenant in the 21st Massachusetts. He was promoted to captain on March 3, 1862. He was transferred to the 36th Massachusetts Regiment and completed his service on March 18, 1865.

Jonas R. Davis entered the military from Templeton, Massachusetts, on August 23, 1861 and served as a sergeant in Company A, 21st Massachusetts. He was promoted to first lieutenant on June 6, 1863 and was transferred to the 36th Massachusetts Regiment, His military service expired on June 8, 1865.

Edward (Tim) Donahue entered the military from Shirley, Massachusetts, on August 23, 1861 and served in Company D, 21st Massachusetts. He was wounded on September 1, 1862 at the Battle of Chantilly and was discharged on September 21, 1863.

Waldo Dwinnell entered the military from Ashburnham, Massachusetts, on January 1, 1864 and served in Company G, 21st Massachusetts. He was captured at the Battle of the Wilderness on May 6, 1864 and imprisoned at Andersonville where he died in September 1864 (buried in an unmarked grave).

Thomas B. Dyer entered the military from Westborough, Massachusetts, on August 23, 1861 and served in Company K, 21st Massachusetts. He was captured at the battle near Bethesda Church on June 2, 1864 and was imprisoned at Andersonville.

George O. Emerson entered the military from Stafford, Connecticut, on August 23, 1861 and served as a sergeant in Company B, 21st Massachusetts. He was captured at the battle near Bethesda Church on June 2, 1864 and was imprisoned at Andersonville where he died of diarrhea on October 8, 1864 (grave #10,542).

Thomas Farrell entered the military from Northampton, Massachusetts, on August 23, 1861 and served in Company C, 21st Massachusetts. He was captured at the Battle of Spotsylvania on May 10, 1864 and was imprisoned at Andersonville.

Richard R. Fiske entered military from Blackstone, Massachusetts, on August 23, 1861 and served in Company E, 21st Massachusetts. He was wounded during the siege of Knoxville on November 24, 1863, and he died on November 27, 1863.

Theodore S. Foster entered the military from Fitchburg, Massachusetts, on August 21, 1861 and served as captain in Company D, 21st Massachusetts. He was promoted to major on May 17, 1862 and was commissioned lieutenant colonel but not mustered because of a disability from a leg wound received in the Battle of Roanoke Island on February 8, 1862. He was discharged with a disability on December 17, 1862.

William L. Fox entered the military from Lancaster, Massachusetts, on August 23, 1861 and served as a sergeant in Company E, 21st Massachusetts. He was discharged on September 24, 1864 as supernumerary.

John D. Frazer entered the military from Holyoke, Massachusetts, on August 21, 1861. He served as a lieutenant in the 21st Massachusetts and was promoted to captain on February 28, 1862. On September 24, 1862, he died of wounds received at the Battle of Chantilly.

Benjamin F. Fuller entered the military from Templeton, Massachusetts, on August 23, 1861 and served in Company A, 21st Mass Regt; he was promoted to quartermaster sergeant, regimental quartermaster sergeant and first lieutenant on October 2, 1862. His military service expired on August 30, 1864.

James Gaffney served in Company F, 11th Massachusetts Regiment. Although he was reported as missing in action near Petersburg, he was captured and was imprisoned at Andersonville where he died of diarrhea on July 30, 1864 (grave #4333).

P. Frank Gethings entered the military from Barre, Massachusetts, on August 23, 1861 and served as a sergeant in Company K, 21st Massachusetts. He was promoted to sergeant major on March 7, 1864. He was captured at the Battle of the Wilderness on May 6, 1864 and was imprisoned at Andersonville. .

Martin Gilson entered the military from Ashby, Massachusetts, on October 23, 1861 and served in Company B, 26th Massachusetts Regiment. He was discharged with a disability on March 6, 1863 at New Orleans.

Thomas Goodness entered the military from Holyoke, Massachusetts, on August 23, 1861 and served as a corporal in Company H, 21st Massachusetts. When he reenlisted on January 1, 1864, he was transferred to Company H, 36th Massachusetts Regiment and then to Company B, 56th Massachusetts Regiment. His military service was terminated on July 12, 1865 (absence—sick).

Charles E. Goodrich entered the military from Fitchburg, Massachusetts, on August 23, 1861 and served as a musician (drummer) in Company D, 21st Massachusetts. He was captured at the Battle of the Wilderness on May 6, 1864 and was imprisoned at Andersonville. On September 14, 1864, Goodrich was transferred to the prison at Florence, South Carolina, where he died on October 10, 1864. After the war, George Hitchcock wrote: "Very often have I thought of him [Goodrich] in these later times as I remember his pleasant, cheerful face, amid so many downcast, despairing ones. Herein we may all find a lesson in this life's struggle. How little costs a cheerful demeanor, yet how much good it does to fellow-man."

Ira B. Goodrich entered the military from Fitchburg, Massachusetts, on August 23, 1861 and served as a corporal in Company D, 21st Massachusetts. He was promoted to first sergeant on July 23, 1862, second lieutenant on September 2, 1862 and first lieutenant on January 15, 1863. His military service expired on August 30, 1864.

Charles Goss entered the military from Sterling, Massachusetts, on August 23, 1861 and served as a sergeant in Company E, 21st Massachusetts. He was promoted to second lieutenant on July 22, 1862, first lieutenant on September 25, 1862 and captain on April 26, 1863. He was killed in front of Petersburg on June 17, 1864.

Marcus Gould, nicknamed "Jule," entered the military from Dudley, Massachusetts, on August 23, 1861 and served in Company A, 21st Massachusetts. He reenlisted on January 1, 1864 and transferred to Company K, 36th Massachusetts Regiment. His military service expired on July 12, 1865.

Samuel N. Gould entered the military from Phillipston, Massachusetts, on August 23, 1861 and served as a musician in Company A, 21st Massachusetts. His military service expired on August 30, 1864.

Alvin S. Graton entered the military from Paxton, Massachusetts, on August 11, 1862 and served as a corporal in Company C, 21st Massachusetts. He was captured at the battle near Bethesda Church on June 2, 1864 and was imprisoned at Andersonville.

Theron E. Hall entered the military from Holden, Massachusetts, on August 23, 1861 and served as adjutant, 21st Massachusetts. He was discharged on July 28, 1862. In July, 1862, he joined the U.S. volunteers as a captain and assistant quartermaster. He was assigned to chief quartermaster with the rank of lieutenant colonel on January 1863. He resigned on December 5, 1864.

Henry M. Harper entered the military from Worcester, Massachusetts, on August 23, 1861 and served in Company K, 21st Massachusetts. He reenlisted on January 2, 1864 and transferred to Company K, 36th Massachusetts Regiment and then to Company E, 56th Massachusetts Regiment. His military service expired on July 12, 1865.

Walter Harriman entered the military from Warner, New Hampshire, on August 26, 1862 and served as colonel of the 11th New Hampshire Regt. He was captured on May 6, 1864 at the Wilderness and imprisoned at Macon and then at Charleston. He was exchanged on September 12, 1864. On March 13, 1865, he was appointed brigadier general for gallant conduct during the war.

William Harrington entered the military from Lunenburg, Massachusetts, on August 23, 1861 and served as a corporal in Company K, 21st Massachusetts. He was killed at the Battle of the Crater on July 30, 1864.

John Frederick Hartranft, colonel of the 51st Pennsylvania Regiment, commanded the Second Brigade in the Second Division of the IX Corps during February and March of 1863. He was named brigadier general on May 12, 1864. He served as governor of Pennsylvania from 1872-78.

George P. Hawkes entered the military from Templeton, Massachusetts, on August 21, 1861 and served as a captain in the 21st Massachusetts. He was taken prisoner at the Battle of Chantilly on September 1, 1862 and was soon released on parole, although not exchanged for several months. He was promoted to major on September 2, 1862 and to lieutenant colonel on December 18, 1862. He resigned due to a disability on July 3, 1864.

Asa E. Haywood entered the military from Springfield, Massachusetts, on August 23, 1861 and served as a sergeant in Company B, 21st Massachusetts. He was promoted to second lieutenant on September 2, 1862 and first lieutenant on December 18, 1862. He resigned on May 14, 1863.

Truman "California Joe" Head served in Company C, 1st United States Sharpshooters commanded by Col. Hiram Berdan, Head, who was born in Philadelphia, wandered across the country to California. A former gold prospector and bear hunter, he was one of many old gunners (46 years old) who became "Sharpshooters."

Sidney S. Heywood entered the military from Royalston, Massachusetts, on August 23, 1861 and served in Company A, 21st Massachusetts. He was promoted to sergeant on July 11, 1862. He was wounded at New Bern, North Carolina, on March 14, 1862, at Spotsylvania, Virginia, on May 12, 1864 and Petersburg, Virginia, on July 5, 1864. His military service expired on August 30, 1864.

George C. Hill entered the military from Shirley, Massachusetts, on August 23, 1861 and served as a sergeant in Company D, 21st Massachusetts. He was promoted to second lieutenant on July 21, 1862, first lieutenant on July 28, 1862 and captain on September 25, 1862. He resigned from the military on April 25, 1863.

William B. Hill entered the military from Gardner, Massachusetts, on August 23, 1861 and served as a sergeant in Company A, 21st Massachusetts. He was promoted to second lieutenant on July 22, 1862. On September 1, 1862, he was killed at the Battle of Chantilly.

George Alfred Hitchcock entered the military from Ashby, Massachusetts, on August 14, 1962 and served in Company A, 21st Massachusetts. He was captured on June 2, 1864 at the Battle of Bethesda Church and was imprisoned at Andersonville, Millen and Florence. He was exchanged at Charleston on December 10, 1864 and was discharged on January 26, 1865.

Henry Sparhawk Hitchcock entered the military from Templeton, Massachusetts, on August 23, 1861 and served as a sergeant in Company A, 21st Massachusetts. He was promoted to second lieutenant on September 25, 1862 and first lieutenant on April 26, 1863. He was wounded at Petersburg on July 30, 1864. His military service expired on August 30, 1864.

Lyman W. Holt entered the military from Ashby, Massachusetts, on October 18, 1862 and served in Company B, 53d Massachusetts Regiment. On March 16, 1863, he died in New Orleans, Louisiana. During this time there were more than 250 men sick with startling rapidity from diarrhea, dysentery and malarial fever.

Edward E. Howe entered the military from Worcester, Massachusetts, on August 23, 1861 and served as a sergeant, Company I, 21st Massachusetts. He was promoted to first sergeant on March 15, 1862, second lieutenant on July 22, 1862, first lieutenant on September 26, 1862 and captain on April 26, 1863. His military service expired on October 10, 1864.

Alvin E. Humiston entered the military from Holyoke, Massachusetts, on August 23, 1861 and served as a corporal in Company H, 21st Massachusetts. His service expired on August 30, 1864.

Chauncey B. Irish entered the military from Millbury, Massachusetts, on August 23, 1861 and served as a corporal and sergeant in Company F, 21st Massachusetts. He was discharged with a disability on October 5, 1863.

John Kelt entered the military from Holyoke, Massachusetts, on October 24, 1861 and served as a corporal and sergeant in Company H, 21st Massachusetts. He was promoted to second lieutenant on September 18, 1862. He was dismissed from military service on August 19, 1863.

Ira J. Kelton entered the military from Holden, Massachusetts, on August 21, 1861 and served as a lieutenant in the 21st Massachusetts. He was promoted to captain on May 17, 1862. On September 24, 1862, he died of wounds suffered at the Battle of Chantilly.

William S. King entered the military from Roxbury, Massachusetts, on August 4, 1862 and served as captain of Company K, 35th Massachusetts Regiment. He was wounded seven times during the Battle of Antietam on September 17, 1862. He was promoted to major on December 15, 1862 and lieutenant colonel on April 25, 1863. On November 14, 1864, he became colonel of the 4th Massachusetts Heavy Artillery Regiment. He was discharged on June 17, 1865, as a brevet brigadier general.

Otis H. Knight entered the military from Worcester, Massachusetts, on December 29, 1863 and served in Company D, 25th Massachusetts Regiment. He was captured near Petersburg on June 15, 1864 and imprisoned at Andersonville. On July 23, 1864, he died of wounds at Andersonville—shot by a prison guard (grave #3842).

John S. Koster entered the military from Palmer, Massachusetts, on August 23, 1861 and served as a sergeant in Company H, 21st Massachusetts. His military service expired on August 30, 1864.

William Samuel Laird served as a corporal in Company I, 185th Pennsylvania Regiment (22d Cavalry). He was imprisoned at Andersonville, Millen, and Florence and was exchanged at Charleston on December 10, 1864.

Walter Lamb entered the military from Templeton, Massachusetts, on September 18, 1861 and served in Company I, 25th Massachusetts Regiment. He was captured at the Battle of Cold Harbor on June 3, 1864 and was imprisoned at Andersonville (according to Hitchcock he was "taken prisoner on June 1st at Drury's Bluff"). He was exchanged on November 20, 1864.

George M. Lander entered the military from Greenfield, Massachusetts, on August 23, 1861 and served in Company K, 21st Massachusetts. He was killed near Cold Harbor on May 31, 1864, at Shady Grove Road during a sharp picket fight.

German Lagara entered the military from Petersham, Massachusetts, on August 23, 1861 and served in Company K, 21st Massachusetts. He was captured at the battle near Bethesda Church on June 2, 1864 and was imprisoned at Andersonville.

George F. Lawrence entered the military from Hardwick, Massachusetts, on August 23, 1861 and served as a sergeant in Company K, 21st Massachusetts. He was promoted to second lieutenant on September 26, 1862 and first lieutenant on March 3, 1863. His military service expired on August 30, 1864.

Daniel Leasure, a colonel who had graduated from Jefferson Medical College, organized and commanded the 100th Pennsylvania Regiment (Roundhead Regiment). He led the Third Brigade, First Division of IX Corps from December 1862 to October 1863; the Second Brigade, First Division of IX Corps from April 1864 to May 10, 1864; and the First Division of IX Corp from May 10-12, 1864. He returned to command the Second Brigade from May 12-14, 1864, but he was "disabled by sickness" and never returned to active duty.

Herbert Leland entered the military from Templeton, Massachusetts, on August 23, 1861 and served as a musician in Company A, 21st Massachusetts. He was discharged on May 15, 1863 with a disability.

Edwin R. Lewis entered the military from Tisbury, Massachusetts, on September 3, 1862 and served in Company A, 21st Massachusetts. He was promoted to sergeant major on December 22, 1862, first lieutenant on April 26, 1963 and captain on June 18, 1864. His military service expired on August 30, 1864.

John F. Lewis entered the military from Templeton, Massachusetts, on August 23, 1861 and served as a sergeant in Company A, 21st Massachusetts. He was promoted to second lieutenant on October 1, 1862 and transferred to Company F. He resigned on March 2, 1863.

Reuben Mann entered the military from Templeton, Massachusetts, on August 23, 1861 and served in Company A, 21st Massachusetts. He reenlisted on January 1, 1864 and transferred to Company K, 36th Massachusetts Regiment and then to Company E, 56th Massachusetts Regiment. His military service terminated by order of the War Department on July 7, 1865.

Isaac March entered the military from Ashby, Massachusetts, on October 18, 1861 and served in Company B, 26th Massachusetts Regiment. He reenlisted on January 1, 1864 and was taken prisoner on September 19, 1864, at Winchester, Virginia. His military service expired August 26, 1865.

Thomas Marshall entered the military from Boston, Massachusetts, on August 23, 1863 and served in Company K, 21st Massachusetts. He was captured at the battle near Bethesda Church on June 2, 1864 and was imprisoned at Andersonville. His military service expired on July 12, 1865.

William H. H. Martin entered the military on September 20, 1861 and served in Company E, 51st Ohio Regiment. He was captured in action at Big Shanty, Georgia, on June 11, 1864 and was imprisoned at Andersonville.

Simon May entered the military from Fitchburg, Massachusetts, on August 23, 1861 and served as a sergeant in Company D, 21st Massachusetts. He was killed in the battle near the Weldon Railroad at Petersburg on August 19, 1864.

John Mayo entered the military from Ashby, Massachusetts, on August 5, 1862 and served as a corporal in Company E, 33d Massachusetts Regiment. He was killed on October 29, 1863 at Wauhatchie, Tennessee (Lookout Valley).

Stephen McCabe entered the military from Boston, Massachusetts, on August 23, 1861 and served as a sergeant in Company B, 21st Massachusetts. He was promoted to second lieutenant on January 12, 1863 and resigned on May 8, 1863.

Barney McNulty entered the military from Leicester, Massachusetts, on August 23, 1861 and served in Company C, 21st Massachusetts. He reenlisted on January 1, 1864 and transferred to Company I, 36th Massachusetts Regiment and then to Company C, 56th Massachusetts Regiment. His military service expired on July 12, 1865.

George Middy entered the military on September 20, 1861 and served in Company E, 51st Ohio Regiment. He was captured in action at Big Shanty, Georgia, on June 11, 1864 and was imprisoned at Andersonville.

James A. Miller entered the military from Templeton, Massachusetts, on August 23, 1861 and served as a corporal in Company A, 21st Massachusetts. He was captured at the battle near Bethesda Church on June 2, 1864 and was imprisoned at Andersonville.

John M. Miller, 2d, entered the military from Boston, Massachusetts, on August 15, 1863 and served in Company A, 11th Massachusetts Regiment. He was wounded and captured at the Battle of the Wilderness on May 6, 1864 and died at Andersonville of "fever typhus" on July 30, 1864 (grave #4329).

Robert Miller entered the military from Spencer, Massachusetts, on August 23, 1861 and served as a sergeant in Company C, 21st Massachusetts. He reenlisted on January 1, 1864 and was transferred to Company I, 36th Massachusetts Regiment and then to Company C 56th Mass Regiment. His military service expired on July 12, 1865.

R. Charlton Mitchell enlisted from New York City on August 3, 1861, and served as captain of Company H, 51st New York Regiment. He was promoted to major on November 20, 1862, and lieutenant colonel on October 8, 1864.

Augustus Morse entered the military from Leominster, Massachusetts, on August 21, 1861 and served as colonel of the 21st Massachusetts. On May 15, 1862, he was discharged from the army by order of the Secretary of War. He was commissioned captain in the United States volunteers on July 14, 1862, with the assignment of assistant quartermaster. He resigned on June 10, 1863.

John F. Mumford entered the military from Frankfort, New York, on November 23, 1861 and served in Company K, 2nd New York Artillery. He was captured at Bowling Green, Virginia, on May 27, 1864. While imprisoned at Andersonville, he signed the petition that was sent to Washington. He was transferred to Millen, Georgia, on November 11, 1864 and was paroled at Savannah on November 26, 1864.

Charles C. Muzzey entered the military from Worcester, Massachusetts, on August 23, 1861 and served as a sergeant in Company F, 21st Massachusetts. He was captured at the Battle of Spotsylvania on May 10, 1864 and was imprisoned at Andersonville.

James Oliver entered the military from Athol, Massachusetts, on July 31, 1862 and served as a surgeon in the 21st Massachusetts. His military service expired on August 30, 1864.

Ansel Orcutt entered the military from Athol, Massachusetts, on August 23, 1861 and served in Company A, 21st Massachusetts. He was wounded at New Bern, North Carolina, on March 14, 1862. He was transferred to the volunteer reserve corps on June 25, 1862.

William L. Orcutt entered the military from Adams, Massachusetts, on August 23, 1864 and served in Company K, 21st Massachusetts. He was captured at the battle near Bethesda Church on June 2, 1864 and imprisoned at Andersonville. He was exchanged on November 27, 1864.

J. Albert Osgood entered the military from Templeton, Massachusetts, on August 23, 1861 and served as a sergeant in Company A, 21st Massachusetts Regment. Nicknamed "Brick-top," he was captured at the Battle of the Wilderness on May 6, 1864 and was imprisoned at Andersonville. He was discharged on May 26, 1865.

George C. Parker entered the military from Worcester, Massachusetts, on August 23, 1861 and served in Company F, 21st Massachusetts. He was promoted sergeant on June 6, 1862, second lieutenant on June 29, 1862, first lieutentant on September 2, 1862 and captain on April 26, 1863. His military service expired on August 30, 1864.

Francis M. Peckham entered the military from Petersham, Massachusetts, on August 23, 1861 and served as a sergeant in Company A, 21st Massachusetts. His military service expired on September 14, 1864.

Buel M. Phelps entered the military from Morristown, Vermont, on October 7, 1863 and served as a corporal in Company M, 11th Vermont Regiment. He was taken prisoner at the Battle of Cedar Creek on October 19, 1864 and was imprisoned at Andersonville. He was discharged on July 7, 1865.

Asa Franklin Van Buren Piper entered the military from Templeton, Massachusetts, on August 23, 1861 and served in Company A, 21st Massachusetts. He was killed on May 6, 1864 at the Battle of the Wilderness.

Thomas Plunkett entered the military from West Boylston, Massachusetts, on August 23, 1861 and served as a sergeant in Company E, 21st Massachusetts. He lost both arms while carrying the regimental United States flag at the Battle of Fredericksburg on December 13, 1862. He was discharged on March 9, 1864 with disability.

Wilbur A. Potter entered the military from Templeton, Massachusetts, on August 23, 1861 and served in Company A, 21st Massachusetts. He was captured at the Battle of the Wilderness on May 6, 1864 and was imprisoned at Andersonville.

John D. Reynolds entered the military from Webster, Massachusetts, on August 23, 1861 and served as a corporal in Company F, 21st Massachusetts. He transferred to Company A. He was killed at the Battle of Cold Harbor on June 1, 1864.

Henry H. Richardson entered the military from Pittsfield, Massachusetts, on August 21, 1861 and served as a captain in the 21st Massachusetts. He was promoted to major on December 18, 1862, but declined a promotion to lieutenant colonel in 1864. His military service expired on August 30, 1864.

Dwight Ripley entered the military from Petersham, Massachusetts, on August 7, 1862 and served in Company K, 21st Massachusetts. He was killed during the siege of Knoxville on November 25, 1863.

Orange S. Sampson entered the military from Huntington, Massachusetts, on August 23, 1861 and served as a sergeant in Company I, 21st Massachusetts. He was promoted to second lieutenant on September 2, 1862, first lieutenant on October 30, 1862 and captain on April 26, 1863. On September 30, 1864, he was killed at Peeble's Farm, Virginia.

Frederick M. Sanderson entered the military from Phillipston, Massachusetts, on August 23, 1862 and served as first sergeant, Company A, 21st Massachusetts. He was promoted to second lieutenant on March 3, 1862, first lieutenant on July 21, 1862 and captain on September 2, 1862. He resigned on April 24, 1863.

William H. Sawyer entered the military from New Salem, Massachusetts, on August 23, 1861 and served as a sergeant in Company K, 21st Massachusetts. He was promoted to first lieutenant on April 26, 1863 and captain on October 12, 1864. He was transferred to the 36th Massachusetts Regiment after the 21st Massachusetts mustered out of service. His military service expired on June 8, 1865.

Levi F. Shepard entered the military from Boylston, Massachusetts, on July 31, 1862 and served in Company C, 34th Massachusetts Regiment. He was wounded and captured at New Market, Virginia, on May 15, 1864 and was imprisoned at Andersonville.

Sidney Sibley entered the military from Barre, Massachusetts, on August 8, 1862 and served in Company K, 21st Massachusetts. He was discharge on May 23, 1864, with a disability.

Charles H. Sperry entered the military from Pittsfield, Massachusetts, on August 23, 1861 and served as a sergeant in Company C, 21st Massachusetts. He reenlisted on January 1, 1864 and transferred to Company I, 36th Massachusetts Regiment and then to Company G, 56th Massachusetts Regiment on June 8, 1865. His military service expired on July 12, 1865.

Frazar Augustus Stearns entered the military from Amherst, Massachusetts, on August 21, 1861 and served as adjutant in the 21st Massachusetts. On March 14, 1862, he was killed at New Bern, North Carolina. General Reno, in his official report of the Battle of New Bern, referred to him as "one of the most accomplished and gallant officers in the army."

Thomas Stephens (Stevens) entered the military from Northampton, Massachusetts, on August 23, 1861 and served as a corporal and sergeant in Company B, 21st Massachusetts. After being wounded at Antietam and Fredericksburg, he was captured near Petersburg on June 17, 1864 and was imprisoned at Andersonville. He was discharged on January 14, 1865.

Joseph M. Sudsburg entered the military as captain of the 2d Maryland Regiment on September 18, 1861. He was transferred to the 4th Maryland Regiment (German Rifles) on November 1861. He was promoted to lieutenant colonel of the 3d Maryland Regiment on May 7, 1862 and then colonel on October 24, 1862. He commanded the Second Brigade, First Division of IX Corps from May 31, 1864 to June 4, 1864, during the Battle of Cold Harbor. He was mustered out of the service on June 24, 1864.

George F. Thompson entered the military from Worcester, Massachusetts, on August 21, 1861 and served as a first lieutenant in the 21st Massachusetts. He was regimental quartermaster and was promoted to captain on September 10, 1862 and lieutenant colonel on March 13, 1865.

Gardiner Tufts, a colonel and a Massachusetts military agent, served as an inspector of government general hospitals and military prisons in the Department of Washington.

William H. Tyler entered the military from Richmond, Massachusetts, on August 23, 1861 and served in Company I, 21st Massachusetts. After his reenlistment on January 1, 1864, he was captured near Petersburg on June 17, 1864 and was imprisoned at Andersonville.

William H. Valentine entered the military from Worcester, Massachusetts, on August 23, 1861 and served as sergeant major in the 21st Massachusetts. He was promoted to second lieutenant on January 1, 1862, first lieutenant on June 19, 1862 and captain on March 6, 1863. He resigned on August 17, 1864.

Charles Folsom Walcott entered the military from Boston, Massachusetts, on August 21, 1861 and served as a captain in the 21st Massachusetts. He resigned on April 25, 1863. On September 24, 1864, he reentered the military as lieutenant colonel in the 61st Massachusetts Regiment and was promoted to colonel on November 9, 1864. On April 9, 1865, he was promoted to brigadier general. He wrote the *History of the Twenty-First Regiment Massachusetts Volunteers* that was published in 1882.

John W. Wallace entered the military from Gardner, Massachusetts, on August 23, 1861 and served as a corporal and then sergeant of Company A, 21st Massachusetts. He was wounded in the leg on June 16, 1864, in action near Petersburg and was discharged on September 24, 1864.

George Webster served as a sergeant in Company I, 181st Pennsylvania Regiment (20th Cavalry). He was captured at Martinsburg, West Virginia, on July 3, 1864 and was imprisoned at Andersonville. He died at Andersonville of chronic diarrhea on November 7, 1864 (grave #11899).

Asahel Wheeler entered the military from Ashburnham, Massachusetts, on August 23, 1861 and served as a sergeant in Company G, 21st Massachusetts. He was promoted to second lieutenant on January 24, 1862, first lieutenant on May 28, 1862 and captain on January 14, 1863. He resigned on April 25, 1863.

Julius Whitney entered the military from Fitchburg, Massachusetts, on August 23, 1861 and served as a sergeant in Company D, 21st Massachusetts. He was promoted to second lieutenant on December 27, 1862 and first lieutenant on June 18, 1864. His military service expired on August 30, 1864.

Lemuel Whitney entered the military from Ashburnham, Massachusetts, on August 14, 1862 and served in Company A, 21st Massachusetts. He was wounded at Fredericksburg on December 13, 1862 and at Spotsylvania on May 10, 1864. His military service expired on August 30, 1864.

Edward A. Wild entered the military from Brookline, Massachusetts, on August 11, 1862 and served as colonel of the 35th Massachusetts Regiment. He was promoted to brigadier general of United States volunteers on April 25, 1863.

Charles S. Wilder entered the military from Worcester, Massachusetts, on August 23, 1861 and served as a corporal in Company A, 21st Massachusetts He was wounded and captured at the battle near Bethesda Church on June 2, 1864 and died in a short time while a prisoner.

Robert Wilson entered the military from Millbury, Massachusetts, on July 13, 1862 and served in Company A, 34th Massachusetts Regiment. He was captured at the Battle of New Market on May 15,1864 and was imprisoned at Andersonville where he died of scorbutus on August 23, 1864 (grave #6769).

Thomas Winn entered the military from Worcester, Massachusetts, on August 23, 1861 and served as a corporal and sergeant in Company K, 21st Massachusetts. He was wounded in the arm and captured near Petersburg on June 17, 1864 and imprisoned at Andersonville.

Samuel Wright entered the military from Pittsfield, Massachusetts, on August 23, 1861 and served in Company I, 21st Massachusetts. He was killed in Columbus, Ohio, on March 30, 1863.

Notes

Editor's Preface

1. Samuel Adams Drake, ed. *History of Middlesex County, Massachusetts*, Volume 1 (Boston: Estes & Lauriat, 1880), pp. 218-226.
2. The 1990 census list 2,717 residents (99.7% White, 0.2% Black and 0.1% Asian).
3. George A. Hitchcock, *Memoirs of Ashby in 1850*. Unpublished manuscript located at the Ashby Public Library, Ashby, Massachusetts.

Chapter One

1. Lemuel Whitney entered the military from Ashburnham, Massachusetts, on August 14, 1862 and served in Company A, 21 st Massachusetts Regiment. He was wounded at Fredericksburg on December 13, 1862 and at Spotsylvania on May 10, 1864. His military service expired on August 30, 1864.
2. Charles Wilkes Wood, George Hitchcock's minister during his youth, was the sixth pastor of the Orthodox Congregational Church in Ashby. He served from 1839 to 1858 and then moved to North Bridgewater, Massachusetts.
3. The *Great Eastern* had arrived in New York from England on August 31, 1862; this "greatest iron ship" was launched in London in 1858, and was five times the size of any ship afloat with a hull 693 feet long (18,915 gross tonnage). There were 800 cabins (some having their own bathtubs with hot and cold running water) and five gilded and mirrored saloons (grandest encompassing 3,000 square feet); the ship was designed to be propelled through the ocean at a mind-boggling 18 knots (never exceeded 14.5 knots) by twin 56-foot paddle wheels and a 24-foot screw propeller that were powered by coal in 10 boilers (carried 3,000 tons of coal). The ship, which also carried 6,500 square yards of canvas on six masts that were available only for auxiliary power, was put on the Atlantic run, but her 4,000 berths were never filled; she was beset by costly accidents and bankruptcies. The Great Eastern Company promoted by Cyrus Field bought the *Great Eastern* in 1864 and fitted the huge ship for the monumental task of carrying 2,000 miles of telegraphic cable to connect England and North America. The second attempt was successful: the *Great Eastern* left Valencia on the south coast of

Ireland on July 13, 1866 and arrived at Hearts Content Bay, Newfoundland, on July 27, 1866.

4. Casualties in Union forces, commanded by Major General John Pope, during the operations from August 16 to September 2, 1862, were: 1,747 killed; 8,452 wounded; and 4,263 missing.

5. Colonel William S. Clark, from Amherst, Massachusetts, was not killed and remained with the 21 st until his resignation on April 22, 1863. However, the regiment (400 soldiers engaged) suffered their heaviest casualties of the war at the Battle of Chantilly on September 1, 1862: 140 casualties—38 were killed or died from wounds, 76 wounded and 26 taken prisoner. Lieutenant Colonel Joseph Parker Rice was killed.

6. Truman "California Joe" Head served in Company C, 1st United States Sharpshooters commanded by Colonel Hiram Berdan. Head, who was born in Philadelphia and wandered across the country to California. A former gold prospector and bear hunter, he was one of many old gunners (52 years old) who became "Sharpshooters."

Chapter Two

1. Long Bridge, crossing the Potomac River at the foot of Maryland Avenue, was the great outlet from Washington into Virginia for Union troops and supplies during the Civil War. The original Long Bridge over the Potomac River was built in 1809 at a cost of $100,000; however, the bridge was destroyed by a freshet in 1831. In 1835, a wooden bridge was erected at a cost of $113,000; the bridge was damaged in 1836 and again in 1840, but was reopened for travel in 1843. The bridge was 4,677 feet long and divided into three sections: the part over the channel was 2,000 feet long with 13 fixed spans of 135 feet and one pivotal span of 182 feet. After being used since 1870 by the Baltimore and Potomac Railroad, the bridge was replaced in 1905.

2. Major General Silas Casey, from Rhode Island, graduated from the USMA in 1826. He is best known as author of *System of Infantry Tactics* (1861), which was adopted by the United States Army in 1862 and also widely used by the Confederates. At this time he was commanding the Provisional Brigade and the District of Washington XXII Corps.

3. Herbert Leland entered the military from Templeton, Massachusetts, on August 23, 1861 and served as a musician in Company A, 21st Massachusetts. He was discharged on May 15, 1863 with a disability.

4. On April 19,1862, the 21st Massachusetts and 51st Pennsylvania regiments landed at Elizabeth City, N.C. and started marching north. Each man carried rations for two days and sixty rounds of ammunition; they marched twenty miles in oppressively hot conditions and then successfully fought the Battle of Camden (South Mill, North Carolina). After a few hours of rest the regiments made the weary return march, encountering severe rain and very muddy roads (the entire expedition took place within twenty-four hours).

5. John W. Wallace entered the military from Gardner, Massachusetts, on August 23, 1861 and served as a corporal and then sergeant of Company A, 21st Massachusetts. He was wounded in the leg on June 16, 1864 in action near Petersburg and discharged on September 24, 1864.

6. Henry H. Richardson entered the military from Pittsfield, Massachusetts, on August 21, 1861, as a captain in the 21st Massachusetts. He was promoted to major on December 18, 1862, but he declined a promotion to colonel in 1864. His military service expired on August 30, 1864.

7. Major General Jesse Lee Reno, who was born in Virginia but lived in Pennsylvania, graduated from the USMA in 1846. He led the IX Corps (September 3-14) until he was killed at South Mountain.

8. Rumors abounded but were frequently false. Thomas Jonathan ("Stonewall") Jackson was mortally wounded by his own men at Chancellorsville on May 2, 1863.

9. Daniel Dailey entered the military from Ashby, Massachusetts, on August 23, 1861 and served in Company G, 21st Massachusetts.. He was killed on September 17, 1862 at the Battle of Antietam.

10. George S. Ball entered the military from Upton, Massachusetts, on November 11, 1861 and served as chaplain of the 21st Massachusetts. He resigned on December 3, 1862.

11. Templeton is a small town southwest of Ashby. George Hitchcock graduated from Templeton High School.

12. Fitchburg was an industrial town of 8,000 in 1860—south of the Village of Ashby. Six members of the Fitchburg Soldiers' Relief Committee visited the Antietam battlefield with supplies for the sick and wounded. Every disabled Fitchburg soldier in the 15th and 21st Massachusetts regiments received a gift of five dollars. The committee included: Alfred Hitchcock (no relation to George),a surgeon; Alva Crocker, paper manufacturer; Alpheus Porter Kimball, deputy sheriff and jailor; Norman Stone, coal dealer; Benjamin Prentiss, blacksmith; and Alonzo P. Davis, former lieutenant in the 21st Massachusetts (resigned on January 16, 1862).

13. Henry Cobleigh entered the military from Templeton, Massachusetts, on July 24, 1862 and served as a musician in the 36th Massachusetts Regiment.

14. John D. Frazer entered the military from Holyoke, Massachusetts, on August 21, 1861, as a lieutenant in the 21st Massachusetts, and he was promoted to captain on February 28, 1862. On September 24, 1862, he died of wounds suffered at Chantilly,Virginia.

15. Ira J. Kelton entered the military from Holden, Massachusetts, on August 21, 1861, as a lieutenant in the 21st Massachusetts, and he was promoted to captain on May 17, 1862. On September 19, 1862, he died of wounds suffered at Chantilly, Virginia.

16. Walter Harriman entered the military from Warner, New Hampshire, on August 26, 1862, as colonel of the 11th New Hampshire Regiment. He was captured on May 6, 1864 at the Wilderness and imprisoned at Macon and then at Charleston. He was exchanged on September 12, 1864. On March 13, 1865, he was appointed brigadier general for gallant conduct during the war.

17. Theodore S. Foster entered the military from Fitchburg, Massachusetts, on August 21, 1861, as a captain in Company D of the 21st Massachusetts. He was promoted to major on May 17, 1862, and was commissioned lieutenant colonel but not mustered due to a disability from a leg wound received at the Battle of Roanoke Island on February 8, 1862. He was discharged for disability on December 17, 1862.

18. Edward Ferrero, who was born in Spain and was active in the New York state militia, was commissioned colonel of the 51st New York Regiment on October 14, 1861; at this time he commanded the Second Division in the Second Brigade of the IX Corps. He was promoted to brigadier general on September 10, 1862.

19. James Ewell Brown ("Jeb") Stuart, Confederate major general who commanded the cavalry of the Army of Northern Virginia, made his second ride around McClellan's Army of the Potomac (October 10-12, 1862), raiding as far north as Chambersburg, Pennsylvania, and on October 12th recrossed the Potomac River north of Poolesville, Maryland, at White's Ferry. Although there was a brief skirmish near the mouth of the Monocacy River, Stuart avoided Union troops waiting near Point Rocks and Poolesville. White's Ferry is two miles below the junction of the Monocacy and Potomac rivers and ten miles below Point of Rocks.

20. George P. Hawkes entered the military from Templeton, Massachusetts, on August 21, 1861, as a captain in the 21st Massachusetts. He was taken prisoner at the Battle of Chantilly on September 1, 1862. He was soon released on parole, although not exchanged for several months. He was promoted to major on September 2, 1862 and to lieutenant colonel on December 18, 1862. He resigned due to a disability on July 3, 1864.

21. Joseph W. Clapp entered the military from Gardner, Massachusetts, on August 23, 1861 and served in Company A, 21st Massachusetts. He was discharged on October 17, 1862 for disability.

22. Frederick M. Sanderson entered the military from Phillipston, Massachusetts, on August 23, 1862, as first sergeant of Company A in the 21st Massachusetts. He was promoted to second lieutenant on March 3, 1862, first lieutenant on July 21, 1862 and captain on September 2, 1862. He resigned on April 25, 1863.

23. Edward A. Wild entered the military from Brookline, Massachusetts, on August 11, 1862, as colonel of the 35th Massachusetts Regiment. He was promoted to brigadier general of United States volunteers on April 24, 1863.

24. Albert H. Davis, who was born in Ashby, entered the military from New Ipswich, New Hampshire, on November 28, 1861 and served in Company K, 6th New Hampshire Regiment. He was killed on December 13, 1862 at Fredericksburg (when the regiment was halfway across the field in front of Marye's Heights, a shell exploded in the midst of Company K).

Chapter Three

1. Edward E. Howe entered the military from Worcester, Massachusetts, on August 23, 1861, as sergeant of Company I, 21st Massachusetts. He was promoted to

first sergeant on March 15, 1862, second lieutenant on July 22, 1862, first lieutenant on September 26, 1862, and captain on April 26, 1863. His military service expired on October 10, 1864.

2. Major General Joseph Hooker, who graduated from the USMA in 1837, commanded the Center Grand Division of the Army of the Potomac (newly formed III Corps and the veteran V Corps) at the Battle of Fredericksburg.

3. Major General Darius Nash Couch, who graduated from USMA in 1846, took command of the II Corps on October 7, 1862, and led this unit in the battles of Fredericksburg and Chancellorsville.

4. James A. Carruth entered the military from Phillipston, Massachusetts, on August 23, 1861 and served in Company A, 21st Massachusetts.

5. Brigadier General Samuel Davis Sturgis, who graduated from the USMA in 1846, commanded the Second Division of the IX Corps of the Army of the Potomac at the battles of South Mountain, Antietam and Fredericksburg.

6. Major General Ambrose Everett Burnside, who graduated from the USMA in 1847, assumed command of the Army of the Potomac on November 10, 1862.

7. William H. Clark entered the military from Pittsfield, Massachusetts, on August 23, 1861, as first sergeant of Company I, 21st Massachusetts. He was promoted to first lieutenant on March 15, 1862 and captain on October 30, 1862. He died on August 16, 1864, from wounds suffered at the Battle of the Mine.

8. William B. Hill entered the military from Gardner, Massachusetts, on August 23, 1861, as sergeant in Company A, 21st Massachusetts. He was promoted to second lieutenant on July 22, 1862. He was killed on September 1, 1862, at the Battle of Chantilly.

9. John Albion Andrews was elected Governor of Massachusetts in 1860 (re-elected in 1862 and 1864). He was responsible for the high state of preparedness of state militia prior to the war and was very supportive of military operations during the war.

10. Brigadier General Orlando Bolivar Willcox, who graduated from the USMA in 1847, was commander of the IX Corps.

11. Charles W. Davis entered the military from Templeton, Massachusetts, on August 21, 1861, as first lieutenant in the 21st Massachusetts. He was promoted to captain on March 3, 1862.

12. Charles Goss entered the military from Sterling, Massachusetts, on August 23, 1861, as sergeant of Company E, 21st Massachusetts. He was promoted to second lieutenant on July 22, 1862, first lieutenant on September 25, 1862 and captain on April 26, 1863. He was killed on June 17, 1864 at the Battle in front of Petersburg, Virginia.

13. George C. Parker entered the military from Worcester, Massachusetts, on August 23, 1861 and served in Company F, 21st Massachusetts. He was promoted to sergeant on June 6, 1862, second lieutenant on June 20, 1862, first lieutenant on September 2, 1862 and captain on April 26, 1863. His military service expired on August 30, 1864.

14. George F. Lawrence entered the military from Hardwick, Massachusetts, on August 23, 1861, as sergeant of Company K, 21st Massachusetts. He was promoted to

second lieutenant on September 26, 1862 and first lieutenant on March 3, 1863. His military service expired on August 30, 1864.

15. Augustus Morse entered the military from Leominster, Massachusetts, on August 21, 1861, as colonel of the Massachusetts 21st Regiment. On May 15, 1862, he was discharged from the army by order of the Secretary of War. On July 14, 1862, he was commissioned captain in the United States volunteers with the assignment of assistant quartermaster. He resigned on June 10, 1863.

16. Edwin R. Lewis entered the military from Tisbury, Massachusetts, on September 3, 1862 and served in Company A, 21st Massachusetts. He was promoted to sergeant major on December 22, 1862, first lieutenant on April 26, 1863 and captain on June 18, 1864. His military service expired on August 30, 1864.

17. Joseph H. Collins entered the military from Athol, Massachusetts, on August 23, 1861 and served as sergeant in Company A, 21st Massachusetts. On January 3, 1863, he died of wounds received at the Battle of Fredericksburg while carrying the colors.

18. Thomas Plunkett entered the military from West Boylston, Massachusetts, on August 23, 1861 and served as sergeant of Company E, 21st Massachusetts. He lost both arms while carrying the regimental United States flag at the Battle of Fredericksburg.

Chapter Four

1. Major General Edwin Vose Sumner, who was commissioned second lieutenant in 1819, commanded the Right Grand Division (II Corps and IX Corps) of the Army of the Potomac at the Battle of Fredericksburg. On January 25, 1863, he was relieved from duty in the Army of the Potomac at his own request. General Sumner died on March 21, 1863.

2. John Mayo entered the military from Ashby, Massachusetts, on August 5, 1862 and served as corporal in Company E, 33d Massachusetts Regiment. He was killed at Wauhatchie, Tennessee, on October 29, 1863.

3. Elias R. Churchill entered the military from Ashby, Massachusetts, on August 5, 1862 and served in Company E, 33d Massachusetts Regiment. He was killed at Wauhatchie, Tennessee, on October 29, 1863.

4. Charles Folsom Walcott entered the military from Boston, Massachusetts, on August 21, 1861, as a captain in the 21st Massachusetts. He resigned on April 25, 1863. On September 24, 1864, he reentered the military as lieutenant colonel in the 61st Massachusetts Regiment and was promoted to colonel on November 9, 1864. On April 9, 1865, he was promoted to brigadier general. He wrote the *History of the Twenty-First Regiment Massachusetts Volunteers*—published in 1882.

5. Julius Whitney entered the military from Fitchburg, Massachusetts, on August 23, 1861, as a sergeant in Company D, 21st Massachusetts. He was promoted to second lieutenant on December 27, 1862 and first lieutenant on June 18, 1864. His military service expired on August 30, 1864.

6. Orange S. Sampson entered the military from Huntington, Massachusetts, on August 23, 1861, as a sergeant in Company I, 21st Massachusetts. He was promoted to second lieutenant on September 2, 1862, first lieutenant on October 30, 1862 and captain on April 26, 1863. He was killed during the Battle at Popular Springs Church, Virginia, on September 30, 1864.

7. This large Georgian mansion known as Chatham had stood on Stafford Heights near Fredericksburg for ninety years before the Civil War. In the 18th century, it was the home of William Fitzhugh, a wealthy landowner. During the war the mansion was referred to as the Lacy House, after its wartime owner, J. Horace Lacy. During the Battle of Fredericksburg, the mansion served as the command post for General Sumner, Right Grand Division Commander. Two pontoon bridges spanned the Rappahannock River immediately below the mansion.

8. The Phillips House was General Burnside's headquarters during the Battle of Fredericksburg. Located east of the Lacy House, it was owned by Alexander K. Phillips and called "Mulberry Hill." General Sumner had occupied the Phillips House but moved to the Lacy House on December 12, 1862. Phillips House burned in February 1863.

9. Brigadier General James Nagle commanded the First Brigade in the Second Division of the IX Corps.

10. Sidney S. Heywood entered the military from Royalston, Massachusetts, on August 23, 1861 and served in Company A, 21st Massachusetts. He was promoted to sergeant on July 11, 1862. He was wounded at New Bern, North Carolina, on March 14, 1862, at Spotsylvania, Virginia on May 12, 1864 and Petersburg, Virginia on July 5, 1864. His military service expired on August 30, 1864.

11. Asahel Wheeler entered the military from Ashburnham, Massachusetts, on August 23, 1861, as sergeant in Company G, 21st Massachusetts. He was promoted to second lieutenant on January 24, 1862, first lieutenant on May 28, 1862 and captain on January 14, 1863. He resigned on April 25, 1863.

12. Edward (Tim) Donahue entered the military from Shirley, Massachusetts, on August 23, 1861 and served in Company D, 21st Massachusetts. He was wounded on September 1, 1862, at Chantilly, Virginia and discharged on September 21, 1863.

13. Frazar Augustus Stearns entered the military from Amherst, Massachusetts, on August 21, 1861, as adjutant in the 21st Massachusetts. He was killed on March 14, 1862, at New Bern, North Carolina. General Reno, in his official report on the Battle of New Bern, referred to him as "one of the most accomplished and gallant officers in the army."

14. George F. Thompson entered the military from Worcester, Massachusetts, on August 21, 1861, as a first lieutenant in the 21st Massachusetts. He was regimental quartermaster and was promoted to captain on September 10, 1862 and lieutenant colonel on March 13, 1865.

15. Major General Franz Sigel, who graduated from the German Military Academy, resigned from the German Army in 1847. He commanded the XI ("German") Corps since September 12, 1862, but he had to resign because of poor health on February 22, 1863.

16. Joel J. Brooks entered the military from Gardner, Massachusetts, in May 1861 and served in Company F, 2nd Massachusetts Regiment. He was wounded in the hand at Antietam on September 17, 1862 but was not disabled. He was promoted to sergeant on September 24, 1862. He was wounded and taken prisoner at Gettysburg while fighting in the meadow on July 3, 1863.

17. John Frederick Hartranft, colonel of the 51st Pennsylvania Regiment, commanded the 2nd Brigade in the 2nd Division of the IX Corps during February and March of 1863. He was named brigadier general on May 12, 1864. He served as governor of Pennsylvania from 1872-78.

Chapter Five

1. George C. Hill entered the military from Shirley, Massachusetts, on August 23, 1861, as a sergeant in Company D, 21st Mass Regt. He was promoted to second lieutenant on July 21, 1862, first lieutenant on July 28, 1862 and captain on September 25, 1862. He resigned from the military on April 25, 1863.

2. Freeman Cole entered the military from Mendon, Massachusetts, on August 1, 1862 and served in Company A, 21st Massachusetts. His military service expired on August 30, 1864.

3. J. Albert Osgood entered the military from Templeton, Massachusetts, on August 23, 1861, as sergeant in Company A, 21st Massachusetts. Nicknamed "Brick-top," he was captured at the Battle of the Wilderness on May 6, 1864 and was imprisoned at Andersonville.

4. Wilbur A. Potter entered the military from Templeton, Massachusetts, on August 23, 1861 and served in Company A, 21st Massachusetts. He was captured at the Battle of the Wilderness on May 6, 1864 and was imprisoned at Andersonville.

5. Major General John Adams Dix, who fought in the War of 1812, commanded the VII Corps in the Department of Virginia from July 1862 to July 1863. From July 18, 1863 until the end of the war, he commanded the Department of the East.

6. Major General William Farrar ("Baldy") Smith, who graduated from the USMA in 1845, commanded the IX Corps from February 5 to March 17, 1863.

7. John F. Lewis entered the military from Templeton, Massachusetts, on August 23, 1861, as a sergeant in Company A, 21st Massachusetts. He was promoted to second lieutenant on October 1, 1862 and transferred to Company F. He resigned on March 2, 1863.

8. Harrison Aldrich entered the military from Williamsville, Vermont, on August 23, 1861, as a sergeant in Company K, 21st Massachusetts. He was promoted to second lieutenant on March 3, 1862, first lieutenant on July 18, 1862 and captain on December 18, 1862. He resigned on April 25, 1863.

9. John D. Reynolds entered the military from Webster, Massachusetts, on August 23, 1861 and served as a corporal in Company F, 21st Massachusetts, before transferring to Company A. He was killed at a battle near Cold Harbor on June 1, 1864.

10. Brigadier General Michael Corcoran organized the Corcoran Legion and commanded the unit at Suffolk, Virginia, from November 1862 to April 1863. The Legion was a brigade composed of the 155th, 164th, 170th and 182d New York regiments and assigned to the VII Corps of the Department of Virginia. He was accidentally killed near Fairfax, Virginia, on December 22, 1863.

11. Battle of New Bern: On March 14, 1862, New Bern, North Carolina, was captured by the Coast Division of the Army of the Potomac led by General Burnside (thirteen regiments of infantry). The official record indicated that the "21st Massachusetts, from its exposed position and the daring of its officers and men, suffered the greatest loss"—58 casualties.

Chapter Six

1. Samuel Wright was killed in Columbus, Ohio, on March 30, 1863. He had entered the military from Pittsfield, Massachusetts, on August 23, 1861 and served in Company I, 21st Massachusetts.

2. The Crisis, published in Columbus Ohio, stated on April 1, 1863: "As several regiments of Eastern soldiers, mostly from Pennsylvania and Massachusetts, were stopping at the depot in this city, on Monday, on their way West; a number of the soldiers, as they had plenty of time, concluded to visit the city, without orders. Our Provost Guard forbid their leaving [the railroad station] and a fight ensued and several of the soldiers were badly wounded. Unfortunately and deeply to be regretted as this affair is, no blame can be attached to the Provost Guard, as they only performed the duty required of them. Where were the officers of these regiments? They are to blame, for not being present. The Provost Guard deserves great credit for their forbearance under the trying circumstances."

Charles F. Walcott, who was a captain in the 21st Massachusetts and present at Columbus, stated in his book in 1882, *History of the Twenty-First Regiment of Massachusetts Volunteers*, that the incident at Columbus was "a murderous attack upon our men, and this inhuman outrage might have provoked a fearful revenge, if the officers of the brigade had not exerted themselves to the utmost to calm the excitement of the men, and keeping them from their guns forced them on board the cars and hurried them out of town."

Comprehensive newspaper coverage of the clash is printed in Appendix C.

Chapter Seven

1. Garret Davis, a congressman from Kentucky, was elected to the United States Senate in 1861 to fill the vacancy caused by the expulsion of John C. Breckinridge. In 1856, he was nominated for President by the Know-Nothing Party. When most Kentuckians were undecided in their course of action in the Civil War, Davis came out for unswerving and complete adherence to the Union.

2. Simon May entered the military from Fitchburg, Massachusetts, on August 23, 1861 and served as sergeant in Company D, 21st Massachusetts. He was killed in the battle near the Weldon Railroad at Petersburg on August 19, 1864.

3. Lyman W. Holt entered the military from Ashby, Massachusetts, on October 18, 1862 and served in Company B, 53d Massachusetts Regiment. He died in New Orleans, Louisiana, on March 16, 1863. During this time there were more than 250 men sick with startling rapidity from diarrhea, dysentery and malarial fever.

4. Martin Gilson entered the military from Ashby, Massachusetts, on October 23, 1861 and served in Company B, 26th Massachusetts Regiment. He was discharged on March 6, 1863, for disability at New Orleans.

5. Major General Jacob Dolson Cox, who on the death of General Reno led the IX Corps during the Battle of Antietam, assumed command of the District of Ohio and the Third Division of the XXIII Corps (Ohio) on April 16, 1863. He was Governor of Ohio in 1866-67.

6. Stephen McCabe entered the military from Boston, Massachusetts, on August 23, 1861, as sergeant in Company B, 21st Massachusetts. He was promoted to second lieutenant on January 12, 1863. He resigned in May 8, 1863.

7. William H. Valentine entered the military from Worcester, Massachusetts, on August 21, 1861, as sergeant major in the 21st Massachusetts. He was promoted to second lieutenant on January 1, 1862, first lieutenant on June 19, 1862 and captain on March 6, 1863. He resigned on August 17, 1864.

8. P. Frank Gethings entered the military from Barre, Massachusetts, on August 23, 1861, as sergeant in Company K, 21st Massachusetts. He was promoted to sergeant major on March 7, 1864. He was captured at the Battle of the Wilderness on May 6, 1864 and was imprisoned at Andersonville.

9. John S. Koster entered the military from Palmer, Massachusetts, on August 23, 1861 and served as sergeant in Company H, 21st Massachusetts. His military service expired on August 30, 1864.

10. Three of the discharged captains received commissions at a later date: Charles F. Walcott, colonel of the 61st Massachusetts Regiment; William T. Harlow, major in the 57th Massachusetts Regiment; and Asahel Wheeler, captain in the 61st Massachusetts Regiment.

11. Alvin E. Humiston entered the military from Holyoke, Massachusetts, on August 23, 1861 and served as corporal in Company H, 21st Massachusetts. His service expired on August 30, 1864.

12. Robert T. Williams was a major in the Kentucky 10th Cavalry (Union troops) in August 1863. He commanded the 14th Kentucky Cavalry (four companies) in the Mount Sterling area.

13. Christopher A. Curtis entered the military from West Boylston, Massachusetts, on August 23, 1861 and served as sergeant in Company E, 21st Massachusetts.

14. Robert Miller entered the military from Spencer, Massachusetts, on August 23, 1861 and served as sergeant in Company C, 21st Massachusetts..

15. Thomas B. Dyer entered the military from Westborough, Massachusetts, on August 23, 1861 and served in Company K, 21st Massachusetts. He was captured at the battle near Bethesda Church on June 2, 1864 and imprisoned at Andersonville.

16. Major General Earl Van Dorn, who graduated from the USMA in 1842 and was a brilliant and daring cavalry leader in the West, was murdered at his headquarters in Spring Hill, Tennessee, on May 8, 1863, by a resident of the neighborhood, Dr. Peters, who stated that Van Dorn had "violated the sanctity of his home."

17. Charles H. Sperry entered the military from Pittsfield, Massachusetts, on August 23, 1861 and served as a sergeant in Company B, 21st Massachusetts.

18. Asa E. Haywood entered the military from Springfield, Massachusetts, on August 23, 1861 and served as a sergeant in Company B, 21st Massachusetts. He was promoted to second lieutenant on September 2, 1862 and first lieutenant on December 18, 1862. He resigned on May 14, 1863.

19. Benjamin F. Fuller entered the military from Templeton, Massachusetts, on August 23, 1861 and served in Company A, 21st Massachusetts. He was promoted to quartermaster sergeant, regimental-quartermaster sergeant and first lieutenant on October 2, 1862. His military service expired on August 30, 1864.

20. Israel Cummings entered the military from Fitchburg, Massachusetts, on August 23, 1861 and served as a sergeant in Company D, 21st Massachusetts. He was wounded during the siege of Knoxville on November 29, 1863 and died on December 2, 1863.

21. Clement Laird Vallandigham, a prominent "copperhead," was a controversial Democratic Congressman from Ohio who symbolized "peace at any price" opposition to President Lincoln. In 1863, he denounced the government for refusing to end the war by mediation. He was tried by a military tribunal and banished within the military lines of the Confederacy in May 1863. Vallandigham's comment that "he did not want to belong to the United States" prompted Edward Everett Hale to write *The Man Without a Country*, which appeared in the *Atlantic Magazine* in December 1863. This fictitious story stimulated patriotism more than any other wartime writing.

22. Ira B. Goodrich entered the military from Fitchburg, Massachusetts, on August 23, 1861 and served as a corporal in Company D, 21st Massachusetts. He was promoted to first sergeant on July 23, 1862, second lieutenant on September 2, 1862 and first lieutenant on January 15, 1863. His military service expired on August 30, 1864.

23. Charles S. Wilder entered the military from Worcester, Massachusetts, on August 23, 1861 and served as corporal in Company A, 21st Massachusetts. He was wounded and captured at the battle near Bethesda Church on June 2, 1864 and died the same day while a prisoner.

24. Charles C. Muzzey entered the military from Worcester, Massachusetts, on August 23, 1861 and served as sergeant in Company F, 21st Massachusetts.

25. Baseball originated from what the English called "rounders," and after considerable modification the Americans called the game "town ball." In 1845, the Knickerbocker Club of New York provided a rule book for the game, but its popularity

really dates from the Civil War, during which it was played with enthusiasm by Union and Confederate soldiers.

26. Thomas Goodness entered the military from Holyoke, Massachusetts, on August 23, 1861 and served as corporal in Company H, 21st Massachusetts.

27. On August 6, 1861, the United States Congress established pay of $13 per month for three years for privates in the Regular Army and Volunteers in the service of the United States. On June 20, 1864, the pay was increased to $16. Soldiers were scheduled to be paid every two months in the field, but frequently the pay was received at four-month intervals and some soldiers had to wait six or eight months between payments. In 1861, lieutenants were paid $105.50, captains $115.50, majors $169, colonels $212, and brigadier generals $315 per month.

28. Barney McNulty entered the military from Leicester, Massachusetts, on August 23, 1861 and served in Company C, 21st Massachusetts.

29. John Kelt entered the military from Holyoke, Massachusetts, on October 24, 1861 and served as corporal and sergeant in Company H, 21st Massachusetts. He was promoted to second lieutenant on September 18, 1862 . He was dismissed from military service on August 19, 1863.

30. George H. Bean entered the military from Biddeford, Maine, on August 23, 1861 and served as sergeant in Company H, 21st Massachusetts. He was promoted to first lieutenant on April 26, 1863. His military service expired on August 30, 1864.

31. Thomas E. Bramlette, a lawyer, was elected Kentucky's last Civil War governor as a Union Democrat on August 3, 1863 and took office on September 1, 1863. He had served as colonel of the 3d Kentucky Regiment in 1861 and resigned to become a district attorney.

32. William King, who entered the military from Roxbury, Massachusetts and originally served as captain of Company K, 35th Massachusetts Regiment, was promoted to lieutenant colonel on April 25, 1863. He was wounded seven times during the Battle of Antietam.

33. John Hunt Morgan was a C.S.A. general and cavalry raider. Morgan's Raiders, officially organized as the 2nd Kentucky Cavalry and calling themselves the "Alligator Horses," attained legendary fame raiding, skirmishing and fighting battles in ten states—especially in Kentucky and Tennessee. Morgan was captured near New Lisbon, Ohio on July 26, 1863, but escaped from the Ohio State Penitentiary on November 26, 1863. He was killed at Greenville, Tennessee by Federal troops on September 4, 1864.

34. Colonel John F. DeCourcy commanded the Fourth Brigade of the Seventh Division of the Army of Ohio. Before leaving Kentucky, General Burnside organized a brigade of new troops under command of Colonel DeCourcy and attached it to the IX Corps with orders to move down the north side of the Cumberland Gap to prevent the escape of the Confederate garrison. General Burnside placed Colonel DeCourcy under arrest for alleged improper conduct for writing what was deemed an improper letter during the siege of the Cumberland Gap in September 1863.

35. Brigadier General John Pegram, who graduated from the USMA in 1854, commanded a brigade in Forest's Cavalry Corps, Department of East Tennessee, from

late October 1862 to August 20, 1863 and led raids into Kentucky. This C.S.A. general was killed on February 6, 1865, near Dabney's Sawmill in the Battle of Hatcher's Run.

36. On July 31, 1863, General Burnside declared martial law throughout Kentucky to preserve the freedom of election, to prevent disloyal persons from voting and to silence any civil authorities who might be disposed to interfere.

37. Moses A. Chamberlin entered the military from Templeton, Massachusetts, on September 25, 1862 and served as a corporal in Company A, 21st Massachusetts.

38. Theron E. Hall entered the military from Holden, Massachusetts, on August 23, 1861 and served as adjutant, 21st Massachusetts. He was discharged on July 28, 1862. In July 1862, he joined the United States volunteers as a captain and assistant quartermaster. He was assigned to chief quartermaster with the rank of lieutenant colonel on January 1863. He resigned on December 5, 1864.

39. Jonas R. Davis entered the military from Templeton, Massachusetts, on August 23, 1861 and served as a sergeant in Company A, 21st Massachusetts. He was promoted to first lieutenant on June 6, 1863.

40. Camp Nelson was named for Major General William Nelson, who founded Camp Dick Robinson; for better protection from invading Confederate armies of Tennessee, the camp was moved to the Jessamine side of the Kentucky River and renamed Camp Nelson by Major General George H. Thomas. General Nelson was killed by a fellow general, Jefferson Columbus Davis, in a Louisville hotel on September 29, 1862.

41. Brigadier General Jeremiah Tilford Boyle, a Princeton graduate and lawyer from Kentucky, helped organize the defense of Kentucky and was Military Governor from 1862 to 1864.

42. Brigadier General Speed Smith Fry, a lawyer and judge from Kentucky, organized the 4th Kentucky Infantry Regiment. He killed the C.S.A. General Zollicoffer at the Battle of Logan Cross Roads, Kentucky, on January 19, 1862.

43. Daniel Boone Cave is located in Jessamine County, Kentucky, a half mile east of Camp Nelson near Hickman Creek. The hill between the village of Camp Nelson and the cave was the Civil War campground. As a boy in Ashby, Hitchcock was always investigating the Indian cave on Jone's hill. He had written that it was "a resort full of mystery for youthful imagination."

44. Francis M. Peckham entered the military from Petersham, Massachusetts, on August 23, 1861 and served as sergeant in Company A, 21st Massachusetts. His military service expired on September 14, 1864.

45. Major General William Nelson, who commanded the Army of Kentucky and was organizing the defenses at Louisville, was killed by Brigadier General Jefferson Columbus Davis in a Louisville hotel lobby on September 29, 1862. Davis, who had been brooding over a rebuke from Nelson, was never punished and returned to active duty.

46. Ansel Orcutt entered the military from Athol, Massachusetts, on August 23, 1861 and served in Company A, 21st Massachusetts. He was wounded at New Bern, North Carolina on March 14, 1862.

47. Samuel B. Adams entered the military from Templeton, Massachusetts, on August 23, 1861 and served in Company A, 21st Massachusetts.

48. Henry N. Allen entered the military from Templeton, Massachusetts, on August 23, 1861 and served in Company A, 21st Massachusetts. He was discharged on August 19, 1864 with a disability.

49. The prejudiced values of the 19th century toward African Americans are evident throughout the diary; however, words did not have the connotations or meanings that they have today. The word *darkies* is considered offensive today but was not in the 1860's.

50. Asa Franklin Van Buren Piper entered the military from Templeton, Massachusetts, on August 23, 1861 and served in Company A, 21st Massachusetts. He was killed on May 6, 1864, at the Battle of the Wilderness.

51. Brigadier General Robert Brown Potter served as major, lieutenant colonel and colonel in the 51st New York Regiment. He commanded the IX Corps in the Army of Ohio from August 25, 1863 to January 17, 1864.

Chapter Eight

1. Joshua K. Sigfried, colonel of the 48th Pennsylvania since September 20, 1862, commanded the First Brigade of the Second Division of the IX Corps and then the Second Division of the IX Corps. He was commissioned brigadier general on August 1, 1864.

2. Brigadier General John W. Frazer, C.S.A., who graduated from the USMA in 1849, surrendered the Cumberland Gap, an important and easily defensible pass, without firing a shot on September 9, 1863.

3. Brigadier General Felix Kirk Zollicoffer, C.S.A., who had served in the U.S. House of Representatives for three terms, was in command of a brigade in eastern Tennessee in 1861. He was killed on January 19, 1862 at Mill Springs, Kentucky.

4. Simon Goodell Griffin, a New Hampshire lawyer and legislator, was colonel of the 6th New Hampshire Regiment. He commanded the First Brigade of the Second Division of the IX Corps and then commanded the Second Division of the IX Corps from August 25, 1863 to October 1863. He was promoted to brigadier general on May 12, 1864.

5. William Gannaway Brownlow, former Methodist minister, was editor of the *Knoxville Whig*. He opposed secession and became a Unionist leader in east Tennessee. He was elected Governor of Tennessee in 1865 and 1867 and United States Senator in 1869.

6. The railroad leading southwest from Knoxville is the East Tennessee and Georgia Railroad, while the line running northeast is the East Tennessee and Virginia Railroad.

7. Lieutenant Samuel N. Benjamin, who had been commended for his action at Antietam, commanded Battery E, 2nd U. S. Artillery.

8. Brigadier General James M. Shackleford, who had captured Confederate General John H. Morgan near West Point, Ohio, on July 26, 1863, commanded the Fourth Division Cavalry of the XXIII Army Corps during the east Tennessee campaign in October 1863.

9. Dr. Calvin Cutter entered the military from Warren, Massachusetts, on August 23, 1861 and served as surgeon in the 21st Massachusetts. He resigned on May 17, 1864.

10. Walter Lamb entered the military from Templeton, Massachusetts, on September 18, 1861 and served in Company I, 25th Massachusetts Regiment. He was taken prisoner on June 3, 1864, at the Battle of Cold Harbor and imprisoned at Andersonville. He was exchanged on November 20, 1864.

11. George T. Barker entered the military from Boston, Massachusetts, on August 23, 1861 and served as first sergeant, Company B, 21st Massachusetts. He was promoted to first lieutenant on October 2, 1862 and captain on April 26, 1863. His military service expired on August 30, 1864.

12. Major General Braxton Bragg, C.S.A., who graduated from the USMA in 1837, commanded the Army of Tennessee.

13. Colonel Frank Wolford, 1st Kentucky Cavalry, commanded an Independent Cavalry Brigade in the engagement at Philadelphia, Tennessee (a few miles southwest of Loudon), on October 20, 1863. Union forces included 1st, 11th and 12th Kentucky cavalries and 45th Ohio (mounted) Infantry. The Confederate cavalry, Army of Tennessee, were commanded by Colonel Morrison and Colonel Dibrell. The Confederates captured 447 Union prisoners.

14. Charles A. Blackmer entered the military from Templeton, Massachusetts, on August 23, 1861 and served in Company A, 21st Massachusetts. He died of wounds received during the battle in front of Petersburg on June 16, 1864.

15. Marcus Gould, nicknamed "Jule," entered the military from Dudley, Massachusetts, on August 23, 1861 and served in Company A, 21st Massachusetts.

16. Henry G. Dillenback entered the military from Derry, New Hampshire, on August 29, 1862 and served as first sergeant of Company E, 11th New Hampshire Regiment. He was wounded on December 13, 1862, at Fredericksburg and promoted to first lieutenant on December 18, 1862. He was discharged on July 22, 1864.

17. Richard R. Fiske entered the military from Blackstone, Massachusetts, on August 23, 1861 and served in Company E, 21st Massachusetts. He died on November 27, 1863, from wounds received during the siege of Knoxville on November 24, 1863.

18. Dwight Ripley entered the military from Petersham, Massachusetts, on August 7, 1862 and served in Company K, 21st Massachusetts. He was killed during the siege of Knoxville on November 25, 1863.

19. Henry M. Harper entered the military from Worcester, Massachusetts, on August 23, 1861 and served in Company K, 21st Massachusetts.

20. William Harrington entered the military from Lunenburg, Massachusetts, on August 23, 1861 and served as corporal in Company K, 21st Massachusetts. He was killed at the Battle of the Mine on July 30, 1864.

21. Major General John Gray Foster, who graduated from the USMA in 1846, commanded the Department of Ohio from December 11, 1863 to February 9, 1864.

22. Major General Gordon Granger, who graduated from the USMA in 1845, commanded the IV Corps (Cumberland) at Missionary Ridge and Knoxville. He had been elevated to command for his outstanding performance at Chickamauga, but he failed to duplicate this success in subsequent action.

Chapter Nine

1. Ransom Bailey entered the military from Lenox, Massachusetts, on August 23, 1861 and served in Company I, 21st Massachusetts. He was captured near Blains Cross Road, Tennessee, on December 23, 1863, and imprisoned at Andersonville, where he died of scorbutus on August 23, 1864 (grave number 6,624).

2. Samuel N. Gould entered the military from Phillipston, Massachusetts, on August 23, 1861 and served as a musician in Company A, 21st Massachusetts. His military service expired on August 30, 1864.

3. Reuben Mann entered the military from Templeton, Massachusetts, on August 23, 1861 and served in Company A, 21st Massachusetts.

4. "Give me three grains of corn, mother, Only three grains of corn. 'Twill keep what little life I have—Till the coming of the morn." This is the first of nine verses of the song: *Give Me Three Grains of Corn, Mother.* This story about a starving boy was printed in school readers during the mid-nineteenth century. According to Carl Sandburg, the 1848 version was long and "it prolongs desolation beyond endurance or healthy art. The latter quality is not found in the variants known among midwest pioneers." The verse mellowed and sweetened as it was passed on over the years and was sung in new ways.

5. R. A. Holden and Company was owned by Reuben A. Holden and Charles E. Houghton. They were wholesale dealers in feathers, ginseng and beeswax.

6. William L. Fox entered the military from Lancaster, Massachusetts, on August 23, 1861 and served as a sergeant in Company E, 21st Massachusetts.

Chapter Ten

1. Francis Burpee entered the military from Sterling, Massachusetts, on August 8, 1862 and served as a corporal in Company E, 21st Massachusetts. His military service expired on August 30, 1864.

2. J. Warren Clark entered the military from Petersham, Massachusetts, on August 12, 1862 and served in Company K, 21st Massachusetts. He was killed during a battle near Cold Harbor (Shady Grove Road) on June 1, 1864.

3. Sidney Sibley entered the military from Barre, Massachusetts, on August 8, 1862 and served in Company K, 21st Massachusetts. He was discharge on May 23, 1864, with a disability.

4. Colonel Albert P. Thompson, C.S.A., commanded the Third Brigade of General Nathan Bedford Forest's Cavalry when he was killed at Paducah, Kentucky, on March 25, 1864. Although the Confederate troops occupied part of Paducah, two attacks were repulsed at Fort Anderson, and they withdrew on March 26th. However, this raid alarmed the Ohio River valley.

5. Sir Henry Havelock, 1795-1857, was a British General who united the graces of religion to the valor of the soldier.

6. Knights of the Golden Circle, which first appeared in 1855 after being known as Southern Rights Clubs with the desire to reestablish the African slave trade and acquire new slave territory, was a secret order in the North of Southern Sympathizers who disapproved of the war.

7. Chauncey B. Irish entered the military from Millbury, Massachusetts, on August 23, 1861 and served as a corporal and sergeant in Company F, 21st Massachusetts.

8. James Emerson was the family doctor in Ashby, Massachusetts.

Chapter Eleven

1. Major General Edward ("Allegheny") Johnson, C.S.A., who graduated from the USMA in 1838, commanded the Stonewall Division in the Army of Northern Virginia. He was captured at Spotsylvania's "Bloody Angle" on May 12, 1864, with some 2,500 of his men.

2. Brigadier General George Hume ("Maryland") Steuart, C.S.A., who graduated from the USMA in 1848, commanded an infantry brigade (four Virginia regiments and 1st Maryland Regiment). He and most of his brigade were captured at Spotsylvania's "Bloody Angle" on May 12, 1864.

3. Colonel John Singleton Mosby, C.S.A., led 100 to 200 irregular troops or partisan rangers in Virginia. They were mustered into the Confederate Army as the 43d Battalion of Virginia Cavalry on June 10, 1863. On May 17, 1864, Mosby, with about 200 men, attacked a detachment from Falmouth within four miles of Belle Plain. Union officials feared that Mosby would attack the depot or wagon trains on the way to the front. Therefore, Union supply wagons required heavy guard. Mosby's Raiders frequently operated in small squads of twenty to eighty men and attacked Union outposts, wagon trains and stragglers with such fury and efficiency that the whole area in northern Virginia became known as "Mosby's Confederacy."

4. William H. Sawyer entered the military from New Salem, Massachusetts, on August 23, 1861 and served as sergeant in Company K, 21st Massachusetts. He was promoted to first lieutenant on April 26, 1863 and captain on October 12, 1864.

5. Major General William Buel Franklin, who graduated from the USMA in 1843, commanded the Left Grand Division (I Corps and VI Corps) at Fredericksburg on December 13, 1862. He was blamed by the Committee on the Conduct of the War for the Union debacle.

6. Brigadier General James Harrison Wilson, who graduated from the USMA in 1860, commanded the Third Division, Cavalry Corps, Army of the Potomac from April 13, 1864 to August 6, 1864, when the division was transferred to the Army of the Shenandoah.

7. Black troops were added to the IX Corps and organized into the Fourth Division commanded by Brigadier General Edward Ferrero. They were the first colored troops to serve in the Army of the Potomac.

8. Major General Winfield Scott Hancock, who graduated from the USMA in 1840, commanded the II Army Corps, Army of the Potomac.

9. Lieutenant General Ulysses Simpson Grant, who graduated from the USMA in 1843, commanded the United States Armies in the Field in May 1864. General Robert Edward Lee, C.S.A., who graduated from the USMA in 1829, commanded the Army of Northern Virginia in May 1864.

10. Major General George Gordon Meade, who graduated from the USMA in 1835, commanded The Army of the Potomac in May 1864.

11. Major General Thomas Leonidas Crittenden assumed command of the First Division of the IX Corps on May 12, 1864, replacing Brigadier General Thomas Greeley Stevenson who was killed in front of Spotsylvania Court House on May 10, 1864.

12. George M. Lander entered the military from Greenfield, Massachusetts, on August 23, 1861 and served in Company K, 21st Massachusetts. He was killed near Cold Harbor on May 31, 1864, at Shady Grove Road during a sharp picket fight.

13. James Oliver entered the military from Athol, Massachusetts, on July 31, 1862 and served as a surgeon in the 21st Massachusetts. His military service expired on August 30, 1864.

Chapter Twelve

1. Two roads connect the Shady Grove Road with Bethesda Church. The road to the west intersects with the Shady Grove Road about one mile from Bethesda Church. At the time of the battle, the area west of this intersection was wooded and the area east, marked as the Bowles farm, was cultivated. This battle took place in these fields and woods near this intersection.

2. Colonel Joseph M. Sudsburg, former commander of the 3rd Maryland Regiment, commanded the Second Brigade, First Division of the IX Corps, from May 31, 1864 to June 4, 1864, during the Battle of Cold Harbor. He was discharged on June 24, 1864.

3. Major General Jubal Anderson Early, C.S.A., who graduated from the USMA in 1837, succeeded Lieutenant General Richard Stoddert Ewell as commander of the II Army Corps, Army of Northern Virginia, on May 27, 1864 (Early had been in temporary command since May 22, 1864). Major General Stephen Dodson Ramseur, C.S.A., who graduated from the USMA in 1860, was placed in temporary command of Early's Division on May 27, 1864. Brigadier General William Ruffin Cox, C.S.A., who

was wounded five times at the Battle of Chancellorsville, was placed in temporary command of Ramseur's Brigade on May 31, 1864.

Colonel Bryan Grimes, who performed flawlessly at Spotsylvania on May 12, was promoted to brigadier general and assumed command of Junius Daniel's North Carolina Brigade on May 19. Major General Henry Heth's Division attacked the V and IX Corps at Bethesda Church on June 2, 1864; his troops were on the far left of the Confederate line. In his journal, George Hitchcock indicated that he surrendered to an officer of a North Carolina regiment. There were two brigades in Heth's Division with North Carolina troops: Cooke's Brigade (15th, 27th, 46th and 48th North Carolina regiments) and Kirkland's Brigade (11th, 26th, 44th, 47th and 52d North Carolina regiments). In *North Carolina Troops*, Walter Clark reported that Kirkland's Brigade charged Union troops on June 2 in a heavy skirmish, "driving them from their first line of entrenchments." General Kirkland was wounded, "receiving a rifle ball through the thigh, and was taken from the field." Clark also stated that "on the evening of June 2, at Turkey Ridge, Cooke's Brigade supported the left flank of Kirkland's Brigade and had a sharp engagement with the enemy until after dark."

4. On June 2, 1864, the Second Brigade in the First Division of the IX Corps lost 137 men: 80 casualties in the 100th Pennsylvania Regiment, 47 casualties in the 21st Massachusetts and 10 casualties in the 3d Maryland Regiment.

5. James A. Miller entered the military from Templeton, Massachusetts, on August 23, 1861 and served as a corporal in Company A, 21st Massachusetts. He was captured during the battle near Bethesda Church on June 2, 1864 and was imprisoned at Andersonville.

6. There were actually eleven soldiers from the 21st Massachusetts captured with Hitchcock: Prentice J. Banks, Daniel E. Barker, James Cane, Thomas B. Dyer, George 0. Emerson, Alvin S. Graton, German Lagara, Martin D. Leach, Thomas Marshall, James A. Miller, and William L. Orcutt.

7. Wilder later died of wounds.

Chapter Thirteen

1. James Gardiner, 1688-1745, British Colonel of a regiment of light dragoons, was slain in a battle at Prestonpans on September 21, 1745, immediately after saying, "Fire on, my lads, and fear nothing." According to Gardiner, he was reading Thomas Watson's *The Christian Soldier*, when he saw a vision of Jesus Christ upon the cross and was immediately converted. *The Life of Colonel James Gardiner: The Christian Warrior* by Philip Doddridge, dated 1745, was one of the most frequently printed books; the 1854 and 1856 editions were printed in New York.

2. In November 1861, President Jefferson Davis requested that the railroad ending at Danville, Virginia, be connected with Greensboro, North Carolina. Construction was delayed for more than two years pending completion of satisfactory surveys, examination of rival routes and arrangements for procuring labor and materials. The connection was completed in May, 1864.

Chapter Fourteen

1. Captain Hartmann Heinrich (Henry) Wirz, C.S.A., who was born in Zurich, Switzerland, in 1823, immigrated to Kentucky in 1849 and then moved to Milliken's Bend, Louisiana, where he functioned as a homeopathic physician. He commanded the interior of the prison at Andersonville, officially known as Camp Sumter, from March 29, 1864 to May 7, 1865 (absent on sick leave during August 1864).

2. William H. H. Martin entered the military on September 20, 1861 and served in Company E, 51st Ohio Regiment. He was captured in action at Big Shanty, Georgia, on June 11, 1864 and was imprisoned at Andersonville.

3. George Middy entered the military on September 20, 1861 and served in Company E, 51st Ohio Regiment. He was captured in action at Big Shanty, Georgia, on June 11, 1864 and was imprisoned at Andersonville.

4. William Henry Clark entered the military on December 23, 1863 and served in Company I, 72d Indiana Regiment. He was imprisoned at Andersonville and died at Wilmington, North Carolina, on March 12, 1865.

5. There was an average of 22,291 prisoners at Andersonville during June, 1864; the prison population was 26,367 on June 30, 1864.

6. Major General Franz Sigel commanded the Reserve Division of West Virginia from May 24 to July 8, 1864, during which time he delayed General Early at Harpers Ferry. He was relieved for lack of aggression.

7. Major General William Tecumseh Sherman, who graduated from the USMA in 1840, commanded the Union forces during the Atlanta Campaign (May-September 1864). Confederate soldiers evacuated Atlanta on September 1, 1864.

8. General Grant ordered Major General William F. Smith with the principal part of Butler's forces to join the Army of the Potomac. They were engaged in the Battle of Cold Harbor, assaulting the Confederate works on June 3, 1864.

9. Major General Frederick Steele, who graduated from the USMA in 1843, led the Arkansas Expedition, Army of Tennessee (Little Rock surrendered on September 10, 1863), and he commanded the VII Corps, Department of Arkansas, from January to December 22, 1864.

10. Thomas Winn entered the military from Worcester, Massachusetts, on August 23, 1861 and served as a corporal in Company K, 21st Massachusetts. He was wounded in the arm and captured near Petersburg on June 17, 1864. He was imprisoned at Andersonville.

11. Thomas Stephens entered the military from Northampton, Massachusetts, on August 23, 1861 and served as a corporal and sergeant in Company B, 21st Massachusetts. He was wounded at Antietam and Fredericksburg. He was captured near Petersburg on June 17, 1864 and was imprisoned at Andersonville.

12. William H. Tyler entered the military from Richmond, Massachusetts, on August 23, 1861 and served in Company I, 21st Massachusetts. He was captured near Petersburg on June 17, 1864 and was imprisoned at Andersonville.

13. Levi F. Shepard entered the military from Boylston, Massachusetts, on July 31, 1862 and served in Company C, 34th Massachusetts Regiment. He was wounded

and captured at New Market, Virginia, on May 15, 1864 and was imprisoned at Andersonville.

14. The Confederate government evacuated Richmond on Sunday, April 2, 1865 and Union troops occupied Richmond and Petersburg, Virginia, on April 3, 1865.

15. Brigadier General David Hunter, who graduated from USMA in 1822, sanctioned the first Negro regiment, the 1st South Carolina Infantry. On May 21, 1864, he assumed command of the Army of West Virginia and was successful in disrupting supplies and communications in the Shenandoah Valley until repulsed by General Early near Lynchburg in June.

16. These villains were called Mosby's Raiders, Mosby's Gang or more frequently "Raiders." The six Raiders, who were hanged at Andersonville on July 11, 1864, are listed on their grave markers as: Jno Sarsfield–144 NY; Wm Collins–88 Pa, Co D; Chas Curtis–5 RI Artillery, Co A; Pat Delaney–83 Pa, Co E; A Mun–US Navy; and W. R. Rickson–US Navy. Official military records indicate that the men were: William Collins, alias "Mosby," Company K and then Company D, 88th Pennsylvania Regiment, who straggled during the retreat from the Rapidan and was captured on October 12, 1863. He was confined at Belle Isle and arrived at Andersonville on March 4, 1864; John Sullivan, Company F, 76th New York Regiment, also straggled during the retreat from the Rapidan and was captured near Stevensburg, Virginia, on October 10, 1863. Confined at Belle Isle with Collins, he too arrived at Andersonville on March 4, 1864; James Sarsfield, Company C, 140th New York Regiment, deserted and surrendered at the Wilderness on May 5, 1864; Charles F. Curtis, Company C, 5th Rhode Island Heavy Artillery deserted and surrendered while confined at the hospital in Moorehead, North Carolina, in April 1864; Patrick Delaney, Company E, 83d Pennsylvania Regiment, deserted and surrendered on October 14, 1863, at Bristoe Station, Virginia; and Andrew Muir, seaman on the Federal steamer *U. S. S. Water Witch,* was captured on June 2, 1864, near Ossabaw Island, south of Savannah, Georgia.

17. Courtland A. Allen entered the military from Gardner (Baldwinville), Massachusetts, on July 27, 1862 and served as a sergeant in Company D, 36th Massachusetts Regiment. During the Spotsylvania campaign on May 12, 1864, he was wounded in the hand and captured going to the rear. He was imprisoned at Andersonville. While being removed from Andersonville, he and five others jumped from the railroad train and escaped into the swamps. They remained for several weeks, subsisting on roots and berries, found a dug-out and made their way down the Altamaha River to the blockading squadron—six weeks after their escape.

18. On July 10, 1864, Major General Lovell Harrison Rousseau, Union cavalry commander, led 2,500 men from Decatur, Alabama, to operate against the railroad lines between Columbus, Georgia, and Montgomery, Alabama. However, Union cavalry did not reach Montgomery until April 12, 1865.

19. The petition, written and supported by prisoners who held similar views, was directed to northern people, state governors and President Lincoln, advising them of the conditions at Andersonville and requesting immediate action for an exchange. The petition was signed by sergeants of 107 detachments, and General Winder permitted six

sergeants to take the document to Washington. President Lincoln ignored the petition and nothing happened. The petition was printed on the back page of *The New York Times* on August 30, 1864. The names of the six sergeants printed in the newspaper were: "Edward Bates, 42 New York; H. C. Higginson, Co K, 19 Illinois; S. Noirot; William N. Johnson; F. Garland; Prescott Tracy, Co G, 82 New York." Many of the prisoners did not approve of the petition.

20. George Webster served as a sergeant in Company I, 181st Pennsylvania Regiment (20th Cavalry). He was captured at Martinsburg, West Virginia, on July 3, 1864 and died at Andersonville of chronic diarrhea on November 7, 1864 (grave #11899).

21. John J. Mumford served in Company K, 2d New York Regiment. While imprisoned at Andersonville, he was one of the detachment sergeants who signed the petition that was sent to Washington.

22. Otis H. Knight entered the military from Worcester, Massachusetts, on December 29, 1863 and served in Company D, 25th Massachusetts Regiment. He was taken prisoner near Petersburg on June 15, 1864 and imprisoned at Andersonville. He was shot by a guard at Andersonville and died of wounds on July 23, 1864 (grave #3842).

23. William Samuel Laird served as a corporal in Company I, 185th Pennsylvania Regiment (22d Cavalry). He was imprisoned at Andersonville and was exchanged at Charleston on December 10, 1864.

24. J. M. Miller served in Company A, 11th Massachusetts Regiment. He was wounded and captured at the Battle of the Wilderness on May 6, 1864. He was imprisoned at Andersonville where he died of "fever typhus" on July 30, 1864 (grave #4329).

25. James Gaffney served in Company F, 11th Massachusetts Regiment. Although he was reported missing in action near Petersburg, he was captured and imprisoned at Andersonville where he died of diarrhea on July 30, 1864 (grave #4333).

26. Major General George Stoneman, who graduated from the USMA in 1846, commanded a cavalry division in Sherman's army. He planned to raid Macon and liberate the Union prisoners at Andersonville. However, unable to cross the Ocmulgee River at Macon, he headed north and a few miles beyond Clinton at Sunshine Church, he was cut off and surrounded by three brigades of Wheeler's cavalry. General Stoneman and 700 men were captured.

27. On August 8, 1864, 33,114 Union prisoners were confined at Andersonville, the largest number on any one day.

28. John J. Buchele served in Company E, 126th Ohio Regiment. He was captured at the Battle of the Wilderness on May 6, 1864 and was imprisoned at Andersonville. He died of diarrhea on August 9, 1864 (grave #5138).

29. Major General Bushrod Rust Johnson, C.S.A., who graduated from the USMA in 1840, commanded the Johnson's Division, Army of Northern Virginia, during the Richmond campaign.

30. The Confederate Army evacuated Atlanta at five in the afternoon on September 1, 1864, and Union troops took possession the next morning. General Sherman wired Washington: "Atlanta is ours, and fairly won."

31. George A. Hitchcock refers to his copy of *The New Testament*, published by the American Bible Society in New York, 1853 (pocket-size army testament that included the Psalms). This army testament was his daily companion in prison, and his copy was marked with his favorite verses: Romans 12; Psalms 37, 51, 90 and 91; John 14, 15, 16 and 17; Hebrews 11 and 12. He carried this army testament from August 7, 1862 to January 1, 1865.

32. Hebrews: Chapter 12, Verses 5, 6 and 7 (King James Version of the Bible)

33. On August 23, 1864, 127 prisoners died at Andersonville, the largest number of deaths on any day.

34. Erastus E. Baker entered the military from Oxford, Massachusetts, on August 2, 1862 and served in Company C, 34th Massachusetts Regiment. On August 25, 1864, he died from diarrhea at Andersonville (grave #6785). Robert Wilson entered the military from Millbury, Massachusetts, on July 31, 1862 and served in Company A, 34th Massachusetts Regiment. On August 25, 1864, he died from scorbutus at Andersonville (grave #6769).

35. Brigadier General Hugh Judson Kilpatrick, who graduated from the USMA in 1861, commanded the Third Division in the cavalry corps of the Army of the Cumberland. General Sherman ordered a raid on the Confederate line of communications south of Atlanta (Kilpatrick's raid to Lovejoy's Station from August 18-22, 1864). This raid failed to destroy the Macon and Western Railroad.

36. Residents of the area had known about this spring for more than thirty years. When the prison stockade was erected in February 1864, the workmen filled up the spring while excavating the trench for the pine fence posts so that the water oozed through the sand to the creek without rising to the surface. The flood, which swept the stockade walls away during the severe August storm, washed the earth from over the spring, and it burst out clear and as strong as ever.

37. German Lagara entered the military from Petersham, Massachusetts, on August 23, 1861 and served in Company K, 21st Massachusetts. He was captured at the battle near Bethesda Church on June 2, 1864 and was imprisoned at Andersonville.

38. Samuel Clark (George Clark in the *Atwater List of Prisoners who died at Andersonville Prison*) entered the military on March 9, 1864 and served in Company D, 60th Ohio Regiment. On September 5, 1864, he died of fever remittent at Andersonville (grave #7919).

39. Waldo Dwinnell entered the military from Ashburnham, Mass., on January 1, 1864 and served in Company G, 21st Massachusetts. He was captured during the Battle of the Wilderness on May 6, 1864 and died at Andersonville in September 1864 (buried in an unmarked grave).

40. Alvin S. Graton entered the military from Paxton, Massachusetts, on August 11, 1862 and served as a corporal in Company C, 21st Massachusetts. He was captured at the battle near Bethesda Church on June 2, 1864 and was imprisoned at Andersonville.

41. This train accident was not a "trifling affair." According to the *Macon Telegraph*, dated September 5, 1864, this "railroad catastrophe" occurred on Friday, September 2, about half past one in the afternoon near Fort Valley (26 miles north of Andersonville). "The two trains approached each other round a curve and were within two or three hundred yards when the alarm was given. The down train was moving at a speed of twenty-five miles an hour, and the up train about eighteen. The speed of neither was perceptually affected by the breaks before they struck. Five of the cars were utterly demolished. The tender of one engine was driven bodily through a grain car behind it, compressing the grain into a solid mass. The other tender was turned up on end and driven through the car behind it. Many soldiers who sat upon the tops of the cars and suspended their legs between, lost them. Twenty-nine were reported dead on Friday night and, about fifty wounded [Confederate soldiers]. Some thirty-five Yankee prisoners on the rear car of the down train, rendered the most efficient service in extricating the unfortunate victims" [there is no record of Union prisoner fatalities]. On September 23, 1864, the Macon Telegraph listed the names and regiments of 41 Confederate soldiers and two civilians who were killed in the accident. The Union soldiers were buried in an unmarked grave that has never been located.

42. On September 17, 1864, General Winder, post commander at Andersonville, issued a pass into the stockade for Dr. Joseph Jones, a Confederate physician and medical researcher, who was investigating the reasons for the very high mortality rate at Andersonville. Dr. Jones spent three weeks at Andersonville. With the aid of his secretary, Louis Manigault, Dr. Jones prepared reports on the abysmal facilities, rampant diseases and the medical condition of the prisoners; these reports are the most detailed and accurate descriptions available on conditions at Andersonville.

43. Daniel E. Barker entered the military from Chesterfield, Massachusetts, on August 23, 1861 and served as a corporal in Company H, 21st Massachusetts. He was captured at the battle near Bethesda Church on June 2, 1864 and was imprisoned at Andersonville.

44. Buel M. Phelps entered the military from Morristown, Vermont, on October 7, 1863 and served as a corporal of Company M, 11th Vermont Regiment. He was imprisoned at Andersonville.

Chapter Fifteen

1. Brigadier General Lucius Jeremiah Gartrell, C.S.A., who served in the United States House of Representative from 1857 to 1861 and in the first Confederate Congress, was commissioned on August 22, 1864 and commanded the Second Brigade of Georgia Reserves, composed of the 1st, 2d, 3d and 4th regiments [provided guards at Confederate prisons in Georgia].

Chapter Sixteen

1. On November 15, 1864, General Sherman started his "March to the Sea" and reached Savannah, Georgia (285 miles from Atlanta) on December 10, 1864.

Chapter Seventeen

1. Colonel Gardiner Tufts, Massachusetts Military Agent, served as an inspector of government general hospitals and military prisons in the Department of Washington.

2. Prentice J. Banks entered the military from Alstead, New Hampshire, on August 23, 1861 and served in Company K, 21st Massachusetts Regiment. He was captured at the battle near Bethesda Church on June 2, 1864 and imprisoned at Andersonville. He died on February 11, 1865, at home.

3. Benjamin J. Church entered the military from Warwick, Rhode Island, on June 5, 1861 and served in Company A, 2nd Rhode Island Regiment.

4. Orville Booth entered the military from Ashby, Massachusetts, and served as a corporal in Company B, 26th Massachusetts Regiment. He was taken prisoner on September 19, 1864, at Winchester, Virginia.

5. Isaac March entered the military from Ashby, Massachusetts, on October 18, 1861 and served in Company B, 26th Massachusetts Regiment. He was taken prisoner on September 19, 1864, at Winchester, Virginia.

6. Henry Sparhawk Hitchcock entered the military from Templeton, Massachusetts, on August 23, 1861 and served as sergeant in Company A, 21st Massachusetts Regiment. He was promoted to second lieutenant on September 25, 1862 and first lieutenant on April 26, 1863. He was wounded at Petersburg on July 30, 1864. His military service expired on August 30, 1864.

7. George Alfred Hitchcock (18 years old) entered the military from Ashby, Massachusetts, on August 14, 1862 and served as a private in Company A, 21st Massachusetts Regiment. He was captured on June 2, 1864, near Bethesda Church (Cold Harbor) and imprisoned at: Libby Prison, Richmond, Virginia (June 3-8, 1864); Camp Sumter, Andersonville, Georgia (June 16-November 2, 1864); Camp Lawton, Millen, Georgia (November 3-21, 1864); Florence, South Carolina (November 27-December 9, 1864). Hitchcock was exchanged at Charleston Harbor, South Carolina on December 10,1864.

The 21st Regiment of Massachusetts Volunteers, which was organized during the months of July and August 1861, reduced to a battalion of three companies on August 18, 1864, and was consolidated with the 36th Massachusetts Regiment on October 21, 1864.

Chapter Eighteen

1. Major General Benjamin Franklin Butler, who the Confederates referred to as "Beast Butler," was appointed a special agent for exchange of prisoners of war on December 17, 1863. His detailed letter on August 27, 1864 to Robert Ould, Commissioner for Exchange, stressing the willingness to renew exchanges whenever the Confederacy was ready to exchange all classes of prisoners, was published widely in newspapers and was printed as a leaflet by the government for general circulation. However, General Grant opposed any exchange: "It is hard on our men held in Southern prisons not to exchange them, but it is humanity to those left in the ranks to fight our battles. Every man we had, when released on parole or otherwise, becomes an active soldier against us at once either directly or indirectly. If we commence a system of exchange which liberates all prisoners taken, we will have to fight on until the whole South is exterminated. If we hold those caught, they amount to no more than dead men. At this particular time to release all rebel prisoners North would insure Sherman's defeat and would compromise our safety here [Richmond campaign]."

2. John Charles Tarsney entered military service from Hillsdale, Michigan, on August 26, 1862 and served in Company E, 4th Michigan Regiment. He was taken prisoner at the Battle of Gettysburg on July 2, 1863 and was exchanged. He was taken prisoner at the Battle of the Wilderness on May 5, 1864 and imprisoned at Belle Isle, Andersonville, Millen and Savannah. He returned to his regiment at Petersburg on January 10, 1865. He was discharged on June 5, 1865. As a Missouri Democrat, he was elected to the House of Representatives in 1889 and served for four terms.

Amos Jay Cummings served as a sergeant in Company E, 26th New Jersey Regiment from September 1, 1862 to June 27, 1863. He was promoted to sergeant major on March 6, 1863. As a New York Democrat, he was elected to the House of Representatives in 1887 and served until his death in 1902.

As reported in the *New York Times* on April 22, 1890, Mr. Tarsney objected to the bill "as indiscriminate, as proposing to reward indifferently the men who had struggled with captivity or chosen to be prisoners rather than serve in the field. It offered a premium to all soldiers of the Union hereafter to surrender." Mr. Cummings stated that "while he would favor the pensioning of worthy prisoner of war, he could not support so carelessly prepared a bill as that before the House." Many representatives objected to the proposition to pay $2 per diem to each of the surviving prisoners of war, because it seemed to be an injustice to other veterans of the war. The opponents of the bill were of the opinion that "no legislation should be enacted that would give one class of soldiers any advantage over another, and certainly none that ranks the soldiers who suffered in actual service below the ones that fell into the hands of the enemy." The commissioner of pensions estimated that 30,000 ex-prisoners have survived. The House bill "For pensioning prisoners of war" was defeated.

3. Brigadier General John Murray Corse, who commanded the Fourth Division of the XVI Corps, was surrounded by French's Division at Allatoona, Georgia, on October 5, 1864. He was ordered to surrender by Maj. Gen. Samuel Gibbs French.

However, General Corse received two messages by signal: "Sherman is coming. Hold out!" and then later, "General Sherman says hold fast. We are coming." By mid-afternnon, the Confederates broke off the engagement and withdrew. This engagement inspired P. P. Bliss, who wrote the hymn "Hold the Fort, For We Are Coming."

4. Colonel Joseph M. Sudsbury commanded the Second Brigade on June 2, 1864, when George Hitchcock was captured. Colonel Daniel Leasure, who organized and commanded the 100th Pennsylvania Volunteer Infantry Regiment—The Roundhead Regiment—was the "well known Pennsylvania officer."

The First Division of the IX Corps had a leadership problem after May 10, 1864, when Brig. Gen. Thomas Greeley Stevenson was killed in front of Spotsylvania Court House. Colonel Leasure assumed command of the First Division on May 10. In a letter to home on May 11, 1864, Charles J. Mills, Assistant Adjutant General of the First Division, wrote: "The division falls to the command of Colonel Leasure, who was in command of the Second Brigade. He did so well at the Wilderness that I had a favorable opinion of him, but I can't say that I retain it. If he is to have command of the division permanently, I shall not stay as A.A.G. that is sure, but my plans are very unsettled at present." Major General Thomas Leonidas Crittenden replaced Colonel Leasure on May 12, and he was replaced on June 9. On May 12, Colonel Leasure returned to command the Second Brigade; however, he was "disabled by sickness on May 14" and was never active in field command again.

The Second Brigade of the First Division changed commands frequently during three critical weeks and appeared leaderless during the Battle of Cold Harbor. The brigade was commanded: Until May 10 by Col. Daniel Leasure; May 10-12 by Lt. Col. Gilbert Robinson; May 12-14 by Col. Daniel Leasure; May 14-31 by Lt. Col. Gilbert Robinson; May 31-June 4 by Colonel Joseph M. Sudsburg. Colonel Leasure's son, Lt. S. George Leasure (Adjutant), wrote to his father that on June 2 "the only General I saw in the front was General Griffin, 5th Corps, who gave some orders which I obeyed, or I suppose the [Second] Brigade would never have received any orders." He wrote on June 4: "I asked to be relieved and sent to my Regiment, as I had become disgusted with Brigade affairs." Lieutenant Leasure was killed on July 30, 1864.

Apendix A

1. Expiration of service was scheduled for August 30, 1864.

2. National Archives, Washington D.C., G. A. Hitchcock's Civil War pension file, general affidavit, dated May 9, 1892, signed by Henry S. Hitchcock.

3. National Archives, Washington D.C., G. A. Hitchcock's Civil War pension file, general affidavit, dated December 27, 1883, signed by Francis W. Wright.

4. National Archives, Washington D.C., G. A. Hitchcock's Civil War pension file, general affidavit, dated December 11, 1883, signed by Joseph Baldwin.

5. National Archives, Washington D.C., G. A. Hitchcock's Civil War pension file, general affidavit, dated December 3, 1883, signed by Levi C. Goodale.

6. National Archives, Washington D.C., G. A. Hitchcock's Civil War pension file, general affidavit, dated 3, 1883, signed by Charles E. Hayward.

7. National Archives, Washington D.C., G. A. Hitchcock's Civil War pension file, general affidavit, dated December 11, 1883, signed by S. Austin Childs.

8. *Proceeding of the Fitchburg Historical Society*, Vol. 5 (Fitchburg, Massachusetts, 1914).

9. Obituary, *Fitchburg Daily Sentinel*, February 6, 1905.

10. Obituary, *New York Times*, May 16, 1957. Pratt Institute, Brooklyn, N.Y., George P. Hitchcock's personnel file in the Reference Library. *Amherst College Biographical Record*, published by the Trustees of Amherst College, 1951.

Appendix B

1. George Cary Eggleston enlisted in Company G, 1st Virginia Cavalry ("Black Horse Cavalry") in 1861 and was a clerk to Brig. Gen. J. E. B. Stuart. In the fall of 1861, he transferred to the field artillery on the South Carolina coast; in 1863, he joined the field artillery in Longstreet's Corps, serving as a sergeant major at Wilderness, Cold Harbor, Petersburg and Appomattox (commanded the Nelson Light Artillery). After the war he was a journalist and novelist. He wrote *A Rebel's Collections*, first printed in the *Atlantic Monthly* (June-December 1874) and was a writer for *New York World*, under Joseph Pulitzer for eleven years.

Bibliography

Addison, Henry. *A Complaint. . .upon the subject of the Potomac Bridge* [Long Bridge], *as an obstruction to the Commerce of Georgetown.* Washington: H. Polkinhorn, printer, 1856.

Alderman, Edwin Anderson, ed. *Library of Southern Literature*, Vol. IV. Atlanta: The Martin & Hoyt Company, 1907.

[Atwater, Dorence.] *The Atwater Report: List of Prisoners Who Died in 1864-65 at Andersonville Prison*, Andersonville, Georgia: National Society of Andersonville, 1981.

Bates, Samuel P. *History of Pennsylvania Volunteers, 1861-5.* 5 vols. Harrisburg: B. Singerly, State Printer, 1869-71.

—*Martial Deeds of Pennsylvania.* Philadelphia: T.H. Davis and Company, 1875.

Bearss, Edwin C. *Andersonville National Historic Site: Historic Resource Study and Historical Base Map.* Washington D.C.: National Park Service, 1970.

Beaver, Patrick. *The Big Ship: Brunel's Great Eastern, A Pictorial History.* London: Hugh Evelyn, 1969.

Black, Robert C., III. *The Railroads of the Confederacy.* Chapel Hill: The University of North Carolina Press, 1952.

Boatner, Mark Mayo., III. *The Civil War Dictionary.* New York: David McKay Company, 1959.

Breeden, James O. *Joseph Jones, M.D., Scientist of the Old South.* Lexington: The University Press of Kentucky, 1975.

Bryan, T. Conn. *Confederate Georgia.* Athens: University of Georgia Press, 1953.

Clark, Walter, ed. *Histories of the Several Regiments and Battalions from North Carolina in the Great War 1861-65.* 5 vols. Goldsboro: Nash Brothers, 1901.

Cogswell, Leander W. *A History of the Eleventh New Hampshire Regiment, Volunteer Infantry, in the Rebellion War.* Concord, N.H.: Republican Press Association, 1891.

Committee of the Order. *An Authentic Exposition of the Knights of the Golden Circle or a History of Secession From 1834 to 1861.* Chicago: Clarke & Company, 1861.

Committee of Publication. *A Memorial of The Great Rebellion: History of the Fourteenth Regiment New Hampshire Volunteers,* 1862-1865. Boston: Franklin Press, 1882.

Committee of the Regimental Association. History of the Thirty-fifth Regiment, Massachusetts Volunteers, 1862-1865. Boston: Mills, Knight and Company, 1884.

Committee of the Regiment. *History of the Thirty-Sixth Regiment — Massachusetts Volunteers,* 1862-1865. Boston: Press of Rockwell & Churchill, 1884.

Coulter, E. Merton. *The Civil War and Readjustment in Kentucky.* Chapel Hill: University of North Carolina Press, 1926.

Current, Richard N., ed. *Encyclopedia of the Confederacy.* New York: Simon & Schuster, 1993.

Doddridge, Philip. *The Life of Colonel James Gardiner.* New York: Carlton & Phillips, 1854.

Eggleston, George Cary. *A Rebel's Recollections.* Bloomington: Indiana University Press, 1959

Emerson, William A. *Fitchburg, Massachusetts — Past and Present.* Fitchburg: Blanchard & Brown, 1887.

Emmerson, George S. *The Greatest Iron Ship: S.S. Great Eastern.* North Pomfret, Vt.: David & Charles, 1980.

Fox, William F. *Regimental Losses in The American Civil War, 1861-1865.* Dayton, Ohio: Morningside, 1985.

Freeman, Douglas S. R.E. *Lee: A Biography.* 3 vols. New York: Charles Scribner's Sons, 1934-35.

Futch, Ovid L. *History of Andersonville Prison.* Gainesville: University of Florida Press, 1968.

Gavin, William Gilfillan. *Campaigning with the Roundheads: History of the Hundredth Pennsylvania Veteran Volunteer Infantry Regiment in the American Civil War 1861-1865.* Dayton, Ohio: Morningside, 1989.

Grant, Ulysses S. *Personal Memoirs and Selected Letters, 1839-1865.* New York: The Library of America, 1990.

Hawkes, George P. Diary. U.S. Army Military History Institute, Carlisle Barracks, Pa.

Hesseltine, William Best. *Civil War Prisons.* New York: Frederick Ungar, 1964.

History and Roster of Maryland Volunteers — War of 1861-65. Baltimore: General Assembly of Maryland, 1898.

Hitchcock, George A. *Memoirs of Ashby in 1850.* Manuscript at Ashby Public Library, Ashby Massachusetts.

Jackman, Lyman. *History of the Sixth New Hampshire Regiment in the War for the Union.* Concord, N.H.,: Republican Press Association, 1891.

Johnson, Allen, ed. and Malone, Dumas, ed. *Dictionary of American Biography,* Vol. III. New York: Charles Scribner's Sons, 1958.

Long, E.B. and Long, Barbara. *The Civil War Day by Day:* An Almanac 1861-1865. New York: Da Capo Press, 1971.

McGee, Benjamin F. *History of the 72d Indiana Volunteer Infantry of the Mounted Lightning Brigade.* Indianapolis: S. Vater & Company, 1882.

McPherson, James M. *Battle Cry of Freedom.* New York: Oxford University Press, 1988.

Marvel, William. *Andersonville: The Last Depot.* Chapel Hill: The University of North Carolina Press, 1994.

—*Burnside.* Chapel Hill: The University of North Carolina Press, 1991.

Massachusetts Soldiers, Sailors and Marines in Civil War. 8 vols. Brookline: published by adjutant general at Riverdale Press, 1935.

Mills, Charles J. Letters. U.S. Army Military History Institute, Carlisle Barracks, Pa.

Morrison, James L., Jr., ed. *The Memoirs of Henry Heth.* Westport, Connecticut: Greenwood Press, 1974.

National Cyclopaedia of American Biography, Vol. 1. New York: James T. White & Company, 1892.

Ohio Roster Commission. *Ohio: Official Roster of the Soldiers of the State of Ohio in War of the Rebellion, 1861-1866.* 12 vols. Cincinnati: published by general assembly at Werner; Wilstach Baldwin; Ohio Valley; and Laning, 1886-1895.

Pingrey, Jennette D., ed. *Birth, Marriage and Death Records of the Town of Ashby, Massachusetts from 1754 to 1890.* American Data Services, 1989.

Priest, John M. *Before Antietam: The Battle for South Mountain.* Shippensburg: White Mane Publishing Company, 1992.

—*Antietam: The Soldiers' Battle.* Shippensburg: White Mane Publishing Company, 1989.

Quint, Alonzo H. *The Record of the Second Massachusetts Infantry, 1861-1865.* Boston: James P. Walker, 1867.

Record of the Massachusetts Volunteers, 1861-1865. 2 vols. Boston: published by adjutant general at Wright & Potter, 1870.

Record of Service of Michigan Volunteers in the Civil War, 1861-1865. Vol. 4. Kalamazoo: published by adjutant general at Ihling Brothers & Everard, 1915.

Record of Officers and Men of New Jersey in the Civil War, 1861-66. Vol. I. Trenton: published by adjutant general at John L. Murphy, Steam Book and Job Printer, 1876.

Rhea, Gordon C. *The Battle of the Wilderness: May 5-6, 1864.* Baton Rouge: Louisiana State University Press, 1994.

Report of the Adjutant General of the State of Illinois–Containing Reports of the Years 1861-66, Vol. III (Roster of Officers and Enlisted Men from 36th to 55th Regiments). Springfield: Phillips Brothers, State Printers, 1901.

Sandburg, Carl. *The American Songbag.* New York: Harcourt, Brace & Company, 1927.

Sears, Stephen W. *Landscape Turned Red.* New York: Ticknor & Fields, 1983.

—*George B. McClellan, the Young Napoleon.* New York: Ticknor & Fields, 1988.

Sifakis, Stewart. *Who Was Who in the Civil War.* New York: Facts on File Publications, 1986.

Sword, Wiley. *Sharpshooter: Hiram Berdan, his famous Sharpshooters and their Sharps Rifles.* Lincoln, Rhode Island: Andrew Mowbray, 1988.

Stone, James Madison. *Personal Recollections of the Civil War: By One Who Took Part In It as a Private Soldier in the 21st Volunteer Regiment of Infantry from Massachusetts.* Boston: published by the author, 1918.

Swinton, William. *Campaigns of the Army of the Potomac — A Critical History of Operations in Virginia, Maryland and Pennsylvania from the Commencement to the Close of the War, 1861-1865.* New York: Charles Scribner's Sons, 1882.

Trudeau, Noah Andre. *Bloody Roads South: The Wilderness to Cold Harbor, May-June 1864.* Boston: Little, Brown and Company, 1989.

Underwood, Adin B. *The Three Years' Service of the Thirty-third Massachusetts Infantry Regiment.* Boston: A. Williams, 1881.

United States War Department. *The War of the Rebellion: A Compilation of the Official Records of the Union and Confederate Armies.*, 128 vols. Washington: Government Printing Office, 1880-1901

Vandiver, Frank E., ed. *War Memoirs of Jubal Anderson Early, Lieutenant General, C.S.A..* Bloomington: Indiana University Press, 1960.

Vermont Volunteers, 1861-66. Montpelier, Vt.: published by the adjutant general, 1892.

Walcott, Charles F. *History of the Twenty-first Regiment Massachusetts Volunteers in the War for the Preservation of the Union, 1861-1865.* Boston: Houghton, Mifflin & Co., 1882.

Welcher, Frank J. *The Union Army, 1861-1865: Organization and Operations,* Volume 1. Bloomington: Indiana University Press, 1989.

Wert, Jeffry D. *General James Longstreet: The Confederacy's Most Controversial Soldier — A Biography.* New York: Simon & Schuster, 1993.

Wheeler, Kenneth W., ed. *For the Union — Ohio Leaders in the Civil War.* Columbus: Ohio State Press, 1968.

Wilkinson, Warren. *Mother, May You Never See the Sights I Have Seen — The Fifty Seventh Massachusetts Veteran Volunteers in the Army of the Potomac,* 1864-1865. New York: Harper & Row, 1990.

Williams' Cincinnati Directory. Cincinnati: Williams & Company, June 1865, 1867 and 1868.

Willis, Henry A. *Fitchburg in the War of the Rebellion.* Fitchburg: Stephen Shepley, 1866.

—*The Fifty-third Regiment Massachusetts Volunteers.* Fitchburg, Ma.: Press of Blanchard & Brown, 1889.

Woodbury, Augustus. *The Second Rhode Island Regiment: A Narrative of Military Operations in which the Regiment was Engaged from the Beginning to the End of the War for the Union.* Providence: Valpey, Angell & Company, 1875.

— *Major General Ambrose E. Burnside and the Ninth Army Corps.* Providence: Sidney S. Rider & Brother, 1867.

INDEX